THE OVERLAND TRAIL

The
OVERLAND
TRAIL

By

JAY MONAGHAN

●

Essay Index Reprint Series

BOOKS FOR LIBRARIES PRESS
FREEPORT, NEW YORK

Originally published as part of the American Trails Series

Copyright © 1947 by The Bobbs-Merrill Company, Inc.

Reprinted 1971 by arrangement

INTERNATIONAL STANDARD BOOK NUMBER:
0-8369-1999-8

LIBRARY OF CONGRESS CATALOG CARD NUMBER:
73-107726

PRINTED IN THE UNITED STATES OF AMERICA

To MY FATHER
who permitted his son to
go West in the early days—
that is, in my early days.

FOREWORD

THE name Overland Trail, as used in this book, is a general term for the north central route of migration to the Pacific Ocean. Some students have tried to restrict the meaning of the Overland Trail to the route followed by the Union Pacific Railroad. Much of that same route is called the Cherokee Trail by other students. The Overland Trail described in this book was known contemporarily as the Oregon Trail, but parts of it were traveled by many more Mormons and Argonauts than by Oregon-bound pioneers. With so many points of beginning and diverse terminals, it has been possible to sketch only in outline its general development. Especially in the western areas, many of the important cutoffs have been left for adequate description in later volumes of the American Trails Series. A great deal of space, perhaps a third of the book, has been devoted to the discovery of the overland way. Explorers were slow to give up the water routes across the continent. The fur traders were essentially boatmen. Lewis and Clark followed the geographical route logical for strangers. They went up the main channel of a known eastern stream and tried to go down the main channel of a western one. But the navigable streams led into the highest, most impassable peaks.

The history of the overland route after the discovery of Lewis and Clark is an account of later explorers' attempts to find a more open way farther and farther south until at last, within a little over a generation, open country was found practically all the way. The final wagon road was surprisingly free from obstructions. Pioneers might emigrate from the Missouri to the Columbia without really encountering any mountains. Week after week they saw in the distance, far to the north, to the south, to the west, mighty ranges steeped in the ultramarine of distance, but the road led across vast flats, gentle slopes mottled with cloud shadows that seemed as big as continents. The Wind River Mountains, the Uintahs, the Sawtooth Range towered high in the sky—but always it was a distant sky. The road up Bear Valley was skirted on both sides by high green hillsides splotched with spruce and aspen, but none had the breath-taking majesty of Switzerland or parts of Colorado. Burnt Fork out of Snake River cut a steep defile through bare hills but it led to open, rolling country. Even the Blue Mountains beyond Grande Ronde were not so impressive as Mount Kearsarge in New Hampshire. On the crest of the Blue, emigrants in the later days—Oregon emigrants—entered the only forest on the entire overland trip west.

The extremely level nature of the country followed by the Overland Trail should not lead anyone to conclude that the way across was easy. A guide in the center of an ocean of sagebrush had to know exactly which way to go. Thirty miles to the left or right invariably put travelers among tangled peaks and chasms, as Lewis and Clark and the Astorians all learned to their dismay.

The achievement of these overland explorers was great, but their explorations must be viewed in relation to those of other explorers of their time. Mackenzie's trip across Canada, Lewis and Clark's trip down the Columbia, Mungo Park's discovery of the head of the Niger and Bruce's journey up the Blue Nile all occurred within a little over a generation. Of the four, Lewis and Clark's was certainly not the most daring but its significance in world development is beyond all comparison with the others. So, too, the later overland migration to Oregon and California looms in importance above its contemporary South African trek or the earlier hegiras of Selkirk's Red River colonists. Argentina, Russia and Australia have plains equal to North America's, but none of them ever witnessed a comparable overland migration. In history generalizations are dangerous. The temptation is always great to magnify familiar deeds with the lens of nationalism. The danger becomes doubly great when the volume describing the Overland Road is to be followed by descriptions of other great roads. But in spite of the risk of overstatement, let us hazard the opinion that the Overland Trail is remembered by most people as the pattern for all emigrant roads—the symbol of pioneer America.

JAY MONAGHAN
State Historian of Illinois

CONTENTS

LIST OF ILLUSTRATIONS

THE OVERLAND TRAIL

Chapter 1

Hail Columbia—Happy Land

Or lose thyself in the continuous woods
Where rolls the Oregon, and hears no sound,
Save his own dashings...

"THE MEN, at Columbia's River, are strait limb'd, fine look-ing fellows, and the Women are very pretty." Eighteen-year-old John Boit laid down his quill pen and tossed his long hair back over his shoulders. He was one of the first Ameri-cans to visit Oregon—a coast claimed by Spain. Instead of com-ing overland like later emigrants, he had spent twenty months on shipboard sailing around Cape Horn. The Americans, five officers in knee breeches, buckle shoes, cocked hats and great-coats, and a crew of Yankee sailors, had discovered a great river in May 1792. The captain, Robert Gray, named it "Columbia" for his vessel. John Boit seemed more interested in the savage natives than in the river. After all, it was Spanish territory. He dipped his goose quill in the ink and continued writing: "They are all in a state of Nature, except the females, who wear a leaf Apron—perhaps '*t was* a fig leaf. But some of our gentlemen, that examin'd them pretty close, and near ... reported, that it was not a leaf, but a nice wove mat in resemblance!! and so we go—thus, thus—and no War!—!"[1]

John Boit's brother-in-law was one of the ship's owners. She had been named *Columbia* as a slur at George III. The recently liberated colonists preferred to revere an Italian discoverer of Central and South America rather than the man employed by an

15

English king to discover their own land. The *Columbia* had circumnavigated the globe on her last cruise—the first vessel to carry the American flag around the world—but on that trip she had not found the fabled Oregon.

John Boit could remember the excitement when Captain Gray sailed into Boston. He had left port second in command of two ships in 1787 and had returned in 1790 as chief.[2] John Kendrick, the ranking captain, had remained in the Pacific—too slow, no pusher, never on time, never demanding performance from the men under him.

Captain Gray's books showed a deficit but he was sure that a hustler could make a fortune on another cruise. The shipping merchants listened to his money-making scheme. Two things, he said, made it important that they finance him at once and let him be on his way. First, England was insisting that Spain open the Pacific Northwest to trade. Gray knew; he had been near Nootka Sound when a British trader was arrested there. The Spaniards had been very friendly to Gray as an American. They feared war with England and wanted allies. He must get back in time to "make hay" while their friendship lasted. With a cargo of sheet copper, cheap cloth and iron he could pick up sea-otter pelts along the Spanish coast for a song, sell them at $50 apiece in China, and come home with silk, chinaware and tea for sale in Boston. The cruise could not lose money, Gray said. He offered to put some of his own capital into the venture.

The Boston merchants knew that the Nootka Sound incident had set all Europe on the verge of war. Why not slip in and get sea-otter pelts while Spain and England quarreled about monopolies on the Pacific coast? The necessary cash was raised quickly. John Boit, with youthful eagerness, had joined to make his fortune. In a little over one month after landing in Boston, Captain Gray had the *Columbia* ready for another voyage. His first mate was Robert Haswell, an officer on the previous cruise. For a personal servant Gray had a Hawaiian boy whom he had brought back from the islands. In all, fifty men enrolled. On the last day it is reasonably safe to believe that the womenfolk came down to Boston's Long Wharf to see the wooden home their men would occupy for the next four years. With a chair attached to the yardarm women were often hoisted to the deck. On the *Columbia* they could admire twelve ponderous cannon to be used against pirates or Indians. A goat promised fresh milk for the officers. Indeed, Captain Gray had lots of ideas that would make this trip succeed where the last one had failed.

On September 28, 1790, the *Columbia* had set sail with a west wind, and the next day she passed the long sandspit known as Cape Cod. The sun was bright, the sky and sea a brilliant blue, as the cape, dazzling white, disappeared under the horizon.

Now, at the mouth of the Columbia River, John Boit could remember every detail of Cape Cod and he longed to see that landfall once more. He had kept a diary and could bring back every day of the cruise by reading it. Four months after leaving Boston the *Columbia* entered the Pacific. During that time John Boit had got to know the captain and crew very well. He still admired the skipper for his driving power but some things about him and the other officers he did not like.

Sailing north in the Pacific with the trade winds meant lazy days for the crew. Day and night the sails remained set and the men had nothing to do. But Captain Gray was not one to waste man-hours on the high seas. He ordered the crew to bring iron up from the hold and kept them busy cutting nails and spikes to be sold to the Indians—the first of his economies that were to bring profit to the owners. The sea was glassy calm, the days fine. The noise of making nails sounded from stem to stern.

In April 1791 Gray's program received a setback. The seamen complained of scurvy, the dread ailment of all long voyages. A few days later another bit of bad luck struck. The captain had ordered the rice brought up from the hold and spread on deck in the fine weather to air and dry. Nancy, the goat, began to nibble the grains. Soon she was dead. The mate explained later that she "eat so much that it swel'd her belly and caused her death."[3] All the men knew what usually happened when dry rice was subjected to moisture, whether in a kettle or inside a goat. The officers missed the milk. Now they, too, might get scurvy like the men.

On June 4, 1791, land appeared—bristling with pines, black as storm clouds, a thin line of white surf on a black rock beach, with rags of fog in dripping mountain valleys. The seamen supposed the forbidding country ahead to be the mainland of western North America. Later they would learn that it was an island to be called Vancouver. Gloomy as it appeared, the Americans knew that the land would provide food that would cure the scurvy. So to many New Englanders the Northwest became a land of hope.

The *Columbia* glided forward on a smooth sea. The men crowded the bulwarks, watching the landfall take shape and size before them. The sun set behind them on the ocean, but the rays shone wanly on the heads of distant snow peaks that peered over the frowning black forest.

Next day the *Columbia* anchored in a great harbor. Indians came out in big dugout canoes. The Boston seamen admired the lines of these savages' craft. John Boit noticed that they resembled Nantucket whaleboats. A dozen Indians sat in each boat. They held up fish, deer meat, and—most precious of all—green leeks and wild parsley. Already they had learned that the white men who came in the great winged vessels needed this cure for scurvy. The Indians also brought sea-otter skins, for they had learned too that the white men would pay well for these velvety hides. Captain Gray brought up his nails, sheet copper and bolts of blue cloth. The chief climbed aboard, barefooted but regally dressed with an elaborate, fringed blanket thrown over one naked shoulder and a conical hat made of woven spruce roots on his head. A price was fixed for the fish and fur, and permission was granted to land the stricken mariners. Ten of the crew, completely disabled with scurvy, were rowed to shore. A tent was pitched. The stricken men were laid on the ground, their swollen limbs buried in the spongy black earth.

Back on the ship a lively trade continued all day. Dugout after dugout came out from shore. Boit estimated that 300 Indians visited the ship with articles for trade. He remembered that the men were mostly naked except for a blanket and conical hat but that the women were modestly dressed from head to heel.

John Boit, glancing over the pages of his journal, could remember that he had not written in his diary for twelve days while he enjoyed studying these strange savages. In this time the men with scurvy had all regained their health and the captain's servant, the Hawaiian boy, disappeared. Gray was not sure whether his servant had run away or been kidnaped. He lost his Yankee temper. The heathen must be taught a lesson. John Boit had thought the Indians friendly people and he believed their coast no place to make trouble—but he did not tell his superior so. Instead, he watched Gray stamp his buckled shoes along the deck in anger. Then the captain became crafty. He invited the chief to come on board and ordered the sailors to seize him. The Indian's canoe was sent back to shore with a tart message: "Deliver the boy or I'll keep the chief." In short order the Hawaiian was returned and flogged for deserting. Then the *Columbia* weighed anchor for fresh trading waters.

The ship sailed north. To John Boit, looking back through his journal, the northern tack must have seemed odd now that the great Columbia River had been found to the south. But Boit knew that furs, not discovery, had brought them all from Boston. True, Captain Gray was prepared to say that he was on a voyage of discovery in case he was stopped by a Spanish man-of-war for trespassing in Spanish waters, but this was unlikely now that Britain had upheld her protest of the arrest of her nationals at Nootka Sound.

Captain Gray knew that the Russians claimed the fur rights up in Alaska, but there were at least five hundred miles of coast along which he could cruise before he might expect to meet their traders. Therefore he sailed boldly along the coast for three days, stopped to trade, then turned back before a northwest wind to the Straits of Juan de Fuca, the broad inlet to the upper Spanish trading country. Here the crew of the *Columbia* saw, for the first time, land that would one day belong to the United States. Here, as before, many natives came out to the ship with sea-otter pelts in their canoes. Boit noticed that these fellows had faces scarred with smallpox, sure sign that they had been associated with civilization. Along with sea-otter fur they brought children captured in war, now for sale as slaves. Captain Gray specified one nail as the price for a salmon. His copper he would trade only for sea-otter fur.

The ship beat back and forth among the straits islands for six days. On July 3, 1791, Captain Gray noticed that he had a strong east wind. He trimmed the ship at once to sail before it back up the coast. At six o'clock in the evening the *Columbia's* crew saw Cape Flattery far to the southeast, the northwest tip of the present state of Washington. It had been named by Captain Cook in 1778 because its appearance "flattered us with the hopes of finding an harbour."[4]

In September the *Columbia* was back again in the straits. The vessel had certainly cruised as far north as the Queen Charlotte Islands, probably to Alaska. Three of the *Columbia's* crew had been killed by Indians. Many rival traders had been sighted, among them Captain Kendrick—with a cargo at last. Gray had circumnavigated the globe and had already partly filled his hold since he had seen his old commander. All the Yankee traders asked if the *Columbia's* crew wanted to send mail back to Boston. The Queen Charlotte Islands were already familiar to Boston seamen, though the coast later known as Washington and Oregon remained a mystery. The islands were a sea-otter paradise—a diminutive continent almost two hundred miles long, cut and crosscut with natural canals, rivers that flowed back and forth according to the tides, a world of contrasts, warm sunny hours interspersed with clammy periods of fog, forests of mighty cedars sailing through tattered wind-swept clouds, gloomy as a dripping cave one moment and dazzling with sunbeams striking a splendor of flashing diamonds from the myriad raindrops the next; and through it all, whether deep in drizzle or in the glory of sunshine, a constant satin rustle of wings—wild fowl, ducks, geese, brant, cormorant.

Two things impressed John Boit in that northern land, the women and the Indians' strange houses. The native women wore labrets or wooden discs inserted in holes in their lower lips. At a distance they appeared to have their mouths open with tongues hanging out. With a toss of the head a woman could flip her labret up over her nose. John Boit thought it "enough to disgust any civilized being."[5] The houses were works of art—not the kind of habitation a New Englander expected an Indian to build. With wide boards split from the great trees with stone hatchets, they constructed walls and gently sloping roofs on which the women sat and looked across the sea. The ground between the houses was sodded soft and green as Boston Common. Men worked around monstrous logs, some as much as six feet in diameter, fashioning them into canoes. John Boit noticed, too, that a few were packing provisions in curious boxes. The Indians had no nails or steel implements for cutting wood, but they had learned to fold thin, split boards into boxes that to Boit seemed "neat." He thought at the time that they were putting away these provisions "against the ensuing *winter.*" It was funny now to look back at that entry in the diary. Far north as this country was, it did not have a New England winter. The Japan current saw to that. John Boit knew now that it seldom snowed on this coast; that ice never froze "thicker than a Spanish Dollar." The sailors had picked blueberries and whortleberries all winter. The country was obviously ideal for orchards. The climate that amazed John Boit and later New England seamen would one day impress thousands of Yankees who would seek an overland road to this winterless land.

John Boit remembered that the upright poles bracing the roofs of the Indian houses were carved with hideous faces. Some had shining teeth made from sea shells. There seemed to be no doors through the vertical slab walls into the houses, but the sailors noticed that many of them were ornamented with an animal's head eight or ten feet tall carved from one block of wood. These heads had their mouths open. The aperture was not over three feet high, but men and women came and went through this opening. The sailors had wondered what the Indians were doing until they discovered that the low hole was a door that led to the top of a ladder on the side of a roofed pit. Pacific Indian houses were twice as large as they appeared to be from the outside, for half the great hall was underground. John Boit and the sailors had entered some of these houses, climbed down the ladder and walked to the glowing fire in the dark interior. When their eyes became used to the blackness, they saw alcoves along the walls. Rude pole beds were covered with skins, some of them the precious sea otter. Under the bunks stood the curious folded boxes painted with symbolic designs to represent whales and various land animals. The smoke made the sailors' eyes smart but they sat down grimly. A woman put bowls of dried fish in their hands and melted grease for "dip," then motioned them to eat. John Boit recorded in his journal: "They treated me quite friendly."[6]

Back on the Straits of Juan de Fuca after the cruise, the *Columbia* drifted among the islands, trading constantly. One day a fog rolled out over the ship. The country down here had as bad a climate as Alaska. The Pacific Northwest all seemed much alike to the New Englanders. Both shores disappeared in the cotton air. In this white darkness the *Columbia* glided silently.

The lookout shouted a warning, "Breakers ahead." Captain Gray tacked the vessel and sailed in another direction. Soon the warning shout came again. The helmsmen turned the vessel. The crew knew that this could not be kept up long. Then the breeze stopped and the men felt relief, but a new danger appeared. Someone leaning over the bulwarks noticed a strong tide racing past the ship. The *Columbia* was moving almost as fast as though under sail. With no wind the crew could not regulate her course. She would probably hit the first rock in her path.

John Boit, thumbing through his journal, remembered that time of anxiety. Gray, with all his crotchets, had risen to the moment. He ordered out the small boats with two lines. Sailors took their places at the oars. Drifting with the vessel, they waited for a command from the misty deck above their heads. Other men with lead lines sounded and called the fathoms constantly. Black spruce trees on a rocky island appeared. Gray barked an order. The oarsmen tugged in their seats, whirlpools from their oars splashing against the wooden sides of the vessel. The great hull of the *Columbia* swung around and the island drifted past in the fog.

Out at sea at last, the ship picked up a breeze. John Boit remembered the general thanksgiving when the ship was safe on the high sea. Out there, too, the fog disappeared. Captain Gray turned north. The country up there seemed a better place to winter than down here in the unknown. Besides, Gray had another of his schemes for making money. With native timber he intended to build a sloop of at least forty-five tons. Such a craft could sail close to shore, tack among the islands, trade with the Indians in the most dangerous waters. The *Columbia*, meanwhile, could scout down the unknown coast hunting new trading grounds. The two would meet later in the summer. When a cargo was made, the sloop could be sold to someone—preferably to the Spaniards.

Captain Gray tacked into a wooded cove up north and spent the winter building the sloop. He christened her *Adventure* and loaded the little lady with four months' supplies. In the open sea the two vessels separated, the sloop to cruise north to the land of the lip plugs, the *Columbia* south into the unknown territory. A rendezvous halfway between had been agreed upon. Next day the *Columbia* again passed the Straits of Juan de Fuca in bad weather. Coasting down the shore that would later be the state of Washington, John Boit noticed that the land looked attractive. The mountains did not slope obliquely into the surging, sucking sea as they did farther north. Fields of grass appeared between low hills. The natives who came out to the vessel talked a different language from the northern tribesmen. They brought sea otter as the northern Indians did but not many of them. This disappointed Captain Gray. He was not interested in the landscape, had no plans for establishing settlements in this distant country. His only interest was in fur. He felt sure that he could get more of it if he could find a place to anchor. He was determined to find an anchorage in such a promising trading country.

On April 28, 1792, Captain Gray spied three vessels. They sailed together. All hove to and a small boat came across to the Americans. The officer in charge was Lieutenant Puget, for whom Puget Sound was to be named. He said that his ships were on a voyage of discovery. Captain George Vancouver was in command. He had recently mapped the coast of Australia and

New Zealand, then touched at the Sandwich Islands. Now he wanted to know the whereabouts of the Straits of Juan de Fuca where the Spaniards had their station. Captain Gray told what he knew. The Britishers sailed away. Captain Gray followed in their wake. For the second time he passed the mouth of the fabled river Oregon without seeing it.

At the Juan de Fuca Straits Captain Gray signaled good-by and started down the coast again to repeat his search for a harbor. On May 7 he discovered a great bay, later called Gray's Harbor. "Vast many canoes" came alongside with fur for trade at remarkably cheap prices. The sailors believed that these natives had never seen a ship or gun before. All day the red men traded and looked over the white men's arms. Next night the Indians returned in a great flotilla chanting a war song, flourishing weapons. The Americans fired a cannon shot over their heads. The reds came on, dipping their paddles furiously. Within easy pistol range Captain Gray fired a nine-pounder point-blank at the leading canoe. The ball split it from end to end. The other canoes veered away and fled.

In the morning the Indians came back to trade as usual. The Americans noticed that the savages pointed at the cannon and chattered about the red lightning that came from them. Surely these scamps were the same men who had attacked last night. Now they traded peacefully all day long. In the evening the *Columbia* made sail and plowed south in the darkness. At four next morning, May 11, 1792, the lookout spied the mouth of a great river with surf breaking along the bar.[7] Captain Gray ordered the pinnace to set sail and investigate. He nosed the *Columbia* toward shore behind her. With lead lines his men began to sound and call the fathoms. The vessel skimmed forward toward the line of breakers on the bar. The pinnace turned this way and that between the shoals and signaled the *Columbia* to follow. The sailors whispered below their breaths at Gray's rashness. Surely they would go aground. The captain shortened sail but the *Columbia* surged forward with heavy momentum straight for the breakers on the bar, rushed through with a splash of spray on deck and glided out into the deep water beyond.

The sailors swung buckets over the bulwarks into the tide, pulled them up and drank. The water was fresh.[8] Huzza!

For eight days Captain Gray explored the mouth of the great river. In the calm water he put the ship in order. The casks were lowered over the side and filled as they floated. Sand bars were numerous, but Captain Gray felt his way carefully fifteen miles upstream. With the ebbing tide driftwood came by. Whole trees with waving roots and branches whipped the roily water. Once the *Columbia* ran aground but backed off unhurt. Every day Indians paddled out with sea-otter and other pelts. They indicated, by tumbling water out of their brown hands and pointing east, that falls and rapids were above. Along the shore the Americans saw at least fifty villages, each with one or two great canoes propped high in the air on stilts. Dead chiefs were buried in them.

On May 15, 1792, Captain Gray and John Boit went on shore "to take a short view of the country,"[9] perhaps the only time Gray set foot on the soil that would be claimed by the United States on account of his discovery. In Boit's journal a note written in different ink, perhaps added later, stated that Gray had taken the country for the United States. John Boit was impressed with the river as a possible site for a trading post. Fur abounded. The river was full of fish and the woods full of deer and moose, he claimed. He may have been mistaken about the moose. Later explorers noted deer and elk. Oak, ash and walnut trees entranced Boit's eyes after months among the gloomy conifers of the north. He liked the Columbia River as well as or better than the Queen Charlotte Islands. With a factory here and another there he believed that an energetic American firm might engross the entire trade of the west coast. Boit believed in big business and freedom of enterprise to form monopolies.

With the choicest furs on the river, safe in the hold, Captain Gray watched the water for a favorable wind to get him out of the river. May 20, 1792, dawned pleasantly with a gentle breeze. Flood tide was due at noon. Then the water would be deep on the bar. Captain Gray decided to run for the open sea. He was proud of his great discovery, but more pleased with the 150 otter,

300 beaver, and twice that number of land furs he had got for a few iron spikes and pieces of copper.

The *Columbia* reached the bar at two o'clock. Suddenly the breeze stopped. The sails hung limp in the yards. The ship lay becalmed in three and a half fathoms of water and the tide was going out every minute. Unless she could move to deep water the *Columbia* was sure to ground and be wrecked. The men looked grimly at the lowering water. Three-quarters of an hour passed. Then a fresh breeze came in from the sea—the wrong direction; but the sails filled and with skillful tacking Captain Gray got the ship into the ocean. At five o'clock the linesmen announced twenty fathoms and all clear. The ship set sail in the gloaming and sped north into the night. The time had come to meet the *Adventure* at the appointed rendezvous.

The Americans arrived at the cove. No *Adventure* was in sight. Indians came out, looked at the crew and asked for the men who had gone with the *Adventure*. The sailors said, "They are asleep below," and made the usual Indian sign. Captain Gray did not want the red men to know how small a crew was left, but the savages paddled away suspiciously. Sentries were posted on deck to thwart a surprise attack.

That night by moonlight the Indians came back. The sentries reported hundreds of them coming across the water. Gray mustered his men on the deck. He hailed the lead canoe. It did not stop. Gray ordered his men to fire. Twenty-five warriors—the whole canoeload—were mowed down. The rest of the war party fled. The disabled canoe drifted alongside the ship. Wounded men writhed among the dead in the bottom. The sailors pushed it clear of the *Columbia* with their boat hooks and watched the craft drift away until it disappeared under the shade of the trees on shore. Sounds of groaning stopped before daylight.

Captain Gray did not care to stay in such a dangerous locality. He nailed a signboard on a tree warning the *Adventure's* crew to beware. Then he sailed north. He anchored at several places but the Indians were unfriendly. His belligerent reputation had preceded him. Unable to get sea-otter by fair means he used foul: deliver skins at his price or watch the village burn. Soon the whole coast feared and hated him. Once, when the Americans landed to cut a mast, they had to kill several Indians who attacked them. At another time a flotilla came out in daylight. The chief sang his war song and urged his warriors to attack. Captain Gray watched the chief lead two or three ineffectual charges. Then he ordered a sailor to kill him with a musket ball.

For two weeks the cruise continued. At last the *Columbia* returned to the dangerous rendezvous. On June 17, 1792, she met the *Adventure*. Captain Haswell came across in a small boat. He had had a successful trip, he said. His hold contained 500 prime skins, "cutsarks, pieces and tails." Cutsarks were otter-skin cloaks made from three pelts by the natives. Tails contained the choicest fur and were often sold separately. The *Adventure's* cargo was worth approximately $25,000, pretty good for a short three-months' cruise.

The *Columbia* and the *Adventure* sailed in close to shore where they transferred the cargo in still water. The *Columbia's* hold was not yet filled. Gray ordered the *Adventure* back to the Charlotte Islands. He followed with the *Columbia*. Both crews traded avidly to make a cargo and be off for China. Gray even swapped his satin knee breeches—his old pair, of course—to an Indian for fur. Racing one night with the *Adventure* up Hecate Straits, the *Columbia* struck a rock and almost foundered. Captain Gray fired his cannon and sent up signal rockets for help but the *Adventure* kept on going. Grim and grumbling, the *Columbia's* crew manned the pumps while the ship wallowed southward. Surely Haswell had seen their signal. Some of the officers remembered that the *Adventure's* commander had been piqued at Captain Gray. Perhaps he wanted to go back to Boston first in command as Gray had done so successfully on the previous voyage. The men on the sinking ship did not approve of carrying competition and individualism so far. *Laissez-faire* was not good for those left behind.

Along the coast the *Columbia* spoke an American that helped her back to the Spanish settlement at Nootka Sound. The governor was hospitable. Evidently he still hoped for American aid in case of war with England for this coast. The American officers were invited to a great banquet served on solid silver plates. Flunkies set five courses before the guests. Soiled dishes were not taken from the room. The guests must see that fresh plates were available for each serving. John Boit estimated that 270 silver plates were used. Knives and forks were also of silver. These Spaniards lived well. Their right to the coast was no new thing.

During the three weeks that the _Columbia_ lay at Nootka for repairs three trading ships came in from London and two from the United States. The North Pacific was fast becoming a well-known coast and certainly Spain held no monopoly there. Patched up again, the _Columbia_ sailed out to find the _Adventure_. The two vessels met in the Queen Charlotte Islands and saluted formally.

Haswell explained that he had not seen the _Columbia's_ distress signals. At dawn he had wondered what had become of her. He had kept on slowly, trading as he went, and now had a good haul of fur.

Fur was what Captain Gray wanted. He ordered the cargo transferred to the _Columbia_. At last the hold was full. Heave ho for Canton, then home! But Captain Gray planned to reap one more profit before leaving. He would grave the little sloop, then go back to Nootka and generously offer her for sale to his hosts. A new cable and anchor were attached to the _Adventure_ to catch the Spaniards' eyes. On September 21, 1792, they arrived.

The harbor was full of strange ships. Vancouver's little fleet had discovered that this coast was part of an island, Vancouver Island. He had circumnavigated it and now claimed it all for Britain, including the Spanish settlement at Nootka. The governor had gone south to Acapulco to get instructions from the viceroy. Robert Gray's commercial scheme seemed to have been wrecked on this latest international complication but he did not give up. A commander who would accept three weeks' hospitality from the Spaniards and then plan to sell them a sloop that he had built out of their own native lumber in their own territory was not one to be easily thwarted in business. A man who had started around the world second in command and come in first, who had established a reputation on the Northwest Coast for telling the Indians what their furs were worth and then insisting with powder and lead that they take the price, who had traded his satin "britches" to get one more hide into the hold was sure to have a ready expedient. He hoisted anchor, set sail and raced down the coast to overtake his friend the governor.

At the Straits of Juan de Fuca the *Columbia*, with the *Adventure* alongside, hailed the Spaniards. Captain Gray displayed the sloop and offered her for seventy-two prime otter skins, $3,960.

The governor delivered the pelts. Gray took the new cable and anchor from the sloop, saluted His Catholic Majesty with nine guns and sailed away. In a cove he anchored to get wood and water for the long trip across the Pacific, Boston-bound. The discoverer of the Columbia River, he was going back by the earliest Oregon trail.

Everyone was gay. With difficulty the men were kept at their tasks. John Boit wrote in his diary: "Full allowance of Grog being serv'd on the occasion, made our worthy Tars join in the *general* Mirth—and so we go."[10]

On October 3, 1792, the anchor was weighed. The sails filled. The gloomy evergreens of the Northwest Coast disappeared under the horizon. Three weeks later the *Columbia* picked up the northeast trade winds and on October 29 she raised the island of Owyhee—Hawaii. Sailors told one another that the distant mountain peak was where Captain Cook had been killed by the natives. Next day the *Columbia* hove to near shore. Hawaii from now on would be the last stop on the sea route to Oregon from both the East and the West. Hawaiian servants would give names to the new Northwest and add much blood and artistic culture to the Pacific Indians. Boit, in his diary, noted that natives came out in outrigger canoes like great insects to trade live hogs and vegetables. In his cabin he wrote: "They were all in a state of Nature, except a small covering round the middle. Not many of the *Columbia's* Crew prov'd to be *Josepths*."[11]

For five days the *Columbia* cruised among the enchanting islands. Gray built pigpens on deck. In them he put over a hundred squealers. To feed the crew he bought "dunghill fowls," sugar cane, breadfruit. The *Columbia* moved from beach to beach with a flotilla of outrigger canoes racing beside her. Boit wrote in his diary: "The shore made a delightful appearance, and appeared in the highest state of cultivation. Many canoes alongside, containing beautiful *Women*."[12] At one island Gray's Hawaiian lad was given an opportunity to go ashore and return to his people. He refused.

On November 3, 1792, the *Columbia* made sail for Canton. The temperate sea was smooth. All hands were put to butchering hogs—more exciting than cutting nails. The meat was stored in casks of brine. A little more than a month later the *Columbia* raised Formosa, pale in the distance. The next day the Americans sighted the mainland of China. "Above 100 sail of fishing boats in sight," Boit recorded. This was like being back in civilization after two years in the Oregon wilderness. At Whampoa forty-seven European and six American bottoms lay at anchor, among them the ship commanded by Captain Kendrick—the great dawdler. Captain Gray unloaded $90,000 worth of sea-otter fur and took on his Boston cargo. Fully loaded on February 2, 1793, the *Columbia* hoisted anchor and dropped down the inlet. "The Ship's Crew are all well and hearty," Boit wrote a few days later, "and looking forward, with anxious solicitude, to a happy meeting of *Sweethearts* and *Wives*. How can we be otherways than happy, when anticipating the joys that *awaits* us there!!"[13]

A month later the *Columbia* stopped at North Isles Roads for water. She had sprung a leak but with one pump working day and night, Captain Gray figured that he could make Boston without mishap. Late in April the Cape of Good Hope was sighted off the larboard bow. For a week the Yankees tacked ten to thirty miles from the African shore, seeing gossamer mountains by day and fires by night. Head winds retarded their passage. "Tight winds for men in a hurry," Boit called them. On May 20, 1793, they picked up the southeast trades, blowing straight for home. The great yards were squared. "Box'd her away for St. Helena," Boit wrote gleefully. Five days later the sinking sun revealed the sharp outline of St. Helena, the island rock in the South Atlantic, the last stop on the Oregon Trail to Boston. The *Columbia* en-

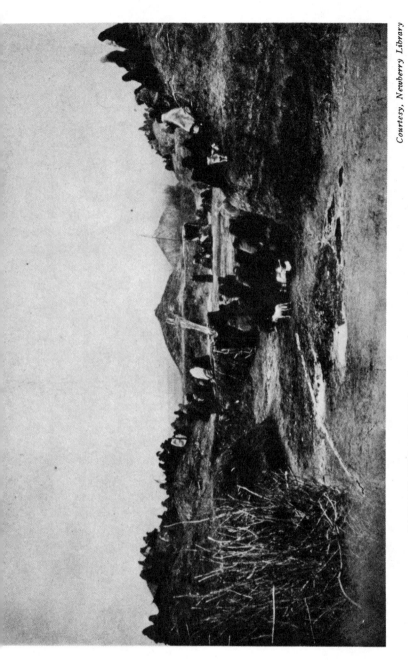

PAWNEE VILLAGE WITH WOMEN SITTING ON THE LODGE ROOFS

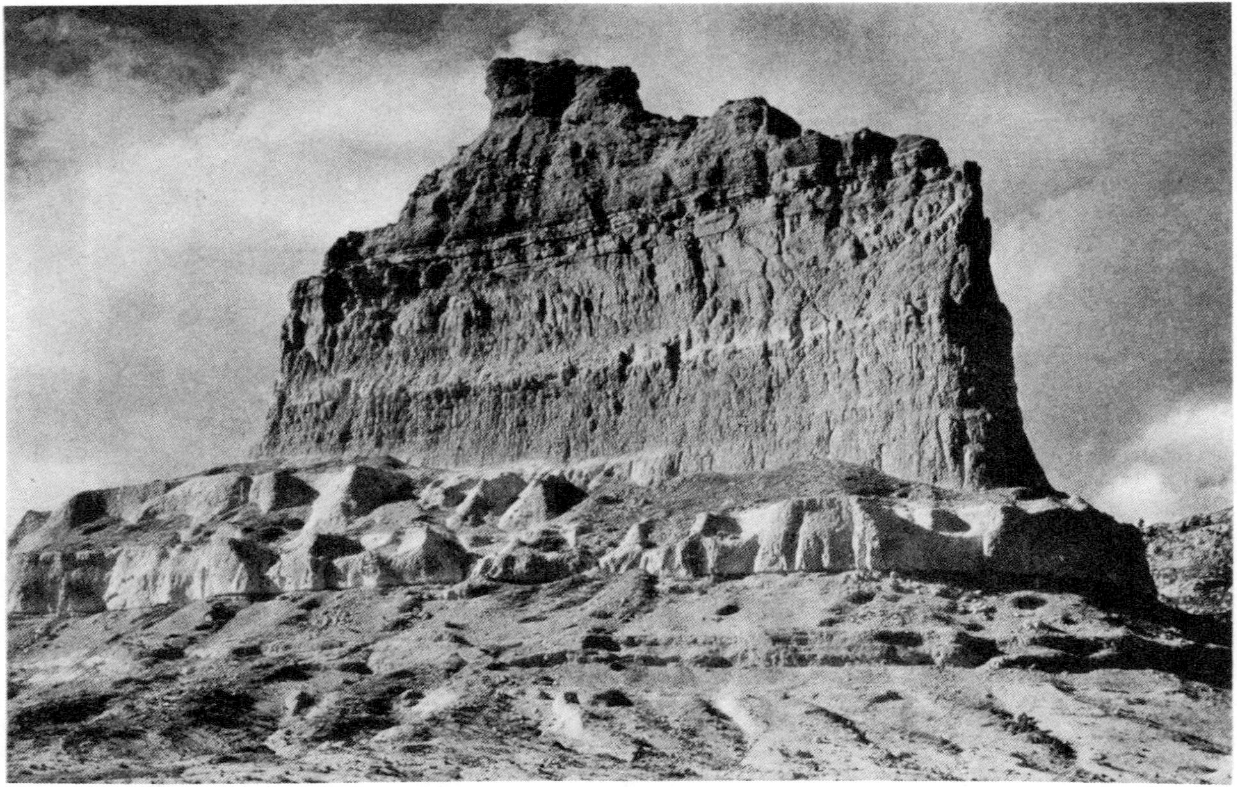

Courtesy, National Park Service

tered the harbor for fresh water. Boit noticed with surprise a great number of ships, a forest of masts, great, pompous and lavishly rigged East Indiamen, mean, greasy whalers. He learned that there was a war in Europe. The vessels were waiting for a convoy. The French Revolution had spread out of bounds. Fanatic French *républicains* had beheaded their king and were overrunning Europe. England had stepped in to stop the threat to her own social order. John Boit observed in his journal for posterity that "poor Louis was a head shorter."[14]

Boit marveled at British efficiency on this rock in the middle of the ocean. Pipes underground brought water to a hose which filled ships' casks without taking them from the hold. "The sight of an English Lady," Boit wrote, "made my heart feel all in an uproar—and alas! the poor Sandwich Isle Girls were entirely forgot. So it is, and we cannot help it." Two days later, May 27, 1793, the *Columbia* sailed at daylight with pleasant trade winds and fair weather. Captain Gray put all hands to painting ship. Men were never idle aboard his vessel. On June 9 they crossed the equator—for the fourth time on the cruise. It was slow going in the doldrums for "men in a hurry." On the twentieth they picked up the northeast trades—good sailing from there to Boston. But the grub was running low and the sailors complained of maggots in the bread. On July 2, 1793, a brig was spoke. She gave her name and her destination, Granada. She said her cargo was livestock. Gray wanted to purchase food but she would not stop. He fired several shots ahead of her. This made the brig heave to. Sheep, hogs and bread were purchased. By the twenty-fourth these supplies were almost exhausted. Cape Cod was known to be close but no land was in sight. The *Columbia* lay becalmed. At last the lookout spied a fishing schooner. Captain Gray sent a small boat out to her. It came back with three barrels of salt mackerel and 300 ship biscuit. With this good luck came a fresh breeze. Sails were set. Next morning at daylight the lookout announced Cape Cod on the southwest horizon. Men stumbled up from the fo'c'sle rubbing their tousled heads. Everywhere around the horizon they saw sails. Soon familiar objects appeared on the coastline—Cohasset Rocks, Hassett Ledges, Boston Light. A pilot came aboard and steered the *Columbia* to Long Wharf. They arrived at candlelighting time and saluted the town with eleven guns.

Captain Gray, Robert Haswell and John Boit walked up the quaint cobble streets of Boston-town. Their cruise had been a success. They had discovered a great river and left the name of "Columbia" on it, as well as on a harbor far to the north. On the opposite side of the American continent that same night an official of the North West Company, Alexander Mackenzie, with an aide, Alexander McKay, and eight *voyageurs*, paddled against time, against the approach of another winter. Only two days before, when the *Columbia* lay becalmed off Cape Cod, they had painted a sign in vermilion on a rock announcing that they had crossed the North American continent, the first Anglo-Americans to reach the Pacific overland. The country that they had traversed would be known as British Columbia. In due time John Boit learned that his and Gray's explorations up the Columbia River had been followed by one of Vancouver's men, Lieutenant Broughton, in the *Chatham*.[15] With a map given him by Captain Gray at Nootka, the Englishman had entered the river on October 21, 1792—while the *Columbia* was racing toward the Sandwich Islands on her homeward trip. Lieutenant Broughton anchored the *Chatham* where the river narrowed. With a cutter and a launch he rowed over a hundred miles upstream, almost to the gorge of the Cascade Mountains.

The Americans had noted the fur and timber resources of the Pacific slope. They had seen that gardens grew successfully in latitudes similar to Newfoundland's. It remained for the Englishmen to be first to penetrate the Coast Range, view the Willamette Valley and see the possibilities of the western third of the future states of Washington and Oregon. But the American name "Columbia" clung persistently to the Pacific Northwest, and the log of the *Columbia's* cruise became the new republic's main claim to the area. An overland trail from the eastern states would be necessary to hold it to the Union.

1 F. W. Howay and T. C. Elliott (eds.), "Reprint of Boit's Log of the Columbia, 1790-1793," *Quarterly of the Oregon Historical Society* (December, 1921), XXII, No. 4, 311-12.

2 F. W. Howay, "Captains Gray and Kendrick: The Barrell Letters," *The Washington Historical Quarterly* (October, 1921), XII, No. 4, 250.

3 Howay and Elliott (eds.), "Boit's Log of the Columbia," 274n.

4 *Ibid.*, 280n.

5 *Ibid.*, 281.

6 *Ibid.*, 279.

7 T. C. Elliott (ed.), "Remnant of Official Log of the Columbia," *Quarterly of the Oregon Historical Society* (December, 1921), XXII, No. 4, 352-53.

8 *Ibid.*, 353; Howay and Elliott (eds.), "Boit's Log of the Columbia," 309n.

9 Elliott (ed.), "Remnant of Official Log," 354.

10 Howay and Elliott (eds.), "Boit's Log of the Columbia," 331.

11 *Ibid.*, 332.

12 *Ibid.*, 332-33.

13 *Ibid.*, 339.

14 *Ibid.*, 346.

15 *A Voyage of Discovery to the North Pacific Ocean, and Round the World . . . under the Command of Captain George Vancouver* (London, 1801), III, 95.

Chapter 2

Lewis and Clark

THE year Captain Robert Gray sailed into Boston Harbor to report the discovery of the Columbia River, nineteen-year-old Meriwether Lewis called at Monticello, the plantation home of Thomas Jefferson, Secretary of State under President Washington. Young Lewis had heard that Jefferson was planning an expedition across the Spanish wilderness to the northwest coast that Great Britain had opened with the Nootka Sound incident. Jefferson knew the young man. He was a neighbor who had combined dutiful attendance at the Latin school with a passion for woodcraft. An ardent hunter, he was also a seeker of knowledge like Jefferson himself.

Jefferson had been toying with the idea of an overland expedition to the Pacific for years. A decade before, when the treaty of peace had been signed with Great Britain in 1783, he had proposed such a trip to the great soldier, George Rogers Clark, who had won the country west of the Alleghenies for Virginia. Three years later, as minister to France, Jefferson had met an adventurous Yankee, John Ledyard, who had written a book on his experiences with Captain Cook on the expedition which cost Cook his life in the Hawaiian Islands. Ledyard and Jefferson talked about the northwest country claimed by Spain and Russia. Ledyard was sure that he could cross Russia and the North American continent, too, alone. He would go first to the Russian fur factory at Kamchatka, take a boat there to Nootka Sound, cross to the Missouri and float down to the American settlements—as easily as that! Jefferson wished him Godspeed. Ledyard set off, but he was arrested by the Russians in Siberia and sent back to Europe. This was when Meriwether Lewis was seven years old, before he had been allowed his first gun.

Jefferson had not given up the idea of the exploration. The State Department had no money for this purpose, but the members of the American Philosophical Society subscribed a small sum. The purpose of the expedition that Jefferson planned was scientific, of course, and not political. He must have a mature leader. Jefferson liked young Meriwether Lewis but he was, after all, only a boy. The lad left Monticello without the cherished appointment.

Jefferson, always partial to the French, selected André Michaux, a scientist visiting in America. He was a recognized botanist who had traveled extensively in the Tigris and Euphrates valleys. The Michaux expedition did not materialize. The French Revolution had progressed amazingly since John Boit had recorded in St. Helena that "Louis was a head shorter." England had declared war at that time to stop the spread of the revolution. Now the French minister in America, Citoyen Genêt, was declaring that America must save France as France had saved America in her revolution. President Washington objected. Genêt ignored him and enlisted men and outfitted ships in spite of the United States' avowed neutrality. One expedition was to float down the Mississippi and take the Spanish city of New Orleans. George Rogers Clark enlisted for this adventure. Michaux joined it, too. Meriwether Lewis, on his mother's plantation, saw the proposed trip to the Pacific evaporate in the heat of threatening war.

The next year, 1794, Meriwether Lewis enlisted as a private in the militia which President Washington called out to enforce a federal tax on whisky in the Pennsylvania mountains. A year later he enlisted in the regular army. By 1797 he had become a captain, having served with distinction in the Northwest under Mad Anthony Wayne. He had also formed a deep friendship for a brother of George Rogers Clark whom he had met in the army. William Clark was four years older than Meriwether

Lewis. Vigorous, red-headed, a natural leader, he made an excellent foil for the more imaginative and scholarly Meriwether. Both of the young men had learned all that they needed to know about soldiering on the frontier, fighting and treaty-making with wild Indians, when, in 1800, Jefferson was elected President.

On March 4, 1801, Thomas Jefferson walked from his boardinghouse to the national Capitol, the first president to take the oath in the new city of Washington. Shortly after his inauguration he wrote to Meriwether Lewis. He wanted the young captain to come to Washington as his private secretary. Meriwether Lewis came at once. In the next two years he learned that Jefferson was still interested in exploring the western country. In January 1803 Jefferson asked Congress for permission to send a small expedition. His interest seemed to be largely commercial and scientific: to open the Indian trade there and also to acquire knowledge of the geography, the plants and animals of the interior. Almost at once Jefferson was forced to buy Louisiana in order to make an outlet down the Mississippi for western settlers. Immediately the western exploration took on political significance.

Meriwether Lewis petitioned his chief once more to be made leader of the expedition. He was now twenty-eight years old and an experienced frontier soldier. President Jefferson granted his request. Lewis asked for his friend, William Clark, as second in command. Congress appropriated $2,500 for the expedition. To save expenses, regular army soldiers already on the payroll would be selected for the trip. Jefferson suggested further, as an economy measure, that the party organize on United States soil where it could be supplied by the War Department. A camp site was selected in the Illinois country across from the mouth of the Missouri. Here, in December 1803, twenty-nine men assembled for training in the rudiments of woodcraft. Nine of them were recruits picked up in Kentucky. Captain Lewis divided the company into three platoons with a sergeant over each. It was a stiff and formal little army with leather collars and hair in pigtails. Captain Lewis and Lieutenant Clark looked down the line of their men. They were only names on the roster now but soon each would have a personality. Hardship would test the character of every one of them—including the commanders.

In the line of faces that stared blankly to the front Lewis and Clark saw some privates who would become the real heroes of the expedition. There were John Potts and John Colter, both destined to like the wilderness better than civilization. Both would elect to remain in the Rockies rather than come back, one of them to die from an Indian arrow and the other to discover the site of future Yellowstone Park. In the ranks, too, stood Patrick Gass—good noncom material, the commanders would learn. Perhaps too good! He intended to keep a journal of the journey himself. Near him stood a youth of seventeen, George Shannon, out for adventure. Lewis and Clark would learn that this boy was courageous and able but absent-minded, apt to wander off and get lost. Boylike, he had not learned to concentrate. He was forever leaving a powder horn or tomahawk at the noon rest and remembering it hours later. George Shannon would grow from a boy to a man on this expedition. He was probably the only one in the ranks who, out of service, might have met Lewis and Clark as social equals. Another private, John Shields, was a blacksmith by trade. His knowledge of metals would make him a man of magic among the Stone Age men in the Rockies. Also in the ranks stood Reuben and Joseph Fields, both recruits from Kentucky. Inseparable companions, they proved to be crack shots and indefatigable hunters. The elk and buffalo they killed would keep the expedition from starvation. Two French rivermen were employed along with a half-breed interpreter, who knew the Indian sign language. The Americans called him Drewyer. His French ancestors spelled the name Drouillard. In addition, Lieutenant Clark had a Negro slave, York, destined in time to become a prominent man among the Crow Indians.[1]

Lewis and Clark spent much of the first winter in St. Louis. They left the drilling and discipline to the sergeants in the camp on the river bottom across the Mississippi. A near-by grogshop caused some trouble. Occasionally men had to be flogged for absence without leave. Merchants in St. Louis told Lewis and Clark all about the upper river country. There was a quite extensive Indian settlement called the Mandan villages, some fifteen hundred miles up the Missouri. St. Louis traders went there often. Warlike nomads along the lower river sometimes gave trouble, and traders had to compete with Hudson's Bay men at the Mandan villages, but they usually came back with a profit. The country beyond the Mandan villages was unknown and the Americans could really begin exploring there.

Lewis and Clark learned that it would take them all summer to reach this outpost of civilization. They would have to winter there and start westward again in the spring of 1805. Thus a whole year more would be consumed getting far enough into the interior of the continent to begin real exploration. To guard against the dangerous plains Indians the commanders decided to take an extra corporal and fifteen soldiers, all to be sent back from the Mandan villages. Nine rivermen were added to help up-stream with the boats.

Lewis and Clark selected the usual equipment for a trip to the Mandan villages. They bought a keelboat and two pirogues, traditional river transportation. On the keelboat deck they mounted a swivel and a little mill for grinding corn. Under the decks they stowed boxes and barrels of supplies, casks of whisky, sacks of grain, kegs of powder, bars of lead, flints, spools of rope, a big American flag, wheels and axles to move the boats overland to the Columbia and—dear to the heart of Meriwether Lewis—a sectional iron boat to be put together in the mountains. Dress uniforms, swords, sashes and plumes were packed in lockers. Lewis and Clark also invested in a great quantity of "trade goods"—beads, cloth, knives, tobacco, fishhooks, steel traps, medals and ribbons, theatrical paint, handkerchiefs, looking glasses, burning glasses, tomahawks. On May 14, 1804, the boats were all loaded and they set off with a good wind in the sails. Horsemen were detailed to ride along shore and kill game.

A spring freshet churned the Missouri. Great trees rolled down the turbid current, lashing the yellow water with bare limbs, waving ugly roots in the air. Along the shore, mudbanks, under-mined by the current, thundered into the river with reports like artillery. French villages swung into view. The explorers landed often. They noticed that the settlers were very poor, almost savages. Lewis and Clark noticed, too, that there were no young men among them, only old fellows, women and children. Lewis, the scientific observer, asked the reason. He learned that all the young men were up the river trading with the Indians for fur and tallow, perhaps a thousand miles from their homes, to be gone a year at a time. The explorers were told that the great American, Daniel Boone, lived near by. On the tenth day out, May 25, 1804, the last village was left behind.

The mouth of the Osage River—below the spot where Jefferson City, Missouri, would one day stand—marked the beginning of the wilderness. Great prairies stretched away on both sides of the river. Deer were plentiful and easily killed. Flies and mosquitoes set them almost crazy. With flapping ears and stamping feet deer would sometimes come blindly down a trail and almost run over a hunter. Every day or two the explorers met Frenchmen in canoes or on rafts loaded with buffalo pelts, mounds of tallow, beaver skins. These easygoing, sociable fellows stopped for a pipe, gossiped, then shoved off to see their families after a year or two with the Indians. Lewis asked these men of the upper waters about the country. In one crew he met a remarkable character, Old Man Dorion. This ancient Frenchman was vigorous,

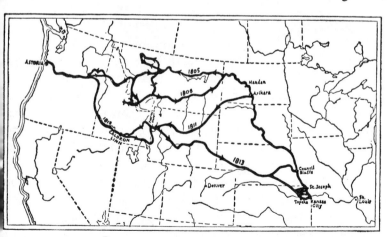

THE ROUTES OF LEWIS AND CLARK AND THE ASTORIANS WITH THE
OVERLAND TRAIL EXTENSION TO ST. JOSEPH AND KANSAS CITY

hard-drinking, jovial. He had traded with the Sioux for twenty years. He knew their language, had half-breed sons. If anyone could get an expedition past this belligerent tribe that claimed to control the Missouri below the Mandan villages, Old Man Dorion should be the one. Lewis hired him to return and help interpreter Drewyer through the dangerous country.

On June 26, 1804, the expedition reached the mouth of the Kansas River, first of the several points that would in time be ports of entry for the Overland Trail. Lewis ordered the men to camp on the point of land north of the Kansas, known later as Kansas City, Kansas. The men set to work unloading equipment. Captain Lewis strolled along the bank. He noticed a flock of parakeets. The grotesque green and yellow midgets turned somersaults around twigs and chattered incessantly. Then they flew and their brilliance disappeared. Strangely enough they appeared to be gray when in flight. The soldiers, not ornithologists like Lewis, cursed the mosquitoes. They got some relief under bars of netting issued by their officers. Then it rained, a downpour. To add to the misery, Lewis reminded the men that they were now in Indian country and each man must be on guard.

The next day dawned clear and sultry. Steam rose from the spongy ground. Captain Lewis decided to remain a day or two and dry the duffel. He set the men to work building a breastwork across the neck of the point between the Missouri and the Kansas. They must be prepared for hostile red men. Inside the fortification the men camped. With leisure on their hands two of the soldiers tapped the whisky in their charge, were caught, court-martialed and sentenced to 150 lashes on the bare back.

On July 2, 1804, the expedition passed below the high hills that were later crowned with Fort Leavenworth, another outfitting place for the Overland Trail. The men noticed that the river was choked with islands. They were not sure which channel was passable. In places driftwood clogged the entire stream. The men landed to hunt the best passage. In the tall weeds the heat was stifling. They discovered a deserted Indian village and the ruins of a French fort. Captain Lewis estimated that it had been built some fifty years before. On the Fourth of July they reached the neighborhood of Atchison and St. Joseph, the next great out-fitting places for the future trail. At dawn the Americans asserted their independence by firing the bow gun on the keelboat. Four days later they reached the Nodaway and encamped on an island in the channel. The riverbank showed the water to be falling rapidly. At dark some of the hunters had not come in and Lewis worried. In the days ahead he would become more philosophical. Hunters would sometimes be out for a week without coming in.

From the Nodaway north up the Missouri the travelers noticed that the country changed rapidly. The prairies gave way to the great plains. The border of trees along the river became narrower, the weeds lower, the horizon seemed farther away, the dome of the sky higher. A man seemed more alone, more in a geographic vacuum. Even the Missouri became broader, flatter. Long white sand bars divided it. The French boatmen said that the mouth of the Platte was close, the stream that would in time become the main route to the Pacific.

On July 21, 1804, the men pointed to the open mouth of the Platte—600 yards wide with water seeping down many channels choked with sand and boulders. No passage appeared deep enough for navigation. The stream obviously came straight from the Rocky Mountains but boatmen could not use it. They would have to keep on going north and turn west when the Missouri turned. The Frenchmen said that several Indian villages could be found a few miles up the Platte but that they would be deserted at this time of year. Everybody would be out hunting buffalo.

The explorers moved on. A few miles above, some hills on the east side of the river appeared like turrets on the edge of an ocean of grass. Here was shade and camp wood, oak and elm on the hills and a chance to climb up and look out across the emerald world as far as the eye could see. Lewis ordered his men to pull the boats to shore. He would rest here and invite all the Indians he could find to come and smoke and learn that the United States owned this country.

Captain Lewis sent out couriers with presents of tobacco. The

Fields brothers and other hunters strode off to get fresh meat for the little army. The sail was stretched like a great awning for the council. Idle soldiers washed their clothes and hung them on the bushes to dry. Some set fishlines in the river. Others set traps for beaver. Lewis brought his journal up to date. He noticed that the air at this longitude was very dry. His inkwell had to be refilled every day.

The hunters were not gone long. They came back to camp with red-coated white-tailed deer, the dead does thin from suckling fawns, the bucks with horns in the "velvet." The hunters also killed wild turkeys and, best of all, young goslings. John Colter, the Kentuckian, understood living off the country. Already he was standing out of the ranks in the estimation of his commanders. The simplest bits of woodcraft baffled the other soldiers but not John Colter. When a flock of turkeys roared up out of the tall grass novice hunters followed them eagerly. Colter knew it was better to sit down quietly and wait. The flock would come together at the place where it had been scattered. The turkeys would come back gobbling to each other and give a silent hunter a good shot. The men lived well on John Colter's rifle.

Some minor chiefs appeared in camp on August 2, 1804. Drewyer and Dorion stepped forward to act as interpreters. Captain Lewis looked at the Indians' squaws and pack ponies. They looked grimy, feeble and poor. The ragamuffins said that the great men of the tribe were away from the villages hunting buffalo. The interpreters translated. Lewis told the savages to camp outside his lines. He would council with them in the morning. Then he turned to his men and warned them to be on guard against treachery. The wealth on board the boats yonder would make these miserable barbarians rich as Croesus.

In the morning Lewis and Clark sat down under the awning and received the Indians formally. Both of them had seen Mad Anthony Wayne's buff-and-blue-clad soldiers treat with Indians back in the Ohio country. Peace pipes were produced and filled with tobacco. Indians had a peculiar manner of drawing the smoke from the long-stemmed pipes. Each took three or four quick, short "pulls" like greedy animals grazing, then handed the long-stemmed pipe to the next in the circle. Lewis and Clark received the pipe in turn. The red men and the white talked. Then the Americans hung medals around the chiefs' necks and told them not to recognize British traders. From now on their "fathers" would be the Americans. The Indians grunted, took the presents given them and walked away silently.

Lewis and Clark both wrote about the incident in their journals. They noted, too, that the site was ideal for a trading post and fort. Good building timber was available. Clay suitable for bricks was at hand. Moreover, the location was central to many large villages, albeit the inhabitants were temporarily absent. Clark, who never mastered spelling, wrote that the place was "Senteral to Several nations." He also called the place "Councile Bluff"—the first use of a name that would be familiar to west-bound travelers for 150 years.[2]

Beyond Council Bluffs the country looked different to the travelers. This was the second change encountered since they left St. Louis. To them, as to many who followed, Council Bluffs was the gateway to the plains, to the boundless ocean of grass, the transparent air. From here on, every day the men saw new wild animals. Prairie dogs, erect on the craters of their burrows, coughed continually like apoplectic aldermen—a cough some called a bark. A great hare, new to the Americans, had black-tipped ears. The first one they saw skipped away with a lop-sided canter, then laid back his ears and raced off like greased lightning. In the distance he made a "sky hop." The hare wanted to see the Americans as much as they wanted to see him. The men learned that these "sky hops" were characteristic of jack rabbits.

At one camping place a soldier killed a pack rat—a fawn-colored rodent with a bushy tail, long whiskers and a creamy soft belly. Pack rats seemed to have no fear of men. The Americans learned that pack rats scampered around the camp while the men were asleep and stole any bright article they could carry away. Another curiosity to the men was a bird the size of a small crow, a noisy, inquisitive fellow. Checkered like a harlequin, he flapped out from the riverbank on black and white wings, looked at the boats with one eye, then the other, and scolded raucously. Captain Clark, the unorthodox speller, wrote in his journal that the magpie was a "butifull thing." The sight of buffalo swimming across the Missouri gave all the men real excitement, the first sure sign of the Far West. At night around the campfire the two leaders heard the staccato yelps of a coyote, maniac laughter flickering like heat lightning on the horizon.

Soon the river became serpentine. Lewis noticed that they sometimes floated ten miles and advanced only two. On August 11, 1804, a hill four or five hundred feet high appeared. Clark landed with ten men and climbed to the summit. Blackbird, king of the Mahar nation, was buried there sitting upright on his horse. A later generation would call Blackbird's people the Omahas, but both Lewis and Clark called them the Mahars.

On August 20, 1804, Sergeant Floyd died on the ship as she sailed along under a gentle breeze. Two days before, he had been too ill to continue writing in his journal. The men buried him with military honors on a hill where Sioux City, Iowa, would later stand. Private Gass was promoted to his position. Already, Gass was showing his mettle. The expedition had now reached the edge of the Sioux country and all knew that trouble was ahead. The Sioux claimed a monopoly on the river trade. They would probably object to the Americans' going farther. Captain Lewis sent old Dorion ahead to notify the chiefs to come for a council. He then selected a suitable meeting place and ordered his men to erect a tall flagstaff near a shady oak. He spread out suitable presents and prepared his speech.

The Indians straggled down toward the camp, dismounted near by, erected brush shelters and lay in them while the squaws painted their faces, plucked out offending whisks of beard, put beaded moccasins on their feet. Among them was Dorion's half-breed son with his dusky family. The time for the council was fixed. Dressed in handsome buckskins embroidered with porcupine quills, the Indians came and sat in a half circle before the Americans. The pipe of peace was passed from mouth to mouth. Captain Lewis made a "talk." The two Dorions translated. Presents were distributed. Medals were hung around the necks of the principal chiefs. They were told that they were American subjects. To the grand chief Lewis gave a richly embroidered artillery coat and a cocked hat with a red feather. Then the Indians retired to their lodges. Captains Lewis and Clark ordered their own dinner. Proud of their achievement, they sat down together. The Dorions were left to shift for their meal between the soldiers and the Indians. As interpreters they felt themselves as good as the headmen. Clark noticed that the Frenchmen were offended. He soothed their feelings with a bottle of whisky. The Americans then packed their duffel and sailed away, leaving the Dorions maudlin and happy with their red kinsfolk. The expedition had run the Sioux gantlet without casualty.

September passed and the pirogues moved slowly up the river. Councils were held at the tepee villages of the Tetons and Gros Ventres — French names better not translated — also with the Chiens or Dog Indians — another French name later spelled Cheyenne. In October the Americans came to the Arikara villages, an early starting place for Oregon exploration. Hundreds of horses grazed on the broad plains all around. The river was dotted with bullboats—round hide canoes—paddled by women towing loads of wood. The Arikara lived in lodges covered with dirt. The structures appeared like mounds of earth, great anthills. Pale blue smoke fanned from the top of each. Blanket-wrapped squaws squatted on top also and watched the boats in the river. Lewis and Clark landed. They walked up through the mounds, which seemed to be built without order. The doors were at the ends of short tunnels of upright logs. Buffalo robes hung across the openings. Inside, the lodges were warm, pungent and gloomy, with shafts of light from the smoke holes piercing the blue haze. That night Clark wrote in his diary: "Those people are much pleased with my black Servent. Their womin verry fond of carressing our men &c." Next day Clark added another note: Two young "squars" determined to follow the expedition. The guard was ordered to keep them out of the lines.

In October the high plains became tawny. Winter was coming fast in this northern country, but Lewis and Clark knew that they would easily reach the Mandan villages in time to make good winter quarters. Trees had become scarce along the river-bank. A few stood almost leafless and forlorn. In the current, dead leaves tumbled past the boats. The men noticed that the game animals had put on their winter coats. The deer up here were different—blue-gray in color, with forked tines on their antlers. They had small tails and big ears like a mule. These upcountry deer did not throw up their tails like rabbits when they ran. Instead they bounded away with stiff-legged jumps, striking the ground with all four feet at the same time. Antelope—"goats" the Americans called them—were also plentiful. They, too, seemed bigger up here. Perhaps it was their spongy winter hair.

Most noteworthy of all, the Americans found a new kind of bear, bigger than any yet discovered in America. Lewis and Clark were the first to describe the grizzly, but they called him the "white bear." They also saw bands of elk, sway-necked like camels, swinging along on a trot. The Fields brothers, Joseph and Reuben, were becoming great hunters like John Colter.

On October 26, 1804, the explorers reached the Mandan villages, the great barbarian metropolis of the plains, terminus of the boat trade from St. Louis. Here the Americans planned to rest during the winter and prepare for the exploration of the unknown country ahead.

Lewis and Clark looked over the entire area. They wanted to select a suitable place to build a fort and barracks. A North West Company trader in town offered to show them around. The villages clustered on seven hills, like ancient Rome. Dirt lodges, some of them sixty feet across, were surrounded with sodden gardens of withered corn, bean plants, squash vines and tobacco stalks. The trader talked to the natives in broken Indian with an Irish accent. Men and boys galloped to and fro. Horses were plentiful here as they had been below. Here, too, groups of blanket-wrapped people sat always on the tops of the hovels watching the horizon. The young men rode across the sky line hunting buffalo every day. Raiding parties of Sioux also came across the horizon to steal horses and kill unwary Mandan hunters. The Americans learned that the Indians took their best horses into the houses with them at night. They also noticed that dead Indians, swathed in buffalo robes, were "buried" on scaffolds.

Lewis and Clark chose a site for their fort and set the men to work building a stockade. A detail of hunters kept the company in meat. John Shields set up his forge and began blacksmithing. Indians strolled in every morning and watched the work. Several French traders came in from the plains to join their Indian families for the winter and chat with the Americans. Shields soon had more business than he could attend to, mending broken tomahawks and making new ones out of scrap metal. Amid this sociability, the fort was soon finished.

Every night, guard was mounted and all loafing Indians were ordered out. The gates were closed. Lewis knew that his stockade was not invulnerable but it had a martial appearance. Soon he learned that his men, coming in late at night from the Indian villages, vaulted the wall instead of calling out the guard for admittance. Lewis ordered this practice stopped at once. It might put an idea into the Indians' minds.

With the fort completed, Captain Lewis increased the number of his hunting parties. He set other men to work building carts to bring in the meat. Axmen cut timber for the frames of six canoes. One day Indians galloped along the riverbank shouting that the prairies were on fire. Men, women and children, on foot and on horseback, were known to be scattered far and wide across the grasslands, hunting buffalo and roots and berries. From the fort it was hard to see the course of the fire. The vicious red line crackled up broad slopes, leaped across valleys, roared in the tall weeds along washes. Smoke billowed high in the blue sky and bits of black ash floated down to settle on the anxious watchers along the river. Far into the night word passed from village to village, asking for news about this and that person known to be out on the plains. Lewis heard, finally, that all were accounted for. One man and woman had burned to death. A trader's half-breed son had been saved by lying flat on the ground under a green buffalo hide.

In November the nights became very cold. The river rustled with mush ice. Day after day the crystals tinkled past. Lewis and Clark issued the men a grog ration. During the night of December 6, 1804, the river suddenly became still. It was frozen solid. Sub-zero weather followed. The men shivered around the stone fireplaces in their daubed cabins. Captain Lewis knew that busy soldiers were contented soldiers, but when he looked out the door and saw the arctic atmosphere glittering with suspended frost prisms in air that cut human lungs like steel, he decided that they had better not venture out to hunt.

One day of idleness chafed Joseph Fields. On the second day he asked permission to go out. A mile from the fort he killed a buffalo. The Kentuckian had already become a mountain man. The next day red-headed Clark, more rough and ready than Lewis, decided that he could stand the winter weather. With a camp outfit on a sleigh, he took a detail of men hunting and bivouacked in the open. Back in the fort the next day, Clark thawed out his fingers before the open fire and wrote in his diary, "the Murckerey Stood at O."[4]

Now that the river was closed with ice, the game moved back from it. They licked snow for water. Lewis and Clark discussed the best way to victual their men. They decided to send hunters to the game country. Eighteen miles away a camp was established. With sleighs the men made regular trips into the fort with meat. Once the teamsters were pounced upon by a band of raiding Sioux. The savages cut loose all the horses and with a whoop galloped away with them in a cloud of snow thrown up by flying hoofs. Captain Lewis detailed a squad of men to pursue and punish them, but the Indians were too fast for his Americans.

In February the commanders began to make their preparations to move as soon as the river opened. They estimated that over two thousand miles of unexplored country lay ahead of them. Late in March the ice went out—great blocks covered with snow spinning endlessly down the brown river water.

Lewis ordered his own men to drag the canoes to the river in readiness for launching. The masts on the pirogues were rigged. Goods were repacked and assembled on shore. Lewis insisted that all essentials be distributed in different packs. In case of accident to any one cargo, the explorers could thus be supplied from another. The men were set to work carrying bars of lead, canisters of powder, casks of liquor, bolts of trade cloth on board the pirogues. The unwieldy metal joints and girders of Lewis's portable boat no doubt made them swear sometimes. Captain Lewis, half-defiant, half-ashamed, bragged about the boat's excellence, its possible great service ahead. Like his mentor, President Jefferson, Captain Lewis enjoyed gadgets.

During the winter Lewis and Clark had met a French half-breed named Charbonneau with three squaws, one a Shoshoni whom he had purchased from a Hidatsa war party. Charbonneau could not talk English, but he and his women had proved to be useful interpreters for the explorers. The squaws had translated the Mandan dialects to their lord and master. He repeated the words to a French mulatto in the village, who relayed the messages in bad English to the Americans. Charbonneau's Shoshoni or Snake squaw, Sacagawea or Bird Woman, a girl of eighteen, might be invaluable for translating among the Snake Indians in the unknown country ahead.

Lewis offered wages to Charbonneau if he would accompany the expedition with this woman. Charbonneau was not enthusiastic. The trip promised to be a hard one but the pay attracted him. Then, too, he watched Americans work around the fort like squaws. The half-breed did not intend to do such drudgery. He wheedled promises of immunity from all military duties and at last consented to go. He brought his little squaw, Sacagawea, and her household duffel to the fort. She carried a tiny baby on her back in a papoose board.

Charbonneau loafed around the stockade a couple of days, then announced that he would stay at Mandan. However, he thought this decision over for a day and changed his mind again. Captain Lewis, in the meantime, organized his men into two parties. One, under Corporal Worfington, was assigned to the barge. With six soldiers, four Frenchmen and an Indian, Worfington was to take the official report along with a collection of curios to President Jefferson. He had instructions to pick up a

load of peltries, some chiefs and another Frenchman at the Arikara village. All were to go to St. Louis. Then Corporal Worfington was to take the Indians on to Washington to meet the
President.

Captain Lewis mustered the remaining twenty-six soldiers into
another party for the explorations ahead. He planned to take
also the two half-breed interpreters, Drewyer and the new fellow, Charbonneau, his wife and baby, the Negro servant York,
and Lieutenant Clark as second in command. One Mandan
Indian joined to go as far as the Snake country. The entire party
was to embark in the two pirogues and six canoes.

Captain Lewis, with a flair for the dramatic, ordered both parties to their respective boats at the same time. At a given order
all shoved out into the Missouri, the barge to sail down to civilization while the flotilla turned west into the unknown. Captain
Lewis on shore strode off on foot. He would join his command
at their night camp. Overhead long lines of wild fowl were flying north, wavering lines sweeping northward like deploying
soldiers in the sky. That night Lewis wrote in his diary:

This little fleet altho' not quite so rispectable as those of Columbus or Capt. Cook, were still viewed by us with as much pleasure
as those deservedly famed adventurers ever beheld theirs; and I
dare say with quite as much anxiety for their safety and preser-
vation. We were now about to penetrate a country at least two
thousand miles in width, on which the foot of civilized men had
never trodden.[5]

The next day was cold with a wind against the explorers. They
made slow progress. A squaw caught up with them and wanted
to go along. Captain Lewis sent her back. Day after day they
moved forward on the ribbon of water through the golden
plains. At first, snow was in the air. The skies were overcast and
cold. Lewis and Clark took turns walking on the shore. They
passed the Little Missouri, the Yellowstone, the Musselshell. Two
months passed. Clark killed a jack rabbit mottled with brown
and white. It was changing color for spring. In May, green
grass carpeted the plains.

On June 8, 1805, the explorers reached a fork in the Missouri. The men wanted to take the north branch. Lewis and Clark thought the south the better. They had a North West Company map which indicated that the left branch penetrated deeper into the mountains. The commanders decided on the southern branch and, by so doing, turned into the high Rockies of Montana instead of going by a good pass through Canada to the Pacific. Lewis named the right fork "Marias River," for Maria Wood whom he admired back in Virginia. "It is true," he wrote, "that the hue of the waters of this turbulent and troubled stream but illy comport with the pure celestial virtues and amiable qualifications of that lovely fair one."[6] Lewis wrote also that he believed this river destined to be the scene of strife as the boundary line between the United States and British territory.

In the distance the Rocky Mountains peered above the horizon. Would the explorers be able to find a passage through them to navigable water on the other side? To carry their supplies over such a wall seemed impossible. The commanders decided first to bury their heavier equipment. The French boatmen understood how to dig a cache, how to carry the dirt away, throw it in running water and replace the sod so that passing Indians could not discover the hidden treasure. This was common practice with the traders. Lewis and Clark watched them hollow out a small round hole, pile the dirt on a buffalo hide, then excavate the cellar underground. The goods were buried— but Meriwether Lewis insisted that they take the portable iron boat with them.

At last the explorers reached the great falls of the Missouri. Sacagawea began to recognize the country, but she also became very ill. Captain Lewis bled her, then experimented with medicine. Her husband tried his usual cuffing and beating. The baby cried in his papoose board. Captain Lewis was annoyed. The little Indian woman compared unfavorably with his Maria Wood. Most of the men respected Bird Woman. They admired her quiet fortitude. Clark began to feel an affection for her that would grow with the passing months.

To get the canoes around the falls the men unloaded the wheels and began the slow portage. Above the falls proper the explorers found many other portages and miles of necessary towing. The time had come to abandon their big boats and try Lewis' portable iron vessel that had caused so much worry and ridicule. The supply of goods would also have to be reduced. Lewis announced that the men could drink up all the liquor. With gusto the iron boat was jointed. July Fourth came and the men, still working on the boat, dissipated by dancing in the evening until 9:00 P.M.

When finished the boat's iron framework looked quite impressive. Lewis ordered hunters to go out and kill sufficient elk for hides to cover it. Before long the craft was ready to launch. She had a carrying capacity of 8,000 pounds, and there was only one thing wrong with her. Water leaked in at all the seams between the hides. She would not float! Captain Lewis wrote gravely in his diary: "The boat in every other rispect completely answers my most sanguine expectations."[7] Obviously the Jeffersonian experiment in portable boats would have to be left on the edge of the Rocky Mountains.

The soldiers probably got amusement out of the captain's discomfiture but of course said nothing—within hearing. Clark, excellent soldier that he was, never mentioned the contraption or its failure. The men buried more supplies in another cache and built two more canoes out of wood. They wondered why they had seen no Indians. This was the country of the Snakes, Sacagawea's people, but as yet no tribesman had appeared. Both Lewis and Clark knew that they would never be able to find a path across the mountains unless they had guides. They suspected that the Indians heard their guns and fled before them. At last Captain Lewis announced that he and a picked party would strike out ahead and keep going until they found the red men. Dressed in tanned skins and moccasins with a cocked hat and feather, he strode away with his party. For days Lewis trudged along shooting game to eat, sleeping with the men in the open, the watch in his rolled trousers ticking in his ear. They came to the three forks of the Missouri. Lewis named them Jefferson,

Madison and Gallatin, for the President, the Secretary of State and the Secretary of the Treasury. Going up the Jefferson, the little party came to high green meadows under towering mountains. The porous ground froze every night and in the morning crackled frostily under their moccasins. At noon the sun was piping hot. Lewis had never before felt such sudden changes in temperature. He knew that the Continental Divide must be close.

One day the river had become so small a man in the party straddled it and joked that he stood with one foot on each side of the mighty Missouri. From a mountain pass on August 12, 1805, the men looked west to a chaos of peaks and many deep defiles, all apparently too rough for boats. A short way down the slope they came to water tinkling through the rocks under bluebells and marsh marigolds. One by one they bent down, drank from the icy stream and bragged that they had tasted the "Columbia." At last the explorers found some Indians, but they could not talk to them nor ask what they wanted to know. Sacagawea, ill with the main party on the eastern slope, was of no service.

Captain Lewis explained and re-explained that he wanted to buy horses and hire the Indians to pack supplies across the mountains. With many small presents he finally got them to understand—or thought he had—but the Snakes, or Shoshoni, were slow to agree. Always on the verge of starvation, they had to hunt game constantly to keep alive. Lewis did not have enough supplies to feed the village, so his pleas and presents were minor inducements. Besides, the Indians seemed to suspect that the Americans wanted to lead them into ambush on the eastern slope of the mountains. The savages feared to leave their own lofty valley. Finally, however, Lewis persuaded them to move. His own hunters with guns helped kill meat for all, but the farther the red men went down the eastern slope the more unhappy and suspicious they became. Constantly they accused Lewis of treachery. To reassure them, Captain Lewis put his cocked hat on the chief's head, said over and over that his men must be very, very near. At last they found them. Sacagawea embraced her relatives. Tears ran down her copper cheeks. She smiled at the Americans and sucked her fingers, the Indian sign that these were her kinsfolk.

The men in the main party said that Bird Woman's health had improved during the last few days. She had pointed out familiar landmarks and showed them the place on the river where she had been captured by the Hidatsa. With much noise and laughter the Indians packed the explorers' camp and carried it back into the mountains. Lewis noticed that the women were as adept as the men in lifting bags and bundles onto a horse's back and lashing them there with ropes of hair and sinew. On the march the cavalcade spread out for several miles. In every grassy park the Indians raced with one another to be first at the distant forest wall where the trail made them travel single file.

A few days' work and travel were enough for the Indians. Fickle always, they wanted to go about their own business—and did. Sacagawea stayed with her man, and Lewis and Clark struggled on as best they could. They had purchased some thirty-eight horses. The men had made packsaddles and had learned to load them, but they did not know which way to go. Many a time they struggled to the top of a mountain to find that the stream on the other side flowed back into the one that they had left. Clark went ahead and tried to find a way through by what was later known as the Salmon River country of central Idaho. He came back and reported that this stream sank into deep canyons below snow-capped peaks. The way was impassable and the game scarce. The explorers turned and groped their way farther north. They met primitive bands of Indians, the most degraded people they had yet seen. These red men had no direct contact with white traders. Only an occasional piece of iron put them out of the Stone Age. Usually they ran when they saw the white men. With presents they could sometimes be enticed to talk. Occasionally they helped the explorers for a day or two but they were afraid to leave the borders of their own valleys.

On September 10, 1805, a party of Indians showed fight, surely a different breed. The interpreters beckoned them with signs. The savages put down their weapons and came forward. They were Flatheads from west of the mountains. The Shoshoni, they said, had stolen some of their horses. To get revenge they had come to the highlands. The warriors consented to lead the Americans to a river which flowed to the western sea. Five "sleeps" would be required, they said. The Indians guided the Americans for a day, then decided to do something else. They pointed their bronze hands at distant purple canyons and galloped away.

Captain Lewis ordered his men to march in the direction the Indians indicated, but the country did not appear as they had anticipated. The streams all flowed the wrong way. Time and again the men led their struggling horses up steep ridges and slipped down to streams on the other side, but the water did not flow west. John Colter and the Fields brothers, with all their skill as hunters, could not find a path in this maze of mountains.

At last, still in country later known as Idaho, the wanderers came to a village of well-made brush wickiups. The people came forward dressed in handsome clothes of snow-white buckskin decorated with shells. Their moccasins were embroidered with porcupine quills. They brought presents of fish and bread made of floured roots and dried berries. They said that they were Nez Percés.

The Americans ate hungrily. They noticed that these Indians were well-to-do. Many horses grazed in the mountain valley above their lodges. Snowshoes hanging in the trees indicated that the winters were severe here. The Indians smiled and indicated the depth of imaginary snowdrifts on the trunks of trees. They said that they went east across the mountains every summer to hunt buffalo. They knew a good trail. The Americans were pleased and helped themselves to more of the root bread, then looked at one another questioningly. Their stomachs had begun to turn handsprings. Lewis learned, as many other explorers have, that men have trouble adapting themselves to new food and new climates.

Slowly and with considerable misery, the men moved on to the forks of the Clearwater. In north central Idaho, where the town of Orofino would later stand, they stopped. Below the junction there was enough water to float boats, and on the banks the men saw ample timber for canoes. Overland travel on foot and on horseback had not been pleasant. The men were eager to be back on the water. All were confident that this stream flowed into the Columbia.

Still ill and weak, the men set to work in short shifts, chopping trees. Lewis ordered a horse killed for food. The meat helped the men's intestines. Friendly Indians came to watch the work. A toothless old savage, brown and wrinkled as a windfall apple, beckoned with a skinny arm and by signs said that he had floated down the stream "many suns" to a fort kept by white men, who had traded him white beads. Captain Lewis knew that some old Indians were garrulous. He doubted the story. No settlements were known on the Columbia. But a man could never be sure. Had the British slipped in from the north and established a fort? Mackenzie had crossed the continent twelve years before. The British fur companies had probably been busy since that time. Lewis asked the interpreters to get more details from the old man. With the sign language they set to work. The old fellow could give no new details. He repeated his first story without embellishment; he seemed to know no more. Captain Lewis decided that the old man was romancing.

On October 7, 1805, six canoes were finished and launched. All floated and proved seaworthy. A successful trip to the Pacific seemed assured, but something must be done with the horses until the men returned. Captain Lewis called a council of the Indian chiefs. With Clark and the interpreters they sat down and smoked. Lewis offered to pay the Indians two guns and a keg of powder to herd his horses until he came back next summer. The red men agreed.

Lewis knew that the Indians had hundreds of horses of their own. He ordered his own mounts branded with a *US*, and then, so that they could be easily identified, he had his men cut off the foretop of each animal before turning it loose. At night after dark, when the Indian visitors were gone, the Americans buried their saddles in a cache. The next morning they pushed the canoes into the stream. The men scrambled on board.

The riverbanks slipped past them rapidly. The explorers waved to Indian fishermen. The houses in the villages down here were different from those above. The brush wickiups of the mountains were replaced by low, sloping-roofed lodges of matting.

On October 11, 1805, Lewis and Clark saw a larger river ahead of them. Their boats floated out into the Snake River in what would later be the state of Washington. Soon the mountains dropped below the eastern horizon. Ahead on both sides the open desert appeared dry as ashes, without a tree in sight, not even along the water's edge. Here and there on the banks the men saw Indian villages. They landed, discovered that the people lived almost entirely on fish. Captain Lewis remarked that the timbers in their houses must have floated down from above. The red men had great numbers of horses. They occasionally varied their diet with antelope meat—the "goats" that Lewis and his men had seen in the east.

On October 16, 1805, the Americans came to the Columbia. There was no mistaking the great river. Lewis ordered the canoes to shore and pitched camp. Hundreds of Indians appeared from dozens of villages. The red men chattered, waved their paddles, grinned and pointed. Lewis noticed that many of the savages had deformed heads. They had evidently been flattened in babyhood. The line of the nose on these people extended to the top of the peaked cranium, and the forehead bulged unnaturally on both sides. The women were shorter and more corpulent than the Nez Percés, and they wore no clothes except a girdle. All seemed to have bad eyes and teeth. Lewis thought the glare on the water and the diet of fish were responsible. He noted that many of the men's teeth were worn to the gums. As Lewis watched and mused he heard Indian drums—musicians come to entertain the strangers. Lewis called for the chiefs. He and Clark sat down with them and smoked. Presents were exchanged; then the Americans got in their boats and floated away.

They noted a great quantity of dead salmon in the river and along the banks. Lewis wondered what had killed them. He did not know that these fish went up the river each spring to spawn, die and drift back to sea. From the canoes he watched the distant mountains in the west become clearer and higher each day. Evi-

dently the Columbia cut through the mountain wall ahead. From
Indian fishermen the Americans learned that a powerful tribe had
a village at the edge of the mountains. They collected toll on all
goods and canoes that passed through the canyon. As middlemen
they bought Indian supplies from the coastal red men and exchanged it for the roots, dried berries and grasses harvested by
the Indians above.

Captain Lewis did not have any supplies to be wasted as toll
for piratical Indians. He ordered his men to inspect their arms
and pick their flints. The threatened hostility ahead was notice-
able in the changed attitude of the Indians along the shore. The
mountain wall grew higher each day and the red men more truculent.

Lewis sighted a chasm ahead, The Dalles, the location of the
village that controlled trade through the canyon. An outlying
village came into view. The men saw two beautiful canoes, large
as whaleboats, dugouts scraped thin as boards and shaped su-
perbly. Both ends tapered and curious figures had been carved
on the bow. Evidently the explorers were coming to a new civilization, the culture John Boit had described to Bostonians a
decade earlier.

At last Wishram and then The Dalles proper! These villages
consisted of several large houses built of split planks—obviously
the board houses of the northwest coast, half underground, with
the entrance through the gable end, often through a hole in a
rafter post carved like a face with open mouth. Outdoors, between the slab houses, hundreds of split salmon dried on frames.
Captain Lewis landed his men in one village, looked at the jungle
of racks and estimated that they held at least 10,000 pounds of
fish. Women were busy pounding the dried fish and packing the
pulp in containers like sausages. Salmon would keep indefinitely
in this form, and the packages were a medium of exchange on the
river. These barbarians were wealthy.

Captain Lewis noticed that the chiefs, old and dignified, were
walking toward him. The red men asked for toll, payment for
the right to pass. Lewis lined up his soldiers and refused to pay.
The chiefs looked at the flintlock rifles and stalked away. The

Americans expected an attack. With a detail on guard they let their canoes down through the rapids. In many places they portaged the duffel, but always they were careful to keep the supplies guarded. Captain Clark noted in his journal that the Indians were in a "bad humer."

Every few miles the explorers came to a small village of a few great family houses containing twenty to thirty souls. In front of each stood elaborately carved totem poles. The Americans noticed that some houses were deserted. They prowled into them and found the planks alive with fleas. Perhaps the Indians had been driven out by their own vermin. The white men came back to their boats scratching. They had no clothes except the leather shirts on their backs. To get rid of the insects became a real problem.

Below the gorge through the Cascade Mountains the country opened into beautiful timbered valleys. On the water, white pelicans, round as china pitchers, paddled away from the canoes. Black angular cormorants dived at the approach of the boats and swam off underwater. The men saw sea otter, playful as porpoises. This was the fabled land at last.

On both banks of the Columbia clear tributary streams flowed into the river under a gray veil of the bare branches of elms and maples. The uplands were black with noble conifers. The Americans had never seen such forests. They landed and walked across the yellow carpet of fallen leaves into the gloomy woodland beyond. Red trunks, straight as shipmasts, towered two and three hundred feet into the sky. At the giants' splay feet, ferns stood tall as a man's head. The air was soft and misty. Wan rays of the sun penetrated the cathedral gloom. Both commanders wrote in superlatives about the luxuriance of the vegetation. They wondered how severe the coming winter would be. They saw no sign of frost and guessed the climate to be mild. Entranced with the beauty of their surroundings, they looked back up the river and spied snow-covered Mount Hood.

Such was Lewis and Clark's first impression of the Oregon country that would lure the emigrants a generation later.

In addition to the natural bounty of the Columbia, Lewis and

Clark were impressed by the great population of Indians along the shore of the lower river. The savages seemed to subsist almost entirely on fish and on a root known as wapatoo. Both could be found in abundance, and the natives lived in comparative indolence. A short way below the Willamette Valley the Americans met a gang of canoes filled with red men in sailor jackets, overalls, shirts and hats. The ragamuffins carried muskets, pistols and tin powder flasks[8]—a mean crew, impudent and saucy. Firearms had made them lords of the river and they seemed disposed to contest the Americans' rights. Captain Lewis outnumbered them in fighting men and felt no danger. He invited them to shore for a smoke. He hoped to get some information from them about the country ahead, but failed. Instead, his guests pilfered everything they could lay their hands on. They "stold"—Clark's spelling—his best tomahawk pipe while it was passing around the circle. Unable to carry away a capote, they hid it under a tree root, evidently intending to come back after the explorers had gone. All the whites were glad when their guests departed.

In the days that followed, the explorers met many canoes—almost as thick as the cormorants and pelicans. Indians still in their native culture were friendly, offered food and talked with the sign language. The Columbia soon widened to a bay or estuary, and wind whipped the water into high waves. The men became seasick. Squeamishly they watched Indians come out from their villages and go galloping across the billows in canoes. The Americans noticed that these down-river natives wore different clothes and talked a different dialect from those above. They were Chinook.

The explorers knew that the ocean must be close. Fog kept them from seeing far ahead. The wet curtains of moisture hung so thick that men at the opposite ends of a canoe appeared dimly as through a heavy veil. The men could see, by marks on the riverbank, that the tides rose six to eight feet. They wondered how far away the ocean really was.

At last the great day came. It was November 7, 1805. The explorers were camped among the river boulders close to the water. In the fog over their heads gulls screamed. The men could hear the rustle of wild-fowl wings all around them. Silently the sun dissolved the fog. The Americans saw two points of land and between them the Pacific Ocean. They clambered into the boats and paddled toward the west. Soon they could hear the roar of the surf on the rocky shore; plumes of spray leaped around Cape Disappointment and fringed the coast beyond mile after mile into the distance. The journey was over, but Lewis and Clark still had the problem of survival during the winter and the long trip home with the record of their discovery.

Had the explorers but known it, the brig *Lydia* from Boston lay in the Columbia. Through her they could have announced to the world the success of their journey and acquired much-needed supplies for the winter. The Indians, through craft or stupidity, had said nothing about the sailing ship. Repeatedly the Americans asked the names of traders who brought their cloth and metal. The red men described thirteen vessels, the number of their masts, the deformities of the commanders.[9] The Indians said that the traders talked like the explorers, said "powder," "shot," "file," "damned rascal," "heave the lead," and "sun of a pitch."[10] Yes, they spoke English all right, but there was no indication that any of them were still here, no reason to expect them again until spring. In the meantime Lewis and Clark must find suitable winter quarters.

On the south bank of the Columbia they built Fort Clatsop, and in the spring deeded it to a neighboring chieftain, Comcomly. With him, too, Captain Lewis left a list of his party's members and a memo on the route they intended to follow back to the States. In case they all perished, the captain of the next trading vessel would learn that they had at least crossed the continent.

Late in March, Lewis and Clark set off in their boats. They entered the Cascade gorge, passed the Bridal Veil, Horse Tail, Oneonta and Multnomah waterfalls, wreaths of vapor cascading down beetling battlements that shut the river from the sun. At the Indian village of "Wallahwallah" they were received hospitably. They abandoned their boats and they marched up the Clearwater to the Nez Percés. The reds delivered their horses as agreed and led the explorers across the mountains to the forks of the Big Blackfoot and Bitterroot near where Missoula, Montana, would one day stand. Here the Indians left them and the whites separated into two parties. Lewis intended to explore the country to the north across the mountains to Marias River while Clark rode south to the headwaters of the Yellowstone. They met again below the junction of the Missouri and Yellowstone rivers. Sacagawea went with Clark. His attachment to her and the baby had increased. Clark called the little fellow Pompey and named a mountain for him in Montana.

Captain Lewis' side trip was less romantic and more dramatic. He had a fatal conflict with the Blackfeet. Some historians maintain that this fight turned the tribe into mortal enemies of the Americans and made exploration in their country impossible for a generation, thus deflecting the possible route of the Overland Trail far to the south.

Reunited and back at the Mandan village John Colter and John Potts asked to be discharged. Colter remained there along with Charbonneau, Sacagawea and nineteen-month-old Pompey. The rest of the party floated rapidly down the Missouri to civilization. They met many boats on the way, learned that they had been given up for lost and that the war between Britain and France, which John Boit had seen begin thirteen years ago, still dragged along. Among the boatmen, Lewis and Clark met a scout they had known in the Ohio country, Robert McClellan, a small wiry, intense man, loud in talk about his experiences and always threatening to kill someone. In McClellan's crew they recognized Old Man Dorion, on his way upriver to visit his Sioux kinsfolk again. On September 25, 1806, Lewis and Clark were back in St. Louis. A great dinner and ball were tendered them. Next day Clark wrote solemnly and with his usual spelling in his journal: "a fine morning we commenced wrighting &c." Both men took the task of authorship seriously. They were sure that they had crossed the continent at the most accessible place—except for that little strip through the mountains,[11] and they realized the importance of informing the world about their explorations.

Courtesy, Jay Monaghan

DEVIL'S GATE

The Trail Passed Around the Righthand Bluff.

Photo by the Author

INDEPENDENCE ROCK

EMGRANT GUIDEBOOKS

1 Reuben Gold Thwaites (ed.), *Original Journals of the Lewis and Clark Expedition, 1804-1806* (New York, 1904), I, 185n.

2 *Ibid.*, 98-99. See also Elliott Coues (ed.), *History of the Expedition under the Command of Lewis and Clark . . . A New Edition* (New York, 1893), I, 66n.

3 H. M. Brackenridge, *Views of Louisiana, together with a Journal of a Voyage up the Missouri River, in 1811* (Pittsburgh, 1814), 229-30; Washington Irving, *Astoria, or Anecdotes of an Enterprise beyond the Rocky Mountains* (Philadelphia, 1841), I, 171ff.

4 Thwaites (ed.), *Lewis and Clark Expedition*, I, 237.

5 *Ibid.*, 284.

6 Coues (ed.), *Lewis and Clark*, II, 354n.

7 *Ibid.*, 406n.

8 Thwaites (ed.), *Lewis and Clark Expedition*, III, 197.

9 *Ibid.*, IV, 178.

10 *Ibid.*, III, 327, 344

11 *Ibid.*, IV, 68.

Chapter 3

John Jacob Astor Opens
the Way: 1811

EWIS AND CLARK worked diligently but they were slow in getting their journal ready for the publisher. Sergeant Patrick Gass, always independent, got his in the hands of a printer in 1807. Reprinted several times, it was translated into German and French. From this booklet, rather than from the Lewis and Clark journals, people first learned about the overland route to the Oregon country. In 1809 a counterfeit publication, compiled from the Gass diary, several notes, documents and fur-trader accounts, was published as the true journal of Lewis and Clark. The genuine printing did not appear until 1814. By this time other notable travelers had crossed the continent.

Before the real journal was published John Jacob Astor, an immigrant boy become rich in the Midwest fur trade, decided that the time had come to expand his operations. He saw opportunity for large profits in a series of trading posts up the Missouri and over the Rockies with a headquarters factory at the mouth of the Columbia River. A small fleet would engross the coast trade as far north as Russian Alaska. Astor planned to send a shipload of Indian trade goods annually around the Horn to the Columbia factory. From here they would be distributed up the great river and along the coast. He would take the furs collected at the factory across to China, as Captain Gray and the Boston men had done. With Oriental goods he would come back to the United States. The plan seemed to be a money-maker as Astor outlined it in his mind. He even hoped to make a trade alliance with the Russians and supply Indian goods to the Alaskan posts. A combination of John Jacob Astor and the great trading monopoly chartered by the Czar could surely squeeze England, France and Spain from the Northwest coast Indian trade. Between them they could keep out both the Hudson's Bay and the North West fur companies and nullify the rights claimed by Mackenzie's overland trip to the Pacific. Astor explained his dream to President Jefferson, adding that the United States political empire might spread with trading establishments. Jefferson seemed interested.

Astor's first problem was to select suitable men for his commercial adventure. His rivals, the Hudson's Bay and North West companies, possessed men with the requisite skills. Astor turned to them. He knew that many excellent young men in these Canadian firms must be discouraged at the slow prospect of advancement in such large organizations. Several young Scotsmen attracted him. There was Alexander McKay, who had accompanied Mackenzie on the first expedition across North America to the Pacific while Captain Gray was sailing back to Boston from the Columbia. Certainly he was a seasoned trader and explorer. Astor had an interview with McKay and employed him. The wealthy New Yorker next approached Duncan McDougal and David McKenzie, two ambitious clerks, also in the North West Company. He outlined the opportunities of advancement in a small concern and enlisted both of them. To head his new company, Astor selected Wilson Price Hunt of New Jersey, the only American in the organization. The partners were to put up their services against Astor's money in a joint-stock company. On June 23, 1810—with Jefferson no longer President—these four men incorporated themselves with John Jacob Astor as the Pacific Fur Company. Astor agreed to advance up to $400,000 for equipment and supplies. For this he was to retain a half interest in the concern.[1]

McDougal and McKay enlisted a party of French *voyageurs* in Canada and with them embarked on the ship *Tonquin* for the mouth of the Columbia. Wilson Price Hunt and McKenzie went

to Canada to start the overland journey. At Montreal they hired
a crew of *coureurs de bois*. Such men, they believed, would be
ideal for the adventurous exploration. With keelboats common
to the Canadian fur companies they set off up the Ottawa for
Lake Huron and the island of Mackinac. They found the French
boatmen cheery and philosophical but lazy. They plied their oars
to boat songs but stopped for a pipe at the least provocation.
They showed no independence of spirit and the prospect of going
into the Far West dismayed them. Hunt was disappointed. At
the North West Company factory at Mackinac he wanted to enlist more Frenchmen, westerners. These fellows, too, were sunny
and good-natured but unwilling to embark on a long adventure.

Wilson Price Hunt was perplexed. Then he met a friend,
Ramsay Crooks, a stockily built man who had come from Scotland as an employee of the old North West Company. Making
money was the controlling interest of Crooks's life. He had left
the big company to speculate on his own account, going to the
upper Missouri in partnership with Robert McClellan, the wiry
little trader whom Lewis and Clark had met on the Missouri.
Hunt explained Astor's great scheme and his own troubles enlist-
ing boatmen. He offered Crooks an interest in the company if
he would go along.

Crooks accepted but he said that a large number of men would
be necessary to put the goods through the Sioux and Blackfoot
countries. Lewis and Clark had made the last-named Indians
especially hostile to Americans. Hunt agreed to hire the men but
how could the loafing Frenchmen be induced to go? Crooks,
oval-faced, solemn with thoughts of money, knew the way to a
French boatman's heart—and a cheap way too. Soon a few gay
fellows were dancing up and down the steep streets of Mackinac
with bright feathers in their hats. Friends asked where they got
their gay ornaments. The men replied, "From Mr. Hunt!"
Featherless boatmen came to him for the gewgaws. Hunt handed
out cocks' tails, ostrich plumes, white feathers tipped with red,
but with each gift he exacted a promise that the recipient enlist
for the Columbia. In no time the gay badge was fashionable.
Crooks and Hunt had all the men they needed.

To get them into boats and off the island was another problem. Out in Lake Michigan at last, the new partners took a deep breath of relief. On the west shore, in Green Bay, the trouble started again. The Frenchmen begged to stop at every cottage. At night they wanted to go to the nearest light or stop where a fiddle whined. These men were forest-bred but they had no ambition to explore a new route to the Pacific. If the adventure proved successful, Hunt and Crooks would alone be responsible for it.

The happy-go-lucky *voyageurs* rowed up the Fox River, portaged to the "Ouiskonsin" [Wisconsin] and floated to the Mississippi along the fur route used by traders for generations. Down the Mississippi through the Des Moines rapids they traveled to St. Louis, metropolis of the West.

Hunt and his Canadians landed and walked up the levee into the great fur mart. They passed brick houses occupied by Yankee shopkeepers and old French mansions standing among shade trees. Rivermen, merchants in stovepipe hats, French Canadians, dark-skinned Spaniards with earrings and here and there a lank Kentuckian in fringed hunting shirt strode along the streets. Indians squatted in their blankets before the stores. Hunt had noticed since he left Montreal that the northern wilderness was controlled by the big fur companies. He knew that St. Louis was not in the jurisdiction of the Hudson's Bay or the North West companies but he soon discovered that another organization, the Missouri Fur Company, monopolized the trading rights on the Missouri. Manuel Lisa, a Spaniard by blood but a long-time fur trader in this country, controlled the Missouri firm. He had recently expanded his operations. The dreaded Blackfeet had harassed his fort at the forks of the Missouri and the factor, Andrew Henry, had crossed the mountains to establish a post in safer country on the headwaters of the Columbia. Lisa did not look with favor on competition with outside capital from John Jacob Astor. Hunt found many obstacles thrown in his way in St. Louis. Supplies were difficult to purchase and the men he tried to hire claimed previous engagements with the local company. At last Hunt met an independent trader, Joseph Miller, who was not associated with the monopoly. Miller hailed from Baltimore. He had served as an officer in the army but resented the discipline and found trading with the Indians more to his liking. Hunt offered him an interest in the Astor company and Miller accepted.

With Crooks and Miller, Hunt had two veterans. The three men decided to employ a few more men and get out of town. The season was too far advanced to cross the mountains this year, but the men could move into a good game country this side of the dangerous Indian range and winter there, economically. In the spring they would start for Oregon. This plan was agreed upon. On October 21, 1810, with two barges and one keelboat, the expedition started up the Missouri. Occasionally they used sails but most of the way the boats moved tediously by oars, poles and long cordelles. The Frenchmen in harness plodded slowly along the bank singing their boat songs. To work in gangs, stop regularly for a pipe or cup of tea and a joke suited their gregarious natures. They passed La Charette, the westernmost settlement when Lewis and Clark had come down the river only four years ago. Now pioneer cabins appeared along the bank for 275 miles above it.[2] At the mouth of the Osage in what would later be central Missouri a fort had been built.

The boats moved slowly past the high bluff, site of future Kansas City, through the island-choked channel near where Leavenworth would be, around the great horseshoe bend later known as St. Joseph until they came to the mouth of the Nodaway. Here, almost five hundred miles from St. Louis, Hunt called a halt on November 16, 1810. The bare trees and leaden skies warned the outdoor men that winter was coming. Hunt put his crew to work chopping trees for cabins. He had stopped just in time. Two days later the river froze above their camp.

One day a short wiry man came to the wilderness camp. He was Robert McClellan. A tall long-legged Virginian also strode into the temporary settlement. John Day was an older man than McClellan. About forty, he was six feet two inches tall, walked with an elastic step, stood straight as a pine tree and had a reputation for being a dead shot. Both men had been associated with

Ramsay Crooks. They were immediately taken into the new venture. Independent spirits seemed willing enough to enlist against the Lisa monopoly, but all said that Hunt would have a problem getting past the Sioux and Blackfeet.

Hunt decided to go back to St. Louis. His men were well encamped with plenty of deer and turkeys. He must enlist more help if possible to get through the dangerous tribes that blocked the Lewis and Clark route to the Columbia. Hunt's new partners told him that there was a French half-breed in the employ of Lisa who spoke Sioux and had great influence with that warlike nation. He was Pierre Dorion, son of the old Frenchman whom Lewis and Clark had used to get by the Sioux. Pierre was in St. Louis with his squaw and children waiting to go up the river as interpreter with Lisa's boats, come spring.

Hunt determined to get the half-breed for himself. In St. Louis he found Pierre willing to evade his winter whisky bills and Lisa also, and go with the American, provided his squaw and children were taken along. Hunt enlisted also some more hunters and boatmen. Two English scientists, John Bradbury and Thomas Nuttall, asked to join the party. Hunt started back to the Nodaway with all of them.

Manuel Lisa learned that his rival had taken the invaluable Pierre Dorion. He needed the scamp to get his own boats past the Sioux. Lisa swore out a complaint and sent officers to bring the half-breed back to stand trial for jumping his liquor bills. Dorion learned that the law was after him. With his Indian family he slipped from Hunt's camp, hid in the brush and rejoined the Astorians above the pale of the law.

On the way to the Nodaway, Hunt met a man famous on the frontier. John Colter, who had left Lewis and Clark at the Mandan village in 1806, had finally had enough of the Rocky Mountains. He had discovered what would later be known as Yellowstone Park and had suffered a terrifying experience as prisoner of the Blackfeet. They had stripped him of his clothes and let him run for his life with all the tribe's warriors after him with spears, bows and arrows. A fast runner, he had outdistanced the pack, turned and killed one man as fast as he was, and then dived into the Missouri. He swam under water to some driftwood and lay submerged while the baffled savages hunted for him.³ Night after night he drifted downstream, naked and without weapons, for hundreds of miles. He knew the ferocity of the Blackfeet all right and he warned Hunt about the danger of taking the Lewis and Clark route to the Columbia. Hunt offered Colter a job to go back with his party but the frontiersman declined. He had come 3,000 miles down the racing Missouri in thirty days, and did not intend to go back. He was bound for civilization at last.

On April 17, 1811, Hunt and his recruits arrived at their winter quarters on the Nodaway above the big St. Joseph bend. On April 2 Manuel Lisa, jealous of the interloper, had started after him with a picked crew in a keelboat. The Spaniard was intent on getting through to his man, Andrew Henry, on the Columbia. He had lost Pierre Dorion but he could get by the Sioux if he could overtake the Americans. The race would be exciting. Hunt was almost five hundred miles ahead but Lisa started a good three weeks earlier in the spring. A man of great energy, he bounced from place to place among his men. He helped row, hauled on the cordelle and led in the singing. His picked crew would surely overtake the poorly organized Americans.

Hunt found things in his camp in poor shape to pack and start. Rain poured down every day. The river rose ominously, eating into the mudbanks. There was great danger of wetting his goods while he was loading the boats but he dared not wait on the weather. The men carried the cargo over the muddy trails and stored it under canvas on the decks. The boats seemed almost as wet inside as out.

Hunt urged his men to get the boats loaded. He had almost sixty men, five of them partners, forty *engagés*. His four boats were all equipped with sails and one mounted a swivel and two howitzers. They shoved off on April 21, 1811. On the twenty-eighth they arrived at the mouth of the Platte, the boundary between the upper and lower Missouri. Newcomers were initiated here much as sailors celebrate the crossing of the equator. Above Council Bluffs some of the partners left the boats and climbed to the summit to look across the fresh green plains, the ocean of grass. Was there no route across this trackless waste to the mountains except by way of the Missouri and the Sioux and Blackfoot country? The Platte stretched straight as a string to the horizon toward the mountains but its shallow channel would not carry boats with supplies.

Near Council Bluffs the local Indians said that the Sioux were prepared to stop the expedition. They had gathered in force on both sides of the river. Hunt's men talked about the danger. A few deserted, to drift 600 miles downstream with no chance of help until they met Lisa's boatmen. Hunt kept grimly on up the stream. He passed the grave of Blackbird, the Omaha chieftain. In the dreary country above, his men met a canoe carrying two trappers back to civilization. The white men had spent two years on the upper Missouri. Hunt employed them at once to return with him. Then he received an unwelcome dispatch. From the bank a white man hailed the boats. He was a messenger from Manuel Lisa with a letter. The Spaniard wanted him to wait in order that they might unite forces to pass through the Sioux country. Hunt consulted Crooks and McClellan. Crooks advised Hunt not to wait. Lisa was a treacherous fellow, he said. If they combined, he might prejudice the Sioux against the Astorians. McClellan, always mercurial, boiled over. He would shoot the Spaniard at sight, he said.

Hunt thought it best to beguile his rival. He sent back word that he would await him at the Ponca village a short distance above. Then as the messenger returned, Hunt ordered his men to go forward with all haste. Surely they could keep ahead of the rival keelboat. At breakfast next morning, a short distance above the Niobrara, Hunt spied two canoes a half mile away across the river. He squinted at them through his telescope and discovered the canoemen were white. He ordered a gun fired to attract attention. The canoemen proved to be three Kentuckians returning to the States from employment with Lisa's Missouri Fur Company. They had been with Henry on the upper Missouri and had crossed the Continental Divide to the fort he had established on the Snake, or Lewis, fork of the Columbia. One of them, sixty-five-year-old Edward Robinson, wore a handkerchief around his head to cover a scar left when Indians had scalped him years ago on Kentucky's dark and bloody ground. His companions were John Hoback and Jacob Reznor.[4]

Here at last were men who had been across to the Columbia. Moreover, they had no scruples about joining the Missouri Company's rival organization. Hunt hired them instanter. The men unloaded their scant duffel and shoved their abandoned canoes out into the current. Good-by.

During the days that followed Hunt talked to them often about the country ahead. They all maintained that the best pass across the continent was at the head of the Platte and the Yellowstone, a country south of the dangerous Blackfoot territory. To cross there the travelers should leave the river at the Arikara village a short distance above, trade for horses and go overland. Experienced men all recognized the danger of following the Lewis and Clark route. Hunt decided to take his new employees' advice and let them guide him to the headwaters of the Snake. They had just come over part of the route.

On the last day of May the expedition came upon the Sioux. The boatmen watched a formidable array stream down the hills to the bank of the river. The Indians were armed with spears, bows, arrows and round shields. A few carried carbines. The river was swift and the boats had to keep close to shore. From the top of the banks the Indians could shoot down into the vessels without danger to themselves. Hunt called his men together for a council. All agreed that the whites must meet the Indians in a pitched battle, settle the issue and determine the right of passage. Hunt ordered the boats across the river. On the far bank the men's arms were inspected. The howitzers and swivel were fired and reloaded. Then the boats set off straight for the hostile Indians.

The red men waited in a fluttering line. The sun sparkled on necklaces and spear points. Painted faces gleamed white above dusky bodies. In the boats the French Canadians complained resignedly, "We are not going to a wedding, my friend." Hunt, on deck, estimated the Indians at 600 against his sixty. The boats came within rifle range and the hunters prepared for action. On the shore the Indians waved buffalo robes above their heads and then spread them on the ground. Pierre Dorion warned the Americans not to fire. The Sioux wanted to talk.

Hunt, with McKenzie, Crooks, Miller, McClellan and Pierre Dorion, landed. The Indian chiefs awaited them, squatting in a solemn semicircle. The Americans advanced and sat down. A peace pipe, with a stem six feet long decorated with paint and feathers, was produced. All took a whiff, then the speeches began. The Indians said that they objected to the whites' going to trade with their enemies. Why not trade here? Hunt replied in French that he was not going above to trade but to travel to the distant big salt water. In case the Sioux opposed them the Americans were prepared to fight. Pierre Dorion translated. Then some of the Frenchmen brought suitable presents of tobacco and corn from the boats. The Indians thanked Hunt and the expedition proceeded.

Above the Sioux encampment the Astorians entered the buffalo country. The plains, clothed in new grass, were dotted with bison to the horizon. At every turn in the river the shaggy brutes were seen ahead drinking along the banks. They stared stupidly at the approaching sails. Hunt stationed his best marksmen at the bows of his boats to pick off the fattest animals to feed his crew. Among the dark shaggy monsters the hunters occasionally saw dun-colored antelope, dainty as fairies. On July 3, 1811, an Indian came running along the bank. He announced that a boatload of white men was coming up the river behind them. Hunt suspected that this must be Manuel Lisa overtaking him at last. Both had succeeded in getting past the Sioux. What treachery would Lisa plan up here with the rich Arikara and Mandans who were to furnish horses for the overland trip? In any event further flight was impossible. Hunt ordered the vessels to stop until his rival came up.

The twenty-oar keelboat came around the bend and was received with outward civility. For two days it traveled with the Astorians. McClellan still muttered but no longer threatened to kill the Spaniard. Now he said that he would shoot Lisa if he tried to pass above them to reach the Arikara village first. Two days later the old grudge came to a head. A thunderstorm stopped the travelers. Lisa tied up 100 yards behind the boat carrying Hunt and Pierre Dorion. The half-breed was enticed onto the Spaniard's boat and offered a drink. Shortly thereafter Dorion burst into Hunt's tent, smelling of liquor and swearing that Lisa had tried to hold him by force. Suddenly Manuel Lisa himself threw back the tent flap and came in. The half-breed struck him, then snatched Hunt's pistols and dared him to come forward. Lisa, trembling with rage, returned to his boat.

In the Indian country each man was his own law. The Spaniard returned with a knife in his belt and one of his own men beside him. McClellan heard the loud talking. He came with his rifle. Excited men ran along the riverbank. Hunt ordered Mc-Clellan to put down his gun. Behind him Lisa accused the American of dishonorable conduct. Hunt's temper flared up. In a rage, he challenged Lisa to a duel with pistols. John Bradbury, the English naturalist, and Lisa's second, mollified the principals. Both retired to their own boats and the parties proceeded on opposite sides of the river.

On June 11, 1811, they came to the anthill houses of the Arikara. Two chiefs with a French squaw man, resident in the village, paddled out to meet them. The interpreter announced, as the Sioux had, that the white men must not proceed farther and trade with enemy tribes above unless they would agree to leave at least one boatload of goods to be traded here.

Hunt explained that he did not want to trade above. He wanted horses and would trade here. Much pleased, the Indians paddled back to their town. Lisa also sent word that he had come independently with goods to trade.

Next morning Hunt and Lisa made it a point to land at the village at exactly the same time in order that neither might accuse the other of taking undue advantage, of being the first to arrive.[5] Together, but with mutual distrust, they marched among the dome houses to the council lodge. Here they sat in a circle around the fire. The town crier squatted on the roof by the hole which served as both chimney and window. From the lodge, the chief called orders and the crier shouted the news across the housetops.

Soon warriors came trooping in through the tunnel corridor to the council chamber.

Manuel Lisa spoke first. McClellan and Hunt watched him suspiciously. The Spaniard explained that he did not belong to the Astorian party but that he would resent any wrongful act to them as much as to his own people. He then proceeded to describe the goods he had brought to trade. Hunt, a little disappointed at this friendly gesture, spoke next. He stated that he was not a trader but had come instead to get horses for an overland trip to the big salt water. Then Chief Gray Eyes arose and said that the Arikara did not have sufficient horses to trade but if the white men would wait, their warriors would steal some from their enemies.

Thus the rivalry between the two traders was settled amicably. Perhaps Crooks and McClellan had displayed undue jealousy. Both parties settled down for a period of peaceful trading and the English naturalists prepared their specimens and made plans to go back with Manuel Lisa. Hunt established a camp on the plain above his boats. His baggage was unloaded and the trade goods spread out to dry. Tents were pitched and the men unfolded buffalo skins on which they bivouacked in the open air.

Weeks passed in purchasing horses. The Arikara village was built in two sections, each occupied by a different clan. Blanket-wrapped women and children sat all day long on the housetops, thick as starlings, watching the plains where their menfolk gathered horses. The mounts were brought in and Hunt inspected them. When he agreed that an animal was sound he paid the previously agreed price and the horse's tail was cropped to distinguish him from his unsold fellows.

Eighty-two horses were purchased. This was enough to carry the baggage, the trade goods, supplies and beaver traps, but many of the travelers would have to walk. However, the Indians had no more for sale. On July 18, 1811, the cavalcade set off, most of the men afoot leading pack horses. Each of the partners was mounted, as was Pierre Dorion, who also led a pack animal carrying his two children. His squaw trudged along in the column.

By good fortune Hunt had employed a second interpreter, named Edward Rose, a mulatto who had lived among the Crows. He promised to be invaluable when the party came to the high country. The route Hunt was undertaking was at least six hundred miles longer between the heads of navigable streams than the path Lewis and Clark had described.

Manuel Lisa watched them ride off. He shook his head. Would the motley array ever find its way across the sea of grass to the Pacific? How would they feed themselves? Would not the savages kill them if they separated to hunt? Most fur traders considered it unwise to go far from the safety of their boats.

The Astorians traveled south of west. The plains were hot and dusty in midsummer. There was no shade, but the dry air had a stimulating buoyancy. The guides urged Hunt to bear more to the south and thus evade the mountains where the Blackfeet were sure to make trouble. One morning Crooks complained that he was ill, unable to travel. The stocky Scotsman was subject to such spells. A litter was made for him and the cavalcade went on with Crooks groaning in a hammock suspended from poles between two horses.

Sixty-five miles out from the Missouri the conical tepees of a Cheyenne village were sighted. Here was a chance to get more horses, lay in a supply of buffalo meat and let Crooks recuperate.

For a fortnight the Astorians camped with the Cheyenne. They traded for thirty-six more horses and had great sport chasing elk and buffalo with their red friends. On August 6, 1811, they resumed their journey. Most of the horses were packed with goods but every two men had one horse to ride now. Crooks, still unwell, was confined to his litter. Each morning hunters rode out to replenish the larder, for meat spoiled almost overnight in the hot weather. One evening Pierre Dorion and his two companions did not come in. Next morning they had not arrived. Hunt ordered a smudge of smoke left on the plains to disclose the location of the camp. Dorion's squaw packed his things and the column moved away.

For days the traders shuffled slowly westward but the hunters did not catch up. Hunt began to fear that something serious had happened to them. Then by luck, rather than by good management, they met on the Little Missouri—near the future Montana-Dakota border. The reunited party wandered on to Powder River and beyond into the Big Horn Mountains. The guides were not so helpful as they had hoped. They had crossed the Continental Divide, true enough, but the country was so vast they did not recognize the few landmarks in this area. Certainly they had got the party into high mountains much sooner than the Lewis and Clark route would have done. Hunt ordered his men to skirt south of the Big Horn Mountains. They came to the Wind River canyon and followed up Wind River—keeping in open country but always seeing the mountains in the distance. At night water froze. The August days were hot but the men felt a new elasticity in the atmosphere.

One day in camp, at the foot of the Big Horn Mountains, Hunt saw two wild-looking human beings, undoubtedly Crows, sitting on horses as wild as themselves. Hunt sent Rose out to parley. The mulatto brought the savages back into camp. Their village, they said, was not far away. Next morning at dawn a troop of dusky horsemen whooped into camp with an invitation for the Americans to come visit their lodges only sixteen miles away. The troop offered to act as guides so the Americans followed them. The Indian escorts scampered about the slow-going travelers. On half-broken horses they careened around the column like antelope at play. They dashed up and down among the rocks and over the most dangerous places with perfect ease and unconcern, more like birds than men on four-footed animals. Some of the Americans wondered if they were being led into an ambuscade. McClellan, no doubt, fumed that he was going to kill somebody at the first sign of a sellout.

The Crows proved friendly, traded sound horses for the travelers' broken-down steeds and packed up to travel along with the white men. The cavalcade of red men, women and children, dogs and horses, pack animals and travois moved much more rapidly than the Astorians. Chattering, waving, spurring and whipping their pack ponies, the Indians left the whites behind altogether and soon disappeared in the mountains. The

Americans plodded along, glad enough when the last yelping savage was out of hearing. They kept doggedly to the west up Wind River. Game was plentiful, the weather superb. Only one thing marred the travelers' composure. The rumor grew that Edward Rose was plotting with some of the men to steal the horses and run off to the Crows. The deserters would all be rich men among these red fellows, have plenty to eat, good hunting and women to wait on them.

Hunt worried. He offered Rose half a year's salary to leave at once. The mulatto accepted the offer cheerily[6] and jogged away alone to join the red men. On the morning of September 9, 1811, the Astorians came to the north fork of Wind River. For five days they traveled up this stream passing from the desert to uplands of sagebrush, occasionally eight and ten feet high. The pack horses crowded through the aromatic shrubs, breaking the gnarled stalks. The riders' clothes became dusty with yellow pollen. At night sagebrush was the only fuel. It burned with a furious blue flame, sending up billows of smoke and white ashes. Game became scarce in this country but Hunt did not waver. He knew that he was traveling in the right direction to reach the Columbia.

The party headed for the wastes of spruce and pine later known as Yellowstone Park. Game disappeared altogether and starvation stalked along with the explorers. Dorion's squaw, with no food for her babies, did not complain but her stoicism impressed Hunt with his responsibility. He turned to the mountain men who had come out from Henry's fort on the Columbia. They appeared confused, admitted that they knew merely the general "lay" of the land, not the details of the geography. The mountains looked different from this side. They were not sure about the way. One of them told Hunt—incorrectly—that only one divide ahead separated them from the headwaters of the Columbia. To push desperately forward was tempting but Hunt knew that his guide was unreliable. He decided to turn south where buffalo might be found and kill a supply of meat. Had he continued on his course he would have crossed only into the headwaters of the Yellowstone and ahead of him would have been the chaos of mountains that had twice perplexed Lewis and Clark.

They changed their direction and rode southwest. On September 15, 1811, they left Wind River and followed an Indian trail up into the western mountains. The country changed rapidly. They came to bushes loaded with berries, willow-bordered brooks babbling with icy water. Under the summits of high bare ridges Hunt noticed little groves of aspens already turned to yellow gold by approaching winter. Late in the day the traders crossed a saddle in the highlands, Union Pass, Wyoming. Drifts of old snow clung to the north slopes. Ahead of them the sun sank behind a maze of magnificent mountains. The men dismounted to look, marvel and discuss the confused geography. One of the guides who had come out from Henry's fort pointed his fringed arm at three peaks, the Tetons, so called because of their nipple shape. It is easy to believe that he said, "Them pinochles is dreened by Lewis Fork of the Columbia. Henry's fort is on yan side, due west."

The party dropped down into the shadow of the valley to make camp. The Tetons sank behind the near-by mountains but the Astorians remembered their location. Hunt named them Pilot Knobs. Next day the Astorians rode beside the clear water of Green River. They had reached the western slope at last but not the Columbia. Ducks and geese flew up from Green River and the banks disclosed many beaver slides—channels on the bank down which beaver slid into the water in case of emergency. Great trees, two feet thick, cut down by the energetic rodents, lay with their tops in the stream. The men noticed that Green River flowed south instead of west. They left it and turned toward the Tetons. In a meadow they found buffalo sign. Meat at last! Hunt ordered his men to encamp and prepare for a big hunt. With rifles across their saddles the huntsmen jingled away. Hours later they came back loaded with cured meat and beaver skins. They said that they had met some Shoshoni hunting buffalo. This was Crow country and the Shoshoni had fled when they saw the strangers. The whites overtook them and made signs of peace. Then the redskins took them to their village and loaded them with supplies.

For five days Hunt's party feasted, rested and hunted. They accumulated two tons of meat—enough to load every horse except those ridden by the partners and Dorion. On September 24, 1811, they broke camp, traveled fifteen miles over a ridge to a brook that they followed down to a fifty-foot stream which they named Mad River, later known as the head of the Snake. Here under the shining Tetons, Robinson, Reznor and Hoback claimed to be at home. A pass south of the Tetons, they said, led straight to Henry's fort.

The Frenchmen wanted to build boats at once. They were tired of walking and leading horses. Miller, as disgruntled with the expedition as he had been with the army, backed the Frenchmen. He, too, was done with horseback riding. Some Shoshoni visitors said that the river was not navigable but the boatmen would not be convinced. Hunt put the question to a vote. The boatmen won. They began to work. Hunt, still dissatisfied with the decision, sent scouts down-river to spy out the way. He selected lanky John Day, Pierre Dorion and John Reed, an Irish clerk who had distinguished himself for hardihood and self-reliance.

Next Hunt turned his attention to business matters. He was a fur man at heart and this region was virgin beaver country. He detached six men with traps, guns and horses. They were to spend the winter trapping in the majestic mountains surrounding what was later known as the Jackson's Hole country, then, with their accumulated pelts, follow the main party's trail a thousand miles to the mouth of the Columbia.

The trappers shuffled away on their gaunt horses, long unwashed hair hanging on their fringed-buckskin shoulders, brassbound rifles across the pommels of their saddles, steel traps clanking in bags on the pack horses. Plenty of dangers were ahead, and many hardships, but also independence, leisure and good meat. Let's not forget, too, that simple men have a sharp sense for the beauty of the mountains.

The woodcutting continued. Two visiting Indians watched the axmen and shook their heads. The river was not navigable for canoes. Then the down-river scouts came back and reported narrow canyons and waterfalls below. The Indians were right. But the men insisted that they make boats.

That night, perhaps a few of the men noticed that the stars appeared in misty halos. Mountain men knew the meaning of this phenomenon. In the morning a ceiling of clouds pressed down on the camp. Gusts of wind brought eddies of sleet. The campfires hissed in the storm. Fine weather to be wading in icy water with homemade boats! Robinson, Hoback and Reznor urged Hunt to pack the horses and cross the Tetons to Henry's fort. They knew the way. It must be close. Boats could be made readily there.

Hunt stood around the fires in the mud. He asked the Shoshoni visitors about the fort. They said that they knew it, yes. They would guide the Americans there. It was truly enough "big short way."

The weather cleared on October 3, 1811. The clouds lifted, broke into rags and blew away through the peaks. The cold sun in a blue sky shone down on a glittering white world. While rain fell in the valley it had snowed all around the encampment. Hunt ordered the men to prepare to move in the morning. Miller grumbled at the work wasted on the logs strewn along the stream.

Bright and early the packs were lifted on the horses. The men mounted. Indians muffled in buffalo robes led the way across Snake River. Water came to the saddle girths. On the west bank the Shoshoni rode up a well-beaten path across the Tetons and down on the other side into what would be known as Pierres Hole. Reznor, Hoback and Old Man Robinson said that they had come out by this same pass on their way east. Four days later the horsemen dismounted at Henry's fort.[7]

The men prowled through the deserted cabins. They estimated that Henry had left last spring to go east and meet Lisa—probably at the Arikara village. He must have gone down the Yellowstone or Missouri while the Astorians were searching out the overland route.

The horse feed hereabouts was good—grass cured on the stem. Trees along Henry Fork were large enough for boats. The men still clamored for river travel and Hunt gave in. He negotiated with the Indians to watch his horses until he returned, then set the men to work chopping trees to make canoes. He detached four more trappers to "work" the area during the winter and come along to the Pacific in the spring. Hoback, Reznor and Robinson knew the country. Hunt chose them. He selected old Robinson to be chief of the little party and told off one more man to make the even number considered correct for trapping. Men in the mountains worked in couples, to guard each other. Horses, ammunition, trade goods were given to the little party. Then, before they left, Joseph Miller announced that he was going with them. Hunt was astounded. Miller had joined as a partner in the enterprise. An ex-army officer and man of education, he was, in short, a "gentleman." For him to live the wild animal life of a mountain trapper was unbelievable but Miller was obdurate.

Hunt appeared mortified. He urged Miller to change his mind, offered to give him passage back by boat when they all reached the Pacific. Miller replied that his mind was made up. Hunt could give him a trapper outfit or not as he wished. He had quitted the United States Army when he made up his mind to, and he would quit Astor. Hunt gave him four horses, powder and lead and watched him jog off with the three trappers.

The party remaining consisted of Crooks, McClellan and McKenzie, all with an interest in the company, the clerk John Reed and the French boatmen. All embarked in fifteen recently completed canoes and sailed away. Over a hundred horses were left grazing on the bank. Perhaps the two Snake Indians would guard them until next summer.

Hunt's decision to take boats was the worst error of his entire trip but the men insisted on it. For a short way the canoes sped along. They came to the confluence with the Mad River that they had crossed on the east side of the Tetons. The stream became a real river here, with a light pea-green color. Snow fluttered in the air all day long but the men sang their boat songs. They believed that their rapid pace would soon take them to the low Columbia country. On October 21, 1811, they came to bad rapids, near where Idaho Falls would later stand. The home-made canoes were let down with ropes from the shore. Some of them upset and their burden of Indian goods was lost. However, the river below provided good sailing. Willows and cotton-woods lined the stream. Geese and ducks rose from the water ahead of the canoes with great flapping and paddling of feet. Magpies sailed down from the cottonwoods on black and white wings to scold the boatmen. On the banks Hunt noticed beaver signs everywhere.

Two days of pleasant sailing brought the travelers to the mouth of the Port Neuf. The plains here spread out like those west of the Missouri. The men spied an Indian village and landed. The Indians fled. Hunt coaxed them to come back and talk but the primitive people were timid. His men rummaged through the lodges, looked around the smoldering fires. The poor people had little food, only a few minnows, roots and berries that they were drying. Hunt's men picked up and examined a net made of nettle fiber and some baskets of woven willows and grass. The Astor-ians left a few trinkets to show friendship and re-embarked. On the river below they saw three naked Indians on a raft of rushes. These fellows fled also and refused to talk. At the head of Ameri-can Falls the party portaged to the foot of the narrows. Then they floated for eighty miles on the river, sinking deeper and deeper below the level plain.

On October 28, 1811, they had a bad accident near where Milner, Idaho, would stand. The little flotilla was racing along merrily. The second canoe, manned by Crooks and four boat-men, hit a rock. All the men tumbled into the turbulent water. Four clutched the rock and were saved. One man and all the goods were lost. The flotilla darted to shore and the men jumped out. Hunt ordered camp pitched. He was afraid to follow the river farther. With three men he scouted downstream and found a fearful abyss with the river roaring to a tumultuous whirlpool. He named it Caldron Linn.[8]

There was nothing to do but abandon the boats and go afoot. To make things worse rain poured down upon the drenched and miserable men. The situation was desperate, for the party had only five days' rations. Hunt decided to send out scouting parties to look for relief in Indian villages or for a trail that would lead to the Columbia. Crooks started with five men for Henry's fort, 340 miles away, to get the horses, come back and save the party. McClellan, cocky, confident, always talking about wanting to kill somebody, was allowed to go down the Snake with three companions and save himself if he could. McKenzie, with four men, climbed the canyon wall to the plains on top and started north for the distant mountains, perhaps to find a pass to the Columbia up there. Had he but known it, he was heading for the roughest country on the North American continent.

Hunt, left alone with none of his partners and no mountain men, set his thirty-odd people to work digging caches to hide the trade goods from prowling Indians. Knives, mirrors, cloth, paint, his own precious books were buried. The dirt was carefully carried away in blankets and thrown in the river. They had not finished after two days' work, when Crooks and his companions stumbled into camp. The Scotsman had found the task of walking across the endless flats to Fort Henry more than he could bear. Better for all of them to end their existence with the crowd instead of dying one by one alone on the desert. Later two messengers from downstream came back to report that the canyon was absolutely impassable below Caldron Linn.

The party could not stay where it was without food. There was no alternative but to march, yet how could they ever find enough to feed so many? Obviously there was only one solution—divide into two groups, separate and get away as best they could. The supplies of corn, dried meat, grease and bouillon tablets were divided. Each man had a pack weighing twenty pounds. Nineteen men, including lanky forty-year-old John Day, went with partner Crooks across to the south bank. Nineteen others, including Dorion's squaw and two children, went with Hunt. It was raining and both parties splashed along down opposite sides of Snake River. Two days later Hunt's party found a trail with horse tracks in it. The wanderers followed the track to an Indian village. Squaws saw them coming and fled. A few men remained, nervous as wild animals. Hunt heard a murmur under a pile of straw. He turned it over and found a baby there. Hidden by its mother! Hunt picked it up. The red men watched him and trembled with fear. An Indian, bolder than the rest, held out a knife. Hunt recognized it as one that must have been traded from McClellan. So he had found this village on his way down the river!

The Indians offered to share what they had but there was barely enough to feed themselves. In this country the natives lived close to the margin of famine. They had no surplus beyond their own stark needs.

The party moved to other villages. All were on the verge of starvation. The white men traded for a few bits of food. They picked up the fish heads and bones cast out of the lodges. Occasionally they caught a beaver. Dorion's wife was heavy with another child. For her they got a horse, then a few more for themselves. They crossed the desert, north toward the misty mountains, watching the peaks appear naked and cold in the dawn sun, dissolve to gossamer and glow white like distant clouds at sunset.

On November 21, 1811, they saw a stream ahead bordered with cottonwoods and willows, Boisé or Wooded Creek. An Indian village stood close to where Boise, Idaho, would be. The Astorians traveled down the Boise through a flat, pleasant country, until they came again to the Snake running due north here. Across on the west side they could see fluted bluffs. They crossed the Boise, came to the Payette and waded it waist-deep. Ahead lay the Weiser at the foot of towering mountain walls. They had come to the end of the plains at last. Snake River flowed, smooth but rapid, into a narrow canyon between steep grassy slopes a thousand feet high. A few hundred feet above them snow appeared on the slopes level as a water line. To go down the steep and narrow canyon seemed impossible. The Weiser Valley opened toward the north and the party started up it. Soon they came to the snow. A few wet patches changed quickly to a blanket several inches deep. Scouts ahead spied great pine-covered mountains some nine thousand feet high, the wildest, roughest, most mountainous country they had yet seen. In midwinter it was folly to attempt to go farther. Hunt turned west toward the Snake again. On the heights, the snow was knee-deep and more fell constantly. Hunt ordered the horses killed for food. Camps were pitched under the giant pine trees where the snow was less deep and the heavy boughs gave some shelter from the falling flakes. The men built fires and melted snow in kettles for drinking. This snow water tasted flat and failed to quench thirst. Campfires set the pine boughs overhead to dripping.

Finally Hunt and his party came to the Snake River canyon and started down the drifted slope. They could not see the stream through the falling snow but they could hear it. All at once the snow changed to a quiet rain and below them they saw through the mist the great river. They had got below the snow line once more. For six miles they crept along the edge of the Snake, tiny insects at the base of a mighty wall. Supplies, except horse meat, were now completely gone. On the morning of December 6, 1811, across the river at the foot of the west wall, they saw a group of men, Crooks and his party. They, too, were in desperate condition. Hunt ordered a canoe made out of the hide of the horse killed the day before, and some meat was sent across. Crooks, John Day and one of the Frenchmen, Le Clerc, came back. The Scotsman's health had given way again. He was ill as he had been last summer on the plains. He said that some of his party had explored three miles farther down the canyon. It walled up down there to a gash cut with one chop of God's ax. The precipices rose perpendicularly 1,500 feet above screaming rapids. The sun at noon shone in that dismal crevice only an hour. No men would get through it.

The gaunt and haggard appearance of Crooks and his companions dismayed Hunt's men. They had not noticed their own slow degradation under scant diet but the sight of John Day, the Frenchman and stockily built Crooks shocked them. The men looked at themselves with new eyes and began to murmur that they were all starving to death, that they might soon have to cast lots and eat one another. Hunt lay awake far into the night wondering what to do. In the morning he had made up his mind. Their only hope was to get back to the nearest Indian village. But did the men have strength to get there?

In the morning they started. Crooks, Le Clerc and John Day could not keep up. "Leave them," the men murmured. "Save ourselves while we yet have strength." They crowded around Hunt and begged him to give the order. Hunt turned to Dorion and his skeleton horse. The animal must be killed to save them all. The half-breed turned away truculently. His wife would have a baby shortly. His two-year-old child could scarcely walk. No, he would not kill the horse. Dorion raised his club, struck the animal's "cow hips" and drove it out of camp. The men followed him in twos and threes. Only five remained loyally with Hunt. This was mutiny but under such conditions Hunt did nothing. Next day Crooks was worse. With no horses to move him, he would have to lie where he was. Hunt ordered three men to stay with him. He gave them two beaver skins for food and struck off up the trail with the remaining two men.

An iron cold had settled over the lower end of the great Snake River desert. In the sky sundogs—rainbows of suspended frost crystals—glow cold as fire opals in such bitter weather. Hunt traveled all day and, on the morning of the next, overtook his men. He implored Dorion to kill his horse and feed them all. The half-breed refused. Glum, ugly and discouraged, the men stumbled forward irregularly. In the afternoon they spied an Indian village erected since they had passed down. Several horses grazed around the lodges. The men decided to take no chance with these Indians. They slipped forward stealthily, captured the horses and killed one on the spot. The amazed savages peered out of their lodges, then fled to the brush. The whites built great fires and feasted. A supply of meat was sent back to Crooks, and across the river to his people who had followed along on the west bank.[9]

The Americans left a few trinkets, trade knives, etc., in the Indian camp and moved on hoping to find more hospitable hosts. They prayed that the savages would not follow them and take vengeance for their thefts. At the mouth of the Weiser they came to more Indian villages. Exactly twenty days had passed since they had been here, days of extreme hardship in the snow. Hunt bought a horse or a dog here and there to keep his men alive. He learned that there was no route north through the mountains. McKenzie's effort to get out that way must have failed. What had happened to him?

The Indians said that the only trail to the Columbia led over the mountains west of the Snake. The trip in summer took twenty-one "suns." In winter the mountains were impassable with snow waist-deep.

Hunt offered a high price—a gun, pistol, three knives, two horses, a sample of everything in his possession—for a guide to take his party across. The Indians refused. Better to stay with them until spring, they said.

Hunt lost his patience. He called the Indians women, cowards afraid of the snow. One red man became piqued. He stepped forward and agreed to act as guide. Two others volunteered. With five horses to carry camp equipment they all set off. At the Snake River they spent three days ferrying themselves across in a horsehide canoe. On the west side they met thirteen of Crooks's miserable followers. Some of them were too weak now to join the expedition. Hunt sent them back to subsist through the winter with the Indians and if possible to find Crooks and John Day somewhere over there at the mercy of the Shoshoni his men had robbed.

The stronger of Crooks's men and Hunt's party turned toward the high, sloping mountainside that skirted the west bend of the Snake. A trail across the face of the mountain rounded into the steep canyon of the Brulé, or Burnt Fork. At the head of the gulch the trail turned north and crossed the open tableland drained by Powder River. Hunt looked back at his party. He had in all thirty-two whites including the half-breed Dorion, his wife eight-months pregnant, two children and three Indians. The pack horses were weak from wintering out, "cow-hipped" from scant forage and their heels knocked together. Animals in that shape might give up any hour. Hunt ordered them nursed along. His men might have to eat the horses to keep alive themselves before they reached the Columbia.

They traveled about fourteen miles a day, rested long around the campfires and ate only one meal in every twenty-four hours.

To the west the mountains rose in a wall with snow-tipped spruce trees etched against the sky, like feathers on an Indian war bonnet. Ahead the rolling country appeared to be open. The weather was overcast with a drizzle of rain and flurries of snow. Such dull days in this country mean a low cloud ceiling. At sunset they usually end with the sun breaking out under the clouds, setting the bare peaks aglow, illuminating little groves of leafless aspens near the summits with changing colors—a luminous rose, then red, then yellow-gold. In all probability Hunt's brigade— as such parties were called—rested in camp, hungry and worried, but watching in spite of themselves the vivid display.

On the morning of December 30, 1811, Dorion announced that his wife was in labor. All the men were concerned for her welfare. She had withstood so much with uncomplaining philosophy. Dorion told them to go on. He would stay in camp by her and catch up later. With some misgivings the men straggled off. Before long they came out on a promontory and looked down on a great lake of grass twenty miles long and six or eight across. A willow-bordered stream meandered across the level floor. This was Grande Ronde, an oasis in the mountains. The men saw a few Shoshoni lodges and hurried to them. The Indians sold the Astorians four horses, three dogs and some camass roots, a great delicacy that grew abundantly in this level valley. Next day Dorion came in leading his skeleton horse with his wife in the saddle carrying the newborn baby in her arms. The two-year-old was wrapped in a blanket beside her. Hunt had never seen anything like that in New Jersey. In his diary he wrote: "One would have said, from her air, that nothing had happened to her."[10]

The following day was New Year's. The Canadians petitioned Hunt for a holiday. With food abundant, the climate balmy in this snug pocket in the hills, why not? Hunt granted the request. The day was passed in repose and revelry, the Frenchmen singing and dancing.

Next day the work began once more. The Indians had pointed to the trail. North of the Grande Ronde the ridge of the Blue Mountains was high and level-topped, iced like a cake with dark pines that spilled down the sides in little valleys. The men followed the trail into a canyon. The sunny open country changed to a gloomy forest, cold and dank as a catacomb. The Indians had said that the trip across would take "three sleeps." Hunt was prepared for six. The snow became knee-deep. The trail passed through the dark trees as though in a tunnel. In many places the trunks stood close together as palisades. A horse with a pack on his back could not go between them. Occasionally Hunt could look through the forest as through prison bars to an open meadow blanketed white with snow. The men became dry and nibbled at snow crust, which seemed cool and moist but soon made their mouths burn. Surrounded with snow, they suffered from thirst.

On January 6, 1812, the travelers saw in the distance a great golden plain below them. They noticed, too, that the climate on this side of the divide was much more mild—the fabled Pacific Northwest. The men hailed the sight like the Israelites come to the Promised Land.

A trail led down a deep gorge. Soon the snow disappeared. the eager travelers saw herds of black-tailed deer. They noticed, too, that there were many horse tracks in the trails. Indians must be close. The explorers scattered in a race for the village. Let the best man be first. But darkness overtook the leaders—and still no Indian town. A great fire was built. Stragglers came in all night. Others bivouacked by themselves along the trail. In the excitement Pierre Dorion's baby died.

Next morning the men pushed on again without discipline, without waiting for their fellows. At last their inflamed eyes beheld a village of thirty-four matting lodges. On all the grassy hills they saw horses grazing, at least two thousand of them. Red men came out cordially. The Cayuse Indians were well dressed in buckskin shirts and leggings. Unlike the poverty-stricken Shoshoni back on the Snake these Indians were well-to-do. They had warm buffalo robes and in their houses the Americans noticed copper pots and kettles and some metal axes, all sure signs of contact with Europeans. The Indians said that two more days' travel would put the party at the Columbia.

Hunt paid off his red guides and rested six days at the Indian camp while his men straggled in—all but one Frenchman, whose fate was never known. The desperate men feasted and regained their strength. Hunt kept them busy making new moccasins. He purchased some horses. Then the Astorians moved over to the Umatilla, rode down it and across to the Columbia near the mouth of the Walla Walla.[11] Hunt looked across the broad stream, three-quarters of a mile to the far shore. He recognized this as the place described in the Gass journal.[12] From here on he would not be an explorer, but he knew that there might be trouble ahead at The Dalles.

At a near-by Indian village the Astorians purchased a supply of dried salmon. They crossed to the north bank of the Columbia and rode west on a plain trail. The fishing Indians along the river seemed much more degraded to the Americans than the horse Indians but the climate was ideal. Midwinter was like October back east. The village of Wishram, with its split-board houses and acres of racks for drying salmon, reminded Hunt of a New England fishing village. The great snow-covered mountain on the left, he thought, must be Mount Hood. Hunt kept his horses guarded carefully but in spite of his care a few were stolen—including Dorion's.

Hunt knew that he would soon have to embark in boats. He began to trade for canoes as he passed into the canyon below The Dalles. Some of the Indians talked a little English. Hunt learned from them that a fort had been built at the mouth of the Columbia. So his partners had arrived by sea! He heard, too, that one of their ships had cruised north along the coast. Indians had swarmed over the side, butchering most of the crew. The survivors had blown up the powder magazine, killing red and white alike and sinking the vessel.

Hunt suspected that this ship must be the *Tonquin*. The Indians also asked him about Lewis and Clark. Hunt was surprised to learn that these savages had already learned about the mysterious death of Meriwether Lewis on the Natchez Trace less than three years before.

The thieving Indians were friendly enough and Hunt soon traded all his horses for canoes. He transferred his small supply of baggage and on February 5, 1812, shoved off. On the eleventh they were out of the canyon and next day passed the Willamette Valley. They noticed seals sporting in the water and looked back at Mount Hood. The river here was over a mile wide. Fogs rolled down around the canoes and blotted out all landmarks, but the men realized that they were skirting a great bay. Then on the afternoon of February 15, 1812, the fog lifted and they beheld on the neck of land before them the palisaded fort of Astoria. A cheer broke from the canoemen. On shore they could see tiny men running down toward the beach. The travelers plied their oars vigorously. The canoes leaped forward and soon ran their prows into the strand. The men leaped out and embraced those on shore. The Frenchmen shouted one another's names and kissed on both cheeks. Here on the beach were John Reed, the clerk, little McClellan and David McKenzie, the Canadian. They had arrived a month ago.

Up at the fort the partners planned a great celebration. Grog was issued, the colors were hoisted, guns and cannon fired. At night the Frenchmen held a dance, a dance without women. Only two things marred the gaiety. Crooks and his party, including John Day, had probably perished back in the wilderness and the story about the *Tonquin's* being overpowered by the Indians proved true. Poor Alexander McKay, the distinguished partner who had crossed the continent with Mackenzie in 1793, had died in the fight. But in spite of these tragedies, a road—of sorts—had been opened to Oregon.

---

1 Washington Irving, *Astoria, or Anecdotes of an Enterprise beyond the Rocky Mountains* (Philadelphia, 1841), I, 43-44.

2 Reuben Gold Thwaites (ed.), *Original Journals of the Lewis and Clark Expedition* (New York, 1905), V, 390n.

3 Irving, *Astoria,* I, 158.

4 *Ibid.,* 188.

5 *Ibid.,* 213.

6 *Ibid.,* 249.

7 *Ibid.,* II, 13.

8 Philip Ashton Rollins (ed.), *The Discovery of the Oregon Trail; Robert Stuart's Narratives of his Overland Trip Eastward from Astoria* (New York, 1935), 120, locates this pool.

9 Irving, *Astoria,* II, 51.

10 Rollins (ed.), *Discovery of the Oregon Trail,* 301.

11 *Ibid.,* 304, 326.

12 James Kendall Hosmer (ed.), *Gass's Journal of the Lewis and Clark Expedition* (Chicago, 1904), 158.

Chapter 4

Stuart Discovers the Platte River Route: 1812-1813

J OHN JACOB ASTOR's partners sat around a crude table in the fort which they had named Astoria. Rain dripped from the eaves. The winter of 1811-1812 had been mild, just as Lewis and Clark had described an earlier one. In fact there had been no real winter, just a rainy season. The climate was certainly ideal. The firm's business had had its ups and downs. The successful founding of Astoria was a real achievement, and in addition the partners had established a branch post at the forks of the Okanogan, 140 miles below the British factory at Spokane. Then, too, McDougal planned an alliance by marriage with the daughter of old one-eyed Chief Comcomly, titular owner of the first American fort according to the quitclaim deed furnished him by Meriwether Lewis. Two dozen Hawaiians had come in on Astor's supply vessel. They gave promise of being a docile and more or less permanent labor class. On the debit side of the firm's ledger, the loss of the *Tonquin* was serious. The vessel and her cargo of trade goods represented many thousands of dollars. The death of Alexander McKay and his men hurt the company's prestige. The big quantity of trade goods Hunt had brought overland might still be saved, provided some Indians did not find them in the cache at Caldron Linn. The loss of partner Crooks must be charged up, too, for surely there was little chance that he had

93

survived. Even if he had been able to find enough to eat, the Shoshoni at the camp that had been robbed of its horses would surely take revenge on him.

The partners at the rustic table agreed upon the firm's spring operations. At all hazards they must hold the two posts against their English competitors. Word must be sent to Astor reporting the state of affairs. John Reed, the Irish clerk, had proved himself a mountain man and was assigned the job of going back overland with three men to St. Louis. The trail from the Columbia across the Blue Mountains, the route Hunt had followed, was much traveled by Indians and in summer should be easy to follow. The valley of the Snake was known to be open country. Game was scarce in places, but salmon filled the river in great quantities. For 500 miles travelers could ride inland by this route. The only difficult and unknown part of the way east was the short strip of mountains between the head of the Snake and the plains. Hunt's route was much shorter and less mountainous than the way discovered by Lewis and Clark, but the high country around the Tetons must still be crossed or detoured if possible.

Reed bubbled with his great opportunity. He prepared a tin knapsack for the dispatches, soldered the edges to keep out moisture and admired himself with this shining metal on his back. Little McClellan insisted that he would go with him. The two had become well acquainted in their perilous trip out from Caldron Linn, and McClellan, always impetuous, had decided that his interest in the Astor company was too small. He wanted to quit and get into bigger operations for himself, a fickleness that had marked his earlier business ventures. Ten men were to go with the messengers as far as the caches and bring back the trade goods. Another party was to take goods up to the Okanogan post and bring back the winter's fur. These groups set out together from Astoria on March 22, 1812, under the command of a Scotch youth named Robert Stuart, a nephew of the factor at the upriver post. In the canyon the Indians, as usual, came out to pilfer. The travelers were compelled to employ them to carry the supplies around the various falls. This gave some of the rascals a chance to steal. It gave all of them a chance to admire

SHIPS OF THE PLAINS, BY SAMUEL COLMAN

the shining tin box on John Reed's back. They determined to get it for themselves. At one of the portages near Wishram their opportunity came.

Reed and McClellan, inseparable friends, were alone with part of the supplies while their companions carried up the balance from the lower landing. A great mob of Indians rushed the two men. McClellan shot one of the red men before he was knocked down. Reed jerked desperately at the cover on his gun but a club laid him low. The whites heard the shot, came running and drove the red men from the prostrate Astorians. Another Indian was shot down. The wounded Americans had been stripped of their guns, pistols and, of course, the shiny tin box. No use now to go back across the mountains to Mr. Astor. Instead the entire party went on up to the Okanogan factory.

The post had done well during the winter and had engrossed considerable fur that had previously been available to the North West Company on the Spokane. The combined parties seemed ample to get this treasure through the pirates at Wishram, so the canoes were loaded and the men set off for Astoria again. Below the mouth of the Walla Walla the canoes floated rapidly on the broad current. Snow-capped Mount Hood stood serenely ahead. The boatmen heard a man shout to them from the bank. He spoke English. The canoes turned and headed for the bare, level bank of the Columbia. Two naked men, with bodies browned like Indians, stood on the shore. They were Ramsay Crooks and John Day. The two wretched fellows were helped into the canoes, fed and clothed. The vessels skimmed on down the stream and Crooks told his harrowing story.

The two men, Crooks said, had come across on the Blue Mountain trail successfully. They had gone down the Columbia to The Dalles. There, the pirates had received them cordially, fed and entertained them, then appropriated their guns and all their clothes. Robbed and naked, the white men had been expelled from the village. Crooks had begged for his flint and steel in order to make a fire, but the Indians had told him to be gone and quickly. Absolutely destitute, the two men had hoped to be able to walk to the friendly Walla Walla village, 100 miles above.

John Day's age began to tell in this hardship, Crooks said. His tall figure still appeared proud, but at times his eyes saw strange things and he talked incoherently.

The rescue party looked at John Day curiously. He seemed as rational as Crooks. Both of them were truly men saved from the grave. The traders went past Wishram and the other fishing villages below The Dalles with little trouble this time. The pirates respected parties strong enough to protect themselves. On May 11, 1812, they were back at Astoria. A ship from Astor, the *Beaver*, lay at anchor there. A dozen more Hawaiians had come on her. The partners held another council and read the dispatches. Astor wanted the *Beaver* to trade up the coast as the *Tonquin* had done and then return to America by way of Canton, China. The partners decided that Hunt should go north on the *Beaver* and make a deal with the Russians in Alaska, offer to supply them with trade goods. Then more posts would be established on the upper Columbia to compete with the British. In the meantime, a report must be prepared and sent overland to Astor. Robert Stuart had shown good leadership in the last trip up the river. His uncle was a stockholder. Why not let him lead the overland expedition across the mountains with the dispatches? Men who had come in with Hunt could go along to point out the old route, and a new and better one might be found.

The messengers and the traders for the new posts all set out together. Between them they would be a match for the tough Indians in the narrows. They left Astoria on June 29, 1812. McClellan was with the party, still intent on getting away from the company. Crooks and John Day also had had enough and were determined to get back east and quit the organization. In all, the party, including the Hawaiians, numbered about sixty. They set off in two barges and ten canoes.

John Day began to act strangely. He did irrational things. In camp the sight of an Indian made him talk wildly. This was the way Crooks said he had carried on last winter. The spell soon left him, but another recurred the next day. At daybreak on July 2 he snatched two pistols and attempted to blow out his brains. The bullets missed but the shots aroused the camp. John Day was overpowered. It was hopeless to take him farther. He was delivered to some westbound Indians who agreed to return him to Astoria.

On July 6, 1812, the travelers arrived at the river pass through the Cascade Mountains. Stuart ordered weapons put in order. Fifteen days were spent between the first rapids and the head of the falls, a distance of eighty miles. Always armed and alert, the men got through without mishap. Near Wishram, Crooks pointed out two Indians who had robbed him. Stuart ordered their arrest. They were bound and put in a canoe. Then the stolen guns were demanded and returned. The prisoners were set free.

In the open country above the Cascade Mountains, Stuart ordered the men to trade for horses to eat. The July sun brought out great quantities of rattlesnakes on the Oregon desert. At night the men spread tobacco around their tents to keep away the serpents. One day they spied a nest of snakes coiled together and shot into it. With sticks they dragged out thirty-seven writhing reptiles. Everyone felt more comfortable riding in the boat. On July 28 the traders reached the mouth of the Walla Walla. The friendly Indians built a great welcoming fire and a dance was held on the sand.

The next morning Stuart made signs to the Indians that he wanted to buy horses—to ride, not to eat. He planned to leave the main party here and take the overland trail for St. Louis. John Reed was to follow with a party twenty days later, pick up trappers who had dropped out and get the Indian goods at the caches. Stuart set his men to work making saddles, arranging packs, tying parcels of rice, macaroni, corn meal, dried fruit and other supplies.

July 31, 1812, dawned hot and dusty. The saddles were finished and Stuart set off with six men and twenty horses. Robert Stuart was the youngest and also the only man who had not been over the route. Moreover, he was an inexperienced horseman, but his companions were all veterans. Stocky, wrinkled Crooks and small, wiry McClellan had both led expeditions across this country. Le Clerc and the other Frenchmen knew the way, but

Stuart, with his family interest in the company, was the recognized captain.

The boatmen were not used to land travel. On the first day the
heat nearly suffocated them. There was no drinking water on the
desert and the men complained. Mercurial Le Clerc, usually
sunny, sometimes furious, became desperate with thirst. The piny
top of the Blue Mountains showed pale as clouds in the distance.

A dog gave up in the heat. Stuart's brief entry in his journal,
written over a hundred years ago, will bring an unforgettable
picture to all desert travelers who have seen a dog go crazy from
thirst. The writer remembers a collie that trotted behind his
horse in the furnace heat for two or three hours, looking up,
whining, tongue dripping. Suddenly the dog turned at right
angles and started off down a wash at a fast trot, head and tail
down, oblivious to whistles, shouts or even a rope cast over him.
Perhaps Robert Stuart's dog also lost its mind with thirst. All
that his master wrote in the journal was: "Had a fine young dog
(our only companion of the kind) given up for want of water."[1]

The party did not find water until they reached the Umatilla
late at night. The next morning they slept, drank and rested until
eight in the morning. Then they rode up the stream into the
mountains where the trail tunneled into cool evergreens near the
top. The smell of resin and balsam came as a respite to the water-
men's sunburned bodies. Their relief was short-lived, however.
Drinking water was scarce across the mountains and grass for the
horses did not grow in the timber. Then, too, the handmade saddles began to break. In Grande Ronde the men lay over a day for
repairs and let the animals fill up on grass. The beauty of this
inland sea of verdure impressed them in summer as much as it
had during the previous winter. Reluctantly, they crossed to the
southern ridges and climbed out to the rolling Powder River
country. Fresh breezes blew straight from near-by snow fields.
Across the rolling sagebrush hills they could see the Powder ruf-
fled by the wind and sparkling in the sunshine with a thousand
points of light. At one side the men spied a distant band of nineteen antelope, unusual game in this country. Hunters rode off
after them but came back without any meat.

Along the main trail the party crossed the Powder River flats to Burnt Fork, passed between the great bare canyon walls, and came out below on Snake River. Over the smooth-gliding stream they saw the tree-lined Weiser, Payette and Boise Rivers, a network of streams in great meadows. The horsemen did not cross, but instead followed Crooks's old route along the south side of Snake River. A cloud of mosquitoes, thick as snowflakes, rose before the riders. Swarms of gnats settled on the horses' eyes and nostrils drawing little drops of blood from the tender skin. The men guessed rightly that their winged tormentors came from the lush meadows across the river. They whipped, fanned and slapped their horses until they left the Boise bottoms behind, and with them the insect pests.

Near where the present town of Grandview, Idaho, stands, the horsemen went to the river for a drink. They found a white man fishing on the bank. He was John Hoback. From the willows Reznor, ancient Robinson, and "gentleman" Miller all emerged, dressed in ragged skins. They had a fantastic story of adventure to tell. With their beaver traps they had made two small fortunes since Hunt left them at Henry's fort the previous fall. Each time as they accumulated wealth, a roving band of Indians had robbed them. They had kept their guns, but had lost all their horses and beaver.[2]

Stuart unpacked and cooked the fugitives a good meal. Miller, who had been so eager to leave the Army for the fur business and to leave Hunt for a trapper's life, was thoroughly fed up with the mountains. True to form, he wanted to quit again and go back at once to St. Louis. With the hapless recruits, the party set off up the river toward the caches at Caldron Linn. The three derelicts had walked past the treasure. Had they known its whereabouts they might have traded for saddle horses and ridden out of the country in style. The route to the caches did not follow the stream. The Snake meandered in great coils at the bottom of a deep canyon. Stuart's men rode on top of the rim. The leader was no plainsman, and the men showed him many short cuts from bend to bend. Out on the flats the river could not be seen. At a distance of half a mile the two rims merged and they looked across what seemed to be an unbroken flat stretching to the pale mountains far to the north. In this desert world the travelers jogged along. Then suddenly they came to the rim once more and looked down into another universe of hills and ridges and rippling water. The canyon brink was often straight as a wall for ten or twenty feet; below, the bank sloped down three or four hundred feet to the river. A few Indians lived in the canyon. Stuart noticed that they were small, dirty and miserable, so poor that they could not spare a single salmon, much less three horses to mount his three vagabonds. Stuart led his party past them with contempt. Soon he came to rapids. Here were more Indians, Shoshoni, standing in the water spearing salmon. On the shore Stuart counted 100 lodges, with fish racks on the steep slope thick as stakes in a vineyard.

Stuart stopped and traded for a good supply of fish. He learned why the Indians below were so destitute. Their villages lacked the strength to get and hold a place at the riffles where salmon could be speared in the shallow water. The poor Indians downstream lived on the salmon that these strong Indians wounded, lost, and let drift below, belly up, dead and dying. Stuart rode away pondering an economic system old as the Old Testament in which the strong got food to make them stronger while the weak lost even what little strength they had. Paradoxically, this human tragedy was being enacted within fifty miles of the hidden treasure that would have made any Indian who found it fabulously wealthy. Stuart kept the secret to himself and led his men toward the cache.

On August 29, 1812, the party arrived at Caldron Linn. Stuart noticed several weather-beaten books with pages fluttering in the wind. The caches were open and the treasure gone. Stuart suspected that a coyote must have smelled some of the green hides and dug for them, thus leaving a mark on the ground that attracted some passing Indian. The men told Stuart that there were three more caches some eight or ten miles farther up the river. Would they too be rifled? The party set off to see.

The upper caches were intact. Stuart opened them and took out enough to pay his way to the Missouri. Reznor, Hoback and

Old Man Robinson begged him to stake them again. They wanted to stay in the mountains until they had made another fortune. Mr. Miller insisted on going back to the States, penniless though he was.

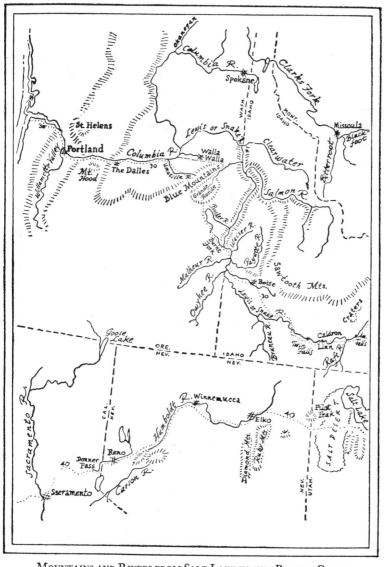

MOUNTAINS AND RIVERS FROM SALT LAKE TO THE PACIFIC COAST

Stuart counted some goods out to the ambitious old-timers. Then the cache was re-covered. Stuart wrote a note and left it in a forked stick for Reed to find when he came for the remainder of the goods. Another note was given to Old Man Robinson, and the three hunters were told to wait hereabouts, live as best they could on beaver until the Astorians arrived.

Mr. Miller bragged that he knew a new way across the mountains. His year in these regions had not been spent without learning the geography, he said. A trail through lower, smoother country could be found south of Fort Henry and the Tetons. Stuart let Miller take the lead, and the seven men mounted their horses and started with the pack animals. Miller led the way across the great flats south of the Snake. They came to footprints in the dirt that made them halt and wonder. The dangerous Crow and Blackfoot country was close. The trail in the dirt was made by a large party of horse Indians. Were they enemies? If so, eight men, even with trigger-happy McClellan, could not make much of a fight against so large a band of warriors. One thing about the suspicious trail encouraged the travelers. Many tent poles were being dragged. Such luxuries usually meant women and children. Surely a war party would not have so much equipment.

A short way above American Falls, near where Pocatello would later stand, Miller led the way up the Port Neuf, a steady but not steep climb among sweeping hills, bare for the most part except for serviceberry bushes heavy with fruit. Aspens grew in the deep hollows and occasional tufts of evergreens appeared on the summits. At last, on September 9, 1812, the men rode through a pass in the hills, and to everyone's surprise came out on a small high plain. This lofty floor, carpeted with lush grass, lay like a broad avenue between tall mountains. The valley of Bear River opened an easy way toward the south. They had come to it at the bottom of its great U-turn. In the meadows, Crooks and McClellan noticed buffalo sign and also pole marks of an Indian village ahead of them. So the red men were following the same trail that Miller thought so good, eh? Moreover this was

Blackfoot and Crow hunting ground. Indians to be met with here were almost sure to be truculent.

On September 12, 1812, camp was pitched near the stream. At suppertime some Indians rode up to the fire. They were Crows and said that they were friendly. A short conversation in signs ensued. Then the red men rode away and came back with a present of buffalo meat. The leader, a big grinning giant, stood six feet four inches tall in his moccasins. His village was only a few miles away, he said. During the evening more Indians rode into the firelight, dismounted and squatted on their heels. They wanted to trade for powder and ball. Stuart ordered the guard doubled around the horses, and warned every man to keep his gun in hand. Young as he was, Stuart understood his responsibility. Midnight came. Stuart kept the fire burning brightly. He counted twenty-one red men to his own seven whites. He noticed, too, that the Indians were becoming insolent. They seemed to resent being unable to get powder and lead. Morning dawned. Stuart discovered that his visitors had stolen a sack of cooking utensils. The eight whites packed up, each with one eye on the Indians. They mounted ready to ride away. The giant chief strode across to Stuart. He wanted to "talk trade." The young man offered to buy more meat, but not trade it for his own gunpowder. The grinning giant slapped himself on his copper breast, looked up at Stuart on his horse, and said that he was a big chief. Yes, chiefs presented one another with great presents. He, for one, wanted Stuart's horse. The young leader shook his head. The Crow put out his brown hand, grasped the bridle and jerked back the horse on its haunches. Stuart, no horseman—he had been riding less than three months—almost fell, but he snatched out his pistol and pointed it at the Indian's head. The chief let go, ducked away and laughed the incident off as a joke. Stuart laughed, too, but not heartily. He gave the Indian twenty rounds of powder and they parted with apparent friendship, but Crooks was solemn and McClellan made no remark about killing anyone.

The Americans rode south through the level Bear River Valley. The aspens on the mountainsides had turned yellow. With the dark spruce they made fantastic designs. Ahead Stuart noticed tall columns of smoke, signal fires. Were the Crows calling friends to come and wipe out the eight white men?

The broad valley of the Bear River proved to be marshy in places. Beaver traps set at night almost always provided breakfast for the men, but the horses mired down in the black mud. Packs had to be taken from them to let the animals get up. This made slow progress and spoiled merchandise. Rice had a way of swelling to twice its usual size when wet. Stuart decided to leave the Bear, strike off up a side creek and evade the Indians if they were gathering. The way led south of the Gannet Hills, across the border into what would later be Wyoming, and thence north along Greys River toward the Tetons, a lush and pleasant country. Aspens and spruce grew down to the margins of green meadows. Beaver dams mirrored mountain headlands and gloomy forests. For six days the men rode hard, looking back over the rumps of their horses. Stuart estimated that they had moved 150 miles. No sign of an Indian had been seen. Stuart decided that they were safe again. The travelers turned out their tired horses to graze and rest. The men themselves relaxed, lounging on their packs. Bear River seemed a long distance behind. Surely the red giant and his insolent warriors did not range in this pleasant region.

At dawn on September 19, 1812, the camp was astir. Cooks had started breakfast and Stuart walked down to Greys River. The hobbled horses grazed near by. A shout from camp made him turn, "Indians! Indians! To arms! To arms!" Stuart saw a lone Crow Indian with a red flag gallop past the camp. The Indian stopped on a knoll, waving his banner. Instantly a war whoop broke from the timber opposite the camp. A troop of redskins dashed out with terrific clamor. Away went the white men's hobbled horses with great leaps, straight for the conspicuous red flag. The first rider turned and dashed off. The horses, filled with terror, instinctively followed the waving banner. Stuart, the tenderfoot, stood amazed for a moment, then raced to camp. With his men Stuart ran helplessly after the thieves. Behind them they heard whoops at the breakfast fire. Indians hopped around the equipment helping themselves. Stuart ordered his men back to drive them away. He recognized the giant joker giving orders from horseback. With a shout of glee the big chief veered away, then jerked his mount to a stop, raised himself in his stirrups and clapped his hands to his bare posterior. Ben Jones, a hunter, raised his rifle at the target's bull's eye.

"Not for your life! not for your life!" Stuart shouted. "You will bring destruction on us all!"[3] Stuart had learned enough about Indians to know that stealing was considered honorable, but to kill a single red man challenged the whole tribe to retaliate, two for one. Hadn't Captain Lewis refrained from killing the Blackfeet until the last extremity?

The unhorsed travelers listened to the distant whoops of the Indians racing away with their horses. Forlornly the marooned men looked at their ponderous equipment. They stood afoot and alone in the heart of the Rocky Mountains. A more desperate situation would be hard to imagine. Rations for only one day were left to them and, worse still, only one beaver trap for sustenance. Stuart talked over the dilemma with the older men. They decided that there was only one course open to them—divide the equipment into packs all could carry on their backs and set off on foot for Fort Henry. Over there they might find the horses Hunt had left last year or trade for new animals from the friendly Shoshoni, then continue their journey.

All day the men sorted the goods and wrapped twenty-pound packs. Jones set the steel trap. In the morning he brought in a fat beaver. The men ate a good meal, piled the goods they could not take in a heap and set it on fire. Nothing was to be left for the rascal Indians. At ten in the morning the men shouldered their burdens and marched away—Crooks, Miller, McClellan, Le Clerc and the rest.

The going was slow. In the woods limbs reached down and snatched at the packs. The meadows were marshy with beaver ponds. The men's shoulders galled with the weight, and they developed stone bruises on their moccasined feet. Camp was pitched early. A few trout helped their menu, but the prospect of walking at least one hundred miles discouraged them. In the morning they set off once more. At the end of eight miles the stream seemed large enough to float a raft. They stopped and cut down some trees. On these they shoved off. The river took them back into the Snake but they made good time, lived well on beaver and calculated that they traveled ninety miles in three days. Only one thing marred the trip. The weather became very cold. The wet logs bobbing in the river became torture vehicles. The raftsmen camped near where Heise, Idaho, would later be, and resolved to go on afoot.

The river had taken them far to the west. The Big Hole Mountains to the north had tapered down in size and the men decided to cross them to Henry's fort, which must be on the north slope. They spent the day making extra moccasins, then trudged away. Soon they came to a broad Indian trail. The pony tracks were not fresh, but the men proceeded cautiously. They camped at night in a deep gulch where their fire would not show. In the morning they came to a stream running north into Pierres Hole, the country Hunt had crossed a year ago.

Stuart gave up the idea of going on to Henry's deserted fort. What assurance had he of finding Shoshoni there? His men knew this country and pointed to the saw-topped Tetons where the eastbound trail crossed. Stuart decided to turn toward the peaks.

Food became short. The men disliked walking. The long grueling was beginning to test the fiber of their characters. Then Crooks suffered one of his spells of illness. He developed a fever. McClellan became surly. On his tour of duty to carry the trap he refused, neither would he carry his share of the meat. By God, he could kill enough meat to eat near suppertime. Stuart did not openly notice the insubordination. He ordered his men to stay close to the hills and not to go out into the broad valley of Pierres Hole where Indians might see them. McClellan grumbled that his feet were sore. By God, he could kill any Blackfoot on his own terms. He wasn't going through "no rough hills." The wizened little tough set off alone.

During the day Crooks's malady became worse. Stuart gave

him a dose of castor oil. This made him very weak. The men urged Stuart to come on and leave him. They would all starve if they stayed here. Besides, a snowstorm might come any day and trap them in these mountains. The young man wavered, then made up his mind. He sent Jones out to hunt and ordered the others to rest near camp. In an hour Jones came back reporting that he had killed five elk. The men carried Crooks along to the carcasses and camped amid the fresh meat. The next day Crooks was still ill but without his pack he could walk. Finally they came to the last ridge on the southwest of Pierres Hole. Across the broad basin the jagged Tetons glittered in the sun. The men pointed to the pass over which they had come with Hunt the previous summer. Stuart ordered them to march straight across the flat toward the pass. Before they reached the bottom of the ridge they saw a small figure ahead. It was Mc-Clellan. He made no sign to them but trudged doggedly along.

On October 7, 1812, the party crossed Teton Pass. The air was cold but little snow had fallen. The deer and elk seemed to have gone to a lower altitude for the winter. The lonely rocks sparkled, cold and destitute of game. Surely this high country was no place for human beings at this time of year.

The men hurried down the east slope, crossed the Snake below Jackson's Hole, and climbed the divide toward Spanish River, later known as Green River. The upgrade slowed their pace. They had become weak from lack of food. On October 11 they stumbled down to the Spanish River and found the ashes of a dead campfire. The mountain men recognized McClellan's tracks around it. They examined them, noted the "freshness" critically, and said that he had left only twenty-four hours before. They pointed to some bones. Look, he had eaten a wolf for supper.

The desperate men scattered out along the river bottom looking under the big cottonwoods for buffalo tracks. They soon returned with sour faces. Jones went into the willows with the beaver trap and came back with another discouraging tale. He had set the trap, he said, but beaver were scarce. He would go back in an hour or two and see if they were going to have any supper.

The seven squatted on the cold ground under the bare trees. In the distance they saw a column of smoke. Did it come from an Indian camp, friend or enemy? Starvation frightened the men more than the Blackfeet. Le Clerc asked permission to investigate. Stuart let him go. Dark settled over the dreary encampment on the bank of Green River and Le Clerc did not come back. The men lay down to sleep on empty stomachs and to speculate on the Frenchman's fate. At daybreak Jones hurried off to the trap. He came back with bad news. The trap held a beaver's foot, nothing more. Their meal had escaped. Grimly they shouldered their packs and resumed the eastward journey. Le Clerc overtook them. The smoke, he said, had come from McClellan's campfire. The little fellow had been off hunting and the flames had burned the few things he owned. Now he lay ill and starving, unable to move. Twelve days alone with little food had broken his sullenness. Le Clerc talked with compassion. McClellan's willfulness was gone. He had sent word that he hoped Stuart would forgive him and that the men would come to him.

Stuart gave the order. Soon the bearded mountaineers stood in a circle around their stricken comrade. McClellan appeared like a skeleton. His eyes burned with unusual brightness but he was scarcely able to lift his head or speak. The men helped him to his feet, took his gun, and with two men beside him the party staggered forward hour after hour. The sun set and they all lay down, estimating that they had traveled seventeen miles. None had had a mouthful of food for three nights. Le Clerc, wild with hunger, came to Stuart, gun in hand. He said that it would take three or four days for them to cross the flats to the mountains where they might expect game. Without food they could not make it. Why not cast lots to see who should be killed for food? "Better," he said, "that one should die to save the rest."[4]

Stuart grasped his own rifle, faced the frantic Frenchman and threatened to kill him for the suggestion. The Canadian fell to his knees whimpering. Then the men lay down to sleep, Stuart himself trembling and weak from excitement and hunger. At daybreak they set off again. They staggered past white buffalo skulls, a mockery to their misery. Hours of agony, delirium!

Their morbid eyes saw a tousled old buffalo bull, skinny, weak and ragged as themselves. They killed him and fell upon the carcass, sucking the hot blood, eating chunks of quivering meat as they flayed and quartered the dead animal. Stuart feared that the men might kill themselves overeating. He warned them of the danger and ordered them to carry the meat to a near-by stream, build fires, put on the kettles and make soup. For twenty-four hours the men supped and rested. Strength came back to them quickly. They were young. At noon on the second day they set off once more. In the distance they saw the Wind River Mountains and believed them to be the Continental Divide. They traveled south and east. One day they met six Snake Indians who led them to a village of lodges made of pine boughs. The savages had been raided recently by a band of Crows. They had lost all their horses but one. Several of their women had been stolen and their village was practically bereft of everything. Yet the red men took it stoically. They received the Americans hospitably, gave them meat, and for an ax, a pistol and a few trinkets sold their last horse—a miserable animal but better than none. The Indians also told about the trappers Hunt had left in Jackson's Hole. They had made a big catch in beaver, the Indians said, but were later robbed by the Crows. One of them had been killed. The others had fled to Snake River and fallen in with some of Hunt's stragglers. Stuart suspected that these fellows, instead of the coyotes, had raided the caches back at Caldron Linn.

The next day, October 19, 1812, the Americans packed six days' rations of buffalo meat on the old horse. With their bedding on their own shoulders they set off, south and east. The mountains receded and the desert before them became very wide and flat. Crooks pointed solemnly to the distant mountains where he had crossed coming out, but Stuart remembered that the Indians spoke of another pass farther south. He hoped to find this South Pass to the Platte. It would be the most direct route to St. Louis. Watching the far-off mountain sky line, the eight men came unexpectedly to the forks of the Sandy, a pleasant stream sunk ten feet below the floor of the plain and invisible a short distance away. On the bank Stuart could look west across interminable flats that swam in the blue distances of the horizon. He knew that the Green River was over there and that he had made a great loop to the north since leaving it. Surely the best road must go straight across. Stuart turned and looked east. The sagebrush flat at his feet sloped gently and almost imperceptibly to a closer horizon, South Pass. North of the pass the Wind River Mountains peeped over the sky line like the top of a high wall. The pass itself was a plain twenty miles wide. The southern extremity ended in some low mesas, and blue ridges sprawled one after another as far as the eye could see.

Stuart led the way up the flat between the forks of the Sandy. He came to a broad trail made by a village of Indians—no doubt the same Crows who had raided the Shoshoni. The trail led off northeast. Evidently the Crows had gone through the north edge of the pass, skirting the mountains where wood was plentiful. Perhaps they were encamped there at this moment.

To evade the red men Stuart skirted the vast plain, keeping close to the barren southern mesas.[5] Squalls of snow whipped the white men's faces. The distant mountains, where the Indians might be encamped, were hidden in clouds. Stuart did not come to the Sweetwater at the place where wagon trains would later cross. Instead, his detour from the Indians put him into the broken country to the south. At last he came to the Muddy and followed this stream back into the Sweetwater route, which became famous later.

The explorers found game plentiful and soon forgot their period of starvation. McClellan killed buffalo for the entire party and probably regained his old pugnacity. Crooks's mathematical mind no doubt mulled figures of profit and loss. Jones brought in fat beaver daily with his trap. Stuart let the men rest and feast every few days. The weather was chilly and he knew that they would have to build winter quarters soon, but if the game remained plentiful the party had little to fear.

The eight men marched down the open Sweetwater Valley that would later be the route of the Oregon Trail. They passed Devil's Gate and trudged out into the broad basin where Independence Rock stands. Buffalo became more plentiful with every mile. At last, on October 31, 1812, the men came to the rim of a deep canyon. Stuart looked down into the dizzy chasm at a torrent tearing its way through a channel choked with rocks big as houses. He called the gorge, with its red and white stratified walls, the Fiery Narrows. Stuart believed the stream to be either the Niobrara or the Cheyenne, and thought that he was near the trail over which Hunt had come out two summers before. None of the men who had been on that expedition retained sufficient memory of the country to set him right. Stuart decided that he had best stay up here in the mountains. The plains below he knew to be ruled by the powerful Sioux, who were sure to find and rob such a small party. Back here in the mountains the Indians were apt to be remnants of broken villages hiding from the warlike nations below. These weak red men were usually friendly.

Stuart examined the country below the portals of the Fiery Narrows critically. Near some red buttes thirty miles down-stream a "water gap" was dotted with cedars. The broken ground gave shelter from the cold winds that blew across the flats. Deer and mountain sheep wintered in great number in the cedar breaks, and buffalo could be had on the near-by flats. Stuart announced that this spot was ideal for winter quarters. He set the men to building a cabin. His hunters were ordered to put in a big supply of meat. Soon the men had a home with a cheery fireplace. Outside, the trees were laden with chunks of buffalo hump, hams of black-tailed deer, and mountain sheep. The party feasted, rested and reveled in abundance.

On the morning of December 10, 1812, Stuart was startled at daybreak by a savage yelp outside the cabin. His men looked at one another. Barks, yips, howls, could be heard all around them. The men saw painted faces peering at the cabin from behind rocks and cedars. They reached for their guns. McClellan shouted to knock the chinking from the cabin logs so that they could shoot through them. "Not yet," Stuart ordered. "It will not do to show fear or distrust."[6]

With one Canadian he stepped outside the door. A chief came forward to shake hands. He was an Arapaho, he said, slapping his breast. The Crows had raided his village and stolen horses and women. For sixteen days his warriors had been hunting the thieves in these mountains. Now their food was gone. They were hungry.

Stuart noticed that they were armed with bows, arrows, tomahawks and scalping knives. He saw a few guns. It would not do to let this savage mob into the little cabin. On the other hand Stuart did not want to appear afraid. He asked if any other chiefs were present. A second savage stepped from the circle of painted warriors. Stuart told the two headmen to come into the cabin. Food would be passed out to the braves.

The Indians stayed at the cabin for twenty-four hours, eating and sleeping by turns. The bounteous supply of meat vanished. At last the red men prepared to go after their enemies. They looked covetously at the hams and slabs of ribs hanging from the eaves. Stuart told them to take a supply. With hunks of frozen meat tied on their horses, the Indians trooped away. Stuart thanked his stars that they had spared him the old nag. He was sure, however, that they would return with reinforcements and rob them completely. The white men talked it over and decided that they must move to a new hiding place. They knew that in a few weeks many hundreds of Indians would spot their location for word traveled fast in the mountains.

The weather was bitter cold. Fresh snow fell on the red hillsides and draped the cedars like white feather beds. The men grumbled about leaving the snug cabin that had sheltered them for five indolent weeks and the bountiful sheltered hills where game wintered by hundreds. But they knew that there was nothing else to do but move. Even "gentleman" Miller, who usually revolted at majority discipline, acquiesced.

On December 13, 1812, the men packed the old horse reluctantly and set off across the cold plains. The open flats made them shiver after the shelter under the Red Buttes. The snow stood halfway to a man's knees. In daytime the sun melted it but the nights were bitter cold. In the morning the crust would barely hold the men up, and every step or two they broke through. It was the hardest kind of traveling. The stream's northward course turned east around what would one day be called Casper Mountain, then in the rolling country beyond, it bore away to the southeast. Stuart knew for sure now that he was on the Platte. Far to the southwest he could see Laramie Peak, tall and pale. Before long the snow became lighter underfoot and he believed that they were coming to a more hospitable country. Round-leaved cottonwood, great winter forage for horses, grew along the stream. Stuart ordered his party to camp in the shelter of the brush and chop down a tree for the old pack horse.

Downstream the snow disappeared altogether. They camped on the north bank opposite the mouth of a stream later known as Laramie Creek. The brushy bottoms were alive with white-tailed deer. The little fellows sneaked away with their heads low in the tangled growths. When the hunters pressed them too closely, these deer ran boldly through the thickets waving their white tails like flags, "catch me if you can." On the surrounding plains, buffalo dotted the sky line. The men could tell that they were getting out of the mountains. Laramie Peak looked far away to the west now.

Stuart reckoned that his party must have traveled over three hundred miles from the cabin, far enough to shake off any pursuing Indians. Besides, his men had noticed as they traveled swirling white clouds behind them—sure sign of a snowstorm. Their tracks must be covered. No sign would show prowling Indians which way they had gone. Everyone began to watch for a suitable site for a new winter cabin.

They traveled down the Platte, pointing out suitable house logs. The stream bed became very broad. Smooth-frozen water changed to rough chunks of ice, dirt and stumps, in what appeared to be a thousand channels. Worst of all, the fringe of woodland disappeared. On Christmas Day the wanderers came to the tall cream-colored butte later known as Scotts Bluff. To the east they could see other pinnacles, lone sentinels of rock along the watercourse in the distance. They could see no trees for firewood down there. Moreover, the great plains beyond were white with snow. More might fall any day.

The men turned back into the saucer of bare ground. In a river bend with tall trees, twelve miles west of the bluff above Horse Creek, they built a cabin.

New Year's Day came and the cabin was not finished. They asked for a day off to celebrate. Stuart gave them a holiday and suggested a feast. Jones and McClellan killed a lavish supply of meat. All day long the men feasted on the choicest morsels, buffalo tongues and hump meat. Le Clerc, no doubt, kept everyone gay with his French songs, and Crooks, the money-maker, probably forgot figures and plans for a few hours. Tobacco was completely gone, but Mr. Miller produced an old tobacco pouch. This was cut up eagerly and smoked with satisfaction.

They fared well in the new winter quarters. The cabin proved comfortable and buffalo were abundant. Two great trees were felled and the men spent hours shaping them into boats for the spring run across the plains to the Missouri. March came. The ice went out and the smooth-flowing Platte promised a fast journey to civilization. Duffel and hides were loaded into the two boats. Part of the men agreed to walk with the old pack horse. The rest shoved off downstream. The boatmen soon learned that the lower Platte was seldom navigable. The channels had a way of ending in shallows a few inches deep. The men stepped constantly out of the boats into icy water to lighten the draft. Sometimes this sufficed to float the canoes to the next deep water. At other times they had to go back for miles and take another channel. Stuart and McClellan decided to walk at all times. Finally the rest gave up too, and joined them. The home-made canoes were abandoned.

The fine spring weather changed. A March snowstorm swirled across the flats. For two days they crouched in camp on the riverbank and waited. Then, with the suddenness of the plains, the sky cleared and the travelers set off again across the vast glittering world.

On March 26, 1813, they looked over the Platte at a serrated bluff stippled with cedars. A gulch there would later be known as Ashtree Hollow and still later as Ash Hollow, famous on the Oregon Trail. The men did not cross on the route the road would take. Instead, they plodded along the north bank. Miles below the bluffs ended like a promontory in a sea of grass. Across a narrow tongue of land Stuart could see the south branch of the Platte. His party had come to the famous "Forks," almost two hundred miles from the cabin.

Myriads of geese and brant flew north overhead. A flight of gabbling swan, white points against dark March clouds, attracted the attention of the wayfarers who began to look for signs of the Missouri. Like sailors, they hailed changes in the ocean of grass and assured one another that each change was a harbinger of the Big Muddy. The grass down here looked more like the Midlands; some pointed out forage six feet tall in the bottoms. Others noted a prairie chicken—so different from a sage hen. The sight renewed hope. "Gentleman" Miller would soon be out of his unwilling enlistment in the fur business. Crooks could sit at a table once more with plans and figures. One night a bit of driftwood with unmistakable marks of an ax set the Frenchmen to jig-stepping.

In the last days of March the weather turned hot. On the thirtieth the party passed three deserted Indian villages. Stuart examined the wrecked huts and speculated on the owners' tribe. Signs indicated that the villages had been occupied the preceding fall. Pegs in the ground showed where hides had been staked out to dry. A few corncobs disclosed that these people practiced some agriculture. They were probably Pawnee or Oto. If so, Grand Island must be close. The men had heard that it was more than fifty miles long and well timbered. Beyond it they should find the Loup River, well known to the Missouri traders at the mouth of the Platte.

The desperate Astorians came to several islands but none proved to be Grand Island. On April 4, 1813, at another deserted Indian village, they found three old squaws left behind to die because they were unable to ride with the village. The ancient Pawnee crones expected instant death from the white men. Presents of food did not allay their nervousness.

Two days later the explorers came to Grand Island sure enough. There was no mistaking it. The plains had been burned here and the island furnished the only grass for the old horse. The men crossed the shallow water and camped under the trees. They figured that they must now be within 150 miles of the Missouri. On April 11, 1813, they met an Indian. He said that he was an Oto. His village stood near by. Yes, the white men's geography was correct. The Indian said, too, that the United States was fighting a war with Great Britain. In fact, the war had begun almost a year ago.

The tattered travelers followed the Indian to his village. They saw blanketed women and children watching them from the distant domed roofs. In the village they walked between the dirt lodges and entered the council chamber through a tunnel ten feet long. Inside it was cool, cellarlike and sweet with smoke. McClellan had wanted to kill Manuel Lisa the last time he sat in one of these lodges. At that time Crooks and Miller had both been full of hope for success in the Astorian adventure. The mishaps of the last two years had changed their ambitions mightily.

Two French traders resident in the village came to see the Astorians. *Oui, oui,* the Missouri she was only thirty-five mile. Yes, by Gar! The war she was a fact.

The Americans speculated on the war's effect. Would Americans or Canadians, St. Louis or Montreal, get the Indian trade along the full length of the Missouri? Stuart realized that his own company at Astoria might be wiped out. Perhaps the British Navy would capture the fort!

The Americans smoked with the Indians, offered to give them their horse if the red men would build an elk-hide canoe twenty-one feet long. The Indians agreed to make such a craft. On April 16, 1813, the Americans set off in it. Merrily they floated down past the mouth of the Elkhorn and out into the current of the Missouri. Downstream they sped light as a floating leaf, past the Black Snake Hills and the Nodaway and Fort Osage. They came to houses in clearings 198 miles above St. Louis. The country was settling fast, mostly by Kentuckians, followers of Boone who had learned the pioneer way of life on the Wilderness Road.

On April 30, 1813, a little before sunset, Stuart's party reached

St. Louis. They had successfully crossed the continent by the Platte River route in a trip that had taken ten months without the loss of a single life. Only two parts of this long trail remained to be discovered and pointed out. From South Pass eastward, Stuart had not come down the Sweetwater by the best route; and from South Pass westward across the interminable flats to Green River and on to Bear River Valley, a road remained to be worked out. In both places Stuart might have found the path if the Crows had not stolen his horses. Henceforth, pack animals would undoubtedly compete with boats for penetrating the country to the Pacific. Stuart wrote the narrative of his own explorations and announced for the world to read that wagons would be practicable for the overland journey.[7]

1 Philip Ashton Rollins (ed.), *The Discovery of the Oregon Trail; Robert Stuart's Narratives of his Overland Trip Eastward from Astoria* (New York, 1935), 75.

2 *Ibid.*, 86.

3 Washington Irving, *Astoria, or Anecdotes of an Enterprise beyond the Rocky Mountains* (Philadelphia, 1841), II, 140.

4 *Ibid.*, 156.

5 For more data on the discovery of South Pass, see: W. J. Ghent, *The Road to Oregon* (London, 1929), 18-19; Rollins (ed.), *Discovery of the Oregon Trail*, 182; and Donald McKay Frost, "Notes on General Ashley, the Overland Trail, and South Pass," *Proceedings of the American Antiquarian Society . . . 1944*, LIV, part 2 (Worcester, Mass., 1945), 210-16.

6 Irving, *Astoria*, II, 172.

7 Hiram Martin Chittenden, *The American Fur Trade of the Far West* (New York, 1935), I, 459.

Chapter 5

Ashley's Men

John Jacob Astor in his palatial New York home planned a great eastern fur organization while Crooks, Hunt and Stuart struggled to establish Astoria on the Pacific. In 1808 Astor had organized the American Fur Company to compete with the two big Canadian firms, the North West and the Michili-mackinac fur companies. He had raided their ranks for his Pacific Fur Company and in 1811, the year Wilson Price Hunt started for the Pacific, Astor combined with his eastern rivals to form a trust.

On the upper Missouri the fur business continued in the hands of conservative St. Louisans. Locally, Manuel Lisa and the Chouteaus were competitors. Astor's new combine hung above them like a threatening thundercloud. No doubt the New York financier wanted an international monopoly.

The War of 1812 gave him a setback. His Pacific Fur Company was wiped out. Under threat of a British naval vessel, the ex-North West Company partners whom Astor had engaged with such shrewdness sold out to their old firm. The peace treaty with Great Britain stipulated that all land captured by either nation be returned to the original owner. This did not affect private ownership so Fort Astoria remained in the possession of the North West Company. The British flag had been hauled down belatedly from the fort after the treaty of 1818 proclaimed the Oregon country open to settlement by citizens of both the United States and Great Britain.

In 1821 the North West Company was consolidated with the

Hudson's Bay Company, and Parliament gave the combine a monopoly—excluding only British subjects—and the right to administer justice over the inhabitants. Thus British law was the first
in the Oregon country. The territory was open to Astor once
more but he did not return. Instead, he put Crooks and Stuart in
charge of his Mackinac station, opened an office in St. Louis in
1822 and threatened to invade the upper Missouri field. Then a
man with new ideas entered the fur business—ideas that would
revolutionize the old fur trade and lead to the exploration of
every gulch and mountain along the Oregon Trail.

William Henry Ashley was a Virginian. He came to Missouri
at the mature age of thirty in 1808, just two years after Lewis
and Clark had returned from the Pacific. A man with some education, considerable means and tremendous versatility, he built a
gunpowder factory near Potosi, Missouri. He met Andrew
Henry for whom Henry Fork of the far-off Snake River had
been named. Henry, an old partner of Manuel Lisa, had given
up fur trading in 1811 to mine lead. Thus powder and lead drew
Henry and Ashley together.

Ashley was what would be called a go-getter. Besides his investments in business enterprises and a trusteeship in an academy,
he took an active part in the militia and in politics. By 1819 he
had become a colonel and was lieutenant governor of Missouri
Territory. The governor was William Clark, the great explorer,
who now lived in a fine mansion in St. Louis. Ashley, too, had
ambitions for a big estate. He owned stock in many ventures and
was also reputed to have debts amounting to $100,000—large even
for a go-getter.

In 1822, the year Astor opened his St. Louis office, the fur business looked unusually good. The government had relaxed the
old factory system of regulated Indian stores which restricted
individual initiative. The business was thrown wide open and, in
addition, the government promised to use the army to police the
Indians and keep out Canadian interlopers. Several new companies organized to take advantage of this government support.

Lieutenant Governor Ashley, a general in the militia now,
combined with the experienced Andrew Henry to make a new

fortune. The two men planned to play a different game from the old-timers'. The customary procedure had been to buy a stock of goods, load it on a keelboat, move slowly upriver to a suitable location and build a trading fort. Here the Indians were invited to come with furs and hides to trade for the trinkets and manufactured goods they had learned to require. The worst flaw in this procedure was the Indians themselves. Sometimes the red men did not come in to trade. Often the strong tribes would not let weak neighbors cross their lands to the fort. Moreover, the area surrounding the trading post was soon denuded of beaver. The firm of Ashley and Henry intended to try an entirely different method.

On March 20, 1822, Ashley advertised in the *Missouri Republican* for "one hundred young men to ascend the Missouri river to its source, there to be employed for one, two or three years."[1] Other firms might wait at trading posts for the whims of the savages. Ashley and Henry intended to do their own trapping with sufficient men to enter the country of the strongest tribes.

The young men who joined their service were very different from the old-fashioned *voyageurs*. In time they became famous mountain men, pathfinders and guides on the Oregon and California trails. There was Jim Bridger, eighteen-year-old Virginia farm boy; Thomas Fitzpatrick, later known as Broken Hand, an Irish lad of twenty-four. The general knowledge of South Pass would stem from a letter he wrote to Ashley. Jedediah Smith, "Bible-backed" New Yorker of twenty-five, was destined for a short life but one of prodigious travels. James Clyman would stand in ranks with Abraham Lincoln in the Black Hawk War and then return for a lifetime of adventure in the Rockies. The notorious Mississippi riverman, Mike Fink, "half-horse half-alligator tipped with a snapping turtle," joined the hardy throng and soon succumbed. The most successful of them all was William L. Sublette, a Kentuckian whose grandfather was said to have killed Tecumseh. One of a famous family of Indian traders, he would die a man of wealth and a cutoff on the Oregon Trail would bear his name. Another of the Ashley men who became famous was Hugh Glass from Pennsylvania, who would fight a grizzly bear singlehanded and win. Then, too, there were the mulattoes Edward Rose, whom Hunt had left with the Crows, and Jim Beckwourth, teller of tall tales who had a way of turning up on every trail from California to Santa Fe. The fact that so many of the boys whom Ashley employed became great men in the trade explains his own success.

In April 1822 the first Ashley expedition set off in two keelboats under the command of Andrew Henry. He planned to go to the headwaters of the Missouri, then send trappers across the Great Divide into the Oregon country, where he had been in 1810—the year before Wilson Price Hunt had found his deserted fort there. Ashley was to come up the Missouri himself a year later with more trade goods.

Henry had bad luck before he got out of the settlements. Below Fort Osage, one keelboat hit a snag and sank with $10,000 worth of goods—a serious blow, but expected profit from the other boat would keep the firm from bankruptcy. Henry went on upriver, passed the mouth of the Platte and Council Bluffs, where the army had established a post in 1821.[2] Traders did not yet leave the river here to follow Stuart's route to Oregon. Boats were still considered essential for carrying large quantities of goods. Henry kept on to the Arikara and Mandan villages. He went above, with horsemen scouting along the banks, trading with the Indians. Opposite the mouth of the Yellowstone his men were surprised by a war party and all his horses were stolen— a second jolt to the finances of the new firm.

Henry decided that he would have to winter where he was. He set his men to building a fort. Throughout the winter he trapped and traded for more horses. In the spring he loaded his pack animals with "Indian goods" and set off for the upper Missouri, almost a year behind schedule but still intent on recouping his first losses. The inhospitable Blackfeet treated him as they had Meriwether Lewis. They killed four of Henry's men and drove the survivors from their country. In June 1823 the beaten men congregated at the forks of the Yellowstone once more.

In the meantime Ashley outfitted his expedition in St. Louis and set out in the spring of 1823 at the very time that Henry's men were trying to save themselves from their third disaster. Ashley brought a hundred more men and boys including Sublette, David E. Jackson, pious Jedediah S. Smith, Hugh Glass and the notorious mulatto, Edward Rose. Ashley intended to trade for horses at the Arikara village and send part of his expedition inland to meet Henry on the Yellowstone. A message from his partner told him of the disasters and the urgency of bringing as many mounts as possible. The Arikara owned many horses. Ashley pulled up to their village to trade as Hunt had done twelve years before.

The red men came out of the stockade around their domed houses and met the Americans with apparent friendship. Yes, they would trade horses. The price was agreed upon. Goods were spread out on the riverbank and brown boys trotted the horses back and forth for Ashley to see. He should have known that these villagers were noted for their treachery. They had been friendly enough with Lewis and Clark and with Hunt, but many small parties of traders had been pillaged by their warriors. Edward Rose warned Ashley to be on guard. Something in the careless insolence of the boys displaying the horses or the undisguised contempt of the blanketed women on the dome roofs told him that trouble was brewing.

Big businessman Ashley distrusted Rose as Hunt had done. He was not afraid of the red men, who seemed friendly and brought their horses to trade. On the night of June 1, 1823, Ashley retired to his boat, the trading completed. He intended to start the two expeditions forward in the morning. On the bank below the village, forty of his men including Jackson, Sublette, Hugh Glass and Jed Smith encamped with the horses. At three o'clock in the morning Ashley was awakened and told that one of his men had been killed by the Arikara. Ashley called all men to arms. With daylight, red flashes spat from loopholes in the Indian palisade and from along the crest of the moat below. The white men on the sand bar were mowed down as by a scythe. Horses plunged, reared and fell. Some huddled stupidly together. Ashley could see white puffs of smoke above the sides of dead horses. His men were putting up a fight. Ashley ordered the keelboats to shore. He would reinforce them. The *voyageurs* complained about the danger. To expose themselves meant death, they said. Ashley was only a militia general. War was not his element. He became flustered, shouted orders impossible to obey. The men lost all confidence in him, and the keelboats, ninety feet from shore, floated impotently at anchor. The marooned riflemen watched their chances and plunged into the Missouri to swim for shelter in the boats. Some wounded men sank before help arrived.

The scrimmage was all over in fifteen minutes. Ashley's men cut the cables and the boats floated downstream. Out of range of the Indian rifles, Ashley mustered his force. More than half of the land party were casualties—fourteen killed outright and the rest wounded. Hugh Glass nursed a bullet hole that would heal before his historic encounter with the grizzly bear.

The business venture of Ashley and Henry seemed to have come to an ignominious end, but both partners were men who could not be discouraged by bad luck. Ashley sent word downriver to Fort Atkinson at Council Bluffs for the army to come up and chastise the red men. He called for volunteers to take a message to Henry above, get him to come down and help the party past the Arikara. For two men to venture out across the Indian-infested plains and find Henry some three hundred miles away, seemed an impossible mission—but not for Jedediah Smith and a nameless French-Canadian who volunteered to help him. The New York boy, still untrained to the great open spaces, believed that God would protect them on this perilous journey—and He did. Soon Henry came floating down the Missouri with his supply of fur and extra fighting men.

In the meantime, Lieutenant Colonel Henry Leavenworth at Council Bluffs had got word and came upriver with a detail of United States soldiers.[3] The Arikara were punished, but not severely. Instead of opening the upper Missouri to traders, incensed and undefeated Indians closed it.

Ashley and Henry were caught in a bad way with their goods and no market. They devised their second great experiment in the fur business. The innovation proved a great success, revolutionized the trade and opened the overland route to Oregon. The two partners decided on the plan to the last detail. Ashley watched Henry ride off with a band of eighty picked men, among them Jedediah Smith, Jackson, Sublette, Rose, Bridger, Clyman, Glass, to trap the Columbia country, that is, upper Green River and beyond. Ashley returned to Missouri to run for governor in 1824.

The westbound mountain men were almost two years behind schedule but they were off for "Oregon" at last. During the fall and the following spring they divided into small parties and trapped the entire drainage of the upper Green River, the passes from the head of the Platte and Big Horn, and beyond to Bear River Valley. Each learned a part of the vast country across which Stuart had stumbled uncertainly. In the summer of 1824 they held the first Rocky Mountain trapper rendezvous, an annual gathering that would be famous for the next seventeen years. The mountain men, with red friends from the wilderness, came for supplies, news from the States and a brief period of revelry. They told one another about their recent discoveries, then jogged off, spurs jingling, for another twelve months in the gulches. The blind spots in the future Overland Trail thus became well known to all of them. As guides they would be invaluable in escorting travelers from the head of the Platte across the confusing country to the Snake. The entire route across was free from mountain obstructions. The trouble encountered by Lewis and Clark, Hunt and Stuart came from the fact that they did not know the way.

Jed Smith brought to the rendezvous of 1824 better news than the knowledge of a way across the continent. In the Oregon country—that is, in the country west of the Missouri drainage—he had met a party of Hudson's Bay traders. With God's help he had relieved them of their supply of furs. Perhaps the details of his negotiations will never be known. Did he rob them outright? Did he find their cache and rifle it? Were they in some desperate predicament which enabled Jedediah to buy their treasure for a song? Perhaps the Canadians turned traitor to their company. No matter. Jed Smith brought the plunder to the rendezvous to prove God's miracle. This haul alone assured the success of the year's operation. With Jed Smith, his fur, and the collections of other trappers, Andrew Henry returned to St. Louis. Supplies would be sent to another trapper rendezvous the next summer.

In St. Louis Henry learned that his partner, Ashley, had not been elected governor. Their two-year venture in the fur business had been saved from complete failure by the novel rendezvous, but the business was too hazardous for Andrew Henry. He decided to go back into lead mining. Ashley, discredited politically and deep in debt, looked back at the fur trade with hopeful eyes. Surely with Jed Smith, who had saved the last expedition, he could make a fortune in the mountains if he devoted all his time to it. Ashley drew up an agreement with the young zealot to serve as his right-hand man. A new supply of goods was purchased, another crew enlisted, and in October 1824 Ashley started up the river by boat. At Fort Atkinson, or Council Bluffs, he unloaded the supplies, and with twenty-five men, including Jim Beckwourth for personal servant or handy man, he started along the north bank of the Platte with fifty pack horses, a team and wagon. At last the overland route was to be tried to the Pacific slope.

Winter weather on the plains was bleak and cold, but Ashley, the go-getter, was escaping from defeat and the worry of tremendous debts. Snow lay like a white blanket over the dreary landscape. The horses' feet soon polished like agate in the hard crystals. Breath gushed from their nostrils in long plumes of vapor. Under the snow many parallel trails could be seen. They led to the Pawnee villages. Ashley promised his men a warm rest with the red men and at the same time cut rations in half. Jim Beckwourth dearly loved to eat. Around the fire at night with icicles on his mustache, the mulatto complained of the lack of food, hinted to his master that the men were becoming discouraged before they were well out from the Missouri. Ashley did not listen to him.

The traders came to the Pawnee village. The great dirt lodges, with fragrant wood smoke, thin and blue, whipping from the smoke holes into the cold prairie breeze, tempted the travelers. The lodges were warm and gloomy. The white men threw off their coats and warmed their fingers before the fires. Some wanted to tarry until better weather but Ashley ordered them to saddle and march again.

As they traveled up the Platte, wood became very scarce. Stuart had noticed this eleven years ago. He had stayed out of the country in bad weather on account of it. Ashley's party kept doggedly on—a centipede with a wagon for a tail creeping across the endless white waste. One day a small party of Pawnee caught up with him. The red men, balls of fur on horseback, peered out of their frost-tinted buffalo robes. They said that they were going to the forks of the Platte. Let's all go together! How?

Ashley welcomed the company. The red men knew the country and also the best way to exist in this frigid world. From them he learned that no wood would be found until they came to the forks of the Platte. The horses would go hungry until they came to cottonwoods. Then trees could be cut down and the animals would recoup by eating the bark. The cavalcade reached the forks on December 12, 1824. Ahead the country appeared rougher, more sheltered and easier for winter traveling. The Pawnee stopped here, but one told Ashley: "Go South Fork. More wood." The Indians traded the whites some fresh ponies, for the animals were starting to waste under the grueling. Five of the Indians hired out to go farther. Soon buffalo became plentiful. Their trails etched lacework on the white plains. The bulky beasts dotted distant snowy swells. Hunters killed them daily, staining the snow with blood, bringing the meat half frozen to the camps. Jim Beckwourth ceased to complain of lack of food, but the horses suffered acutely. Hobbled and on picket lines, they could not get enough to eat. Cottonwood limbs must be found for forage. The scene one morning when four horses were found lying in the snow may readily be imagined. The men kicked and whipped them, but the chilled half-starved brutes could not get up. Finally the strong men of the party were called to "tail 'em up." Husky fellows grasped the animals by the tails and lifted their hind feet clear of the ground. It

BREAKING CAMP

Contemporary Painting by W. H. Jackson.

CAMP AT WHITE RIVER

was no use. Numbed legs collapsed and let them down again in the powdery snow. Ashley ordered the brigade to leave them and march forward. Back in the trampled snow of the deserted camp the horses lay, with drooping, listless heads, ears hanging sideways. Wolves circled and came closer.

On January 1, 1825, the men sighted the tassel tops of bare cottonwoods ahead, bark at last for the horses. They whipped forward. Under the trees they made camp and rested a fortnight, filling the horses with cottonwood bark and themselves with fresh buffalo steaks. The Indian guides left them and rode south across the frigid horizon with bundles of firewood on their horses. Off for the Arkansas, they said.

Ashley's men did not find another camp site with enough cottonwoods for their horses until January 20, after almost ten days on sparse horse feed. Then they stopped again. In the distance they could see the purple sides and glittering peaks of the Rockies. The plains became rougher, too, as the men approached the mountains. The weather was not so cold here in the low foothills. The wind was less sharp, and on the south slopes the snow had melted. Dry grass stood brown and dead. The horses ate it eagerly and Ashley noticed that it gave them strength.

The South Fork of the Platte turned sharply south toward a high wall of snowy mountains. To the north the country appeared open. Ashley led his horsemen north of the river and around the end of the high mountains. He did not go north to the North Platte and therefore did not go toward South Pass by the route Stuart had come. Instead, he skirted the Medicine Bow Mountains by a route similar to that taken by the Union Pacific Railroad forty-five years later. The gloomy, frowning mountains, the vast rolling plains of Wyoming, the thousands of buffalo and antelope and bighorn sheep excited Ashley's expansive nature. It was good to be in this land of plenty, far from debts, disappointments and worries.

Wood was still scarce but the men found an herb that burned readily. Ashley called it "wild sage." Grass, thick as hair on a dog's back, stood cured on the stem. The streams were full of beaver. In places they burrowed in the banks but more often they lived in houses out in ponds that they had made with dams. The rodents had gnawed down big cottonwoods that lay with their branches in the water. Under the ice they could feed on the trees' bark. Beneath the green ice the men could see many limbs peeled white by beaver.

Ashley ordered his company to unload their traps and set them every day. He would move slowly, camp every five or six miles and thus move toward the spring rendezvous, collecting fur.

Late in March the trappers crossed the Continental Divide at what would later be known as Bridger Pass—not a pass to the Columbia but into the Spanish or Green River watershed. A few days later, at a patch of good grass, Ashley ordered a halt. With a companion he went ahead ten miles to scout. They climbed a promontory, probably Pilot Butte in the vast country north of Rock Springs, Wyoming. Far to the north across the Big Sandy flats that would later be the route taken by the Oregon-bound wagons, they saw gauzelike mountains against a pale blue sky, the sharp peaks of the Gros Ventres and Tetons in the Snake River drainage. Ashley believed them to be the watershed of the Yellowstone and the Columbia. The two men climbed down and started for camp. In the morning Ashley intended to bend his route to the north into this country that must be familiar to his men who had been here with Andrew Henry. He did not know that a war party of Crows had spied him on the butte. The red men tracked him back to camp and stole seventeen of his best horses. Ashley pursued the flying savages. They dropped a few of the stolen animals but got away with most of them. Ashley had to pack his extra trade goods on the backs of his men. With a few pack horses and with many men stooped under heavy loads, they moved off north and west across the upland desert. April snowstorms made the going disagreeable. Every six or eight miles they camped. At last they came to Big Sandy, the western exodus from South Pass. They plodded on to the green waters of the Spanish River. Ashley named it "Green," and the name stuck. The Green River appeared to be trapped out. Ashley thought that the Hudson's Bay people must have been over here three or four years before. He decided to try one of those original expedients which made him a great fur man in spite of his excitable temperament and frequent indecisions. First he would split his party into small groups as Henry had done, instruct them to trap, trade for fur with the natives, watch for the trappers left in this country last year and tell them to come with their fur to a rendezvous he would pick out down-river. Next Ashley determined to take a boat and explore the lower and unknown reaches of Green River while his mountain men were coming in.

The Indian goods were spread out on the bank of Green River where, in two decades, covered wagons would pass by hundreds. Ashley allotted the trade trinkets and all the horses to his parties and watched them jog away into the open wilderness. He ordered the men left behind to construct the framework of a boat and kill buffalo for hides to cover it.

Ashley loaded his goods and men and started down between the butter-colored banks of Green River. He saw at once that his boat was scarcely seaworthy. His load was much too heavy for such a craft. Forty miles downstream he landed and set the men to work making another boat. With two, he distributed his goods and went on down the green water, past the future site of Rock Springs and the mouth of Blacks Fork. High mountains loomed ahead. At the next stream entering from the west, Ashley left a mark designating it as the place for rendezvous. Henrys Fork—of the Green River, not the Snake—had good grass, wood and sufficient room for a large party of horsemen to encamp. Downstream the country appeared to be even more verdant but the mountains blocked the way.

Ashley left the site of the rendezvous and entered the wall of the mountains by a narrow canyon. His two hide boats passed through Flaming Gorge, Ladore Canyon and Split Mountain, a series of chasms sometimes two thousand feet deep and so narrow that the sun penetrated to the river only a brief hour or two a day. The men came out at last in the Uintah Basin of Utah. Here Ashley traded for horses from the Ute Indians and rode westward. In the Wasatch Mountains he met some Hudson's Bay trappers who explained the confused geography of the Weber River on its course to Great Salt Lake. Ashley pronounced the Canadians "very intelligent men." They belonged to a party under Peter Skene Ogden.

Ashley met also Etienne Provost and with him jogged back to the rendezvous with well over a hundred packs of beaver bobbing on their pack saddles. Estimated to be worth from $75,000 to $200,000, this one haul assured the success of Ashley's expedition—provided he could get the fur back to the States. Just where or how Ashley got possession of these pelts has never been thoroughly explained, but one thing is certain: they had not cost him much and they had formerly belonged to Peter Skene Ogden. The "deal" was a repetition of Jedediah Smith's in 1824. Hudson's Bay men seemed ready enough to sell out to Americans.

A hundred and twenty men gathered at the rendezvous on July 1, 1825, reckless fellows with tousled hair hanging on the shoulders of their fringed buckskin shirts, scalping knives in their belts and long rifles in their arms. Some of them had been away from civilization two years. Many wore Indian dress and all prided themselves on their familiarity with sudden death. Ashley noticed twenty-nine "free trappers"—independent fellows on their own in the wilderness. They had deserted from the employ of the big fur companies. Many had been Hudson's Bay men.

They traded bales of fur for "Indian goods." Ashley added to his stack of beaver, a veritable haymow of fur. The wild fellows swapped yarns and drew with their fingers in the sand the watercourses of half a continent; then rubbed out their maps with a flip of the hand. Jed Smith told tales of the fabulous furs to be had in the Snake River and in the Columbia since that region had been evacuated by Astor's men. Eighty thousand beaver taken in the last four years!

General Ashley promised to come back next year with more supplies. He had made a fortune. His debts, his disappointments, three years of disasters in the fur trade were all wiped away, provided he could get the pelts back to St. Louis. Ashley knew from bitter experience that horse travel was precarious among horse-stealing Indians. He knew that the Platte was not navigable. He decided not to go back by the route of the future Oregon Trail, but instead to hire men and horses to take his treasure to the Big Horn, construct boats there and float by the old trade route to the settlements. Soon after he started, he picked up an additional forty-five packs of beaver, cached the year before by Thomas Fitzpatrick, who told about a great boulder, Independence Rock, bigger than a steamboat, in the middle of an open valley. Twice attacked by Indians, Ashley lost some horses, and his servant, Beckwourth, was slightly wounded.[4] Below the Big Horn Mountain canyon the horses were sent back.

In skin boats Ashley and a picked crew went down to the Yellowstone and thence to the Missouri, where one of the precious boats was wrecked and thirty packs of beaver rolled away in the muddy water. Ashley "in a perfect ferment"[5] shouted to his men. The bales were retrieved and set dripping on the bank. The wet and breathless men then looked up and saw that they were surrounded by soldiers. General Atkinson had come up the river to force the new government policy on the Indians.[6]

Ashley noticed that the officer had seven stout keelboats, enough to transport his fortune in fur safely to the States. Atkinson did not plan to return until fall. Ashley offered to let his men act as guides for the soldiers, as killers of meat—perhaps even have Jed say prayers—if Atkinson would give him room in his keelboats for the furs. The army officer agreed, and Ashley with his men reached St. Louis in the fall of 1825 with a grizzly bear chained on the cabin deck of one boat and Jim Beckwourth strutting in embroidered fringe on another.

Ashley feasted and feted his mountain men in St. Louis. Jim Beckwourth said later that he drank at the boss's expense for a week. Then the whole gang was outfitted and sent on horseback to the mountains, by the Platte River and South Pass route—the Oregon Trail—now reasonably well known. Ashley himself married and prepared another big caravan to take to his men in the spring.

During the winter William Sublette came down from the mountains. Ashley employed him and Jedediah Smith to act as his lieutenants on the spring excursion. They set off in March 1826 with fifty men and 100 horses and mules: Ashley expansive, well-to-do at last, exhilarated with the prospect of more open-air traffic; Sublette slim and graceful in the saddle, his bright gray eyes flashing under a thatch of dark hair as he looked along the line of horses and horsemen; Jed Smith watching the birds and blossoms, more interested in nature and lonely exploration than in commerce, always trusting in God and ready for any hairbreadth escapade. Their route lay up the Platte from Council Bluffs. Snow did not mantle the plains as it had a year earlier when Ashley took this route after his defeat at the polls. The grass was still brown, in many places burned black, but streams and springs were bordered with new sprouts. Suddenly, and before the horsemen realized it, the flat tableland turned green. There was feed everywhere for the horses, and buffalo meat for the men, cheap transportation and free board for employees. The rendezvous had become a recognized success and with it the Overland Trail supplanted the tedious upriver route by boat.

At the forks of the Platte the horsemen crossed to the north channel. Sublette had come down that way in the winter. Thence, past the bluffs and buttes that stood like monuments along the shallow river, they came to the hunter's paradise at Laramie Fork, with the Black Hills—later known as the Laramie Mountains—in the distance. They journeyed on through the rolling plains of central Wyoming to the Sweetwater, up its broad valley to South Pass, over and gently down to the flats drained by Big and Little Sandy and across the purple sage to Green River. This was the Overland Trail.

Couriers were sent ahead to notify the trappers that the goods were on the way. The rendezvous was ordered in Great Salt Lake Basin at the mouth of the Weber. The Echo Canyon-Weber route through the Wasatch Mountains was still considered difficult. Ashley's men skirted the high country, crossed the deserts west of Green River to Bear Valley and went down into the basin. This route became known as the Sublette Cutoff. William Sublette, riding beside Ashley, could tell him in soft

Kentucky accents how he had ordered the men to comb the Salt Lake, Green and Bear River areas for furs the preceding fall. He had not left them until the hunt was over. They had built winter quarters on the edge of the mountains—near where Ogden, Utah, would later stand.

The rendezvous of 1826 in Salt Lake basin was much larger than the Henrys Fork meeting the year before. The men had built winter cabins. With Indian women and their relatives the settlement numbered six or seven hundred souls. Ashley rode down to the river, unpacked, shook hands all around and established headquarters. Jim Beckwourth, his teeth shining below his kinky mustache, came forward with the trappers who had left St. Louis with him last winter. Everyone had bales and bales of fur. Ashley saw that he was going to make another fortune. Operation by rendezvous was a great success.

The mountain men had many tales to tell. During the winter a war party of Bannock had found their cabins and raided their horses, a big mistake for the poor warriors. The trappers had followed them, got back their own mounts and forty belonging to the thieves. In the spring the mountain men had gone on a great hunt up Bear River Valley, a region of fine horse feed and good timber. They had passed hot springs with water that tingled in the mouth like soda. Over the divide they had ridden down the rolling hills to the Port Neuf until it disappeared in a gorge of black lava a short way above Snake River. They had met Hudson's Bay trappers with big catches over there.

Ashley liked these wild fellows. He liked the trader's life—but he was forty-eight years old, a bridegroom and wealthy. His lieutenants, Sublette, Smith and Jackson, came to him with a proposition. They offered him 150 percent over cost for the goods piled on the ground around him. They would take another caravan load here in the mountains each year and would agree to sell him their fur. The deal looked good to Ashley. He drew up a contract giving his old partners five years to finish their payments. Then he made an impassioned speech to the assembled mountain men. The politician in him was not yet dead.

Ashley returned to St. Louis by land, not by the water route he had used the year before. Men were beginning to realize that the Overland Trail was the best and shortest. Ashley covered the distance in seventy days, and *Niles' Register*, a nationally read newspaper, reported that he had found ample grass for his horses and abundance of meat for the men. "There was no day in which they could not have subsisted a thousand men, and often ten thousand."[7] Surely the Platte River route was a bounteous roadway for emigrants into the West.

During the next three years Ashley sent the supplies he had agreed upon to his successors. His extraordinary prosperity astonished the staid Creoles of St. Louis. Even John Jacob Astor took notice. Estimates of Ashley's sudden fortune varied from $50,-000 to $80,000, a tidy sum in the 1820's. With his new wife he retired to a mansion on an eight-acre tract north of St. Louis, a house finer than the one owned by William Clark, ex-governor of Missouri. Ashley, now a gentleman of leisure, oversaw his estate, and began to dabble again in politics as he purchased goods for his annual expedition to the mountains. His caravan in the spring of 1827 went equipped with a four-pound cannon hauled by mules, said to be the first wheeled vehicle to cross the Continental Divide on the Oregon Trail. The ordnance was destined for a trapper fort in the Great Basin and thus could not claim to be the first wheels to reach the Pacific. Strangely enough, Astor had an interest in this expedition. The New Yorker continued to have a suave hand in any fur enterprise that made money.

The rendezvous of 1827 was held at Bear Lake on what would be the Utah-Idaho line west of the state of Wyoming. The congregation of trappers continued to be very important for the dissemination of knowledge about all possible overland trails. Jedediah Smith was back again with stories about a long march he had made to California. He was the first American to go there overland. Eighteen of his companions were still in that foreign territory, he said, and he intended to go back for them. He had in mind a two-year journey through California and Oregon. The boys might look for him to be coming back through the Snake River Valley in the summer of 1829. He hoped to bring with him the men he had left on his last trip. If he made the circle without being captured by the Californians, killed by the Indians, choked on the deserts or buried in Sierra snows, he would certainly be the greatest living authority on trails from the Salt Lake Basin to the Pacific.

The rendezvous came to an end. Sublette started for St. Louis with the fur bales bobbing on his pack mules. He and his partners had made enough to pay Ashley in full. Henceforth profits would be their own. Jed Smith set off with Bible and gun to make his two-year trapping tour of California and Oregon. The third partner, Jackson, stayed in the high country with the remainder of the trappers, establishing headquarters in Jackson's Hole.

Two years passed profitably. In the summer of 1829 Jackson and William Sublette set off to find Jed Smith and his companions in the upper Snake River country. They found him on Henrys Fork beyond the Tetons with one companion. Of the eighteen who had set out to explore the Pacific ranges, only two had survived. Jedediah Smith had suffered hardships and escaped death by miracles as fabulous as those in his adored Bible. He said that he had gone south to the Mojave Desert, had been attacked and robbed by the Indians there. For nine and a half days he had trudged with his men across the desert to California. In a Spanish mission the ragged refugees had been fed and nursed back to health, then imprisoned by the authorities for entering California illegally. At last they were released with orders to leave the country at once. Instead, Smith led his followers north up the pleasant California valleys, trapping as they went. They wintered in what became known as American Fork of the Sacramento. Smith said that he broke camp in April 1828 and started north for Oregon. Up there, on the Umpqua, his party had been surprised by Indians and all but Smith and two others were killed. The Indians stole all their horses and a year's catch of beaver pelts. Absolutely destitute, the survivors reached the Hudson's Bay post on the Columbia.

Dr. John McLoughlin, the chief factor, took them in. The

post had been established here in 1826. The doctor was a tall, handsome, long-haired man. In charge of the vast Columbia River area with trappers working the tributaries as far east as Snake River and the Wasatch Mountains bordering Great Salt Lake, he had abandoned Astor's fort, which his company had purchased, and established headquarters across from the mouth of the Willamette. Ashley had based his fortune on furs taken from Dr. McLoughlin's firm, and the Canadian might have been expected to retaliate. Instead, he welcomed the three destitute Americans and told them not to say anything about the massacre of their companions. He would try to make amends. Then the factor sent out Thomas McKay, half-breed son of the Astorian who had been massacred by the Indians on the ill-fated *Tonquin*. Dr. McLoughlin had married McKay's squaw and adopted his son. McKay crossed the river and went to the Indian villages. He ordered the savages to bring in their furs. Jedediah Smith identified his pelts. McLoughlin took them from the Indians without pay and demanded also the stolen horses. Practically everything, including one of the men's diaries, was recovered. The three survivors rested all winter at the Hudson's Bay post. Dr. McLoughlin paid them $20,000 in drafts on London for their beaver. He also exacted a promise from Smith that his firm would stop trapping west of the Continental Divide. Smith agreed. One of his companions joined the British company, the other had been sent with Smith to one of the subfactories, Flat Head House. From there they had come down to the Snake, as Smith had boasted they would do, two years before.

Smith and Sublette did not like the agreement not to trap west of the divide in the Oregon country. However, the drafts for $20,000 were more than the partnership had a right to expect after such horrible hardships. Smith, the senior, had made the agreement. Jackson and Sublette acquiesced. The fall hunt was ordered in the dangerous Blackfoot country at the head of the Missouri, and in December Sublette went out for supplies for the next summer's rendezvous. In April 1830 he started back with an elaborate outfit of eighty-one men mounted on mules, ten wagons pulled by five mules each, two dearborn buggies each pulled by one mule, twelve head of cattle and one milch cow—the first wagon train on the Oregon Trail. The beef cattle were to supply meat until the buffalo country was reached. The cow furnished milk for the officers' table. The place of rendezvous was east of South Pass, probably on the head of the Popo Agie, and the wagons did not cross the Continental Divide.

At the meeting the partners figured the value of their furs. They estimated that they had made a great profit in the last four years, marred only by one bad deal, Smith's forced agreement to stay out of the Oregon country. Perhaps they had better sell out to their best employees as Ashley had sold to them. Fitzpatrick, Sublette's brother Milton, Jim Bridger and a few others offered to purchase the business. They organized as the Rocky Mountain Fur Company, received right and title to the Smith-Sublette-Jackson assets, excepting the agreement to stay out of the Oregon country, which Jackson, with his headquarters in Jackson's Hole, had never taken too seriously.

The retiring merchants loaded their wagons. With the great fur harvest—190 packs of beaver—they rolled down the wagon trail to St. Louis. No one had ever come in with such a treasure. A messenger rode ahead to announce the wagon train's approach. Citizens met the travelers with an ovation.

Jed Smith turned his attention and wealth to adventures on the Santa Fe Trail where he was shot in the back and killed by a Comanche arrow the following year. Sublette built a big store and fine house like Clark's and Ashley's. He filled his mansion with museum relics from the mountains and in the yard he kept an Indian family in their native lodge. Word of the fame and fortune to be made in the far western country spread across the United States. Ashley went to Congress. Senator Thomas Hart Benton from St. Louis began to thunder about the country's manifest destiny to control the Pacific. The contagion spread. Young men everywhere planned and dreamed about the golden West and a land called Oregon.

1 Hiram Martin Chittenden, *The American Fur Trade of the Far West* (New York, 1935), I, 261.

2 Harrison Clifford Dale (ed.), *The Ashley-Smith Explorations and the Discov-*

ery of a Central Route to the Pacific, 1822-1829 (Cleveland, 1918) , 86; Chittenden, *American Fur Trade*, I, 251.

3 Donald McKay Frost, "Notes on General Ashley, the Overland Trail, and South Pass," *Proceedings of the American Antiquarian Society . . . 1944*, LIV, part 2 (Worcester, Mass., 1945), 186.

4 Beckwourth's injury is questionable. See Dale (ed.) , *Ashley-Smith Explorations*, 159n.

5 *Ibid.*, 161n.

6 Jay Monaghan, "North Carolinians in Illinois History," *The North Carolina Historical Review* (October, 1945) , XXII, No. 4, 422-29.

7 Dale (ed.) , *Ashley-Smith Explorations*, 169.

Chapter 6

Nathaniel Wyeth: 1832

I~N~ 1831 Nathaniel J. Wyeth was attracted to something printed in the paper. His active mind was eager for new business opportunities. He had already distinguished himself as a money-maker. With no hope of reaping agricultural wealth from the rock-bound soil near Cambridge, Massachusetts, he had gone into the ice business. Cutting ice in winter on Fresh Pond, he had loaded the cakes in a sailing ship and sold them profitably in the West Indies. People said that he had been a supersalesman—going south ahead of his ship to teach the islanders to like cold drinks before the ship arrived. In any event, things generally happened when Nat Wyeth took hold of them, and now he was interested in a formal published "Memo" which read:

The Oregon country forms the western section of the United States. It is bounded on the west by the Pacific Ocean, on the east by the Rocky Mountains, on the north by the Russian territory, and on the south by Mexico. It extends about 400 miles on the ocean, and reaches about 500 miles inland. It is intersected by the Columbia River, which is 600 miles in length, and six miles wide at its mouth. Three large rivers are tributary to it—Clark's in the north east, Lewis's [the Snake] in the centre, and the Multnomah [Willamette] from the southeast, and nearest the mouth of the Columbia.[1]

The article was written by a Boston neighbor of Wyeth's named Hall J. Kelley. For years the writer had been urging Congress to send troops to the Northwest, keep out the British "race

of slaves, and the domination of tyrants."[2] Kelley had taught
school in Boston at the close of the War of 1812. Wyeth read
further:

The frost seldom appears till January, and then it is so slight,
as scarcely to freeze over a pond of still water, or to impede, on
low grounds, the progress of vegetation. The oldest Indians have
never known the bays entirely frozen over. During the winter,
which seldom continues more than six or eight weeks, the snow
sometimes falls to the depth of three inches, but it is generally
dissipated by the warm sun in a few days. Rains are frequent
in the winter, often accompanied by a southeast wind, which
serve to preserve vegetation, so that cattle may live comfortably
in the woods through the winter. In April, warm weather
commences, shrubbery is in blossom, and vegetation proceeds
briskly. In June, most kinds of fruit are ripened, and weather,
delightfully pleasant, succeeds.[3]

Kelley wanted to organize a colony, let New Englanders take
their families to the new land and start a settlement as the Puri-
tans had done at Plymouth. Kelley told prospective emigrants
that it would be easy to reach the Pacific:

The open and comparatively level country between the Mississippi and Columbia rivers, formed by a depression in the
Rocky Mountains; the ease by which it can be travelled, while
in a state of nature, with carriages, will secure to the Western
States a commerce of unparalleled advantage.[4]

Even the Indians, according to this man Kelley, seemed to be
ideal. Wyeth read on:

The Indians are friendly to the whites and trade freely with
them. The men and women generally dress very much alike,
but on the sea coast their clothing resembles that of white people. They have an unpleasant custom of flattening the heads of
their children in infancy, by binding them between two pieces
of board, which gives the top of the head a broad, flat appear-

ance. They generally live in houses with pitched roofs, from 20 to 60 feet long and from 10 to 20 wide. The ridgepole is frequently the trunk of a large tree, resting on strong posts set firmly in the ground. The sides are made of boards, or of logs placed close together, and covered with cedar bark. The Indians are the rightful proprietors of the soil, and are willing to sell it to the whites.[5]

Wyeth could tell that Kelley did not think much of Britain's claim to the Northwest. True, the Hudson's Bay Company controlled the fur trade from the Pacific to the head of the Snake River, but the treaty of 1818 with Britain renewed again in 1827 proclaimed the country "free and open" to both Americans and Britishers. Wyeth thought that he saw a great opportunity there—certainly a better chance of getting rich than by selling ice in the West Indies. He read that Kelley had called a meeting. Emigrants were to be enlisted and moved to an island in Boston Bay to get lessons in woodcraft. The schoolteacher died hard in Hall J. Kelley.

Nathaniel Wyeth rubbed the fringe of whiskers on his lantern jaw. The overland adventure appealed to the twenty-eight-year-old businessman. "I cannot divest myself of the opinion," he wrote, "that I shall compete better with my fellow men in new and untried paths than in those to pursue which requires only patience and attention."[6] Wyeth went to see Hall Kelley, and enlisted to start on January 1, 1832.

Christmas came and Kelley still talked, but nothing was ready. Practical businessman Wyeth became disgusted. A Yankee fully as ingenious as Captain Gray, Wyeth was a man of action. He liked to build, to plan, to drive things through successfully. People said that he could carve a full-sized wagon out of wood with a jackknife. He looked forward to using his skill in the open country. Kelley seemed good for nothing but the dissemination of words—a pedagogue ready to rave about "the rills rippling from the declivities of the Rocky Mountains, and swelling into murmuring streams, [to] form most of the tributaries of the Columbia." He could rant about the promise of "a western empire"—how democrats relished that royal name!—but he could not get his emigrants ready by the first of January as he had promised.

Wyeth knew that fine words would cook no beans. He announced that he planned an emigrant organization of his own and he would start across the continent March 1. At once he wrote to New York for forty dozen steel traps, each to weigh five pounds. He specified the length of the chains, the number of swivels. His practical, inventive mind grasped every detail. He drew plans for three boats on wheels—good for land and water—experimented with tents, prescribed each emigrant's uniform.

Kelley continued to extol the virtues of Oregon and his own plans to colonize there. Wyeth noticed that the propaganda was attacked scornfully by one W. J. Snelling in the *New-England Magazine*. Perhaps the dissenter was merely seeking notoriety. On the other hand, the energy of his attacks indicated that he might be employed by the rising industrialists who feared that they would lose their labor supply by a mass migration into the West.

Nat Wyeth paid no attention to either of the ranting journalists. He got the money he needed from three capitalists, Henry Hall, Tucker and Williams. To the most minute detail he perfected his travel plans. He had access to the writings of Lewis and Clark, as well as Sergeant Patrick Gass's journal. The exploits of Wilson Hunt, of Robert Stuart and of Ashley's men had all been published in the papers. Wyeth read that Indians were eager to trade for vermilion, glass beads, cheap knives, buttons, nails, small looking glasses, things "on which young Indians of both sexes set a high value, and white men little or none."[7] He purchased his trade goods accordingly.

Wyeth planned to take a company of fifty men. The time came to start and only twenty-four volunteered. Unlike Kelley, Wyeth had everything ready and did not delay. He moved his men across to an island and began their outdoor training. In the party were three of his relatives: an older brother, Dr. Jacob Wyeth, who was a graduate of Harvard and was now thirty-three years old; a nephew of eighteen named John B. Wyeth; and a cousin, Thomas Livermore, who was not of age but got his father's consent to go. For geologist, Wyeth enlisted John Ball, a Dartmouth graduate. He enrolled also a gunsmith, a blacksmith, two carpenters and two fishermen. The other members of the party were farm boys and laborers, mainly from New Hampshire. Nat Wyeth issued each man arms and uniform—a coarse woolen jacket and pantaloons, a striped shirt and cowhide boots. Every man was given a musket, a bayonet on a broad belt, a large clasp knife for eating and a greatcoat in which to sleep. A small ax was also to be slung from the belt. Captain Wyeth and one or two others carried a brace of pistols.

A ship loaded with trade goods and tools for the colony was started around the Horn to meet the overland travelers at the mouth of the Columbia. On March 11, 1832, Wyeth embarked his landsmen on another vessel for Baltimore. There the baggage and boat-wagons were unloaded. The hardy explorers, dressed in their striped shirts and clanking arms, marched to the edge of town. To save expense they pitched camp and cooked their meals. Wondering citizens stared at them and said, "Yankee all over!"[3]

Railroad trains and canalboats moved the travelers to Pittsburgh. In the black and smoky coal town they boarded a palatial Ohio River steamboat and floated away.

The party arrived at St. Louis on April 18, 1832. Wyeth found a very different town from the one described by Lewis and Clark. St. Louis had changed in twenty-four years. Most disappointing of all, Wyeth learned that the fur trade was an old established business, well organized by men who knew the Indians and knew what they wanted. Veterans, grown gray in the mountains, lounged in front of the stores and stalked silently along the muddy streets. Merchants told Wyeth that Mr. William L. Sublette was purchasing a supply of goods to take to the mountains. Better see him!

Wyeth introduced himself to the tall Kentuckian and explained his plan to establish a colony and trading station in the Oregon country. The wealthy fur man invited the Yankee to go with him as far as the rendezvous. Indians or trappers out there would be able to lead the way on to the forbidden Oregon country, the fur paradise that God-fearing Jedediah Smith had agreed to vacate. Sublette looked over Wyeth's outfit. He suggested that the New Englander sell the amphibious carriages. They were too heavy to haul and would be unseaworthy in turbulent mountain streams. Sublette also suggested that Wyeth go on up the Missouri to Independence, a little depot town below the entrance of the Kansas. Santa Fe traders outfitted there. Sublette had wintered his own pack animals near by. At Independence, Wyeth could camp, buy animals and train his men for the overland journey. Sublette would pick him up as he came by and the two outfits would ride together to the mountains.

Wyeth sold his wagon-boats at half the cost price. His relatives snickered. Their inventive leader with all his theoretical plans did not look so good out here among professionals. The New Englanders all felt a little foolish in their striped shirts beside real mountain men in frock coats that would have looked right in Boston. The reduced equipment was loaded on an up-river steamboat. For ten days the men tarried at Independence. The prospect did not look good. Slant-eyed Mexicans in enormous hats, rawboned American backwoodsmen, Indians in blankets and paint, all conjured pictures of a savage life beyond this stark river settlement. Three of the New Englanders deserted. Several others discussed abandoning the project. Then Sublette arrived with sixty-two *engagés*. The slim and courtly mountain man looked over Wyeth's outfit again. He suggested that Wyeth buy fifteen sheep and two yoke of oxen. Meat would be scarce on the plains until the buffalo range was reached. A few head of livestock could keep up with the column and be slaughtered as needed.

Sublette gave the New Englanders new courage. His ample company of slim and agile packers, sun-tanned and with legs bowed to the saddle, reassured the novices, but their respect for their own visionary leader went down.

Sublette's party started down the dirt road in a long column of twos. Each man led a pack horse. Wyeth fell in behind with his men, bayonets and hand axes swinging in broad belts. The way led under great trees bright with new leaves in May. The well-beaten track was rutted by Santa Fe traders. On the second day out, the New Englanders came to the prairie. Sublette left the road and struck off across the greensward. Seventy miles from Independence the column came to an Indian village—peaceful Kansans who lived in stockade huts, cultivated corn and pumpkins and went yearly to the high plains to get buffalo meat.

The travelers kept on, crossed the Kansas River, the Little and Big Vermilion, the Big Blue. Near what would one day be the Kansas-Nebraska line, three more of the New Englanders deserted. One of them was Wyeth's young cousin, Thomas Livermore, who had come with his father's consent. The sea of unvarying tall grass, the expanse of great plains across which a man could see the crest of three or four ground swells ahead and nothing more, had discouraged the boys.

Sixteen more days in the geographical void took the travelers to the Platte near Grand Island, the spot that had seemed such a haven for Robert Stuart and his forlorn band in the spring of 1813, nineteen years earlier. For twenty-seven days they traveled up the endless valley of the Platte. At night they pitched their tents in a great square with the horses picketed inside, the men constantly on guard for thieving Indians. Every six men had a tent and cooked their own mess on a separate fire of buffalo chips—dried dung—for there was no wood along the Platte. The water gave them dysentery. Dr. Wyeth became very weak. The last of the livestock was killed. Hungry and disconsolate, the men grumbled about Nat Wyeth, their chief. What would have become of them except for the slim, silent and capable William Sublette?

At last they came to the buffalo country. As far as their eyes could see, the black monsters dotted the grasslands. In the distance it appeared as though the ground itself were moving like the sea. The men killed ten or twelve the first afternoon just for the fun of it. They brought to camp all the meat they could eat. In the morning they went back for more and found that wolves had picked the carcasses clean in the night.

Soon the column came to the forks of the Platte, the long tongue of flat low land dividing the desert stream. Sublette led the way up the South Fork. The trail was more open and better timbered that way. Six days later he forded the Platte and turned the column toward the North Fork. The horses plodded up the elevated tableland between the streams. Near the summit they stopped for breath. A mountain man pointed south across the plains. Let us believe he said, "Yan way's the trail to Bent's Fork on the Arkansas!"

Young John Wyeth, disillusioned about his uncle's leadership, marveled at the ability of these mountain men to keep their directions. How lucky they all were to be with Sublette who never took a false step! Without him they surely would have become lost and wandered aimlessly in circles on this sea of grass. Their greenhorn leader with his heavy amphibious carriages would have left them all as helpless as fish out of water.

The long column crossed the tableland. Suddenly the lead riders disappeared. Like a snake the column dropped into Ash Hollow. Under the rim they wound through the sand hills and sugar-loaf pinnacles dotted with cedars. The New Englanders looked curiously at Spanish needle plants and prickly pears. At the mouth of the hollow they forded the North Fork and rode out again on endless plains. Dr. Wyeth became so ill that he was afraid he could not sit his horse.

In the distance tiny objects like houses came into view. Soon they looked as big as churches. The mountain men said that they were "badlands"—grotesquely carved buttes along the banks of the Platte. One, yellow as cheese in the rising sun, was called Scotts Bluff for a trapper who became ill and was abandoned sixty miles above. The next year his faithless companions found Scott's grinning skull near the yellow cliffs. He had crawled the long distance before death overtook him. Sublette's men warned the New Englanders to beware of the giant grizzly bears that ranged these flats. As large as steers, they might charge a man without provocation and several rifle balls in vital spots were required to knock them down.

On June 12, 1832, the fur brigade crossed a shallow stream in the grassy river bottom called Horse Creek where Stuart and his party had wintered. The next day they saw in the distance the pale outline of the Laramie Mountains. The buttes and badlands had looked tall to the New Englanders, but the sharp-edged peaks ahead made anything in New Hampshire look like molehills. The men noticed, too, that the plains had changed from treeless flats to swelling ridges. Cedars were common on the steep rocky slopes. Box elders and cottonwoods lined the streams.

Below Laramie Creek, Thomas Fitzpatrick, Broken Hand himself, met the column. He had made a hard ride from the mountains to bring important news. The American Fur Company trappers, he said, were gathering at the rendezvous. Their own caravan had not yet arrived. If Sublette hurried he would get all the American Fur Company's trade and his own besides.[9] Horseflesh must not be spared. The fur men urged the packers to double their efforts. Rest periods were cut and the length of marches increased. Wyeth's ill and inexperienced men feared that they could not keep up the pace. Hustler Nat gloried in the extra activity—the hustle and bustle, men with mouths full of food striking tents, running from campfires to pack the animals.

Near the present site of Casper, Wyoming, the brigade came to what the trappers called The Crossing. A tall round-topped mountain blocked the south side of the Platte. Sublette's men set to work to construct a bullboat out of hides. Mechanical-minded Wyeth and his Yankees watched the mountaineers cut willows and stick them upright in the sand, bend them together in a great inverted basket pointed at both ends. Over this the mountain men stretched green buffalo hides and stitched the seams. Underneath they kindled several slow fires to heat and dry the skins. In the smoke the men brushed away the sand with their brown hands and rubbed the bloodshot surfaces with buffalo tallow until the hides became watertight.

Captain Wyeth called his men away from the strange spectacle. He had his own Yankee ideas about construction of craft for crossing streams. He could build a raft from cottonwood logs and be across long before Sublette's elaborate craft was dry. Yankee axes began to ring along the riverbank. Sublette strolled across to see what the Yankees were doing. Wyeth, always in the thick of things with sleeves rolled up, pointed to the half-finished raft with pride. Sublette asked how Wyeth would steer the ungainly craft in the swift current.

Ingenious Wyeth had a plan for overcoming that contingency. Watch! A swimmer was ordered across the Platte with a rope in his mouth. This was attached to a tree. The raft would be towed. Sublette asked in his quiet way if such a long rope might not break. Wyeth had used rope to drag great loads of ice on Fresh Pond. He 'lowed he'd try.

The anvil, a heavy iron vise, some bar iron, a load of the precious steel traps, and a keg of powder were placed on the floating logs. The men waded out and started the raft into the Platte. On the north bank other men tightened the rope. The craft moved easily into midstream, hit the comb of the current and shied away. The rope tightened, leaped dripping from the water, stretched like a bowstring and snapped. The raft spun downstream, collided with a half-submerged tree, and dumped the heavy cargo into the muddy water.

The loss of so much iron in a Stone-Age country was irreparable. The already discouraged men, two-thirds of them ill and wan, marked up another failure against their energetic but ineffective chief. Listlessly they watched Sublette's seasoned employees turn over their skin vessel and launch it lightly as a leaf on the water. The Yankees laughed out loud—in admiration, not derision. "The contrivance would have done credit to *old* New-England," they told one another.[10]

The march continued, still racing against time, all determined to beat the American Fur Company supplies to the rendezvous. The long pack train passed the Red Buttes where Stuart had tried to winter, and saw at their left the portals of the Fiery Narrows.

Thence the fur brigade went on up the Sweetwater, Wyeth's New Englanders grumbling about his impractical ideas and Sublette's perfections. What would they do without the great mountain man after he left them at the rendezvous? Then, to add to the discouragement, one of Wyeth's horses gave out. Worse still, the gnats were terrible. Almost invisible, they settled on the tender skin under the men's eyes and behind their ears. Little drops of blood came out when they bit. At night the gnats disappeared, but swarms of mosquitoes made sleep impossible.

On June 22, 1832, the New Englanders saw in the distance a long black object, like a titanic whale, in the middle of the broad plain. At noon they clambered over the broad back of Independence Rock, exclaimed in nasal twang at the names carved on the smooth surface and added their own. Through hot days and frosty nights they marched and camped along the Sweetwater, cross South Pass and rode down into the sagebrush flats. Had the American Fur Company caravan got ahead of them?

Some horsemen were sighted in the distance charging toward them. "Indians!" Sublette assumed complete command at once. He ordered every man to tie up his horse and prepare to fight on foot. Mountain men had learned that redskins relished fighting on horseback, charging recklessly with hair, rope ends and thongs flying. A calm rifleman on the ground had little trouble knocking over such easy marks.

The distant figures galloped nearer. Sublette recognized them as whites—a party of his own hardy mountain men come to escort him to the rendezvous. The fringed and bewhiskered fellows clattered up to Sublette. The whole party rode on to Green River and camped. The next day they crossed to the headwaters of the Snake, a tributary below Jackson's Hole. This was the Columbia watershed at last and the Fourth of July to boot. Young John B. Wyeth wrote in his journal that the men were very homesick 4,000 miles from Boston and that they drank to their homes and friends "in good clear water, as that was the only liquor we had to drink."[11] Their captain was obviously keeping something from them, for Nat Wyeth in his journal recorded: "Drank to my friends with mingled feelings from the waters of the Columbia mixed with alcohol and eat of a Buffaloe cow."[12]

Sublette, always courteous, came down to the New Englanders' camp. He said that the way ahead was rough, the most mountainous country yet. They would drop into Jackson's Hole, then cross Teton Pass to Pierres Hole, the place of rendezvous. He was anxious to get there as soon as possible. Were the ill New Englanders able to keep up? Perhaps they had better "cache" their goods in trapper fashion and relieve the horses for all the men to ride. Wyeth agreed to this, and on July 8, 1832, the cavalcade wound its way up into Teton Pass. The day was clear, brilliant blue sky above dizzy peaks, bluebells bobbing over tinkling rivulets, "Little Chief" hares whistling in the rocks. Some of the men dismounted to lead their horses. The pack animals had to charge up the steep slopes to keep their footing. They almost ran over the weak men leading them. Dr. Wyeth dropped out. Soon the party was scattered for miles through the pass. One horse stumbled and rolled into a gulch 100 feet below. Men climbed down, loosened the pack ropes and got him to his feet, but the animal was unable to go farther. The Yankees divided his pack and scrambled up to the trail. The broken-down horse stood forlornly waiting for the wolves.

Sublette said that the New Englanders could not miss the rendezvous from here. West of Teton Pass a hundred or more men were encamped in the meadows. The American Fur Company supplies had not arrived, and he must get to the rendezvous, unpack and sell his goods without delay. The New Englanders could move in from here at their leisure. The distance was only twelve or fifteen miles, but look out for Blackfoot Indians!

Nathaniel Wyeth waited at the top of the pass until his men caught up. Then they all went down into the Hole and camped on the edge of the plain. That night it snowed. In the morning the New England boys looked helplessly at the gloomy pines floured white with snow. Boston and the old familiar bridge connecting it with Cambridge seemed very, very far away. Yet they all realized that the journey to the Pacific was only half completed. Wyeth, resilient with vitality, strode across the hummocks of green grass clotted with wet snow. "Pack up, boys. Only ten miles to the rendezvous."

The New Englanders rode forward. Within an hour the sun shone warm and brilliant on the green meadows. In the distance the riders saw a line of horsemen several hundred strong coming toward them, white men in fringed buckskin, red men in feathers, scarlet blankets, dazzling white robes. This was a formal reception committee of savages advancing to the distant murmur of Indian song. The New Englanders were due for the stilted intercourse typical of the frontier. They watched the wild men of the mountains curiously as they approached. With military precision their red and white hosts wheeled into line and halted, eagle feathers spinning, braided hair streaming in the wind, restless horses pawing the sod.

Nathaniel Wyeth ordered his pitiful eighteen, in their tattered striped shirts, broad belts and bayonets, to form in line on the green. Then the savages fired three rounds. Wyeth ordered his men to do the same. The white smoke drifted away. Sublette, slim and graceful on a magnificent charger, came forward. With courtly dignity he showed his guests to a camping place. The New Englanders feigned indifference to the savage display. Young John Wyeth said to himself that he and his companions were treating their hosts' elaborate ceremonies with the studied indifference which Franklin and Adams had shown Lord Howe's military display on Staten Island in the Revolution. That night in his journal he wrote: "This parade was doubtless made by Sublet for the sake of effect. It was showing us, Yankee barbarians, *their Elephants.*"[13]

For days the men rested at the rendezvous. Leisure after the exacting duty of the march gave them time to become more homesick. Among themselves they resolved that the company should go back to the States with Sublette's returning caravan. They would never have got this far with Nathaniel Wyeth alone. Why trust themselves with him from here on? A committee of the insurgents went to their chief and demanded their right as New Englanders to hold a town meeting and decide their future course. Captain Wyeth knew what the majority would vote to do. He was committed to democratic principles as much as his men, but he believed also in the democratic right of every man to take advantage of constitutional rules, to make the other fellow do his will and "if he hollers let him go." With all his greenness and enthusiasm for gadgets he had also the elements of great leadership. Suavely Wyeth told the delegation that he would grant them their town meeting, but of course he himself would have to preside. The malcontents succumbed to this compromise. The men assembled. Wyeth called the roll. No man was allowed to voice an opinion. No motion that the company return home was accepted by the chair. Wyeth himself stated the question, "Who will go forward, who return?" The men voted without discussion. Wyeth's political maneuver saved the expedition. Seven of his eighteen voted to return, among them his ill brother and his eighteen-year-old nephew. John Ball, the Dartmouth man, remained loyal.

Wyeth gave the deserters one of the two tents belonging to the expedition. He selected the best guns for himself and left the discards for the returning party. He gave them two horses to carry their baggage. Then he ordered them to pack up and move a quarter mile from camp. He moved a half mile farther the other way. Milton Sublette planned going west to winter with twenty men. Wyeth with his loyal eleven would go along. Somewhere in the Snake River country he would strike out independently for the mouth of the Columbia, open the trail which Hunt and Stuart had used to Oregon, meet his ship with its load of supplies and start his trading settlement.

The loyal New Englanders joined Milton Sublette's professional trappers, a motley hard-bitten crew of half-breeds, Canadian-French, deserters from the Hudson's Bay Company, with squaws and children. The two commanders, Milton Sublette and Nathaniel Wyeth, mounted their horses and rode down the valley with their men. They camped under the pass. The next morning they saw coming through the gap a long line of men and horses. Both leaders looked through their telescopes. Milton

Sublette pronounced them Blackfeet, mortal enemies of all the whites and their red allies at the rendezvous. He ordered two couriers to race back to his brother and get reinforcements. Then he prepared his mountaineers for action, placing the Yankees in reserve. Obviously he did not count on them. Soon an advance party of Indians rode out of the timber, crossed the open ridge and came forward. The chief was wrapped in a scarlet blanket and carried a white flag—two dazzling dots of color against the somber pines. Milton Sublette sent two of his men out to meet them. One was an Iroquois half-breed, Antoine, and the other a Flathead chief. Antoine's father had been killed by the Blackfeet. A white flag meant nothing to him. The two men plotted as they rode forward. The Flathead agreed to take the Blackfoot's hand in friendship and hold it until Antoine shot him.

The plot succeeded. As the chief fell, his murderers snatched the scarlet robe, wheeled away and galloped back to the mountain men's lines. The outraged Blackfeet began to howl. The shrill yip of the war whoop resounded along the mountainside. A horseman with a red flag raced back and forth out of rifle range. Puffs of white smoke blossomed in the tall grass and along the dry watercourses. Bullets hummed over the mountain men's heads and whacked against logs where the Yankees stood. The sound of chopping and the crash of trees told the whites that the Blackfoot squaws were building a fort for their warriors. Milton Sublette ordered his men forward, each for himself like skillful hunters. He went with them, squirming across the ground. Wyeth's men took little part. Arrows terrified them more than bullets. The singing wands struck and trembled in trees beside their heads or darted, even when spent, like vicious lizards in the rocks around their feet. The idea of a barbed arrow in a man's body appalled them.[14]

The stealthy fighting lasted six hours. The Blackfeet were great warriors. Milton Sublette called off his men. They held a council. Five of the mountain men had been killed, nine wounded, and no telling how many friendly Indians were dead. Milton Sublette's blood was up. Nothing would do, he said, but to charge the barricade. He himself would lead the way. Every man must crawl forward on his own and not stop until he reached the log stockade or was killed.

The Indian fort was taken by dark. Sublette lost one more Indian and was himself wounded in the arm and shoulder. The victors retreated back up the valley to the main encampment. Without doubt the Blackfeet would follow and get revenge. The enemy appeared to have 400 lodges and 600 warriors. Wyeth wrote in his journal:

If they come they must be met with our whole force in which case the contest will be a doubtful one. We have mad[e] horse pens and secured our camp in as good a manner as we can and wait the result. this affair will detain us some days.[15]

The big camp buried its dead, five whites and six Indians. At least thirty-five more were wounded. Ten scalps had been brought in. Everyone tested his arms and waited. The Blackfeet did not come. Scouts slipped down the valley and up to the pass. They came back and reported that the enemy had gone away. Thus ended the battle of Pierres Hole, destined to live forever in mountain man history.

On July 24, 1832, the white men decided that it was safe to move. They rode down past the scene of battle. The stench was terrible. Vultures rose on whistling wings. Masterless dogs howled and skulked away. Thirty-two dead horses lay on the battlefield with legs bloated grotesquely. Behind the barricade sprawled a few dead warriors and two squaws. The men clucked to their horses and rode on. For seventy-five miles they worked their way south and west down the upper Snake River drainage. Behind them the Tetons remained as landmarks in the sky— sharp and clear in the morning, pale at noon, glowing like nuggets of red gold in the setting sun.

Wyeth noticed that the Snake River desert was much hotter in the daytime than Pierres Hole, but the nights were still cool. Mosquitoes continued to be troublesome, and, worse still, the men began to scratch. They had got lice from the Indians. On the sweeping slopes below the mountains they found buffalo. Milton Sublette said that none ranged in the desert below. Everyone stopped to "make" meat. Then they set off again with loaded horses. A squaw in the party retired into the brush to have a baby. In less than an hour she was back, ready to go ahead with the infant in her arms.[16] The brigade came to the flat along the Blackfoot River. Three miles away the men saw a great smooth knoll that Wyeth would remember when he came this way again. At the Port Neuf, Wyeth noticed black lava. Snake River was near but out of sight in a canyon where it roared over American Falls. Sublette detailed sixteen men to leave the cavalcade, scatter out and trap.

For two weeks more he escorted Wyeth westward across the desert between the canyoned Snake and the southern mountain rim. The New Englanders suffered with the heat. Their gun barrels became uncomfortably hot in their hands. Wyeth ordered them to remove the percussion caps lest the hot sun explode them. At night he allowed the men to prime their guns once more. In this desert the men saw strange insects: crickets two inches long that marched in armies. At noon the bugs "shaded up" like bunches of grapes on the sage bushes. Sublette said that the Digger Indians dried crickets and ground them into flour.

One day the travelers spied some Indians, Shoshoni, the first red men they had seen since leaving Pierres Hole. These Indians were small people, pinched and half-starved. Kept from the buffalo ranges by powerful horse tribes, they eked out a precarious living. Wyeth offered to trade with them but discovered that they had nothing to sell except a few skins of moccasin leather. With one of his own traps he caught a beaver, his first on the trip. Wyeth recorded it with pride in his diary.[17] He was becoming a mountain man, but it was still good to have Milton Sublette and his old-timers to show the way.

The Snake River, deep in a canyon, changed its southwest course to due west. Across on the north bank, the Yankees could see the flats of Snake River basin, but on their side the desert floor was cut with impassable side canyons. They turned toward the southern hills to find a way around, the route Stuart had used. In these rough hills the New Englanders saw red men watching them from a distance, but the timid savages would not come when the whites made friendly signs. Sublette explained that these Indians were Diggers, a people more destitute than the Shoshoni. In reality they were Shoshoni forced down to a miserable cultural level. The trappers would gladly have traded with them for any food, fish or berries. Their own smoked buffalo supply was getting low.

On August 29, 1832, Milton Sublette said that he could go no farther. Business was business. His men must circle back, trapping as they went, until they found winter quarters in a good game country. Nat Wyeth took the news stoically. He appreciated all that the Sublettes had done for him but he had self-confidence. He was a mountaineer of four months' standing now himself. He would find the way to the Columbia.

Left to his own devices, Wyeth rode ahead to spy out the way. The route was exceedingly rough with no regular trail. Wyeth climbed a high point and looked ahead at a scene of wild chaos. All the streams ran through deep chasms difficult to follow. The flats between the mountains and the river were cracked with impassable canyons. Neither stream nor tableland offered a suitable road. Moreover, Wyeth must find food for his people. He ordered them to travel into the rugged country. From evacuated Digger camps his men got a few fish and serviceberry cakes. At last they came to the desert, later known as Owyhee, and their troubles were over. A big Indian village provided salmon cheap, two for a fishhook. Wyeth smoked with the chief and became sick. He hired a guide and moved his men along the Bruneau. Hot springs delighted his inquiring mind. Some of them were deep enough for him to swim and dive in.[18] The Indians were better fed in this country. Near one village the natives brought him firewood and salmon. Wyeth returned a present of awls, fishhooks, vermilion and cheap knives. Then the Indians came in a mob and prowled through his camp. Wyeth suspected one rascal of taking his knife and concealing it under his robe. Nat grasped the fellow and opened the robe. Instead of his knife he saw one of his men's coats. Wyeth snatched it, but the Indian, childlike, held fast. Wyeth drew his pistol. The savage let go, turned and picked up Wyeth's cased fishing rod. No doubt he mistook it for a rifle. The other Indians fell upon their tribesman and held him until he dropped the rod. Then the chief sent him back to the village.

The chief told Wyeth that Snake River was four days' ride downstream. The party reached there September 11. The weather was still hot, reaching eighty degrees in the daytime. The Snake River had a plain trail running along the bank and the men turned their horses down it. They came to one Indian village after another. Dozens of red fishermen were spearing salmon. On September 13, 1832, Wyeth's men crossed the mouth of a stream later known as the Owyhee in Oregon. Across the river, back in Idaho, they saw the great meadow bottoms of the Boise with its groves of trees, the first timber they had seen since leaving the mountains. Indians were everywhere, begging, stealing, grinning. Wyeth asked them all for beaver pelts and soon accumulated a few. One Indian tried to snatch a paper of fishhooks from Wyeth but was not quick enough. The Yankee had learned to hold his own with Indians. John Ball, the geologist, was not so acute. Once he dismounted from his horse to go into a willow thicket and set a trap. He came out and found that a skulking Indian had stolen his greatcoat from his saddle. The temperature was still eighty degrees Fahrenheit so he did not need the coat, but it served as his bed at night. Then on September 17, 1832, it stormed, with rain and hail like a New England nor'easter, Wyeth thought. The next day the sun came out. The high mountains to the north were white with new snow. Wyeth decided to take a side trip and catch some beaver. With two men he was gone for nine days. When he came back his party had moved on, and the Indians teased him. He overtook his men the next day. They had an Indian guide who claimed to know the way to Walla Walla. The men told Wyeth that Sublette and his men had visited them while he was gone.

The trappers had crossed the Snake to trap the Boise, Payette and Weiser rivers on the north side.[19] Wyeth regretted that he had taken the side trip and missed seeing his friend.

The Indian guide said that the Snake canyoned deeply below. They could follow it no longer, but must take the trail up Burnt Fork to the high country and on to the west. He cautioned Wyeth that food would be scarce. No Indian village could be counted on until they passed the Blue Mountains.

Wyeth laid in a big supply of salmon from the Indians. Then he moved slowly up Burnt Fork, trapping as he went. He often rode ahead in the morning to set a trap at the next night's camp and thus provide a beaver for supper. On September 9, 1832, the party came to Grande Ronde. The Indian guide said that a seven-day ride would put them in Walla Walla. The Blue Mountains—high ridges capped with dark pines across the green meadows—were the only obstruction ahead. In the broad meadows Wyeth's men found many old Indian camps but not a living soul.

The guide built a great fire, then covered it with green weeds. A cloud of smoke billowed up. He said it would attract the Nez Percés if any were in the country—but none came. Wyeth ordered an old horse killed for food. Then the party climbed up into the shady Blue Mountain forest. The horse meat spoiled. They reached the Umatilla without provisions. Wyeth left his people with their slow-moving pack animals and struck out alone to find the Hudson's Bay post. A hard thirty-mile ride put him over the grassy divide, and in the evening he arrived at the Walla Walla, a stream seventy-five feet wide and two deep. On the north bank, in the center of a sandy plain, he saw a small square fort with bastions on opposite corners, each with a brass cannon. Wyeth splashed across the stream. Lieutenant Pierre C. Pambrun, Hudson's Bay Company agent, came to meet him with outstretched hand. These Canadian rivals in the joint occupancy of Oregon were cordial fellows.

Pambrun furnished Wyeth with new clothing. In the morning the Yankee looked over the fort. It was built of drift logs and garrisoned by only six men. A small garden contained corn and pumpkins. Chickens and a cow and calf seemed strangely out of place in this distant wilderness. On September 18, 1832, the main party straggled in.

The route west of the fort was well known. Since the days of Lewis and Clark, the Astorians and the Hudson's Bay men had made a thoroughfare of the lower Columbia. Wyeth was eager to get to the Pacific, meet his ship and start his colony. He arranged to leave his horses with Pambrun and embark his men in one of the company's barges. Five eventful days put them through the treeless desert to The Dalles. The boatmen pointed out a stream named John Day for the trapper who had gone insane near its banks.

At The Dalles the Indians were hired for a quid of tobacco apiece to carry the boat a mile around the falls. Three days later the travelers emerged from the mountains. The insolent and aggressive Indians submitted meekly to the white man's ways, now that the Hudson's Bay Company ruled this country. Wyeth wrote in his diary on September 23, "our conductor appears to have a wife at each stopping place 4 already and how many more sable beauties god only knows."[20] The chief at one village came out dressed in a blue frock coat, vest and pants to greet the boatmen. A man of wealth with some four tons of dried salmon hanging on the racks around his village, he invited the Americans to his house and served them molasses. He got it, he said, from the Hudson's Bay factory down at Fort Vancouver. His sister had married an American trader named Bache who had established a post in the canyon three years ago but had drowned the following spring. Wyeth was not coming into a new country by any means.

The Hudson's Bay Company's success in pacifying the river pirates had been aided greatly by a death plague. Down at the cascades, where the barge emerged from the mountains, the ancient Indian village was deserted except for two miserable women. The stripped house frames stood like skeletons on the shore. Dead bodies were half interred. No help was available to carry the boats and baggage. Wyeth looked solemnly at the Indian sepulchers, as Lieutenant Broughton had done forty years before when he explored the lower reaches of the Columbia. There was savage propriety in laying a fisherman away in his great canoe elevated on moss-covered poles near the roaring rapids. A dense fog rolling in from the west added to the dismal dignity of the scene. The travelers had reached the region of almost constant rain during the winter. The air was warm from the Japan current and indescribably soft. The boatmen called these wet west winds chinooks, because they came from the Chinook Indian villages at the mouth of the Columbia. The name would go east along the Oregon Trail and be given in time to the hot, dry winds in Wyoming that melted snow in wintertime. Men who talked "hot air" would also be called Chinooks.

On October 28, 1832, the barge pulled up to shore for the night at a sawmill operated by the Hudson's Bay Company. The man in charge of the dripping buildings had come to the country with Wilson Price Hunt twenty-two years before, but had changed his allegiance to the Canadian company long since. At noon the next day the travelers reached the rain-splashed dock at Fort Vancouver opposite the Willamette, headquarters of the Hudson's Bay Company in Oregon.

The fort was a quarter of a mile from shore. Through the rain, Wyeth could see a stockade. A dozen cabins stood inside. Two hundred rich, wet acres of broken ground showed where wheat, barley, potatoes, peas, pumpkins and Indian corn had been harvested. An orchard of peach and apple trees had recently been set out, and Wyeth saw the upright stakes for a vineyard. The factor—tall, handsome, long-haired Dr. Mc-Loughlin—met Wyeth and presented him to the other two gentlemen residents at the post, his own adopted son Mr. McKay and a Mr. Allen. Wyeth was impressed with the education of his host and the intelligence of his associates. The improvements about the fort, the horses, cattle, hogs and sheep all indicated a degree of prosperity Wyeth had not expected.

Wyeth asked about his ship from Boston. He learned that it had been lost at sea. His whole business venture had come to nought. Wyeth's men asked to be released from their five-year contract. The Yankee could do nothing but grant their request, although it embarrassed him on two counts. First, it hurt to have Dr. McLoughlin see their lack of loyalty, and second, the Canadian factor said that "free" or unattached men made trouble. There was no law in the country. His own company had charter rights to administer justice to its employees; but suppose a "free" man was killed by the Indians. Who had authority to administer justice? Yet if murder went unpunished, the Indians would become dangerous and ugly.

Four of Wyeth's men remained permanently in Oregon. Five waited for the next boat to take them back to New England. Two agreed to return overland in the spring with their chief. Among the men who stayed in Oregon was John Ball, the geologist, who settled on a farm on the Willamette. The letters he wrote home would do their share in influencing future emigrants. Ball described the trip overland with Wyeth in detail and said that food had been plentiful—hunters killed sufficient every day. He described Dr. McLoughlin's successful farming, his advanced agricultural practices, his kindness toward emigrants. Ball wrote, too, about the wonders of the Willamette Valley. His description was more authoritative than any which Hall J. Kelley had written but equally laudatory. New England farmers became convinced that there was good reason to cross to Oregon.

Nathaniel Wyeth started back to the Missouri with his two men on February 3, 1833. He did not follow the Oregon Trail across the Blue Mountains as he had come. Instead he went with a Hudson's Bay party of horseback peddlers into the high mountains of central Idaho and finally dropped down on the upper Snake River where they discovered a swarthy white trader known to the Indians as the Bald Chief and to Americans as Benjamin Eulalie de Bonneville, captain in the United States Army on leave. Financed in New York with some Astor money, he had come west with a wagon train of goods, forded the Kansas, crossed the prairie to the Platte, traveled up the North Fork, thence along the Sweetwater and through South Pass—the first wheels to do this since Sublette's cannon. Captain Bonneville had left his wagons at Green River,[21] packed his animals and crossed Teton Pass to Pierres Hole shortly after the battle. The trampled ground was deserted. He came on to the Salmon Fork of the Snake where he built winter quarters.

Wyeth decided to join Bonneville in a new trading venture, then changed his mind. The 1833 rendezvous was meeting on Green River and the New Englander had a plan to resurrect his Oregon venture. He rode over the divide and found his old friend Milton Sublette trading there as chief representative of the Rocky Mountain Fur Company. An Irishman, Robert Campbell—destined to be one of the rich men of St. Louis—had brought up the trade goods from the Missouri. He had beaten Astor's outfit to the rendezvous and felt arrogant, bragged that he would put Astor out of business. Wyeth, always full of schemes, waited for an opportunity to talk to Milton. New Englanders would finance him for another Oregon trip, he said. He could thus bring up next spring's trade goods cheaper than anyone else. Milton Sublette saw an opportunity for a bargain and agreed to take $3,000 worth. With this contract Wyeth hurried back to Boston. The profitable deal gave him a good talking point with his backers. They financed him for another Oregon venture. Neither Wyeth nor the New Englanders suspected that they were to be duped. They did not understand how big business was played in the Rocky Mountains.

In Boston Wyeth learned that Hall Kelley had gone to Oregon. With no company, the impractical fellow had left for New Orleans and intended to cross Mexico. Wyeth, for his second venture, loaded a brig, the *May Dacre*, with trade goods to be sent around the Horn. She was to come back with a load of Columbia River salmon, thus paying for the delivery of the goods on the Pacific. Wyeth himself left Boston on February 7, 1834, for the overland trip. Two scientists, Thomas Nuttall and J. K. Townsend, and several Methodist missionaries under the leadership of Jason Lee joined the expedition. On the plains Wyeth noticed the trail of another expedition ahead of him. At Laramie Creek he saw thirteen men building a fort. Robert Campbell was in charge. He said that the new post was being built to compete with the Astor stores over on the Missouri and that the tracks headed for the upper country were made by his partner, William

Sublette, who was going to the rendezvous with the annual supply of trade goods. Wyeth suspected that the new firm planned to beat him to the rendezvous as they had beaten Astor last year. When he arrived at Green River he learned that his fears were justified. The trading was virtually over and Milton refused to take Wyeth's goods. The Yankee was stuck with a large supply of trade goods and no market. Versatile always, he worked out a new plan. He pushed on to the Snake River, into the Hudson's Bay country where he had met Bonneville, and built a fort there to protect his goods. With him from the rendezvous went Sir William Drúmmond Stewart of Perthshire, Scotland, a knight hunting adventure in the big-game country.

Wyeth named his post Fort Hall for his Boston backer. He then hurried on to the mouth of the Columbia to meet the *May Dacre*. To his dismay he learned that the vessel had been struck by lightning. She had not arrived in time for the salmon fishing. Wyeth's second venture had failed. Dr. McLoughlin, cordial as ever, showed the New Englander every courtesy. He said that he had received word that a fellow named Hall J. Kelley was coming overland by way of California with a herd of stolen horses.

The ex-schoolteacher and propagandist arrived in October 1834, very ill in health and dressed in a white slouch hat, blanket capote and leather breeches with a red stripe down the seams. McLoughlin, for once in his life, was not cordial. He shipped the propagandist back to Boston, steerage.

Wyeth started a colony on an island opposite the mouth of the Willamette. He made a trip back to Fort Hall, tried desperately to keep his ventures solvent. In 1836, on the verge of bankruptcy, he started back to the States. His second commercial enterprise had failed completely and everyone knew that his scant holding would soon be taken over by the Hudson's Bay Company which had consolidated with the North West Company in 1821 and now held a monopoly in British North America.

---

1 Archer Butler Hulbert (ed.), *The Call of the Columbia (Overland to the Pacific,* IV [Colorado Springs and Denver, 1934]), 41.
2 *Ibid.,* 48.

3 *Ibid.,* 42.

4 *Ibid.,* 31.

5 *Ibid.,* 46.

6 *Ibid.,* 105-6.

7 Reuben Gold Thwaites (ed.) , "Wyeth's Oregon, or a Short History of a Long Journey," *Early Western Travels* (Cleveland, 1905) , XXI, 32.

8 *Ibid.,* 35.

9 Hiram Martin Chittenden, *The American Fur Trade of the Far West* (New York, 1935) , I, 298.

10 Thwaites (ed.) , "Wyeth's Oregon," *Early Western Travels,* XXI, 55.

11 *Ibid.,* 60-61.

12 Hulbert (ed.) , *Call of the Columbia,* 119.

13 Thwaites (ed.) , "Wyeth's Oregon," *Early Western Travels,* XXI, 63.

14 *Ibid.,* 72.

15 Hulbert (ed.), *Call of the Columbia,* 122.

16 *Ibid.,* 125

17 *Ibid.,* 130.

18 *Ibid.,* 136.

19 *Ibid.,* 142.

20 *Ibid.,* 148.

21 Washington Irving, *The Rocky Mountains: or, Scenes, Incidents, and Adventures in the Far West; Digested from the Journal of Captain B. L. E. Bonneville . . .* (Philadelphia, 1843) , I, 97, 151.

Chapter 7

Narcissa Whitman: First Woman Over the Oregon Trail, 1836

ERHAPS it was love at first sight. Narcissa Prentiss was "going on twenty-seven." Blonde, sunny in disposition, curved like a Grecian vase, she loved children and above all wanted to serve the Lord. Marcus Whitman was her opposite in temperament. He was short-spoken, heavy-built. His bushy hair was prematurely gray. His blue eyes were resolute to the point of stubbornness. At thirty-two he had not made up his mind what he wanted to do in life. He had studied for the ministry and also to be a doctor. A remarkable event in missionary circles brought Marcus and Narcissa together.

In 1831 four Indians from west of the mountains arrived in St. Louis. The fur city was accustomed to wild Indians as well as fringe-shirted trappers, but these red men had come from a country farther away than most traders. They claimed that their fathers had seen Lewis and Clark. Old William Clark still lived in St. Louis. The four young Indians from the Far West were told to see the patriarch. William Clark took them in and here, in a spare room, two of them died.

This melancholy event set the religious world agog. The Bishop of St. Louis reported that priests had attended the young savages' last hours. Before death, they had clutched the symbols of the Cross offered to them. The story was told and retold. Soon religious people said that the red men had come to St. Louis to request that the Cross and Bible be sent west of the mountains.

Investigators asked the identity of the four Indians. To what tribe did they belong? A Canadian fur trader pronounced them Flatheads. This name ignited a flame of zeal to send missionaries to Oregon, a flame that burned the fingers of Narcissa Prentiss and immortalized her husband.

The American Board of Foreign Missions had established missionaries in the distant outpost of Hawaii in 1820. For years these brethren had urged the Board to penetrate deeper into pagandom—into Oregon, into the Queen Charlotte Islands—to convert the heathen along all the Northwest coast. Sailors had reported that these coastal Indians wanted the Bible, so the Hawaiian missionaries said. Moreover, the natives of these distant lands mutilated themselves barbarously. They flattened their babies' heads, disfigured their innocent young girls with labrets in their pierced lips.

The Board was impressed by the horror stories but Oregon was much more remote than the Hawaiian Islands, harder to get to than Africa, India or even China, where babies were also mutilated by having their feet bound. The Board did nothing. Then in 1831 word came to Boston from St. Louis about the four Flatheads' quest for the Bible. If savages could cross from Oregon overland, why not missionaries? The Board might have learned from Lewis and Clark's journal that the tribe known as Flatheads did not necessarily flatten the heads of their children. Neither did all the Nez Percés pierce or press flat their noses, nor did the Pend Oreille necessarily have hanging ears on account of their names.

Indian names did not always describe the peculiarities of a people. No matter. "Flathead" connoted deformity—bodies and minds crippled with paganism. Ordinary Indians' souls might be saved along the Missouri River. Souls and innocent childrens' skulls might both be saved west of the mountains. Presbyterians, Congregationalists and the Dutch Reformed Church began to preach a new crusade. Hall Kelley had intimated the advantages of sending missionaries to Oregon. Nathaniel Wyeth and also his malcontents had publicized the area. The Board of Foreign Missions had heard plenty about the rich valley of the Columbia. They decided to send the Reverend Samuel Parker, pastor of the Presbyterian Church at West Groton, New York, and instructor in the Ithaca Academy, out to St. Louis to investigate the possibilities of an overland trail.

Parker came back and reported that fur trains went to the Continental Divide each spring but that he had arrived at St. Louis too late. The last train had already gone.

The Board determined to send missionary scouts with the fur men next year. Marcus Whitman, still uncertain about his life work, applied for the assignment. "I am not marrid," he wrote, "and I have no presant arangement upon that Subject. Yet I should wish to take a wife, if the service of the Board would admit."[1] This was in June 1834. In December the Reverend Samuel Parker met Miss Narcissa Prentiss. He found her to be actively interested in Sunday School work and to have taught children in what would later be called kindergarten.

The records indicate that Parker introduced Narcissa to Marcus Whitman. In January 1835 Marcus was commissioned to accompany Parker on the proposed scout for missionary sites in Oregon. Narcissa acted quickly. In the middle of February Marcus left for the West. He planned to ride horseback to St. Louis, visiting friends in Ohio and Illinois on the way. Brother Parker was to bring his baggage and go by wagon to Buffalo, Erie, Mercer and thence by boat to Cincinnati and St. Louis. Marcus had not been gone a week before Narcissa applied to the Board for a job, "to be employed in their service among the heathen, if counted worthy."[2] A letter of recommendation sent with her application stated that she was engaged to marry Dr. Whitman.[3] Narcissa also wrote a letter to Marcus at St. Louis where he would wait for Parker.

Marcus replied to Narcissa: "In reading your letter I was surprised exceedingly that you should have conceived it practicable for you to have crossed the mountains this spring. Had I known one half as much of the trip as I now do, when I left you, I should have been entirely willing, if not anxious, that you should have accompanied us."[4] Without doubt Narcissa was a fast worker and her hero now had an "arrangement" about being "marrid."

The long summer passed. Early the next winter people were congregated at church in Ithaca, so tradition says, when Marcus Whitman, two Indian boys at his heels, strode down the aisle and took a seat in front. After the services he told about his summer's adventures. With the Reverend Mr. Parker he had traveled to the rendezvous with Fontenelle's supply train. He did not say that the ruffians had pelted him with rotten eggs at first but later he had won their respect by fearlessly attending the stricken men in a cholera epidemic. At the rendezvous Whitman had cut an iron arrowhead from the backbone of Jim Bridger and had witnessed a duel between a freckle-faced little fellow named Kit Carson and a big bully named Shunar, but neither event interested Whitman vitally. He was more concerned about establishing new missions on the Columbia. Cattle should be taken west by missionaries to supply milk, Whitman said, and if women went—he was thinking about Narcissa—wagons could be driven as far as the rendezvous, perhaps farther. The Reverend Mr. Parker had gone on from Green River to the Pacific. Whitman said that Parker would be at the rendezvous next summer to guide incoming missionaries.

The Prudential Committee of the Board of Foreign Missions considered Dr. Whitman's recommendations. On January 5, 1836, they voted to send a party of six, two ministers, their wives, a farmer and a mechanic—all godly people of course. Dr. Whitman and Narcissa would be first. The second couple selected were the Reverend Mr. and Mrs. Henry Spalding, a choice that seemed innocent enough, but Spalding had gone to Prattsburg Academy with Narcissa and had fallen in love with her there. He was the same age as Whitman but a very different personality, more impractical but a better talker. Spalding was lugubrious, introspective. In his application to the Board he said with apparent relish that he had lived "a very wicked life among wicked men till the age of 22 when God in great mercy rescued me."[5] He did not mention his affair with Narcissa Prentiss. Instead, he said he had married the daughter of a substantial farmer near Hart, New York, "for the express purpose of giving my wife the opportunity of pursuing the same Theological studies with myself." Spalding was physically rugged and well suited for pioneer life. The woman to whom he gave theological "opportunity" was delicate but willing.

The Board considered the applications of several mechanics for the mission. They selected one named William H. Gray, a twenty-seven-year-old carpenter with a smattering of education and an urge to talk and write more fluently than his ability warranted. He dreamed of being a minister some day and was certainly no more peculiar than the other tenderfeet selected to escort the first white women into Oregon.

The time for the marriage of Marcus and Narcissa was approaching. Her father, Judge Stephen Prentiss, insisted that Spalding be brought to the house. He wanted an understanding between the two before he would consent to his daughter's union with Marcus. The married man and the engaged girl met. Judge Prentiss talked to them. Then he exacted a promise from Spalding that any former grievance be forgotten or he would not consent to his daughter's marriage. Spalding agreed. Time would show how well he kept his promise.[6]

On February 18, 1836, Dr. Whitman and Narcissa Prentiss were married at Angelica, New York. The ground was covered with snow. Friends who later knew her fate in Oregon remembered with tears in their eyes that she had sung in a strong voice on that fateful day, the missionary hymn:

> Yes, my native land I love thee,
>   All thy scenes I love them well,
> Friends, connections, happy country,
>   Now, I bid you all farewell.

After the ceremony her brusque bridegroom tucked her into a sleigh and they whirled away with jingling bells to Hollidaysburg, Pennsylvania. There, on the Pennsylvania Canal, they began their transcontinental honeymoon that would be famous in the history of the Oregon Trail.

The honeymooners met the Spaldings at Cincinnati. The party boarded a boat for St. Louis and transferred to a Missouri steamer bound for Bellevue, south of Council Bluffs where the fur train was assembling. A wreck caused them to land at Liberty, across from Independence. For twelve days they remained at the little village on the east side of the Missouri. Then they decided that Gray, Spalding and the Flathead boys had better start upriver with the livestock. A man named Dulin[7] was hired to go along. Whitman, with the ladies, the baggage, tent, rubber blankets and theological books, would come on the first steamboat and meet them at Cantonment Leavenworth. With time on her hands, Narcissa wrote her sister Mary:

My health was never better since I have been on the river. I was weighed last week and came up to 136 pounds. . . . Mrs. Spalding does not look or feel quite healthy enough for our enterprise. Riding affects her differently from what it does me. . . . Sister S. is very resolute, no shrinking with her. She possesses much fortitude. I like her very much. She wears well upon acquaintance. She is a very suitable person for Mr. Spalding, has the right temperament to match him. I think we shall get along very well together.

Then Narcissa indulged in a confidence with her sister—a confidence that revealed her own and Marcus' characters:

I have such a good place to shelter—under my husband's wings. He is so excellent. I love to confide in his judgment and act under him. He is just like mother in telling me of my failings. He does it in such a way that I like to have him, for it gives me a chance to improve.[8]

Days passed. Finally a steamboat came around the bend. Whitman and the ladies boarded her. In time the bluffs of Leavenworth, with buildings on top, came into view. The vessel docked. Whitman unloaded and then inquired for Spalding and Gray. He learned that they had crossed the river three days ago and had gone out on the prairie. Spalding, always trusting in God and forgetful of man, thus left Whitman with all the baggage and no means of hauling it. Marcus fumed impatiently. He hired two wagons and teams, loaded them and set off to overtake the absent-minded brethren. Expenses were already more than he had reckoned and the Board would not like this uncalled-for extravagance. Brother Whitman did not feel in a Christian mood. He lashed the horses and soon overtook his party on the prairie. Sisters Narcissa and Spalding watched from the depths of their sunbonnets, and the baggage was no doubt exchanged with surly grunts.

Reunited again, the party was guided by a friendly missionary along the winding road toward Bellevue where the fur train was organizing. On the edge of the prairies many civilized Indians had cabins in the groves along the streams. Forty miles out of Leavenworth, they met a white boy sixteen years of age. He came into camp wearing an old straw hat, a ragged fustian coat, half a shirt, buckskin pants and one moccasin. He begged a little powder for his horn, said that he had not eaten for two days but could kill plenty if he had the ammunition. Marcus looked critically into the lad's light blue eyes. He was thin, hungry-looking but in good health and spirits. Marcus fed him, asked where he lived and urged him to go back to his parents in Iowa. The boy shook his unkempt flaxen hair positively. He wanted to go to the Rocky Mountains. If they would help him get to the fur train, he would earn his passage tending horses. His name, he said, was Miles Goodyear. Whitman decided to let him work for board and keep. None of the famous mountain men made a more unprepossessing start and only a few ended with more renown than did Miles Goodyear.

The party crossed the Platte to the north bank and found the telltale wagon and horse tracks of the fur train. It had passed. The "sign" appeared to be reasonably fresh. Surely the missionaries could overtake the brigade before reaching dangerous Indian country. At the Loup Fork the fur men were bound to spend considerable time crossing. Marcus galloped back to the missions around Bellevue and employed a guide. Narcissa felt that they were really on the way at last. She knew that her trip was epic and kept a diary of passing events. Their outfit consisted of two wagons, one drawn by four horses and the other by a team. Eight extra horses, six mules and seventeen cattle com-

pleted the livestock. Ten people, including the women, made up
the personnel. The women both had sidesaddles but Mrs. Spalding traveled most of the day in one of the covered wagons. Narcissa enjoyed riding with Marcus and the Indian boys behind the
cattle. The plains were fresh and green, sultry at noon, but Narcissa wore her cape mornings and evenings.

At last the guide said that one more day would put the party
at the Loup. They would be sure to catch the fur train at the
crossing. All day the missionaries urged the stock along. As
usual it became hot. The cattle flagged at the pace. Their heads
drooped. Spume threads hung from their open mouths like
spider webs of spun glass. The crack of a whip did not make them
flinch. Whitman knew that the cattle would have to be humored
or left behind. He ordered the wagons and loose horses to be
driven ahead. Find the fur train if they could! He and the Indian
boys would come along with the stock. Narcissa said that she
would stay with "Husband," come what may.

Ahead the wagons shrank smaller and smaller, disappeared only
to reappear again in diminutive size on the next swell of the
plains. Finally they went out of sight entirely. The sun sank—
a golden ball dropping below the horizon. An evening chill settled across the open spaces. The Indian boys told Marcus and his
wife to ride on after the wagons. They would sleep with the cattle and bring them in tomorrow. Dr. Whitman would not con-
sider this. He and Narcissa would stay with the stock.

Dark came. Marcus ordered a halt. From his saddle he untied
a tin cup. Into this they milked supper for the four of them.
Then, thanking God for His kindness, they lay down by their
panting animals for a night's rest.

Next day they reached the Loup. On the far side they saw
the fur camp. Four hundred animals, seventy men—Frenchmen,
half-breeds, Negroes, Missourians—talking, swearing, singing bits
of song, popping whips. Whitman saw his own wagons parked
on the outskirts of the throng. He and Narcissa forded the cattle
and went to their campfire for something to eat. The Spaldings
said that they had arrived at eleven o'clock last night after a
very hard drive.

The Pawnee came across from their village of mud and wattle lodges[9] to see the first white women. With brown gnarled hands they parted the fly of Whitman's tent, looked in, then placed their hands across their mouths in wonder.

The fur company moved away from the Loup with rough military discipline. Thomas Fitzpatrick led the vanguard. Spare, bony, with cadaverous face and flashing eyes, he looked every inch a mountain man. His broken hand did not mar the plainsman's ruggedness. With him rode the British sportsman, Sir William Drummond Stewart—Marcus had met him last year—and some other "gentlemen" with servants and dogs, all out for sport. Behind the hundreds of pack animals, seven wagons rolled along with six mules each. Milton Sublette brought up the rear in a cart hauled by two mules tandem. A malignant growth on one leg had taken him from the saddle but Milton Sublette could not stay away from the rendezvous. He was a mountain man.

In the wake of the brigade and at one side of the long line the missionaries cruised in their wagons with the two women in sunbonnets like ventilators on a gunboat. Narcissa beamed at the romantic scene. She noted the picturesque costumes and the strange drawl of the mountain men. At night the cavalcade camped in a large circle on the plains. Discipline was strict, for lurking Indians might stampede unguarded livestock. The wagons, baggage and tents were placed so as to fence a large tract. Indians did not care for cattle. They were picketed outside but the precious horses and mules were hobbled within. A guard watched them night and day. The fur men's party was divided into a dozen messes of eight or ten each.

The missionaries messed separately. They had one large round homemade tent with a pole in the center. In this the Whitmans and Spaldings and two Indian boys slept. For a table the women spread a rubber blanket on the ground. Around this they sat cross-legged, tailor fashion, or tried to. Narcissa laughed when she first tried it. Her plump knees were not made for such acrobatics. Each person had a sheath knife and he cut a sharp stick for a fork. Tin basins and iron spoons were set on the blanket for tea. Each had also a tin plate, and a large pan of milk was put in the center. At the end of the meal the menfolk wiped their knives on their boots and threw the wooden forks in the fire. Marcus could tell them that they would soon be in a country where even a splinter would be a rarity.

The women were flustered at first by baking outdoors for ten men but they soon "got the hang of it." Bread and milk were the two staples and the flour barrel emptied rapidly. One day was much like the next on the unvarying plains. At dawn the cry to rise set all the mules to braying. They were hungry in the wagon corral and knew that they would be turned out for an hour to fill themselves on grass. Beside the tents and wagons, columns of smoke rose from each mess. Some men rolled and tied the baggage as others cooked. By six o'clock the fur men were off, a long snake toiling across the green swell of plains. The missionaries tarried for divine worship, then followed. At eleven o'clock a halt was called for dinner. The animals were unhooked and turned out to graze. At two the column started again and drove until six.

The fur men pressed ahead eagerly for the buffalo country. At the forks of the Platte, they all said, the animals blackened the hills for miles around—meat for everybody. On June 3, 1836, a buffalo was killed. Where one grazed there was bound to be a herd close. Men rode off from the column and disappeared in the sand hills along the Platte. Marcus, with his gun, galloped away to prove that he was a plainsman and good provider. In a few hours he came back, red meat dripping limp from his saddle. He untied the steaks and explained that each must be roasted in a different manner. Narcissa watched with adoration as the veteran of a year displayed the art of buffalo cookery to his uninitiated companions. Soon the meat was sizzling on spits around the fire. Narcissa cut off a crisp crackling and tasted it. Delicious! Like beef but a trifle sweeter. Thanks be to God and a kind Providence! The bread diet was forgotten. Three times a day the missionaries feasted on buffalo and felt new strength in their bodies. Narcissa craved no other food, or claimed in her epic diary that she did not. Sister Spalding ate heartily too, but the meat upset her stomach.

The party came to the South Fork Crossing. Whitman was obliged to leave a large box of theological books at the ford in order to make his load lighter. The wagons creaked across the tableland to Ash Hollow and down to North Fork. The travelers noticed cedars on the tops of the angular hills—wood once more. In the distance they saw Court House Rock. Three days later they passed it, then Chimney Rock and at last Scotts Bluff loomed into view, white gold glowing in the sunshine. "We feel that the Lord has blessed us beyond our most sanguine expectations,"[10] Narcissa wrote in her journal.

Marcus Whitman did not feel like blessing the Lord. The gulches across the flats between Scotts Bluff and the Platte were too deep to be crossed with wagons. A detour back through the hills was necessary. Marcus complained that he would have to make his load lighter. He insisted that he must sell his extra shirts, his black suit and overcoat as soon as they reached Fort Laramie. Narcissa insisted that he do no such thing. She said that she would sell all of her clothes first. Why should she have nice clothes if he had none to go with her? Marcus made no reply. Narcissa hoped that she had won the argument.

One day the mountain men ahead began to shout and point. Far across the plains, Narcissa saw Fort William on the Laramie—named for William Sublette but popularly called Fort Laramie. Fur trains for the rendezvous always stopped here to repack and repair. The sight of a house, even though it was a fort in the Indian country, gave Narcissa a thrill. The garrison lined the walls to look at the newcomers. Long-haired men came out the great gate to welcome them. Marcus ordered his camp pitched under the walls. Narcissa and Mrs. Spalding walked modestly into the open gate, sniffed at the dark rancid rooms where buffalo hides were stored, peeked at the store—dear to all women's hearts—where blankets, mirrors, hawks' bells and vermilion could be bought. Some easy chairs with buffalo hide for seats caught Narcissa's eye. Such luxury after trying to sit cross-legged around a rubber blanket for a month! That night Narcissa put her clothes to soak for washing in the morning. Think of a whole day without traveling!

The scene at Fort Laramie next day may be imagined from the scant details that have been preserved. Marcus Whitman, no doubt, began tinkering with his wagon gears, tapping a felly here, mending a brake block there, shaking the wheels on their axles to see if the spindles were wearing. Captain Fitzpatrick came along the fort wall silently in his moccasins. He intended to leave the company wagons, he said, except the cart that was necessary for Milton Sublette and his bad leg. Three years ago Bonneville had taken wagons on west to Green River but there was no road. Broken Hand, in his quaint Irish brogue, advised Marcus Whitman to leave his wagons here. The missionary straightened up from his work. No sir! He intended to take wagons to the Pacific—open the Road to Empire. Besides, Mrs. Spalding was ailing. It would be necessary for her to ride.

Fitzpatrick became grave. Why take her to certain death? Let her remain at the fort and go back with the fur train when it returned from the rendezvous. The two women heard the argument and came out of the tent, their hands pink and shriveled from washing clothes. Brother Spalding came too. He urged his wife to do as Fitzpatrick said. Eliza Hart Spalding would not hear them. She had been reared in an atmosphere of preaching. "What mean ye to weep and break my heart," she is reported to have said, "for I am ready not to be bound only, but to die at Jerusalem or in the Rocky Mountains, if need be, for the name of the Lord Jesus. Duty is mine; my life, my strength, the dangers of the way are His."[11]

Thomas Fitzpatrick had no answer for this argument. Brother Spalding, too, knew that there was no use talking back to a Christian woman.

The day came to depart. Whitman decided to leave one wagon but he loaded the other one. The cavalcade pulled out, serpentining for the high country west of the Platte. Milton Sublette followed in his cart. The missionaries' pack animals and livestock kept up easily with the fur men. The wagon and cart dropped behind. The four-wheeled vehicle had more difficulty than the shay. Sometimes the wagon tipped over two

and three times in a day. Often a rut was cut around a steep
hillside to prevent the wheels from skidding to the bottom of a
gulch. Pack horses walked easily between trees that had to be
cut down to pass a wagon. Whitman and Dulin often got the

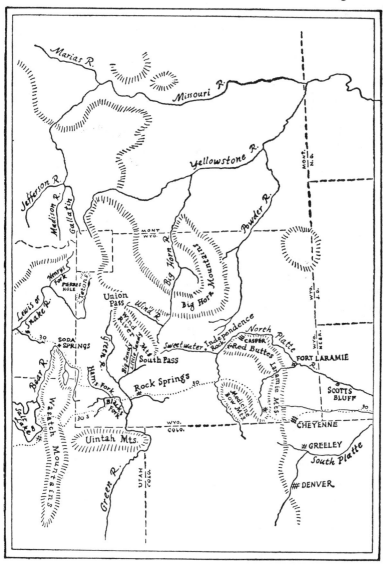

MOUNTAINS AND RIVERS FROM SCOTTS BLUFF TO SALT LAKE

wagon into camp just in time to see the fur men packing to pull out. Miles Goodyear urged the boss to forget the vehicle, put the load on the horses and come along. Marcus would not listen. If fur men could get wheels across the Continental Divide, God-fearing Christians could do so too. Fitzpatrick noticed Whitman's trouble. He assigned two men to ride with him and scout for the best road through the hills. This helped, but the wagon still took long circles around a gulch that pack animals scrambled across.

On July 4, 1836, the party crossed South Pass. In the evening they camped on Little Sandy. Indians from the rendezvous rode into camp. They were not natives of this country but Nez Percés from the headwaters of the Columbia. A chief named Rotten Belly commanded. At the rendezvous they had heard that the supplies were approaching, that "Men Who Talked About God" were coming. They brought a letter from the Reverend Mr. Parker for Marcus Whitman.

Marcus broke the seal. Brother Parker said that he would not be able to meet the missionaries at the rendezvous. He was busy exploring suitable sites for their missions. The Indians would be able to guide the men and their wives better than he, Parker, could do. Rotten Belly grunted assent. Marcus introduced him to Narcissa.

Two more days' travel and the rendezvous, the valley of Green River, was reached. It teemed with Indians wanting goods and trinkets. These red men, as well as the French-Canadians, were fond of elaborate ritual. The New Englanders were told to halt formally and let the Indians greet them in a conventional way. New England leveling did not appeal to primitive men. The missionaries stopped in a long irregular line. Ahead they saw horsemen coming across the flats under the cottonwoods. The strange horsemen pranced forward. In scarlet, white and blue blankets they rode by, feathers spinning and ribbons fluttering. Behind the horsemen came old women on foot. Their brown hands clawed hospitably at the mounted women's dresses and capes. They stroked Narcissa's mannish boots with wonder and made signs for the women to dismount.

Narcissa and Sister Spalding jumped down from their sidesaddles. The squaws wept and kissed them. Flushed and smiling, not too heartily perhaps, they saw another group of fancily dressed people waiting to greet them—free trappers and company employees, Frenchmen, half-breeds, Negroes and Jim Bridger, his back completely well since Dr. Whitman had operated on him a year ago. The mountain men had decked themselves out like Indians except for their beards. Blue eyes smiled incongruously over cheeks burned by the sun to a copper color almost as dark as the Indians'. One mountaineer attempted to raise his tattered hat with the elaborate art he had seen years before on the streets of St. Louis. The missionaries stifled their laughter.

Sister Spalding, weak and sickly, was led away by pitying Indian women. With signs, they recounted their own aches and pains to her and she reciprocated. The mountain men surrounded Narcissa. Her bold carriage and golden hair fascinated them. None had seen a white woman for a year and some had not seen one for three or four. Providence be praised!

The Whitmans pitched their homemade tent beside the wagon. The two Indian boys prowled off among the Nez Percé lodges. They found their families. Relatives presented them with saddle horses and chattered around them like blackbirds. Whitman and Chief Rotten Belly planned the trip ahead. The Indian said that the missionaries might go with his people but that they would all have to stop a month in the buffalo country and "make meat." Marcus did not like the prospect of this delay but bowed to the inevitable. Why had not Parker come back to show them the way through? Narcissa thanked God for His consideration of them and put her soiled clothes to soak.

There was no alternative now for Marcus but to write the Board and tell them the progress of the journey, but he did not like to write letters. He put it off and rode over to settle accounts with Fitzpatrick. The traders were busy exchanging bales of beaver skins, round as barrels, for beads, awls, fishhooks, butcher knives and papers of vermilion. The log storehouses were already full of pelts. Whitman, stockily built, energetic, went up to the gaunt Broken Hand. What was his bill? The tall Irishman's eyes flashed in his cadaverous face, "An' what's yer own account fer doctering me men?"

Whitman said that there was no bill.

"Then there is none on my side," the Irishman replied.

Whitman tarried in the wilderness mart. He heard that the Hudson's Bay Company had some traders ten miles away. The Canadians were giving the Americans a little competition. Captain Wyeth on his way back from the Columbia River was over in the rival camp. Whitman untied his horse and rode away to see him. He found a cluster of dirty tents and makeshift lodges. Nathaniel Wyeth was here all right and with him were two Hudson's Bay officials, John McLeod and McLoughlin's adopted son, Thomas McKay. The Canadians, their *engagés* and Indian hangers-on were going back to Walla Walla. They agreed to let the missionaries accompany them. Thus the month that would be required for the Nez Percés to stop on the way to "make" their winter meat would be saved.

Whitman was delighted. Wyeth gave him a letter to Captain Thing, his factor at Fort Hall. From Wyeth, too, Whitman learned much more about the road to Oregon than Parker's letter had contained. He jogged back to his own camp. The letter to the Board could be put off no longer. Whitman sharpened a pen. With assurance he told the Board that the land route was the best way from Boston to Oregon. There were three possible passages. Straight west from South Pass lay a terrible sand desert and rugged mountains. A northern route through Jackson's Hole and Teton Pass was a long detour impassable for wagons. The best route swung southwest across the Green to the Bear River, thence north to Soda Springs and over the divide to Fort Hall. Whitman told his Board that the Britishers were hospitable and had already suggested a place for their mission. "They say," he wrote, "we may locate where the climate is mild grass soil & timber good   The valleys free from timber. Plenty Elk, Deer & fish & about three days ride from Walla Walla."[12]

Brother Spalding also wrote a letter full of "literary language" —product of Oneida Institute perhaps. Even William Gray felt the urge to send back a letter from this rendezvous in the wilderness, although his hands, used to the hammer and the chisel, found a pen hard to grasp.

The accumulated messages were folded for the post. Then the missionaries packed to go on. McKay and McLeod both urged the doctor to leave the wagon behind. Dulin quit but Whitman still had Miles Goodyear to help him. The wagon must go, he said doggedly. The Indians encouraged him. Chief Rotten Belly said that he wanted to see the strange vehicle in his homeland. His tribesmen promised to find a path for it, YES! The Hudson's Bay men agreed reluctantly. Mrs. Spalding's weak health served as the final excuse for taking it.

On July 18, 1836, the party set off, Canadians, missionaries and Nez Percés in a long picturesque procession. They went down Green River and moved across through the open country to Bear River. The red men were leisurely fellows. They objected to packing and unpacking more than once a day. They usually set camp early in the afternoon. The Indian women rested and the young men hunted. One day it rained. Narcissa learned that rain in the Rocky Mountains is much colder than in lower altitudes. Quick evaporation in the dry atmosphere chilled the women's fingers in no time. The rain turned to hail that pelted them like stones. The horses would not face it and turned their tails to the storm. When it stopped the travelers splashed along, crunching the ice pellets under foot. The Bear River Mountains towered above them green and cold under a mantle of new white snow. Aspen leaves shivered in the steep mountain valleys.

Bear River was too high for buffalo. The party ate "jerky." Narcissa thought that it looked black and dirty but she thanked Providence for anything. The Hudson's Bay men saw their plight and sent some fried cakes from their mess. Manna from heaven. Providence be praised! Secretly in her diary Narcissa wrote:

I would not go back for a world. I am contented and happy, notwithstanding I sometimes get very hungry and weary. Have six weeks' steady journeying before us. Feel sometimes as if it were a long time traveling. Long for rest, but must not murmur.

Feel to pity the poor Indian women, who are continually traveling in this manner during their lives, and know no other comfort.[13]

Next day an accident cheered Narcissa's flagging spirits. The way was rougher than usual and one of the wagon's axletrees broke. Goody-goody! The old contraption would have to be left behind and Marcus would ride with the party and be cheerful.

Narcissa did not yet know her bridegroom. He discarded the wagon box, made a cart of the hind wheels and lashed the front ones to them. He was going to open the Oregon Trail to wheels or know the reason why. Outwardly sweet, resigned, albeit ill-humored, the missionaries got the cart to camp. They were now out of supplies. Even the jerky was gone. The fur men sent them some antelope meat for supper. "Thus the Lord provides and smooths all our ways for us, giving us strength," Narcissa told her diary.[14]

The mountains became higher every day and it was hard to believe that the trail across the meadows led them down instead of upstream. Antelope were plentiful. One day the dainty little runners came near causing a fatal accident. The Indians jumped a small band of them. The animals raced through the cavalcade, Indians after them with feathers and blankets flying. The pack horses took fright and jostled one another. Brother Spalding was driving the mules hitched to the cart. His wife rode a sleepy horse near by. Sudden panic seized the mules. They sprang forward and knocked down Mrs. Spalding's mount. Her husband, tugging on the lines, heard a smothered scream as he thundered past. At last he stopped the mules, tied the trembling brutes and ran back. Sister Spalding lay insensible on the ground. He bent over her and to his joy found that she was not hurt. "Only a kind Providence preserved her," he said.

At Soda Springs the Bear River turned sharply to the west and dropped into a slit of a canyon. The trail from the upper meadows crossed a low ridge and led into the headwaters of the Port Neuf—open, rugged country with black lava boulders among the sagebrush. The sharp rocks made the cattle tender-footed. The men stopped to shoe them, sweating and hammering like fury. Narcissa knew better than to stand around men at difficult work. She strolled off and looked at the country. Never in her life had she seen anything so desolate. The green mountains had been left behind. The barren grandeur appalled her. Across a hundred miles of empty desert she saw gleaming mountains. This world was vast and uninhabited as the moon.

The travelers left the Port Neuf to circle the lava beds and drop into Snake River basin. Dust from the lead horses settled on the women's sunbonnets and capes. The mules coughed with it. Rotten Belly pointed to a low mound in the flat this side of three buttes. Fort Hall was there!

At last the log walls, bastions and adobe chimneys came into view, sharp but tiny like an image seen through the wrong end of a telescope. The women became ecstatic. The sight of man-made walls stirred them with nostalgia. The hewn logs looked like luxury. The neglected garden, scraggly and overrun with weeds, excited memories of central New York. The corn was a stunted Indian variety. The turnips were all gone to tops. The pea pods had been cut by field mice. The onions stood rank and gone to seed. What matter! Narcissa compared herself to Christian in *Pilgrim's Progress* and remembered that he got to heaven in the end.

Wyeth's lieutenant, Captain Thing, came out to meet the missionaries. Dr. Whitman presented his letter. The Americans and their British friends were welcomed. The cart wheels were unhooked from the mules and Marcus Whitman was very proud. Captain Thing said that game could not be killed close to the fort. The Indians moved off to the buffalo range up Snake River to kill their winter meat. Rotten Belly stayed with the white men. McKay and McLeod said that they must go on to Fort Boise, the rival British post 300 miles away. Whitman was eager to go with them. Rest in the fort did not appeal to him. He overhauled his cart and said he was ready. Miles Goodyear balked. He would not go a step farther with the infernal spokes. Leave the wheels or leave him. The Methodists held a conference. Most of them considered that the sixteen-year-old boy was a big help, more important than the wagon, but Marcus did not agree. Let the boy stay. The cart would go through to the Pacific.[15] Miles Goodyear did stay, to be heard of later as a great mountain man with Indian wives and the first white man to cultivate land in Utah.

Early in August the Whitman party set off. Ten miles below the fort they forded the Port Neuf. North of them they heard water roaring deep below the plain—American Falls. They went to the rim and looked down at Snake River dashing with great force against broken rocks in the channel and swirling away under patches of foam. The missionaries estimated the fall to be about fifteen feet high. Brother Spalding remarked that it was not so impressive as Trenton Falls back in New York.

The cavalcade moved on. Grass was scarce. Narcissa was reminded of the things that she had read about the Sahara but it was not so hot here, even in August. The nights were always cool. One morning she found ice in the milk pans.

Indians along Snake River furnished all the fish the travelers could eat. The diet became monotonous and, worse still, the horses began to waste away for lack of grass. The fur men said that they must all push ahead while the horses had strength to travel. Whitman could not move any faster with his wagon. He would not abandon the wheels but he decided to reduce the load. Narcissa's trunk must be sacrificed. It was a needless impediment. He told Narcissa and she acquiesced graciously. She loved Marcus very much but she did yearn for a confidante to whom she could go when he did things that hurt her. She wrote privately to her sister 2,000 miles away:

Dear Harriet, the little trunk you gave me has come with me so far, and now I must leave it here alone. Poor little trunk, I am so sorry to leave thee, thou must abide here alone, and no more by thy presence remind me of my dear Harriet. Twenty miles below the falls on Snake River, this shall be thy place of rest. Farewell, little trunk, I thank thee for thy faithful services, and that I have been cheered by thy presence so long. Thus we scatter as we go along. The hills are so steep and rocky that husband thought it best to lighten the wagon as much as possible, and take nothing but the wheels, leaving the box with my trunk. I regret leaving anything that came from home, especially that trunk, but it is best.[16]

Mr. McKay, the half-breed, looked over the things that Whitman discarded. He asked for the trunk. He could pack it easily enough on the side of a mule and the design pleased him. Narcissa watched her treasure move away in vulgar hands. Next day she wrote again about the trunk: "Dear Harriet ... My soliloquy about it last night was for naught. However, it will do me no good, it may him."[17]

The party forded Snake River where Glenn's Ferry would later be. Many fur men, both Canadian and American, had explored the Snake River basin since Crooks, Stuart and Wyeth had crossed along the south bank in 1811, 1812 and 1832. Most travelers evaded the desert at the north and followed the south bank to the crossing, then cut north to the wood, grass and shade along the Boise. At Glenn's Ferry Crossing, the river was 1,000 feet wide and deep below the floor of the plains. Two islands separated the channel. A scout from Whitman's party rode ahead on one of the tallest of the American horses. The water was sure to make an Indian pony swim. The channel between the second island and the north bank appeared to be deepest, but the scout got across with dry feet by lifting them out of the stirrups. Water came within nine inches of the horse's withers. The men decided that the women must ride on the biggest horses. Marcus insisted that he would be able to get his cart across.

Narcissa and Eliza Spalding mounted. Two Frenchmen took the lead ropes on the women's horses and entered the water. The first two crossings were made easily. At the third channel, the ford crossed diagonally by a route half a mile long. In such great distance both men and animals were apt to become confused by the flow of water and step off the bar. A man's eyes unconsciously followed the current but if he let his horse do so too, they were both lost. The women watched the water rise higher and higher on the sides of the Frenchmen's horses ahead of them. The animals' tails floated out behind. A breaker of foam churned against the shoulders of their own mounts. They felt the animals lean over against the current. Mrs. Spalding could not keep her eyes from the swirling water. She became dizzy. Her husband saw her reel in the saddle. "Look," he yelled at her, "at those deer coming down that mountain; we will have meat for supper." Sister Spalding lifted her eyes from the water. Her head steadied. She recovered her balance. Spalding cautioned her not to look at the water again. Watch the far bank at all times. Thus she reached shore safely.[18]

From a perch high on the north shore the women watched the cavalcade in the water behind them. Some of the smaller horses' backs submerged, but the weight of the riders kept their feet on the bottom. Marcus' cart—perhaps it should be called axle and wheels—almost reached shore, then upset, entangling the mule in the harness. Frenchmen with ropes and knives cut the traces and dragged out the vehicle. It was a narrow escape but an important one for the Oregon Trail.

The men and women dried their clothing, thanking Providence or God, each according to his tradition. The fur men said that they would have to leave the missionaries here. The trail was good to Fort Boise and they were anxious to get there. They left three men to act as guides and said that they would look for the Americans in due time. With a wave of their fringed arms they rode away with their packs.

The missionaries moved slowly with their shod cattle. From Indians along the river they bought salmon. The grass was better on the north side and the animals gained flesh and became sleek and glossy. At last the missionaries sighted the cottonwoods along the Boise, the largest trees they had seen for the past 40 miles. Under the welcome shade they prayed beside still water.

Fort Boise stood near where Nampa, Idaho, would one day be located. The missionaries rested there three days. Whitman made a deal with the Hudson's Bay men to leave some of his foot sore cattle here and be paid for them with sound animals at Walla Walla. His own people and the fur men, too, agreed that he must not try to take the wheels farther. Rotten Belly offered to take the iron tires off the spokes and flatten them for packing on horses to the Columbia if that would satisfy "Man Who Talks About God." The wheels could be got there no other way.

Whitman gave in at last. Perhaps his ears still roared with the waters which upset the cart back at the crossing. Perhaps he realized that he could not expect the Hudson's Bay men to tarry for him on the next leg of the journey to Walla Walla.

Marcus Whitman's show of weakness caused rejoicing by the entire party. Mrs. Spalding relaxed. Her health seemed to be better. Once more Narcissa put some clothes to soak. McKay furnished some corn and rice for a feast, luxuries unknown at Fort Hall. McLeod asked Brother Spalding to conduct divine services come Sunday. Whitman was leaving the wagon!

On Monday the missionaries set off once more with McLeod and his *engagés* in the lead. At the mouth of the Boise River, they came to another ford. Two islands blocked the stream here too. The party forded the first two channels but the third was plainly swimming water. The men scouted up and down the island. No riffle disclosed a bar under the smooth rapid current. One of the men found a little Indian raft made of reeds. It was just large enough to carry the two women and their saddles. Ropes were attached to it. Narcissa Whitman and Eliza Spalding stepped on the shaky craft. Two Indians spurred their ponies off the bank into the river and towed the women into the current. "O! if father and mother and the girls could have seen us," Narcissa exclaimed after she jumped out on the west bank. But for once she did not thank Providence.

Again the party dried out and reorganized. Then they struck off north and west up the narrow one-horse trace, winding above the precipices at the mouth of the Burnt Fork defile. Whitman realized that he could never have got the wagon through here.

In the Powder River country above, the men counted their rations and estimated that they did not have enough food to last them to the Columbia at the slow pace necessary for the mission-

aries' cattle. McLeod suggested that his men and the two Whit-
mans make a race for Fort Walla Walla. They could leave most
of the supplies, and Chief Rotten Belly would guide the Spaldings
and the Indian boys through. All agreed. The Whitmans, Mc-
Leod and the fur men trotted off. Over the divide they came to
Grande Ronde. Narcissa exclaimed over the green lake of grass.
Such a sunny restful oasis! No wonder the Nez Percé and
Cayuse liked to come here to dig and boil camass roots.

McLeod had no time for artistic raptures. Food was scarce.
He urged the horsemen across the Ronde and up the slope into
the gloomy forest. Narcissa had never seen a woodland like this
before. In places the trees grew as close together as pickets. A
horse could not get off the trail if he wanted to. There was no
underbrush. Open parks of tall grass, weeds and flowers made
the forest floor a fairyland. From the trail these green and sunny
open spaces could be seen through the pillars of dark tree trunks.
The riders came to the northwestern edge of the mountains at
sunset. Below them lay the broad gray plains of Oregon. All
stopped.

Narcissa was carried out of herself. On the right and left of
them the pine-clad mountain shoulders were fluted with 1,500-
foot chasms. The depths glowed with a luminous violet light,
attractive but terrifying. Far in the pale distance, snow-capped
Mounts Hood and St. Helen stood sharp against the fiery sunset.
Beyond them, the missionaries thought that they could see the
shining waters of the Pacific. Narcissa, always sentimental, said
that she was reminded of her beloved Onondaga and the twi-
lights there. William Gray had scoffed at American Falls but
this splendor overpowered him. An emotional desire to express
himself mastered his illiteracy. With awe he wrote:

For a moment I forgot the toiles of the day and in my thoughts
I could but Adore the God of Nature and in my soul I could but
admire the works of Creation and quick as thought my mind
assended upward to Him that made the magnificent scenery before me to[o] feeble to express adiquate adoration of the God
who is Omnipreasant in all His works.[19]

The trail down the mountain was filled with small sharp rocks like crushed stone on a road back east, Narcissa thought. The horses flinched. They were getting tender-footed. Uphill trails had not hurt them but the rocks on the downgrade were more than they could stand. Animal after animal balked. They refused to go forward when whipped. Night was falling fast. The beaver in each pack were worth several hundred dollars but McLeod ordered the packed horses left behind. The main column must get down to grass and water. Narcissa's own saddle horse flinched badly. She wanted to dismount and lead it. Marcus would not let her. She was expecting a baby and the steep walk downhill might be dangerous in her condition.

At the first available spot they camped. McLeod fretted around the fire. A fortune in beaver fur was wandering around back up the trail. Wolves might tear the pelts to pieces. At daylight he sent riders back hunting the stragglers. Marcus and Narcissa moved slowly on to better grass on the tawny hills of the Umatilla. Finally the fur men, with all the animals, caught up.

Supplies were completely exhausted. McLeod made everyone's mouth water with descriptions of the fresh meat, milk and vegetables at Fort Walla Walla. All danger from Indians was past, he said. The missionaries could jog in with his pack men. He would gallop ahead and return with a ripe melon for Mrs. Whitman, who had never tasted one. Walla Walla must be paradise.

McLeod cantered away. The Whitmans with William Gray and the fur men with their heavily packed animals plodded across the bare hills toward the fort. The tracks of many horses and some cattle told them that they were close to civilization. Finally on September 1, 1836, they came to the fort garden. Two miles farther and they saw the post on the dusty flat near the junction of the Columbia and the Walla Walla. "To God belongeth all the praise of our safe arrival," said William Gray.

Pierre C. Pambrun, commander of the fort, saw the missionaries coming. With John Townsend, the Philadelphia naturalist, and McLeod, the fur man, he hurried out to greet the first white woman to cross the Oregon Trail. Narcissa was helped from her saddle and escorted to a cushioned armchair. Pambrun's squaw welcomed her in French. Madame Pambrun belonged to a tribe east of the mountains and had never learned English. Narcissa tried to be Christian and tolerant of this intermingling of races but "miscegenation" was an ugly word in English. She looked critically at Pambrun. Certainly he had all the airs of a "gentleman"—very different from a fur company *engagé*. This world was not like central New York. She was reminded again that there was little democracy on the frontier.

Pambrun ordered his menservants to prepare a meal. He himself conducted Mrs. Whitman to a room in the west bastion. A loaded cannon stood in the embrasure. Firearms were stacked along the walls. The only light in the room entered through loopholes. Narcissa told herself that women should be timid in such martial surroundings but she felt immodestly delighted.

At noon a great breakfast was announced. The table displayed fresh salmon, potatoes, tea, bread and butter. William Gray had dreamed of becoming a minister with frequent invitations to Sunday dinner. Here his dream had come true. Narcissa sat down beaming over the little domestic things that delight a country girl, commonplace things in the fort compound—hens, turkeys, cooing pigeons. After the meal she wrote:

> While at breakfast . . . a young rooster placed himself upon the sill of the door and crowed. Now, whether it was the sight of the first white woman, or out of compliment to the company, I know not, but this much for him, I was pleased with his appearance. You may think me simple for speaking of such a small circumstance. No one knows the feelings occasioned by objects once familiar after a long deprivation.[20]

Two days later the Spaldings straggled in with the baggage and cattle. Thus the journey ended from Council Bluffs to the Columbia in ninety-six days. The missionaries were absolutely dependent on the British for supplies. Whitman decided to go down to Vancouver and meet Dr. McLoughlin. The Reverend Samuel Parker should be there to give advice on the best place to establish the missions. Marcus took Narcissa along. A six-day boat trip put them at the Hudson's Bay capital. Below The Dalles

A DESERT RIVER

White River Above Its Junction with the Green.

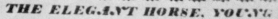

THE ELEGANT HORSE, YOUNG

Arabian Leopard,

WILL stand the ensuing season, (Saturdays, Sundays and public days excepted) from the first day of April to the last day of July, at the subscriber's stable, 2 miles East of Springfield, and will be let to mares at the reduced price of **TWO DOLLARS** the single leap, cash, paid when service is rendered; **THREE DOLLARS** cash, the season, if paid by the first day of October next, if not paid by that time, $4 will be demanded; and **FIVE DOLLARS** to insure a mare to be with foal — which may be discharged in the following articles, delivered at the stand by the first day of December next, viz: Young Cattle, Pork on foot, Wheat, Linen, Beeswax, Wool, Whiskey and Dry Hides for which the market price will be allowed. Pasturage gratis for mares from a distance. Any person putting 4 mares by the season shall have one gratis. Any person putting a mare by the season that does not prove to be with foal shall have the fall season of the same mare gratis.

Any person parting with an insured mare before she is known to be with foal, forfeits the insurance money. All possible care will be taken to prevent accidents, but the subscriber will not be accountable for any that may happen.

PEDIGREE.

Young ARABIAN LEOPARD is a beautiful White, **6** years old, 1½ hands 3 inches high, in full perfection and vigor. He was got by the old imported *Leopard*, an Arabian horse, his dam by Roebuck, and his grand dam by the old imported *Towhead*. A further detail of his *pedigree* is deemed unnecessary, as the horse will recommend himself. Farmers and others are invited to call and see him and judge for themselves.

Geo. Donner.

MARCH 26, 1831.   b. C. MEREDITH, Printer, Springfield

BROADSIDE PUBLISHED BY GEORGE DONNER BEFORE LEAVING
SPRINGFIELD, ILLINOIS

they saw their first Indian with a flattened head. They had long since learned that these curiosities were commonest along the coast, not in the Flathead country. At Vancouver, Dr. McLoughlin was sympathetic. He told the missionaries that the Reverend Mr. Parker had gone home via Hawaii. Thoughts of the trip back across the hunger-haunted, savage-infested mountains had been too much for him. The Overland Trail might be the shortest route in miles but Parker preferred the longer way around the world. Whitman could brag about getting a wagon across the Continental Divide, but the Reverend Mr. Parker would tell a different story.

Narcissa's round eyes reveled in Dr. McLoughlin's great plantation, the fort, the storehouses and resident officers' quarters, the cottages for employees and their Indian wives. Two ocean-going sailing ships lay at the dock. The cultivated fields overflowed with a bountiful harvest. Narcissa came from a farming country. She should know. Particularly, she noticed that fruit did unusually well here. She wrote her friends about it, said Fort Vancouver was the New York of the Pacific. Most marvelous of all, this prosperity had been achieved in twelve years.

Marcus and Narcissa traveled up the Willamette Valley. Here, discharged Hudson's Bay servants had prosperous farms. So did the earlier missionaries who had come with Jason Lee. Surely this country was worthy of Christians.

In October 1836 the Whitmans started back up the Columbia. At Fort Walla Walla they decided to establish missions in the Cayuse and Walla Walla country near by. The Hudson's Bay officials offered suggestions as to the best sites. They sent Hawaiian servants to help build their houses.

Narcissa, heavy with child, watched "Husband," Brother Gray and two Hawaiians build an adobe house thirty by thirty-nine feet at Waiilatpu, twenty miles up the Walla Walla River from the fort. She had no chairs and no table. Blankets covered the gaping windows. Cottonwood branches served as springs for her bed. "Where are we now and who are we that we should be thus blessed of the Lord?" she pondered.[21] On March 14, 1837, tiny Alice Clarissa Whitman was born. A great day! Indians from far and wide came to the mission. There was not standing room in the cabin for the red men and some whites who wanted to see the first white American Oregonian.

One other thing was almost as important as Alice Clarissa. The western country seemed to have unusual health-giving qualities. The air acted like a tonic. William Gray, always eager to express ideas that impressed him, in spite of his difficulty with grammar and spelling, wrote his friends back East:

And shure I am from this experiment and the nature of the Mountain air and the exilirating influence of traveling through romantic sceneries of the Mountains . . . that if scores of the daughters of the Church was to under take this journey instead of remaining inactive on their soffas at home pale and ematiated and pining under sickness they would find health and vigor renovating their whole cistim.[22]

------

1 Archer Butler Hulbert and Dorothy Printup Hulbert (eds.), *The Oregon Crusade: Across Land and Sea to Oregon (Overland to the Pacific,* V [Colorado Springs and Denver, 1935]), 259.

2 Archer Butler Hulbert and Dorothy Printup Hulbert, (eds.), *Marcus Whitman, Crusader, Part One, 1802 to 1839 (Overland to the Pacific,* VI [Colorado Springs and Denver, 1936]), 19.

3 *Ibid.,* 141.

4 *Ibid.,* 143.

5 Hulbert and Hulbert (eds.), *Marcus Whitman,* 30.

6 *Ibid.,* 32.

7 Charles Kelly and Maurice L. Howe, *Miles Goodyear, First Citizen of Utah* (Salt Lake City, 1937), 19.

8 Myron Eells, *Marcus Whitman, Pathfinder and Patriot* (Seattle, 1909), 58.

9 Hiram Martin Chittenden, *History of Early Steamboat Navigation on the Missouri River: Life and Adventures of Joseph La Barge* (New York, 1903), I, 28-30.

10 Eells, *Marcus Whitman,* 66.

11 *Ibid.,* 47.

12 Hulbert and Hulbert (eds.), *Marcus Whitman,* 209.

13 Eells, *Marcus Whitman,* 69.

14 *Ibid.,* 70.

15 *Ibid.,* 43; Kelly and Howe, *Miles Goodyear,* 31.

16 Eells, *Marcus Whitman,* 74.

17 *Ibid.,* 75.

18 *Ibid.,* 45.

19 Hulbert and Hulbert (eds.), *Marcus Whitman,* 227.

20 Eells, *Marcus Whitman,* 83.

21 Hulbert and Hulbert (eds.), *Marcus Whitman,* 72.

22 *Ibid.,* 56.

Chapter 8

Black Robe: 1840-1842

FATHER PIERRE-JEAN DE SMET worried about his weight. He was a short-bodied Belgian. Only five feet six, he weighed 210 pounds, was red-faced, jovial and apoplectic. He had been a stockily built boy of great strength, called "Samson" by his schoolmates. Excelling in athletics as well as scholarship, he came to America at the age of twenty to study for admission to the Society of Jesus. The order was famous for exacting mental and physical discipline of a high degree. Jesuits for three hundred years had given their lives in missionary service to the Indians. They had carried the Cross to the Americas many years before the settlement of Jamestown and Plymouth. In 1827 De Smet was ordained at the age of twenty-six. For more than ten years he served as a priest at the mission near Council Bluffs. Then Joseph Rosati, Bishop of St. Louis, who had broadcast the plea of the four Flatheads, sent Father De Smet on a mission to the far western Indians.

Father De Smet started from Westport on April 30, 1840, with the annual supply of goods for Fort Laramie, the trading store of the American Fur Company—a St. Louis company since Astor had retired from the firm in 1834. Westport was comparatively new. The old river landing below Independence had proved unsatisfactory. In 1833 it had washed out. Another wharf off a rocky point farther up the Missouri immediately became popular. A trader's store near the landing but back on the bench by the Santa Fe Trail had grown quickly into the new outfitting

place called Westport. A settlement at the new wharf was called
"Kansas" and later "Kansas City."

Andrew Drips was in charge of the 1840 fur company expedition. Father De Smet soon learned the grim mountain man's history. Drips had worked for the Astor firm back in 1831 when
the rival Rocky Mountain Company was rising to fame and fortune with a monopoly of the mountain trade. With Fontenelle
and another man named William Henry Vanderburgh, Drips
had come into the Rocky Mountain Company's territory to follow their trappers and learn the best fur areas. Nathaniel Wyeth
had crossed South Pass with the Rocky Mountain Fur Company when supplies were rushed to the rendezvous in order to
thwart Drips and his Astor-controlled firm. That fall Jim
Bridger had tried to shake off Drips and his interlopers by going
into the dangerous Blackfoot country but he gained nothing
from the ruse except the enemy arrow he carried until Whitman extracted it three years later. True, the Blackfeet had killed
Drips's partner, Vanderburgh, but that was part of the fortunes
of the fur trade. The eight years that followed had seen Andrew
Drips rise remarkably in the wilderness world. Yet Drips, with
all his daring history, had sluggish eyes and drooping eyelids.[1]
He had the face of a man who would take pain stoically and be
slow to make decisions. De Smet did not look forward to any
trouble with him, but the two men were as opposite as men
could be—one a squaw man, tall, thin, slow and unschooled but
not illiterate, the other short, heavy, vivacious, highly educated
and a celibate.

De Smet wore his cassock and crucifix whenever possible. He
slept in his own tent with his guide and formally observed grace
before meals. Unlike Whitman, Father De Smet was not pelted
with eggs. He was popular with the men, jolly and full of stories.
Six days out, in the neighborhood of the Little Vermilion in
Kansas, De Smet suffered from fever and ague. He carried the
malarial infection with him up into the mountains and suffered
with it periodically for five months. On May 18, 1840, the party
reached the Platte. De Smet admired the wild loneliness of the
scene and described it in a letter written, no doubt, for posterity

but addressed to the general of his Society at St. Louis. The tree-covered islands, he said, reminded him of flotillas with water surging against their prows. On the surrounding plains, De Smet watched the pale herds of antelope. One day the travelers came to a great quantity of buffalo bones with skulls arranged in a semicircle and painted many colors. The fur men shouted. They knew the work was Pawnee and that the forks of the Platte and the buffalo range must be near. Next day a hunt was planned.

De Smet got up early. He had heard the Indians tell about buffalo hunts for a decade. Now he was going to see one. He walked out of camp alone toward a near-by hill and climbed to the summit. The plain stretched away before him for miles, thickly dotted with buffalo. Tiny horsemen were riding toward the herd. Suddenly they dashed in among the animals, scattering them in every direction, killing until they were tired.

Soon after De Smet reached camp the hunters began to come in with meat dripping on their saddles, staining the sides of their horses with blood. Everyone feasted until dark, then lay down and slept soundly. De Smet was aroused by a lugubrious noise. Suspecting that Pawnee Indians were surrounding the camp, he awakened his guide. The mountain man sat up in his buffalo robe and listened.

"Rest easy," he said. "We have nothing to fear; it is the wolves."[2] De Smet heard him settle back in his robes. Next morning the Jesuit learned that the carcasses of the butchered buffalo had been picked clean.

The party crossed South Fork on May 28, 1840. The angular bench beyond, the Spanish needles and cacti in Ash Hollow and the nakedness of the plains across North Fork impressed Father De Smet. The grass was dead here. The teeming herds of game were gone. The mighty buttresses of Court House and Chimney Rocks and Scotts Bluff seemed very small on the limitless horizon. The fact that these gigantic buttes seemed insignificant intensified the vastness of the plains. The solitude wearied De Smet's ebullient spirits. On June 4, 1840, the cavalcade came to the border of a stream the Belgian called "the Ramee"—Laramie.

On its banks near the fort De Smet saw some forty lodges o: "Sheyennes"—people to talk to, company at last. The fur men rode through the village toward the stockade. De Smet noticec that the Indians were fine specimens physically,[3] clean and civil The men had lithe bodies, aquiline noses and chins strongly developed. The principal chiefs invited him to a feast.

Father De Smet brushed his cassock, rearranged his crucifix and strode down to the lodges. He sat with the headmen on a blanket, blessed a bowl of stewed dog, explained his mission and asked if his hosts would like to have a Black Gown in their village. The Indians accepted his gift of tobacco and answered "Yes."[4]

In the fort, Father De Smet noticed the abundance of half-breed children, the prosperity of the illiterate officials. Here was a new culture—half-Indian, half-European. Young men born in this life were already showing themselves to be more savage than their red mothers. Some were starting little nomadic villages of their own, drifting here and there with a few horses, living on game. Breaking away from tribal ties, they had given up the paganism of the Indians and had substituted no religion to take its place. De Smet was told, too, that the powerful plains tribes had driven their weaker enemies back from the buffalo herds into the Black or Laramie Hills west of the fort. The inaccessible defiles protected them from pursuit. Black Robe, as Father De Smet liked to call himself, prophesied that these renegades would develop into a distinct people and eventually form a dangerous state on the edge of the United States. Highly educated, familiar with the whole panorama of world history, he made a natural enough mistake. To the Reverend Father Roothaan, General of the Society of Jesus, he wrote:

It is to be feared that this immense region forms a limit between civilization and barbarism, and that bands of malefactors organised like the Caravans of the Arabs, may here practice their depredations with impunity. This country will, perhaps, one day, be the cradle of a new people, composed of the ancient savage races, and of that class of adventurers, fugitives and exiles that society has cast forth from its bosom—a heterogeneous and dangerous population, which the American Union has collected like a portentous cloud upon its frontiers, and whose force and irritation it is constantly increasing, by transporting entire tribes of Indians from the banks of the Mississippi, where they were born, into the solitudes of the West, which are assigned as their place of exile. These savages carry with them an implacable hatred towards the whites, for having, they say, unjustly driven them from their country, far from the tombs of their fathers, in order to take possession of their inheritance.[6]

Father De Smet explained further that it seemed reasonable to expect these people to become a race of shepherds and warriors who might prey on the whites and hide their pillage in the remote mountains. He hoped that Black Robes might be sent among these wild brothers but his main purpose was to investigate the opportunities among the Flatheads whom he knew would be at the rendezvous on the Oregon border. The fur train was soon ready to leave Fort Laramie and De Smet set off with it. On his left, the jagged outline of the Laramie Mountains became higher and more distinct each day. Finally, the wagon train left the peak behind and approached the Platte Crossing. West of the ford, De Smet noted the Red Buttes as a famous Indian landmark. The road led up the Sweetwater. At Independence Rock De Smet marveled at the many signatures. He called the rock "the great registry of the desert,"[7] carved his own name and stated that he was the first priest to penetrate these regions.

On June 30, 1840, the brigade arrived at the Green River rendezvous. The traders and missionaries encamped to await the formal reception dear to the savages. In the distance the newcomers could hear drums beating. Three hundred Shoshoni came toward them with a fantastic military display. Hideously painted, armed with clubs, decked with feathers, and with necklaces of animals' teeth and claws, they charged at a gallop and in good order around and around the entire camp shouting with joy. De Smet noticed that the warriors' standard was a pole with dangling scalps upon it.

The red men dismounted and came forward to shake hands. They said that they were preparing an expedition against their enemies, the Blackfeet. De Smet became interested. In the days that followed he visited the Shoshoni village, watched the warriors chant themselves into war ecstasy, noted that every lodge contributed a present to them, that old men harangued them about success in their proposed adventure. De Smet went, too, to the Flathead village. These were the savages whose souls he had come to save. He shook hands with the chiefs and said that he wanted to take the Cross into their country. The Flatheads grunted assent. They would supply Black Robe with an escort of warriors, they said. The Father need have no fear. Had not sixty Flatheads on the way to the rendezvous stood off 200 Blackfoot enemies and killed fifty of them? De Smet appeared convinced. In any event he accepted their guidance and protection.

De Smet announced to the whole rendezvous that he would celebrate the holy sacrifice of Mass on Sunday, July 5, 1840. On the prairie he prepared an altar in a shell of cottonwood boughs decorated with garlands of wild flowers. The brilliant sunshine of upper Green River was very different from medieval cathedral twilight, but the free trappers, *engagés,* half-breeds, Canadian-French, Shoshoni and Flatheads all came—a great concourse of people. De Smet in his long black robe—trimmed with cockleburs no doubt—walked among the people. In French, and also in Latin, he led the Canadians in singing hymns. The red men chanted, too, in their own languages. "It was truly a Catholic worship," De Smet noted.[8]

Next day De Smet set off with his Flathead friends. Indians always had to keep moving to get food. A large number could never stay together more than a day or two. For eight days De Smet rode with his wild guides north and west through the mountains to the Bitterroot country that would one day mark the boundary between Montana and Idaho. Here, in the cool green mountains, he explained Catholic usages, baptized converts and taught them to pray. On August 27, 1840, after a two months' sojourn, he started back to the United States, not by the

Oregon Trail but through the extremely dangerous Blackfoot, Sioux and Arikara territory north of it. These warlike tribes brooked no trespassers. But with one companion, De Smet struck out across their country for the river settlements. With death constantly before their eyes, the two men rode fast, along gulch bottoms when possible, avoiding sky lines. Campfires were built at dusk when the smoke would be invisible. After eating, the two men trotted off into the night to sleep far away on the limitless upland. They had several narrow escapes but arrived unhurt at last on the Missouri and floated down to civilization just ahead of the freeze which might have locked them for the winter in the wilderness.

De Smet reported the Flatheads ripe for salvation. His superiors decided that Jesuit missions should be established in the Oregon country. In the spring of 1841, De Smet prepared to go back to the mountains. This time he arranged for two Jesuits to establish prospective missions. Father Nicolas Point was recognized for his courage and zeal and Father Gregory Mengarini, a linguist just arrived from Rome, came with the traditional courage of the Jesuit Order. In addition, De Smet engaged three devout lay brothers, a carpenter, a blacksmith and a tinner—two of them Belgians, the other a German. An English sportsman, named Romaine, joined the party to hunt big game. Guides, packers and servants made an aggregate of eleven men all told.

At Westport, De Smet learned that no rendezvous was to be held in the Rockies. This was hard to believe. After eighteen years the great summer mart in the mountains had become an institution taken for granted. But the decline was easy to explain. In the first place, beaver had become scarce and their fur was not in such great demand as formerly. Silk, instead of beaver, hats had become fashionable. Traders tried to save the declining business by asking Indians to bring in buffalo robes. The great bulky hides could not be baled readily into pack-horse loads at a rendezvous. Forts with storage warehouses were necessary for them. Moreover, the big hides were worth only a fraction of the former value of the smaller beaver skins. Thus the whole nature of the business changed. Fortunes like those accumulated by William H. Ashley and William L. Sublette had not been made for years. Astor had seen ahead. In 1834 he sold out to Ramsay Crooks, who with Robert Stuart as second in command, continued to rule the fur trade from Mackinac Island. Both of them groused about Old Tightwad Astor but both had become wealthy serving him. Now they both were planning to quit and looking for investments in other fields.

Lesser fur men still clung to the old life and, of course, the various trading forts must be supplied annually. Father De Smet, stranded at Westport, learned that a small party of traders, some forty rifles, was going to Fort Laramie under Thomas Fitzpatrick. De Smet arranged to go alone. He hired Broken Hand to guide him beyond Laramie. The clerics learned, too, that a United States exploring expedition under Jean Nicollet was due to go west with a surveying party from Council Bluffs. Father De Smet knew Nicollet. If by good fortune he could join Nicollet on the Platte, the Jesuits would be well guarded in the mountains.

On May 10, 1841, Father De Smet pulled out of Westport. His plans for crossing the continent were uncertain but the chance of meeting the United States explorers seemed good and his trust in God was complete. With no immediate danger, each wagon and pack horse set its own pace. De Smet had supplied his companions with two-wheeled carts covered with canvas stretched across wagon bows. Each cart was hauled by two mules hitched tandem. Such a rig was more practical than a four-wheeled wagon. The half-breeds in the Red River of the North had found these carts the best means of transportation on roadless plains.

The fur men, with De Smet, were soon scattered for miles along the road. Five days later the party came to the Kansas Crossing, close to the present Topeka. The river was running bankfull. Indians from a near-by village showed the missionaries how to swim horses and provided a pirogue for the baggage and wagons. When they reached the north bank, De Smet ordered his tent pitched. The Indians galloped away in a cloud of dust but the tent pegs were hardly driven when a camp tender announced that the Indians were coming back. The chief presented himself to Father De Smet. The priest ordered a mat spread and they sat down. The chief produced a portfolio. De Smet opened it and read that his host had many honorable titles including title to the land on which they sat. De Smet brought out tobacco and they smoked and meditated. This ceremony completed, the chief assigned two braves to the missionaries as a guard in his realm. One of these naked fellows bore a lance and shield, the other a bow, arrows, unsheathed sword and necklace of bear claws. Thus ably protected, De Smet waited three days as the fur men straggled in and crossed the Kansas. Then the reorganized party continued its journey.

Father De Smet and Father Point, with the British sportsman, left the column to gallop off and repay the visit of the Kansas chief. They rode over the swell of the plain to the west toward the Indian village. Ahead they noticed some twenty mounds, for all the world like stacks of wheat in a harvest field. "There it is," said the Britisher. Dismounting at the edge of the town the white men walked in among the huts. Above the six-foot walls poles rose to a round opening at the top which served as window and smoke hole. De Smet knew that the Pawnee over on the lower Platte constructed similar lodges. The men walked through one of the tunnel vestibules to a fragrant fire smoldering in the center of the room. Judging by the beds arranged around the wall, De Smet estimated that the lodge housed thirty to forty people.

The Indian men produced little mirrors and began to paint themselves. Their wives brought out ornaments, put beaded moccasins on their lords' feet, plucked out stray hairs from their chins and eyebrows. The men's heads looked like peeled onions, bare except for the scalp lock tied in an aggressive roach with a ribbon or feather attached.

A mat was spread and the pipe of peace began to pass. Children crowded in, gaped at Father Point's beard and fled laughing. The elders listened attentively to De Smet's religious teaching. He explained the new God to them and the efficacy of prayer. His humor bubbled over when the red men asked God to make them successful in stealing their neighbors' horses and to deafen their enemies' ears so that they might slip up, stab them and take their scalps.

The two warriors assigned by the chief to escort the missionaries rode with the clerics for two days along the Overland Trail, then stopped. This was the boundary of Pawnee country, they said. They could go no farther. The Kansas had recently raided the Pawnee and a war party was sure to be out looking for them or any other loose Kansas.

De Smet presented his dusky guards with twists of tobacco and they galloped away. Two days later the Jesuits met the Pawnee looking for their enemies. Surely, De Smet mused, here was work for the missionaries. Why had the Protestants with their missions among the frontier tribes failed so signally? The Pawnee seemed fully as savage as the Kansas—perhaps more so. They said that the Kansas had raided their villages in order that the Great Spirit would give them rain. Only a few years before the Pawnee had immolated a fifteen-year-old Sioux girl to induce the Great Spirit to give them good crops. Such religion! De Smet learned that the young captive had been well treated all winter and promised a great feast in her honor in the spring. She had believed and rejoiced as she saw the snow disappear on the plains. Father De Smet described her horrible death to his Father Provincial:

The day fixed upon for the feast having dawned, she passed through all the preparatory ceremonies, and was then arrayed in her finest attire, after which she was placed in a circle of warriors, who seemed to escort her for the purpose of showing her deference. Besides their wonted arms, each one of these warriors had two pieces of wood, which he had received at the hands of the maiden. The latter had on the preceding day carried three posts, which she had helped to fell in the neighboring forest: but supposing that she was walking to a triumph, and her mind being filled with the most pleasing ideas, the victim advanced towards the place of her sacrifice with those mingled· feelings of joy and timidity, which, under similar circumstances, are naturally excited in the bosom of a girl of her age.

During their march, which was rather long, the silence was interrupted only by religious songs and invocations to the Master of life, so that whatever affected the senses, tended to keep up the deceitful delusion under which she had been till that moment. But as soon as she had reached the place of sacrifice, where nothing was seen but fires, torches, and instruments of torture, the delusion began to vanish and her eyes were opened to the fate that awaited her. How great must have been the surprise, and soon after the terror which she felt, when she found it no longer possible to doubt of their intentions? Who could describe her poignant anguish? She burst into tears; she raised loud cries to heaven—she begged, entreated, conjured her executioners to have pity on her youth, her innocence, her parents, but all in vain; neither tears, nor cries, nor the promises of a trader who happened to be present, softened the hearts of these monsters. She was tied with ropes to the trunk and branches of two trees, and the most sensitive parts of her body were burnt with torches made of the wood which she had with her own hands distributed to the warriors.—When her sufferings lasted long enough to weary the fanatical fury of her ferocious tormentors, the great chief shot an arrow into her heart; and in an instant this arrow was followed by a thousand others, which, after having been violently turned and twisted in the wounds, were torn from them in such a manner that her whole body presented but one shapeless mass of mangled flesh, from which the blood streamed on all sides. When the blood had ceased to flow, the greater sacrificator approached the expiring victim, and to crown so many atrocious acts, tore out her heart with his own hands, and after uttering the most frightful imprecations against the Scioux nation, devoured the bleeding flesh, amid the acclamations of his whole tribe. The mangled remains were then left to be preyed upon by wild beasts, and when the blood had been sprinkled on the seed, to render it fertile, all retired to their cabins, cheered with the hope of obtaining a copious harvest.[9]

De Smet was not the first white man to revolt at this custom of the Loup Pawnee. The rite persisted and was hard to stamp out. De Smet meditated its horrors as he plodded along to the Platte. On June 2, 1841, he camped on the river's south bank.

The fur company was again scattered in numerous groups along the back trail. Father De Smet hoped to meet his friend Jean Nicollet and the surveyors in these parts.[10] The priest settled down for a few days of rest. The grass was good. Every day the horses regained their strength. De Smet read Washington Irving, compared his descriptions with the scene before him and kept an eye on the horizon over which he hoped to see his friends emerge.

One day De Smet saw the white tops of wagons against the blue sky above the sand hills south of the Platte. They came forward, rocking down the draw. This was not part of the fur outfit and there were too many for Nicollet's surveying party. Heads appeared at the end of the wagon bows, men on foot and horseback trudged beside the wagons. De Smet counted sixty-nine persons in all. The priests put on their robes to welcome the strangers.

A young man of twenty-two rode forward to meet the Black Robes. John Bidwell was born in New York State and he had an interesting story of overland promotion to tell. He had taught school the winter before at Weston, Missouri, and at the same time organized in several frontier towns what was known as the Western Emigration Society. All members were to meet in the spring on the frontier at Sapling Grove. Then, long before the day set, a letter from California written by a former resident of Peoria, Illinois, named Thomas Jefferson Farnham, appeared in the newspapers both in New York and in the West. The prospective emigrants became discouraged over Farnham's account of California. They backed out of the Western Emigration Society's program. At Sapling Grove when Bidwell arrived, he found only one wagon waiting. With youthful energy and optimism Bidwell had sought last-minute recruits along the border, and here they were, the first overland emigrants to California.

John Bidwell was a striking-looking young man but neither De Smet nor anyone else foresaw his political future culminating half a century later, in his candidacy for President on the Prohibition ticket in 1892. Bidwell's hastily organized party contained many foreigners. De Smet listed them and noticed that his and

Bidwell's parties represented every country in Europe. They all camped together on the Platte. The water was rank with the smell of buffalo. Thousands and thousands of the monsters must be crossing upstream. Everyone was eager to get up to the buffalo range, but dangerous Indians were known to be hunting there, too.

De Smet's little party joined the emigrants and they all set off together.[11] They passed Grand Island, came to the forks and traveled up South Fork to the crossing. It looked dangerous. The stream was a mile wide, shallow but probably full of holes and quicksand. Two Canadians rode out in the water to test the ford. De Smet watched them for over a half hour as they splashed across. Then the mules and wagons followed in a long line. The teams all reached the north shore. They crossed the bench to North Fork, forded again and went on up the trail.

The wagon train had an "Indian scare" one afternoon shortly before supper. Father De Smet, John Bidwell and Father Point had ridden ahead to select a camp site.[12] They found a suitable area and unsaddled their horses. An alarm cry, "Indians, Indians!" came to them from the approaching train. In the distance they saw a party of warriors. One of Bidwell's men, James Dawson, ran in from the prairie out of breath and in a furious temper. Contrary to orders, he had slipped out to hunt. The Indians found him, took his horse and gun and gave him a beating. The enraged fellow wanted to go back at once and kill them.

Fitzpatrick galloped up with flashing eyes. He screamed a command for the wagons to move into close double file. Men seized their arms and prepared for a siege. Then Fitzpatrick rode off to talk with the red men. They proved to be a party of Cheyenne. After smoking they agreed to restore Dawson's horse and gun. Father De Smet chuckled at the settlement. He remembered later that the Indians agreed to give back everything but the blows. The young American was called Cheyenne Dawson for the remainder of the trip.

At the upper crossing of the Platte the wagon train had a much worse experience. It had forded the South Fork without mishap. North Fork at the upper crossing was much narrower but it was also deeper. De Smet, round as a barrel in his saddle, looked across the current and decided to dismount and ride over in a cart. Then he saw his hunter drive the horse carrying his squaw into the current. The *engagé* plunged in the water behind and dragged with him a colt bearing his year-old daughter. To turn back, in face of this nonchalance, was more than De Smet could stand. His ruddy face paled, but he urged his mount into the stream. In the rear he could hear teamsters' shouts and the rumble of wheels as the wagons jolted down the bank and entered the ford.

De Smet climbed out on the north bank dripping wet. He looked back. The wagon train was in wild confusion. One of the largest whitetops had floated out of its standards and was sailing downstream. Another had turned over. Men and mules were splashing in the water. Bidwell stood on the south side with arms extended, calling for help. A German and a mule were appearing and reappearing like porpoises. A horse crawled out of the water without his rider. Two other riders came ashore on one horse. Father Mengarini, the Roman linguist, emerged on the bank with both arms around his horse's neck. Finally all got across.[13] Not a man drowned, and only one mule. Good! Father De Smet began to joke about the ludicrous situations. Around the campfire he told how funny everybody, including himself, had appeared.

In early July the party reached the Sweetwater, the "Eau Sucree," De Smet called it. The travelers were behind schedule. The Flatheads had agreed to meet him on Green River but De Smet wondered if they would wait. At Rock Independence[14]— De Smet's brogue—the party tarried to carve their names. Along the road De Smet watched from his saddle the picturesque buttes and castellated rock formations. In his mind he compared them with the ruins of ancient Gothic castles. At night he wrote that one might believe himself transported "amid the ancient mansions of Knight errantry."[15]

Each day De Smet worried because the summer was passing and he had failed to keep his appointment with the Indians. He decided to send a messenger ahead to find the Flatheads and re-assure them that the Black Robes were coming. After the courier had gone, Father De Smet spent more time looking at the scenery. At Devil's Gate he rode off the trail to stop and wonder. He considered "Heaven's Avenue" a more appropriate name and stood in rapture before the chasm for an hour, so he said. In great detail he noted the wild scene and wrote for his Provincial:

Imagine, in short, two rows of rocks, rising perpendicularly to a wonderful height, and, at the foot of these shapeless walls, a winding bed, broken, encumbered with trunks of trees, with rubbish, and with timber of all dimensions; while, in the midst of this chaos of obstacles, the roaring waves force a passage, now rushing with fury, then swelling with majesty, and anon spreading with gentleness, according as they find in their course a wider or more straitened passage. Above these moving and noisy scenes, the eye discerns masses of shadow, here relieved by a glance of day, there deepening in their gloom by the foliage of a cedar or pine, till finally, as the sight travels through the long vista of lofty galleries, it is greeted by a distant perspective of such mild beauty, that a sentiment of placid happiness steals upon the mind . . . I doubt whether the solitude of the Carthusian monastery, called La Grande Chartreuse, of which so many wonders are related, can, at least at first sight, offer greater attractions to him whom divine grace has called to a contemplative life.[16]

The messengers to the Flatheads came back and reported that the red men had run out of food on Green River. The main party had left for home, but three braves had remained to wait for Black Robe and guide him to their country. On July 7, 1841, De Smet's party reached South Pass and the Jesuits looked upon "Oregon Territory." They traveled down Little Sandy, crossed to Big Sandy, then instead of following the creek, Fitzpatrick led them off on a right-hand road known as Sublette's Cutoff to Bear River. Soon they were out in an ocean of short sagebrush far from shore and the road disappeared. In short they were lost. For three days the caravan wandered at random. Father De

Smet became desperate. He had agreed to meet the Flatheads at the rendezvous July 1. He was ten days late. Would the three red men wait? The priest rode off alone to find the way. He could see ten or fifteen miles in every direction, and mountains fifty miles away stood out plainly in the blue distance. Black Robe rode for a couple of hours and suddenly realized that he was lost from the lost party. His companions were somewhere back on the plain—in sight no doubt, but too small to be seen without a telescope. To be lost in the center of a plain was more terrifying than to be lost in the woods or in the mountains. The distances discouraged a man from even trying to find his way. Father De Smet dismounted and prayed fervently. Then he mounted and whipped his horse rapidly in the direction that he believed right. The scenery did not change. No object came to view and no road. De Smet decided that he was going in the wrong direction. He turned his horse and lashed it irritably in another direction. The sun began to sink in the west.

Then far in the distance, he saw the wagon train. Immediate relief came to the priest. He jogged complacently toward the train. Before dark he arrived. Supper fires were burning. The draft animals were all tied around the wagons with nothing to eat. The travelers were still unable to find the way. They dared not turn the horses and mules out to graze as they would wander away hunting water and be lost permanently. Around the fires, blazing red in the purpling darkness, the men argued about the direction of the road and the shortest way to Green River.

Next morning the horses looked very gaunt, their hides sunken in holes behind their ribs, cadaverous as Fitzpatrick's cheeks. The animals' distressed eyes showed that they were suffering for water. The men hitched them to the wagons, tightened the lines and the train started forward. Before long they came to the rim above Green River and looked down on the stream, its meadows and groves of cottonwoods. The mules began to bray. Soon the entire train reached the river bottom and the animals were turned out to drink and feed. Scouts rode up and down the stream hunting for any living soul. This was the great midsummer mart of the mountains and it was hard to believe that trappers and Indians were not assembled somewhere near by. The three Flathead guides were found. A party of unkempt bearded white men appeared, too, and asked for whisky. They were coming back from California with Henry Fraeb, famous mountain man and onetime partner of Fitzpatrick in the Rocky Mountain Fur Company. Many old-timers were serving as guides now that the rendezvous had been discontinued. Fraeb's party had a doleful story to tell about California. Bidwell's men listened, then talked it over among themselves. The British sportsman and several emigrants decided to give up their trip and go back with Fraeb. Others urged their comrades to go to Oregon. The climate and opportunities described by Hall Kelley, Nathaniel Wyeth and Marcus Whitman sounded better than California. Bidwell, politician at heart, urged, argued and extolled the virtues of California. He failed to convince a few, but most of the men decided to keep going west and continue to argue the comparative merits of California and Oregon as they traveled.

Father De Smet and his missionaries did not wait at Green River to hear the outcome of the debate.[17] With their guides they hitched up their carts and started for Fort Hall. Ten days later they arrived at Bear River and turned north through the meadows. They met a few parties of degraded Shoshoni—Diggers, most people called these Indians. De Smet, in quaint English, called them Uprooters. He had read many accounts of western travelers and explorers but Indians seen through his cosmopolitan eyes were very different from the red men seen by American travelers. Trained in a European, not an American culture, he described the Indians differently from the conventional pattern. The following picture sounds more like European gypsies than American Indians, even Uprooters:

Represent to yourself a band of wretched horses, disproportionate in all their outlines, loaded with bags and boxes to a height equal to their own, and these surmounted by rational beings young and old, male and female, in a variety of figures and costumes, to which the pencil of a Hogarth or a Breugel could scarcely do justice, and you will have an idea of the scene we

witnessed. One of these animals, scarcely four feet high, had for
its load four large sacks of dried meat, two on each side, above
which were tied several other objects, terminating in a kind of
platform on the back of the living beast; and, on the summit
of the whole construction, at a very high elevation, was seated
crosslegged on a bear skin a very old person smoking his calu-
met. At his side, on another Rosinante, was mounted an old
Goody, probably his wife, seated in the same manner on the top
of sacks and bags, that contained all sorts of roots, dried beans
and fruits, grains and berries; in short, all such comestibles as the
barren mountains and the beautiful vallies afford. These they
carried to their winter encampment.[18]

At the tip of the Bear River horseshoe the Jesuits came to the
springs that taste like soda. Many of them gurgled from the tops
of cones four to six feet tall. De Smet walked up the wet sides
of the pyramids and noticed a sugary precipitate that crunched
beneath his feet. He noticed, too, that the ground around some
of the springs resounded under his step as though there was a
hollow vault below. He wondered if the water might have cura-
tive powers like some of the European spas. His men enjoyed
drinking the effervescent fluid.

At Soda Springs the road turned from Bear River Valley and
went down to Fort Hall, only sixty or seventy miles away.
Father De Smet with one companion and a guide decided to go
ahead of the carts. Surely they could make it in two days and
wait for the wagons.

The two priests started off briskly. The way seemed easy, but
they did not know the Port Neuf. By dark they were hopelessly
entangled among black lava walls and treacherous pits that might
break the neck of a horse and rider. The three men groped
around uncertainly. At last the guide admitted that he did not
know the way. De Smet ordered both his companions to un-
saddle. They wrapped themselves in saddle blankets and dozed
until morning. In daylight they found a path around the lava
beds. The peculiar formation interested De Smet. He also noticed the unusual dams along the Port Neuf. The stream was a
series of dark pools separated by white waterfalls.

Trotting, and galloping when the ground permitted, the three men came down out of the mountains. Beyond the basin fifty miles away they could see volcanic buttes. The guide set his course across the flat. Fort Hall lay in the middle of the plain close to where the Blackfoot and the Port Neuf joined Snake River. The riders jogged out on the desert, and soon the long low mound near Fort Hall came into view. They knew that the fort was near the timber along Snake River but night fell before they reached it. The two creeks, numerous sloughs and thickets

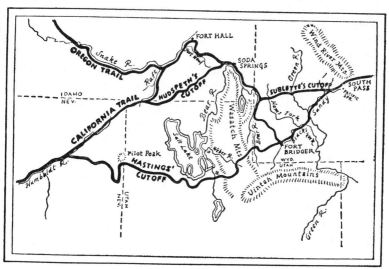

THE PRINCIPAL ROUTES AND CUTOFFS BEYOND SOUTH PASS

baffled the riders. They could hear no sound and see no light from the fort that they knew to be close. Tired from two days' riding and one night without a bed, they unsaddled and slept on the ground again. De Smet's vitality served him well. He rejoiced. This exercise without food would cut down his weight.

Next morning the men found Fort Hall easily. The Hudson's Bay Company had purchased it after Wyeth's second venture failed. Francis Ermatinger, the squaw man who had escorted Wyeth back from Vancouver in 1833, met the priests at the gate and offered them a genial reception. Thirty years' commercial rivalry between the Hudson's Bay Company and the Americans had ended in complete triumph for the Britishers, but Ermatinger understood that a greater force than commerce was coming to Oregon. Like Dr. McLoughlin, his uncle by marriage, Ermatinger was willing to help emigrants and even change his nationality and become an American if need be. Already he was planning to leave the fort for a trip to California. He intended to change with the times. In 1845 he was elected Treasurer of Oregon Territory.

The two priests settled down at the fort. Soon their own and Bidwell's wagons rumbled in all together. The emigrants had caught up with the Jesuits' carts. They were still arguing the merits of Oregon over California. Most of them had turned off at Soda Springs for California by a route somewhat similar to the trace later known as Hudspeth's Cutoff to the Humboldt.

Only thirty-two emigrants had come to Fort Hall. They maintained that they were still undecided between California and Oregon and had come to the fort only to purchase supplies. They would decide here which road to destiny they would follow. De Smet was not concerned about their immediate destination. He was interested to learn that Indians had taken advantage of the emigrants' disputes. One of the small parties of dissenters had been robbed of their horses and massacred.

With the Flatheads, De Smet planned to go north from Fort Hall and leave the emigrants to their dissensions. Most of them were Protestants, including some Methodist preachers. De Smet had explained the truths of Catholicism to all of them who would listen. Now as the time came for him to part with them permanently, he was curious to know if they had retained any of his teaching. Father De Smet walked over to the wagons to talk to the Americans. He came back to his tent disheartened. To his Provincial he wrote that he had not made a conversion. The Americans' minds were closed to the truth, he said, more than the Indians'. However, De Smet added, he had at least destroyed some of the Methodists' prejudice against Catholics.[19]

With his party De Smet turned off the Oregon Trail at Fort

Hall. The Flathead guides led the way up Snake River across a desert more desolate than anything De Smet had yet seen, the only vegetation, cacti and absinthe—as he called sagebrush. To the east he noticed the Three Tetons over sixty miles away, and to the west, within thirty miles, volcanic buttes stood in the desert haze. Below the junction of Henrys Fork De Smet decided to cross Snake River. The guides selected a ford and the lead cart turned down the bank. The vehicle was loaded too heavily for the grade. It pushed against the mules, shoved them into the river and upset on top of them in the water.

The Indians on the bank jumped into the water. The driver was dragged out and most of the supplies saved. Three mules drowned. Father De Smet wondered why God had visited him with this catastrophe when he was on his way to convert souls. It occurred to him that mules get excited when their ears are full of water. Perhaps no more than this caused them to struggle and drown. Finally he remembered that his party had left Fort Hall in a hurry without saying morning prayers.[20]

The baggage was repacked and the cavalcade went forward. At last they came to Flathead country—the Montana-Idaho border. The Continental Divide north and east of them looked like a knife-edge against the sky. The narrow trails seemed impassable for anything but a mountain goat. De Smet looked at his 210 pounds and then at his little saddle mule. She could never carry him over the pass. Father De Smet dismounted and took the little jenny's tail in one hand and a switch in the other. Thus they went over the pass tandem, out of breath but safe and sound.[21]

De Smet wintered with the Flatheads, founded missions and in the spring dropped down to the Columbia until he came again to the Oregon Trail. In a Hudson's Bay barge he floated without mishap to The Dalles.[22]

The river was high with the June floods. De Smet noticed that the water galloped over submerged rocks with sublime fury. Indian fishermen lined the banks netting fish. They had long since given up the idea of exacting toll along the river. In the eddies De Smet saw seals floating with their heads above water. Suddenly they would turn and dash with incredible swiftness after a passing fish.

Next day Black Robe came to what was called the Little Dalles—probably Whirlpool Rapids. Father De Smet walked along the shore as the barge went through. The river path crossed rough boulders. Father De Smet, short of breath, watched the boat with envy. He wished that he were back on his comfortable seat where he could enjoy the frowning bluffs, sniff the fresh-water spray and feel the current tug the boat onward. Suddenly he saw all the boatmen thrown from the thwarts as the clumsy craft hit a rock! Great waves banked against the rear of the barge. She turned broadside to the current and began to spin on the edge of a whirlpool, nearer and nearer the yawning vortex. De Smet saw the pilot shout orders. The men struggled with the oars. The bow rose high in the air. The stern disappeared. Next instant the craft dived into the boiling waters.

De Smet watched with horror. Below the pool he saw oars, bits of wood, then the shiny bottom of the barge come to the surface. Among the wreckage he saw the heads of struggling men. De Smet hurried over the boulders. An Iroquois trapper came to shore floating on De Smet's bedroll. Another man floated in holding the handle of the priest's trunk. De Smet's interpreter came staggering up the beach, his long hair dripping. He had touched bottom twice, he told Father De Smet, but by offering earnest prayers he had been saved.

Five fur men drowned.

De Smet arrived at Vancouver on June 8, 1842. Dr. McLoughlin, a Catholic himself, greeted him as hospitably as he had the Protestants. Two priests, the Reverend Father Blanchet and Father Demers, were already in the Oregon country. They had come with the Hudson's Bay men from Red River and from Montreal. Already they were converting more Indians than the Protestant missionaries. Colorful Catholic rites appealed to the red men.

De Smet started back east on June 30, 1842. With sails and oars the barge moved along to the Cascade range. Long tow ropes pulled them through the canyon to The Dalles. On July 11 they landed at Fort Walla Walla.

De Smet did not go east by the Oregon Trail. With only one companion he traversed the high plains between the Snake and the Spokane, and entered the gloomy forests. Gigantic Oregon cedars impressed him. He wrote:

I measured one forty-two feet in circumference. A cedar of four fathoms, lying on the ground, measured more than two hundred feet in length. The delicate branches of these noble trees entwine themselves above the beech and elm; their fine, dense and ever-green foliage, forming an arch through which the sun's rays never penetrate; and this lofty vault, supported by thousands of columns, brought to the mind's eye, the idea of an immense, glorious temple, carpeted with the hardy ever-greens that live and flourish best in the shade.[23]

Across the mountains of Idaho he found his brethren in good health at the missions. With Father Point and the neophytes he planted a cross at the head of the Bitterroot, one of the sources of the Missouri. Below, on August 15, 1842, the clerics celebrated the Feast of the Assumption on the plains. During the ceremony fifty Flatheads approached the altar. "To my, perhaps partial eye, they resembled angels more than men," De Smet remembered.[24]

Black Robe moved eastward. He found the Crows friendly. With three companions to guide him, he struck off across the dangerous Yellowstone country and arrived at Fort Union on the Missouri. Here he boarded a skiff. Three days later he overtook a steamboat, climbed aboard and landed in St. Louis on October 31, 1842. Father De Smet went to the cathedral, knelt before St. Mary's altar and gave thanks for a safe journey.

---

1 Hiram Martin Chittenden, *The American Fur Trade of the Far West* (New York, 1935), I, opp. 276, prints a photograph of Drips.

2 Reuben Gold Thwaites (ed.), "De Smet's Letters and Sketches, 1841-1842," *Early Western Travels, 1748-1846* (Cleveland, 1906), XXVII, 158.

3 *Ibid.*, 160.

4 *Ibid.*, 137, 162.

5 *Ibid.*, 159-60.

6 *Ibid.*, 162.

7 *Ibid.*, 138.

8 *Ibid.*, 209-10.

9 *Ibid.*, 190.

10 *Ibid.*

11 *Ibid.*, 270.

12 John Bidwell, "The First Emigrant Train to California," *The Century Magazine* (November, 1890), XIX, 116, indicates that this trouble occurred before the wagon train reached the Platte.

13 Thwaites (ed.), "De Smet's Letters and Sketches," *Early Western Travels,* XXVII, 273.

14 *Ibid.*, 215-216.

15 *Ibid.*, 220.

16 *Ibid.*, 241.

17 *Ibid.*, 278.

18 *Ibid.*, 244-47.

19 *Ibid.*, 238.

20 *Ibid.*, 274-77, 327.

21 *Ibid.*, 337.

22 *Ibid.*, 374.

23 *Ibid.*, 340.

24 *Ibid.*, 381.

Chapter 9

Pathfinder Frémont: 1842

SENATOR THOMAS HART BENTON was a pompous old soul who had not been afraid to tackle Andy Jackson himself with a cane and pistol. Benton's daughter Jessie was the apple of his eye. When she decided to marry a weak-faced second lieutenant in the U. S. Army Engineers in 1841, "Old Bullion" Benton loosed the thunder from on high. He soon learned that his daughter was a charming chip off the old block, so he made the best of a bad thing. His constituents in Missouri were vitally interested in the Far West, in the fur business and also in trade along the Santa Fe Trail. For years Old Bullion had watched the activities of William Ashley and all his men. In Congress he had read the petitions of Hall J. Kelley for national aid to settlement in Oregon. He had heard all the gossip about Nathaniel Wyeth's competition with the fur companies. He realized that the Protestant and Catholic missionaries to Oregon were stirring up a great national interest. Territorial expansion was becoming a dominant plank in his party's platform.

His home, St. Louis, was the transfer point between eastern and western boat transportation and promised to be the great metropolis of the Mississippi Valley. With the constantly growing interest in Oregon, a half-dozen other towns were bound to spring up in his state as outfitting places for emigration. Old Bullion, with more than common enthusiasm, arranged to have his new son-in-law inspect the overland route from the Missouri frontier to South Pass—go up on horseback and float back in a rubber boat. It was a great opportunity for the young man—and

217

besides it would leave Jessie where she belonged, with her doting father.

Second Lieutenant John C. Frémont organized his expedition in St. Louis. He employed Kit Carson and L. Maxwell as guides and hunters. A German, Charles Preuss, accompanied the lieutenant as assistant topographer. Twenty-one Creole and Canadian *voyageurs* joined as teamsters, guards, boatmen, helpers and general roustabouts. Nineteen-year-old Henry Brant, son of Colonel J. B. Brant of St. Louis, and twelve-year-old Randolph Benton, Frémont's brother-in-law, went along "for the development of mind and body which such an expedition would give."[1]

In a steamboat the party moved up the Missouri to Cyprian Chouteau's trading house near the mouth of the Kansas River. Frémont employed a "civilized" Indian to lead his column along the forty miles of country roads to the open plains. Then Kit Carson took charge. The little fellow rode beside the lieutenant and his "gentlemen" companions. A color guard led with the American flag. Behind them eight carts carried supplies, scientific instruments and a very fancy India-rubber boat. Armed guards brought up the rear with loose saddle horses and four beef cattle. Late in the afternoon of June 14, 1842, the column reached the ford of the Kansas. A rubber boat, twenty feet long and five broad, was unlimbered. A cart was wheeled on board and ferried to the north bank. The transporting proved to be slow work. At dusk several vehicles were still on the north bank and Frémont became impatient. He ordered two carts put on the boat at once. In midstream the boat upset.

Men plunged into the chocolate-colored water, trying to save what they could. The horses, in the meantime, had been swum across. The cattle were shoved in but they went downstream. Fat and heavy, they swam low, with only eyes, horns and nostrils above water. At last they climbed out on the south side. Darkness found Frémont's expedition wet, divided and disorganized. The men camped as best they could and looked at one another's fires across the stream.

Morning came. Frémont announced that he would spend the

lay getting his expedition together again. Kit Carson was ill from a night's exposure in wet clothes. The Frenchmen complained that the coffee was lost and asked how they could start on a long trip without coffee. Late in the day everyone's spirits brightened. Only part of the coffee was lost and Kit Carson began to feel better. On June 16 they set off again under an overcast sky. During the day heavy rainstorms doused them. Frémont, unable to take astronomical observations, ordered another day's halt. The men, restless with inactivity, prowled off across the prairie. They discovered a bank honeycombed with swallows' nests full of chittering fledglings. The old birds zoomed around on metallic wings. An unusual excitement attracted the men to one of the nests. They saw a prairie snake with a young swallow in its mouth. A well-placed shot brought down the viper. The men cut it open and counted eighteen young birds in its body.

At camp that evening a man rode up to the circled carts. He had come from a party of over a hundred Oregon emigrants, men, women and children, traveling some three weeks ahead of Frémont. The wagon train, the first party of any size to cross to Oregon, was in charge of Dr. Elijah White. The federal government had appointed him Indian agent in Oregon with instructions to enlist white home builders. The messenger from his train said that the wagons were piled high with household goods and furniture. Sickness, probably cholera, had broken out among the emigrants. A child had died and one of the women was very ill when he left. The messenger was taking the sad news back to the States. Frémont wrote a letter to Jessie and sent it out by the rider.

On June 20, 1842, the party crossed the Big Vermilion. Then the Big Blue! They saw their first antelope and Kit Carson brought in a fat deer. The country had changed noticeably. Prairie sod was replaced by sagebrush. Frémont noted in his journal: "The *artemisia*, absinthe, or prairie sage, as it is variously called, is increasing in size, and glitters like silver, as the southern breeze turns up its leaves to the sun."[2] On June 22 the party nooned on the banks of the Little Blue. They saw the dead campfires of the Oregon emigrants, and one of the Frenchmen found a pack of playing cards lying loose on the ground. In the afternoon Frémont noted the first cactus. The expedition had reached Pawnee country now, and in the evening Lieutenant Frémont ordered guard mounted for the first time. Kit Carson and the two boys, Henry Brant and Randolph Benton, were assigned the watch from ten to midnight. The ordeal was almost too much for twelve-year-old Randy. Every shadow seemed to hold a crouching Pawnee, and Frémont heard his young brother-in-law calling out the guard almost constantly. The next morning the men got up asking one another about the Indian alarms. As they talked someone spied a band of Indians, sure enough, out on the plains. The rascals stood in line on their war horses and watched the whites, then scampered off, stopped, turned and looked again. Kit Carson leaped bareback on a fine horse and dashed forward, bareheaded, with his hair, powder horn and strap ends flying.

Frémont noted that this fringed rider, in moccasins and hunting shirt, was the finest picture of a natural horseman he had ever seen. Before long Kit Carson came back, his horse heaving for breath, Kit grinning. The Indians, he said, jumping to the ground, were a band of elk.

At last the travelers came to the place where the road left the Little Blue for the Platte, a twenty-mile hop without water. The men unloaded the kegs, dipped up water with their tin cups and poured it in the bungholes, then lifted the precious water into the carts. They jumped aboard, shouted to the teams and in due time reached the sand hills. Soon they came to the northern rim and looked down on the Platte's ribbon of sandy water stretching east and west from horizon to horizon. Across the quicksands they saw the dense forest of Grand Island.

Frémont estimated that they were about twenty miles from the island's head. The next evening they camped at the western tip. On the following day they met fourteen men walking down the Platte with packs on their backs. The wanderers said that they had left Fort Laramie two months ago to float down in barges. At Scotts Bluff the water became shallow. They had cached their furs and were now footing it to St. Louis. Buffalo, they said, would be found below the forks of the Platte this year, in fact only two days' march westward.

Frémont watched the fur men trudge off down the Platte to St. Louis—only six or seven hundred miles away. True to their prediction, the buffalo were soon found. The lieutenant, like all overland emigrants, was impressed and wrote in his journal:

In the sight of such a mass of life, the traveller feels a strange emotion of grandeur. We had heard from a distance a dull and confused murmuring, and, when we came in view of their dark masses, there was not one among us who did not feel his heart beat quicker. It was the early part of the day, when the herds are feeding; and everywhere they were in motion. Here and there a huge old bull was rolling in the grass, and clouds of dust rose in the air from various parts of the bands, each the scene of some obstinate fight.[3]

Kit Carson and Maxwell galloped off. Before returning they had killed three cows but suffered a bad accident. Kit's horse had fallen, thrown Kit, then scrambled to his feet and run away with the buffalo herd. Maxwell had raced after the excited horse. He had considered shooting him to get back the silver bridle bit but had finally caught the animal. Kit was well shaken but had broken no bones.

The next day a herd of buffalo came up from a water hole in the Platte and crossed a half mile in front of the wagons, grazing as they went. The wind was blowing downstream—from the buffalo to the men. Frémont ordered his hunting horse saddled. With Maxwell and Carson he cantered away. The wind would help hunters to get close before being smelled. The river bottom was wide and level enough for a good chase and the buffalo, full of water, would run slowly. Soon the herd saw the horsemen coming and broke into a rough amble. A few bulls in the rear stopped and faced the riders with tails high in the air, then turned, galloped after the herd a short way and turned to look again. Kit and Maxwell both knew that a buffalo was harmless until he elevated his tail—then look out, he was ready to charge.

The hunters approached within thirty yards of the rumbling herd. Frémont held his loaded rifle ready. The animals, full of water, grunted to one another as they lumbered along. Maxwell shouted for the charge, and the three men swept like dust devils into the moving mass. Blinded with dust, Frémont heard the buffaloes' horns knock and rattle together as they crowded away from him. His horse, a trained buffalo hunter, sprang like a tiger after a racing cow and ran shoulder to shoulder with her. Frémont pointed his gun at the line on the monster's side where the long hair stopped, then pulled the trigger. The cow fell headlong. Frémont checked his horse and turned back to his kill. He saw Kit Carson near by tying his horse to the horns of another dead buffalo. Beyond, he glimpsed Maxwell still with the herd. As he watched, a puff of white smoke told him that the third hunter had got his meat.

Living sumptuously on buffalo steaks, the party reached the forks of the Platte on July 2, 1842. The river was a mile wide but obviously not deep. The main channel seemed to come in from the north. The usual road went up the south side of South Platte to the crossing, but Frémont noticed a great meadow several miles long extending like a tongue between the forks. He intended to come down the North Fork in his rubber boat, and this was a good place to leave a cache to be picked up on the return trip. He ordered the column to cross to the meadow.

The quicksand was bad, trembling under the horses' feet. The riders spurred their mounts. Struggling, splashing and half falling, they reached the north bank. Word was sent back to the teamsters to come quickly, not to stop one instant lest the wheels sink into the treacherous holdfast sand, and not to follow in single file. The path became softer, more yielding, after every animal passed over it.

Amid shouts and a fusillade of popping whips the carts splashed through in echelon. Safely across, Frémont found the meadow was eighteen miles long. Mosquitoes hovered over the grass like mist. They settled on the horses. Bays, browns and sorrels became gray with insects. Horses and mules switched and stamped

DONNER LAKE FROM THE DIVIDE

CONTEMPORARY CONCEPTION OF DONNER LAKE ENCAMPMENT

MAIN STREET, SALT LAKE CITY, WHEN MARK TWAIN SAW IT

with pain. If Frémont slapped the neck of his mount, he left the print of his hand in blood from crushed mosquitoes. He ordered part of the men to turn out, bury a barrel of pork and catch up with the column. The main party moved as fast as they could up South Fork. Twenty-five miles above they encamped. The next day, July 3, they rode up to the crossing of the Overland Road, forty miles from the junction. July Fourth was declared a holiday. Frémont issued a liberal ration of liquor, macaroni soup, preserved fruitcake and coffee. With rich buffalo roast the men feasted.

On July 5, 1842, Frémont divided his party. The main group was ordered to cross to Ash Hollow, go up the Platte to Fort Laramie and wait. Frémont, with some friendly Cheyenne and three of his own party, including Maxwell, planned to scout along South Fork with a small pack outfit and mark locations for a possible chain of forts from the Arkansas to the American Fur Company's post at Laramie Creek.

Frémont observed strict military rank in his little party of six. At night the Indians slept like dogs around the fire. The white men rolled up in their blankets. The lieutenant ordered the rifles stacked and covered with rubber blankets to make a tent for himself. Napoleon is said to have resorted to a similar bivouac.

Frémont knew that there was a trading post owned by Ceran de St. Vrain about ten miles above the mouth of the Cache La Poudre (near where Greeley, Colorado, would be). He decided to go there, then swing along the edge of the mountains to Fort Laramie. One day as they rode they met three men, two white and Jim Beckwourth, the mulatto. Advancing years had given Jim a strong, aggressive face. He was still fond of big stories about being chief among the Crows, but he was content to work for a fur trader, Mr. Charbonneau, Sacagawea's Pompey grown to manhood. Mr. Charbonneau, Beckwourth explained, had attempted to float down from Fort St. Vrain with a load of furs but had run out of water. The shade was good under some big cottonwoods, so he camped. Jim pointed. "You'll find him if you keep goin' straight ahead," he can be imagined as saying.

Frémont rode on up the South Platte. Certainly these western rivers were not navigable. How would his rubber boat cope with them? On the plains, Frémont came to a party that looked like gypsies. The men were white, all free trappers, with Indian wives. Little bright-eyed "buffalo-fed boys" three or four years old tumbled about the camp. Their fathers talked with a New England nasal twang. They told the lieutenant that they had left Wyeth's Oregon expedition at the rendezvous, hadn't got back to New England yet but were on their way, 'lowed it might take them considerable time to get there, seein' as how things stood now—or something to this effect. Frémont noticed that they had accumulated a fine number of horses and mules.

Two miles beyond the quizzical Yankees, Frémont sighted Charbonneau's encampment on an island in the Platte. A Mexican employee of Charbonneau stood on the shore. He said that St. Vrain's fort was only forty miles above.

Frémont's party splashed across to the island. The half-breed proprietor was delighted to have company. Kindhearted like his mother Sacagawea, Pompey also inherited her small stature. Although he weighed 200 pounds he was only five feet six. Unlike the trappers who had been stranded at Scotts Bluff, he did not intend to hoof it to the settlements. He was comfortable where he was. He ordered a servant to gather mint leaves and prepare juleps for his guests. Frémont buried his nose in the pungent leaves. As he drank he noticed that these traders employed Spanish or Mexican help, whereas the fur men on the North Platte and the Missouri used Frenchmen. A young and attractive Spanish girl was pointed out as Beckwourth's wife. The rollicking mulatto always claimed that he had several squaws up among the Crows. Without doubt he had wives of various colors.

The next day Frémont reached Fort St. Vrain. The owner was as affable as Mr. Charbonneau had been. He even generously consented to sell Frémont two horses and three mules, one of them unmanageable, but Frémont did not find that out until the next day. Two trappers asked for Frémont's protection north to Fort Laramie. He took them, hired an extra Mexican and headed north to find a cutoff to Fort Laramie across the plains at the foot of the Rockies.

The going was smooth at first, with the high mountains on the riders' left, but near the place where the Wyoming-Colorado line would one day be, the mountains receded and the landmarks became confusing. Frémont uncased his compass and plotted a course like a mariner at sea. North, across the featureless plains, he led the way. A hot wind burned the riders' faces, but during the nights the men were refreshed by cool air. They crossed Crow Creek considerably east of where Cheyenne would stand, camped on Lodge Pole Creek, crossed several tributaries of Horse Creek far above the mouth where Stuart had wintered when this country was unknown in 1812. Riding through what the men told Frémont was Goshen's Hole, they came to the Platte a little after noon on a hot windy day. The animals thrust their noses deep into the cool green water. The men dismounted and rested under the trees. A plain track of several carts showed where their companions had passed a few days before. Frémont estimated that Fort Laramie must be about thirteen miles upstream.

The men loosened their horses' saddle girths and let them graze for two hours. Then they rode on. Soon tall, irregular Laramie Peak came into view, hazy and blue with the sun directly above it. Later, as the sun sank, the peak stood out black and flat as a silhouette. Evening shadows crept out of the bushes and a cool, refreshing breeze fanned wind-burned faces. At last they saw the tree-lined Laramie coming to join the Platte. At the junction stood a miserable cluster of unfinished cabins, built in the form of a U open toward the river. "That's not the American Fur Company's," Frémont no doubt was told. "That's Sybille & Adams' Fort Platte. Looks like somebody had tried to turn around and had upset, don't it?"

The tired men rode forward. Upriver some two miles they saw the whitewashed walls of an imposing structure with bastions and palisades. Peaked Sioux tepees stood around the fort. Horses were seen on the flat. A tiny rider trotted along a trail, raising a comet's tail of dust. The riders came to the Laramie ford, splashed through, climbed up the ten-foot west bank and stopped in front of the fort gate. Frémont handed his letters of introduction to a stout, bluff little Frenchman who was evidently in command. Bordeau could not read, but he bellowed to the mongrel servants about the place, invited Frémont to dismount and enter the compound. The pompous little fellow said that the lieutenant's men had arrived three days ago and were now encamped on the creek above the fort.

Frémont rode off to see his party. He found Herr Preuss smoking a German pipe excitedly. On the way up the Platte, Preuss said, they had met the great trapper, Jim Bridger, with a party of mountain men. Bridger had told them that the Sioux, Cheyenne and Gros Ventres had all combined to keep the whites out of the upper country. The savages were now in the neighborhood of Red Buttes, the famous landmark northeast of the Fiery Narrows. They had declared war on every living thing west of that point. Bridger said that he had got past them by following a little-known path through the Laramie Mountains. Preuss did not like the look of things. Some of his Frenchmen had wanted to quit at once, but he had got all of them to come as far as the fort.

Frémont went to his tent to fret about the future of his expedition. The long twilight peculiar to the Rockies illuminated the plains and the whitewashed fort with the theatrical glow of a Wyoming sunset. Darkness came abruptly. In the morning Frémont walked down to the fort to learn more about this Indian menace. The great gate stood ajar under a two-story blockhouse. In the compound Frémont looked around. The fifteen-foot adobe walls were lined with rooms opening into the court. Sixteen men with their Indian wives lived here. Half-breed children peered at Frémont from dark entrances, sweet with the spiced earthy air of dugouts. In a large "store," blankets, calico, powder, lead, glass beads, looking glasses and vermilion were for sale, also alcohol diluted with water. After days in the desert the fort seemed restful and attractive. The Indian women kept it clean and well swept.

Frémont sat down with the long-haired fort "gentlemen" on a bench in the entryway behind the gate. The blockhouse overhead made welcome shade. A breeze, cool on the hottest days, always blew here, and the loungers could see what was going on both in the fort and outside. The *bourgeois,* or factor, told Frémont that Jim Bridger's story was the truth and there was much more to it. A party of sixty traders had fought a pitched battle with the Sioux on Snake River last August. Eight or ten warriors had been killed, and the Indians had accounted for four whites, including the leader. Jim Bridger had brought out the survivors. All the past winter the Sioux had beaten war drums for revenge. The Oregon emigrants ahead of Frémont had come straggling into Fort Laramie in small independent parties, complaining that their companions were too fast or too slow, too domineering or too shiftless. At Fort Laramie they learned about the Indian danger. For a week they waited. All arrived and reunited for protection. They traded off their wagons and fine cattle—over a hundred Durhams—for second-rate Indian ponies. The *bourgeois* did not seem to regret the opportunity for a bargain. After the exchange the emigrants had hired Fitzpatrick. With him they went forward, but near Independence Rock the Indians had stopped them. A night of war council followed. Broken Hand's great influence with the Indians had let the emigrants pass, but it was doubtful if any others would get through.

Frémont did not like to think that the United States Army might be held up by rumors of Indians on the warpath. He ordered his horse and rode down to the Sybille, Adams & Company fort at the forks. Here he heard the same story over again, but one of the traders, Joseph Bisonette, a squaw man who spoke French fluently, agreed to accompany the lieutenant as interpreter. Bisonette said that he would join the column when it was ready to start.

Back at his camp once more, Frémont announced that the expedition would go forward at once. Kit Carson, in mischief or malice, made and signed his will, thus upsetting the French *voyageurs'* nerves. Many wanted to go home. Frémont lined them up, preached to them about bravery and offered to let cowards resign. Only one man stepped out of ranks. The remainder were ordered to prepare for the trip. To make the loads lighter Frémont discarded many instruments and all his field notes. A special thermometer that he had brought to test the common belief that water boiled at a lower temperature in high altitudes had broken and thus eliminated itself. Two chronometers, bulky and delicate, were set aside. Then Frémont broached bad news to Brant and young Randolph Benton. They would have to stay at the fort. The lieutenant explained that he did not want to expose them to the dangers ahead. He impressed Randolph with the responsibility of winding the chronometers every day.

Frémont added to his equipment an Indian conical lodge twenty feet high. He had found skin tepees much better in the wind than a canvas tent. For some reason mosquitoes did not enter them, and on hot days the sides could be lifted at the bottom so as to allow a breeze to cool the inside.

On July 21, 1842, the men were ready. Frémont rode to the fort ahead of his men. The *bourgeois* invited him into one of the adobe rooms for a stirrup cup. This bit of hospitality pleased the lieutenant. A little luxury went well with the prospect of days on the wind-swept range lands. Indians crowded around the door. Bordeau screamed to them to stay away. He stationed a guard to keep them off. It was no use. A group of finely dressed powerful-looking fellows shouldered aside the watchman and stepped with moccasined feet into the cool, cellarlike room. One of them handed Frémont a letter. The lieutenant unfolded the paper. In French he read a formal warning from the Sioux not to go up the Platte until the war parties now in the upper country came back. The note had been written by a clerk down at the lower fort for Joseph Bisonette. The interpreter could not write.

The chiefs spoke, one by one. The lieutenant must not go! Their young men would surely fire on him without warning, the Indians said.

Frémont replied that the Great White Father would revenge tenfold any accident to him. Let them send one of their young men to scout ahead and tell war parties that he was not an enemy. He, Frémont, would pay such scouts appropriately.

The chiefs began rebuttal arguments. Frémont walked away, mounted his horse and ordered his men to march. That night they pitched camp on Horseshoe Creek. The men had trouble putting up the new leather tepee. Over the ridge came Bisonette, his young Indian wife and a Sioux scout. They were going with the whites into the dangerous country. Bisonette's squaw laughed at the awkward white men and showed them how women pitched a tepee.

Frémont noticed a change in the country immediately above Fort Laramie. The flat plains turned into rolling foothills. The carts rumbled along, crushing the aromatic sagebrush, filling the air with an odor of camphor and turpentine. Frémont thought the smell might be good for consumption. He noticed that the forage up here was less plentiful. A drought had parched and wrinkled the whole country. The scant grass crisped underfoot. A little spray of grasshoppers leaped and crackled ahead of any man who stepped out of the road. Frémont feared that his horses were in for a hard time.

On July 23 the scouts dashed back to the column shouting, "Indians!" Frémont turned down the ridge toward the Platte to make a stand near water. On the river bluff he placed his carts in a rude corral with the horses hobbled and picketed inside. Then Frémont sent Bisonette and the Indian brave out to talk with the red men. Next he ordered all the guns fired and reloaded. Men were placed in defensive positions along the riverbank, alert and watching. The flag was hoisted gallantly. All waited.

Four men appeared on horseback. The defenders leveled their rifles. Frémont sighted through his telescope. "Hold your fire, it's Bisonette."

The interpreter and the young brave from Laramie Creek galloped in with two Indians—sullen savages, naked for war. The four men rode into the cart corral and dismounted, sitting with rifles across their laps. Frémont asked them questions. Bisonette translated. The Sioux said that their main party was out yonder over the hill. They had all been part of the warrior band that stopped the emigrants near Independence Rock. The Indians had quarreled that night among themselves. Some wanted to fight the whites, some wanted to let them go. Before morning the Indians were on the point of fighting one another. They had let the emigrants go in peace, but the disgruntled tribesmen had broken into a dozen war parties of ten and twenty each. These were scouring the country, hunting for enemies to kill, scalps to bring back to their villages. Some were raiding into Crow country over on Wind River.

Frémont gave his guests each a twist of tobacco. They took the present and smiled wanly, but Frémont noticed that they were nervous, trembling with emotion. He saw, too, that their sullen eyes noted the good guns in his command and the evident preparation for a siege.

The two warriors sprang onto their horses and rode away. Out of sight the whites heard a rifle shot. Scouts crept forward. They learned that the truculent guests had gone, but one of them had given way to his bad humor by killing his own horse.

Frémont ordered the march resumed. With the flag flying defiantly, whips popping, Frenchmen swearing, *"Avance donc, enfant de garce!"* they came to the ford of the Platte on July 28, 1842. The water was low and they crossed without getting the beds of the carts wet. Frémont tested several other fords for his military report, but decided that the usual road crossed on the best one. A short way above, the scouts reported Indians again. Frémont halted and sent forward his emissaries. They came back with a party of red men. These fellows were not sullen or aggressive. They said that they were out of food. They had had little to eat since the big council with Fitzpatrick and the emigrants. No buffalo were on the range to the westward.

Bisonette turned to Frémont and told him in French that it was foolish to go farther. He for one had hired to go only to the Red Buttes. Frémont paid off Bisonette and his red companion and watched them ride away with the Indians toward the buffalo range and Fort Laramie. When they were out of sight Frémont dismantled his carts, buried them in the sand near the Platte, and with his equipment on pack animals struck off for Sweetwater Valley. Kit Carson knew the way.

On August 7 they rode across South Pass with a chilly high-country drizzle smarting on their faces, slippery bridle reins in their wet, numb hands. This was the boundary of Oregon, as far as Frémont's instructions told him to go, but the lieutenant had more than enough rations to get back, and the summer was scarcely half over. Frémont never liked to be held down closely by orders. After all, he was to explore along the route, and a little side trip into the mountains was in line of duty. He ordered the column to leave the familiar tracks of Dr. White's emigrant party and skirt north along the Wind River Mountains. For hours the horsemen rode along close to the mountain wall. South and west the plains stretched away endlessly. The road to Oregon and California—Sublette's Cutoff—traversed that purple ocean of sage. Dim mountains appeared like clouds on the southwest horizon. Night came. The men camped at the foot of the steep slope. In the morning the sun, hidden from the campers by the mountain wall behind them, lighted the distant peaks like a tiara of glittering jewels—glistening snow fields held aloft by long rocky claws. The whole company watched and shivered in the chilly air. Preuss said in broken English that there was no view like it in all Europe. Frémont, the scientist, noticed that the thermometer had dropped a few degrees since daylight. The warm sunshine on distant rocks started a breeze that contracted the mercury in the tube. A half hour passed before the first warm sun rays reached the camp. Then suddenly the tarpaulins, ropes and rubber blankets that had been stiff with cold, softened. It was hard to believe that only a few minutes before the air had been uncomfortable.

Frémont believed the Wind River Mountains to be the watershed of the continent, the divide between the Colorado, the Columbia, the Missouri and the Platte. He was right, but because the four great river systems headed there he made the mistake of believing that they must be the highest mountains on the continent. With this in mind, he led the way north for more than fifty miles along the range, rode back into the green country of lakes, fragrant forests and spongy hillsides under banks of perpetual snow. Frémont climbed what he believed to be the highest peak in the Rockies, planted an American flag there, and of course named it Mount Frémont. He might have gone farther, but his instructions did not call for this detour and he was getting short of rations. Two new animals interested him—mountain goats and a strange little rodent. High in the crags above timber line he heard a chirp that sounded like a kid. Finally he saw a tailless, short-eared little hare at the foot of a rockslide—the cony or Little Chief. Frémont called it "a Siberian squirrel."

The mountain detour consumed ten days. On August 18, 1842, Frémont was back on the Oregon Trail. He turned east along the dim tracks left by the westbound emigrants. Four days later his party came to Independence Rock again. The coffee was all gone, but buffalo ranged all around. The hunters were kept busy, for the crew normally ate two carcasses every twenty-four hours. With ribs and humps roasting around the fire, the Frenchmen sang and laughed. Frémont let them feast and loaf around the elephantine rock. He engraved a large cross on the dark granite surface and covered the incision with a preparation of India-rubber boat patching.

Perhaps Frémont had exceeded his instructions in making a ten-day detour to name the highest mountain he could find for himself. If so, he now atoned for it by obeying with military exactness another part of his traveling orders. He had brought a rubber boat to test the feasibility of floating back from South Pass. The Sweetwater was a small stream. Common sense would have told most men who saw it in August that the creek was not navigable for a twenty-foot craft. However, his instructions were explicit so Frémont inflated the pontoons with air. Dutifully he recorded in his report that he did so "in obedience to my instructions."[4] With a load of supplies and a crew of men including Charles Preuss, Frémont embarked—if wading beside a boat may be dignified with such a verb. For about two miles they dragged the ungainly craft through pools and across gravel bars. Then Frémont concluded that he had made the effort required by his instructions. The men let out the air and rode with the main party to the Platte.

The two streams made a river large enough for a twenty-foot boat. Part of the men were sent downstream with the pack ani-

mals to an island that they all remembered. The remainder
launched the pneumatic boat and once more shoved off. Soon
they were in the canyon known 100 years later as Pathfinder
Reservoir. Through this and the Fiery Narrows below they
guided the boat, cautiously at first with ropes from shore.
Stuart, looking down from the rim in 1812, had recorded a foam-
tossed rapid, sucking the river over a thousand-foot fall with mist
rising from the depths like smoke. Frémont noticed that the walls
loomed higher as his men progressed. In some places the cliff
dropped precipitously into the stream and made trouble for the
men on the bank. Occasionally the current jerked the cables
from their hands. At the heads of rapids Frémont saw breakers
racing up the comb of the stream. The buoyant boat leaped forward as though alive, and went down the current in a shower of
spray. Frémont noticed that the rubber boat glided over submerged rocks that would have punctured and wrecked a wooden
hull. He decided that he had made a great discovery. A buoyant
rubber craft was just the thing for rapid western rivers. Perhaps
he had been overcautious having linemen on the shore. Certainly
they retarded the boat's speed and were themselves in trouble
most of the time trying to find footing or having the ropes
snatched from their hands. Frémont ordered everyone to leap
aboard. They would sail gloriously through these painted canyons.

Away they went into a gloomy slit between the mountain
walls. The Frenchmen chanted a boat song. At the end of each
stanza all hands, including Frémont, chimed in with the chorus.
The speed, the passing walls, the strip of sky overhead, added
zest to the excitement. Suddenly the rubber boat turned over. In
an instant the lieutenant saw boxes, books and bales of blankets
leaping and rolling away downstream. He recognized the sole-
leather case of the sextant, the long black box of the telescope.
Then he, too, went head over heels into the roaring water. A
good swimmer, he righted himself in the current, reached an
eddy and climbed ashore. He saw Preuss on the bank twenty
yards below crawling out on all fours like a drenched otter with
water pouring from his clothes. Across the stream he saw the
Frenchmen. One fellow was towing in a comrade by his long

hair. Another had clutched Frémont's double-barreled shotgun with drowning tenacity and still held it. Downstream, the boat lay bottomside up against a ledge. Boulders, big as log cabins, blocked its passage and the water ran between them in myriad milltails. Above the roar of the river Frémont shouted and motioned for the men to climb up the walls of the canyon, 500 feet high. He started up and noticed that he had lost a moccasin. On top, the men limped along the rim. After dark they found the camp of their friends who had gone around with the horses.

The next day Frémont sent one man back to get the few things rescued from the wreck. With the main party he rode down to the cache, dug up the carts, drove on to the Platte Crossing and made a night camp. He had noticed one thing in the canyon that explained the peculiar characteristic of western quicksand. Mica seemed to be plentiful at the heads of these rivers and when reduced to sand each tiny flake had two flat sides. When water flowed through this sand the grains would be loose or "quick," like quicksand, but when the water was pressed out from between the flat surface the tiny particles would adhere to one another as solidly as rock. Everyone knew that western quicksand let an animal down until the weight of his body pressed the sand. Then, before the unfortunate beast realized it, he was cemented in a substance hard as rock and held fast to struggle until death. A man with a pick and shovel could not free the beast, but a few buckets of water would soften the cement and let it escape.

Below the crossing, Frémont marveled at the change in the country since he had left it a few weeks before. Recent rains had greened the hills. The whole aspect of the range was different. The horses and mules took on new life from the fresh feed. With the American flag flying, the canvas-covered carts rolled down the upland plains. On the last day of August they reached Fort Laramie after an absence of just forty-two days. The traders saluted them with repeated charges of the cannon and Frémont replied with rifle volleys. The adobe fort, which had seemed primitive to him in the spring, now appeared very luxurious.

Brant and Randolph Benton were both in good health and they had presumably kept the chronometers wound. The September weather was ideal for traveling and everybody made ready. The little train pulled out down the Platte eager for home. The expedition passed Scotts Bluff, Chimney Rock and Court House Rock. The Platte was sometimes a mile wide, but the men and horses crossed it at will, seldom finding the water more than a few inches deep—truly a river flowing bottomside up. At Ash Hollow Frémont picked up a cache Preuss had left there, and at the forks of the Platte below he dug up the barrel of buried pork.

The Platte was noticeably larger below the forks. Frémont decided to make one more attempt to fulfill his instructions and navigate it—this time in a bullboat. He sent his men out to kill some buffalo for the necessary hides. The proper framework for a bullboat eight by five was set up on the shore. Four hides were stretched on the frame, sewed, greased and left in the sun to dry and draw snug. The skin tightened quickly. The boatmen tested the skins with their fists. Soon a blow on the bloodshot surface sounded like a loose drumhead. Frémont ordered his men to roll the craft over. She looked seaworthy. The main party was ordered to take the horses downstream twenty miles and camp. Frémont, with Preuss and two other men, shoved off, grounded, stepped out, floated clear and pushed off again. Occasionally they all had to lift the craft across bars and drag it along the sandy beach. After three or four miles Frémont gave up in disgust. "No wonder the Indians call this stream the Nebraska or Shallow Water," he said.

A broad road down the left bank of the Platte made traveling easy for the wrecked mariners. Fifteen miles below they found their camp. On September 18, 1842, they came to the head of Grand Island, really more like a tree-grown delta than an island. Like the other travelers for a generation, Frémont estimated the size of Grand Island and announced that it was over fifty miles long and varied in width from one to two miles. Frémont noted, too, that this would be a good place for an Army fort, the last wood on the road up from Council Bluffs and the natural junction for the road from Westport and the lower Missouri.

Frémont's trip was almost over. To save time he sent three men ahead down the Platte to Bellevue with instructions for the construction of a boat to carry his men down the Missouri to St. Louis. With his main party he came to the domed village of the Pawnee on September 22, 1842. The red men were harvesting corn. Frémont bought grain and also some vegetables—both great treats for men on a meat diet. Two more days' travel put Frémont at the Loup Crossing thirty miles below. The stream was running full and clear and the ford looked bad. Frémont camped two days, waiting for the water to go down. Then he ventured into the stream. Although water flowed through the bottoms of his carts all crossed without accident.

No more obstacles lay ahead of the travelers. On September 30 they camped on the brushy bank of the great Missouri. Frémont arose before daylight the next morning. Across the majestically eddying river he heard tinkling cowbells. The sound made him sentimental. Civilization at last and Jessie waiting.

At Bellevue the boat was almost completed. The expedition's horses, carts and equipment were sold at auction, and on October 4, 1842, the party floated away with ten men at the oars. At the mouth of the Kansas on October 10, they stopped to make astronomical observations. Just four months had passed since they left Cyprian Chouteau's house here. Another week on the river followed. Then, they nosed into the bank at St. Louis, ran the boat ashore and all jumped out for the last time.

Frémont paid off his *voyageurs* and took a steamboat for Washington. He arrived in the capital on October 29, 1842. A letter from Dr. White's overland expedition had had wide circulation. The doctor pronounced the route easy to follow. With wagons he had gone to Fort Hall, then taken packs. Frémont's report would confirm the ease of travel on the overland road. He hurried to get it printed for travelers. Everywhere people were preparing to go to Oregon. In August Daniel Webster had signed a treaty with Lord Ashburton defining the international boundary between the United States and Canada. No line had been agreed upon for the Oregon country. Without doubt the administration in Washington hoped to fill the Northwest with settlers and then drive a stiff boundary bargain.

An excitement called "Oregon fever" was spreading across the land. American love of adventure and the open road, the tradition of Daniel Boone and the Wilderness Trace into Kentucky, still gripped the minds of young men. The flood of propaganda about Oregon since the days of Hall Kelley was germinating a great restlessness in America. Good farms, an ideal climate, fortunes in fish—all combined to make it a personal duty to settle in the Pacific Northwest. Manifest destiny, rivalry with Great Britain—the old enemy of the Revolution—stimulated patriotism. True, land could be had in Missouri, Illinois, Iowa and many other border states, but times had been bad since the panic of 1837. The world market for grain seemed harder to reach from the upper Mississippi than from Oregon where ships could be loaded at the plantations—according to the propagandists.

Great patriotic meetings extolled the virtues of Oregon and the ease of driving there. Thousands gathered to hear the oratory at Springfield, Peoria and Alton in Illinois, at Chillicothe and Columbus in Ohio and at many other places. Overland companies were organized, men discussed proper equipment.

Obviously a great migration would start with the grass of 1843. Senator Thomas Hart Benton's Missouri constituents were going to profit mightily. Old Bullion had timed his agitation for the exploration of the trail with consummate foresight, even if Frémont had accomplished little except naming a peak for himself fifty miles off the road. People were sending to Washington for his report to carry with other guidebooks on the overland journey they planned to make next May. Senator Benton's son-in-law had won a name for himself. The senator seemed pleased. Come spring, it might be a good idea to send the young man west again to survey more trails. Besides, it would be pleasant to have Jessie at home where she belonged instead of dividing her with the young upstart.

---

1 John Charles Frémont, *Report of the Exploring Expedition to the Rocky Mountains in the Year 1842 and to Oregon and North California in the Years 1843-'44* (U. S. Senate Report No. 174, 28 Cong., 2d Sess., Washington, 1845), 10.

2 *Ibid.*, 14.

3 *Ibid.*, 19.

4 *Ibid.*, 72.

Chapter 10

The Great Migration: 1843

I N PLATTE COUNTY on the western border of Missouri, a young
lawyer, Peter H. Burnett, contracted "Oregon fever" during
the winter of 1842-1843. Although he may have believed
that he would be governor of a great state on the Pacific some
day, certainly his townspeople did not. Burnett's immediate ambition was to lead a wagon train of emigrants overland. He called
mass meetings, harangued about good land out west and people's
patriotic duty to keep "haughty Albion" out of Oregon. Burnett's neighbors were wagonmen and frontier farmers, well
suited for the great journey. New farms and buffalo promised
great adventures. The growing political agitation over slavery
disgusted some men and they turned toward a new country
where old prejudices should be forgotten. The recent financial
panic tore loose other men's ties, made many dissatisfied. Most
of the emigrants had some means. They owned wagons and cattle. During the winter months of 1842-1843 they planned the
overland trip, and when spring broke they loaded their camp outfits into their wagons and set off for Independence, Missouri.

The outfitting villages below the mouth of the Kaw had grown
amazingly. Trading stores, blacksmith, harness and saddle shops
were crowded with impatient travelers. The fur brigades and
even the Santa Fe trains were no longer the great topics of conversation, but here and there a mountain man in beaded buckskin
attracted attention. Boys ran after him. Young men asked him
about redskins and scalps, watched his movements and dress, imi-
tated his vernacular: "Waugh!" Family heads busied themselves

with last-minute preparations and purchases. Hundreds of horses, oxen and mules came up the hill from the Kansas City wharf every day. Others trailed in along the dirt roads. The grass around the outfitting towns was trampled out before it had time to grow. Emigrants pushed on along the Santa Fe Trail and camped on the prairie. Burnett, with his wife on the front seat of a covered wagon, rumbled into the emigrants' camping ground on May 17, 1843. A large assemblage was ready to start. Burnett later wrote of it: "The moon shed her silvery light upon the white sheets of sixty wagons; a thousand head of cattle grazed upon the surrounding plain; fifty camp fires sent up their brilliant flames, and the sound of the sweet violin was heard in the tents."[1]

Burnett knew that the inhabitants of those sixty tents were all, like himself, politically minded. A man was going to have to watch his fences if he wanted to hold office here. Burnett had learned in Westport as he came through that Dr. Marcus Whitman was in town. The doctor had left the mission at Waiilatpu last October with one companion to ride to St. Louis. The American Board had sent orders to Oregon to discontinue some of the missions. Whitman had believed that a personal appeal would reverse the ruling. At Fort Hall he learned that the Indians had become dangerous. To evade them he rode far to the south, across the Uintah Basin of Utah and Grand River in Colorado to Taos, New Mexico. Lost in blizzards, Whitman and his Indian guides almost perished but eventually they reached Bent's Fort on the Santa Fe Trail and traveled to Missouri with a party of fur traders. At Washington he interviewed the Secretary of War and urged that Oregon be saved for the Union. Then he went on to plead his case before the Board. Now he was on his way back.

Peter Burnett walked from wagon to wagon talking about the advisability of inviting Dr. Whitman to join the great train. The missionary was a medical doctor, a minister of the Gospel and a man who knew the road. Surely the emigrants would not find a better pilot for the overland journey. Next day, May 18, the wagonmen assembled after chores and appointed a committee to wait on Marcus Whitman and invite him to join their expedition.

Dr. Whitman decided to go with the party. His life's ambition was to settle Oregon with Protestant Americans. To come back to Waiilatpu the leader of the largest wagon train yet to cross the continent would surely make Narcissa and the baby proud. For guide the expedition employed Captain John Gantt, army man, trapper, trader and onetime companion of Kit Carson.

There was much merrymaking and horseplay around the camp. A number of wags became conspicuous. A fellow named J. M. Ware walked among the wagons creating laughter. One of his stories concerned a Dutchman back in Kentucky named George Swartz. According to Ware's story the Dutchman failed repeatedly as a farmer and finally concluded to become a preacher. At a camp meeting he had addressed the congregation in a commanding voice: "Me tinks I hear my Savior say, 'Shorge, what you doin' up dar in dat bulpit?' Me say, 'Neber mind Shorge—he knows what he's 'bout—he's goin' breachin; brethren, let us bray.' "[2]

The story got funnier every time Ware told it. People began to laugh when they saw him coming. They wrote letters home to tell about how much fun they were all having.

On May 20, 1843, the wagon men decided to elect officers and adopt a constitution and bylaws, a procedure dear to all politically minded Americans. The wags were mainly interested in amusing their comrades but they made trouble for dignified citizens. George Wilkes, a New York journalist, remembered later that a dozen men wanted to distinguish themselves with oratory. Mr. Dumberton from Big Pidgeon, Tennessee, dressed in a snuff-colored suit began a "eulogium on the character of Washington; made patriotic allusions to the Revolution, and the late war; touched on the battle of New Orleans; apostrophised the American eagle, and then wound up his introduction with a very meaning sentiment leveled with great force and earnestness at the 'iron arm of despotism.' "[3] After capturing the ear of the assemblage he proposed—and eyewitnesses agree to this—that the emigrants should adopt the criminal laws of Missouri and Tennessee for guidance across the plains.

Many able speakers replied. One of the wags suggested that they take along a penitentiary. A code was adopted but the main election of officers was deferred. Parties of wagon travelers were still coming in daily and the little state on wheels did not yet have its full population. On May 22, the horde moved out to Elm Grove, a dogwood swamp on the prairie with two trees and no wood, according to one unhappy traveler. Eight miles farther they turned from the Santa Fe Trail near where Gardner, Kansas, would one day stand. Burnett felt that they were off at last. He pronounced the expedition "one of the most arduous and important trips undertaken in modern times."[4] But the officers were not yet elected. On May 26, they reached the Kansas River. The water was a quarter of a mile wide and too deep to ford. A Frenchman operated a rickety ferry at an exorbitant charge. The wagonmen called a mass meeting and for three days they debated. A majority agreed not to pay. They would build a ferry of their own. A few of them set to work to join canoes with planks. As they worked they learned that a minority of their fellows had dealt secretly with the Frenchman. The traitors rolled their wagons on to his barge. In the middle of the stream the craft foundered. By good luck none of the women and children drowned but the disloyal people paid heavily for their treachery. Moreover, the democratic assemblage had become an aggregation of distrustful factions.

The improvised ferry put the main party across the Kansas in three days. More wagons came in continually from Westport, among them one with two Catholic priests traveling to the Flathead country. Burnett chafed at the confusion and disorder. He counted over a hundred wagons, 5,000 cattle, 260 men, 130 women and 610 children, all moving with no system, no organization, no one willing to take orders, no one to stand guard at night. What would happen when they reached the Indian country?

On June 1, 1843, the people decided to form a government. An election was held. Peter Burnett was chosen captain—a great honor for so young a man. James W. Nesmith, later a senator from Oregon, was elected orderly sergeant, and nine other men were chosen for a council. Every able-bodied man registered and the officers divided them into guards. Camp sites were selected in advance and the wagons parked in a hollow square with the rough discipline which Gantt said was used by fur traders.

Movement and organization did not stop the quarrels. Men who had not been elected to office complained about the management. Men who owned no cattle objected to herding animals in which they had no interest. There was continual grumbling and much shirking of duties. Then the clear weather changed to the daily torrents common on the plains. On June 5 and 6 the great party crossed the two forks of the Blue. Both streams were running high but they were forded by jacking the wagons up on the bolsters. The weight of the loads held the wheels on the bottom. One night black clouds came up out of the horizon and a storm broke with terrible fury. Half the tents blew down. A sheet of water flooded the entire camp. With dawn the emigrants loaded the wagons and splashed off. Gantt ordered everybody off the road and onto a new route where they would find dry ground. Wet and hungry, the men laid their misfortunes on the shoulders of Peter Burnett.

Out on the plains they met a war party of Osage and Kansas Indians, about ninety of them with shaved heads and painted faces. The scamps displayed a Pawnee scalp and said that they had not eaten for three days. They wanted food. The emigrants gave them a calf and corn meal. The incident took some of the men's minds off their injustices but in the night another thunderstorm flooded the camp. On June 8 it rained again, a cloudburst with gusts of rain ripping along the flooded road and beating into the covered wagons. The cowboys who had no interest in the big herd refused to guard it any longer. This was mutiny. Burnett, future governor of California, resigned in disgust from the presidency of what he had so proudly called "one of the most arduous and important trips undertaken in modern times."

The great cavalcade split into two parties, the Light Column with few or no loose cattle and the Cow Column, the big herd. Each elected a separate captain. The Light Column chose William Martin; the Cow Column, Jesse Applegate. Jesse was tall, wiry, grim. He had attended Shurtleff College in Illinois, understood surveying and in 1845 would open what was known as the Applegate Cutoff for wagons from the Humboldt down the Willamette to the Columbia. Dictatorial by nature, nonco-operative, he succeeded where the democratic principles of Peter Burnett failed. Jesse Applegate did things. He cared nothing for oratory.

The two columns remained close enough to communicate and they soon forgot their animosity. They split again and again, eventually traveling as four companies. Their rocking whitetops met and passed four wagons coming down the road from Fort Laramie. The drivers were long-haired mountaineers in fringed shirts and moccasins—Waugh!—very different from farmer-emigrants. The wagons from the mountains were loaded with buffalo robes trembling like loads of hay. As pets they brought a few buffalo calves—small hints of the great herds ahead. The traders passed them with a nod and wave of the hand. Then the monotonous horizon encircled the emigrants once more. Marcus Whitman rode back and forth along the line of wagons. He asked about the health of the women and gave advice to the men. Determined and always optimistic beyond the bounds of judgment, Whitman revived flagging spirits merely by his tonic presence.

On the night of June 10, 1843, word passed from fire to fire that outriders had seen the body of an Indian with head cut off and scalp gone. He was undoubtedly the victim of the Osage war party. On June 12 a flurry of shouts from wagon to wagon excited the whole party. Captain Gantt and a few companions had killed a buffalo bull. With horse pistols they had chased him and fired seven balls into the huge animal before he fell. The buffalo range was still far ahead. Had one strayed from the herds? In winter buffalo sometimes came over here to eat the rushes in the Blue. Perhaps he had been left behind. The dead bison was very old and thin. Pieces of his meat were distributed among the wagons. The men did not think much of their first buffalo steak.

Three days later hunters brought in an antelope. The dainty little animal was not big enough to feed many but everybody knew now that they were nearing the game country. Next day an excited prongbuck ran the full length of the caravan close enough for everybody to see the broad stripes on its neck, the black, hooked horns and the white disc of rump. Dogs ran out barking furiously but none was able to keep pace with the little racer. People told one another later that an antelope ran so fast its legs seemed to blur like a hummingbird's wings.

On June 17 the rear teamsters saw a party of horsemen over-taking them—Pawnee coming back from a buffalo hunt in the south. The red men rode past half-insolently, mocking the emi-grants by shouting at them, "Gee-haw-whoa." The Indians had a great quantity of jerked buffalo meat. They gave this freely to the travelers. The Pawnee were rough-looking fellows but they had adopted some of the white man's culture. They had guns, wore clothes and, unlike the shaved-headed Osage, they cut their hair like white men. The teamsters told them about the Kansas war party and its scalp. Immediately savagery gleamed in the Pawnee eyes.

On June 18 the long cavalcade left the Blue to cross the divide along a fine level road. At sundown they reached the top of the sand hills and beheld the vast valley of the Platte. The men set their brakes and with screaming wheels jolted down to the bot-tom where they camped without wood or water two miles from the river. In the morning they hooked up before breakfast and rolled on to the Platte, cut willows for fuel, cooked and ate a hearty meal.

They had struck the Platte at the head of Grand Island. The channel appeared to be at least two miles broad. Across the waste of wet sand they noticed a fringe of trees. The country seemed entirely different from the bare bank on which they encamped. Far beyond, the distant sand hills appeared like those on the south side. The emigrants estimated that the river bottom must be fif-teen to twenty miles across. The road turned and went up the Platte. Grass grew stirrup-high. Antelope lifted their heads above the forage and barked alarm. They did not run here as they did on the plains. They jumped with stiff-legged bounds in the tall grass.

The teamsters watched the sand hills endlessly. On them,

Gantt said, the first buffalo would be seen. The drivers noticed hundreds of trails from the bluffs to the river. Grooved like corduroy, some of the paths were six and eight inches deep. The wagon wheels jolted over them, jostling the loads, making the canvas wagon covers wrinkle and flap on their bows. Buffalo chips became plentiful. Whitman told the travelers how to dig a ditch for burning them. Occasionally a rider came in dragging a stick of driftwood with his saddle rope. At night that man's cheery campfire would attract many visitors in the gloomy chip-burning camp.

For four days the men watched the bluffs for buffalo. Then on June 22, 1843—they marked the date in their journals and wrote it on wagon boxes—buffalo were sighted. On the green-sward near the river grazed fifty of the shaggy animals. A party of horsemen galloped toward them and killed two, not enough to go around but a good beginning, and from then on buffalo were killed almost continually. Every wagon had its heavy chunk meat. Gantt showed the Easterners how to hang it high at night and let it chill in the cool air, then wrap it in the bedding during the heat of the day.

A grand buffalo hunt in sight of the entire train occurred on June 27. The wagons were parked at noon a half mile from the river. On the opposite bank seven large bulls appeared walking deliberately upstream. Opposite the wagons they turned and marched straight across the wet sand. All the men got their guns and ran toward the bank, spreading out like a fan. The buffalo paid no attention and came on slowly. When within range all the men fired, a terrific bombardment. Three or four of the monsters fell; the rest, though obviously wounded, galloped off.

Jesse Applegate, with the Cow Column, luxuriated in the daily routine of his command. Thirty-three years later, in 1876, he read before the Oregon Pioneer Association the following classic account of a typical day's march:

It is four o'clock A.M.; the sentinels on duty have discharged their rifles—the signal that the hours of sleep are over—and every wagon and tent is pouring forth its night tenants, and slow-kindling smokes begin largely to rise and float away in the morning air. Sixty men start from the corral, spreading as they make through the vast herd of cattle and horses that make a semicircle around the encampment, the most distant perhaps two miles away.

The herders pass to the extreme verge and carefully examine for trails beyond, to see that none of the animals have strayed or been stolen during the night. This morning no trails led beyond the outside animals in sight, and by 5 o'clock the herders begin to contract the great, moving circle, and the well-trained animals move slowly towards camp, clipping here and there a thistle or a tempting bunch of grass on the way. In about an hour five thousand animals are close up to the encampment, and the teamsters are busy selecting their teams and driving them inside the corral to be yoked. The corral is a circle one hundred yards deep, formed with wagons connected strongly with each other; the wagon in the rear being connected with the wagon in front by its tongue and ox chains. It is a strong barrier that the most vicious ox cannot break, and in case of an attack of the Sioux would be no contemptible intrenchment.

From 6 to 7 o'clock is a busy time; breakfast is to be eaten, the tents struck, the wagons loaded and the teams yoked and brought up in readiness to be attached to their respective wagons. All know when, at 7 o'clock, the signal to march sounds, that those not ready to take their proper places in the line of march must fall into the dusty rear for the day.

There are sixty wagons. They have been divided into fifteen divisions or platoons of four wagons each, and each platoon is entitled to lead in its turn. The leading platoon today will be the rear one tomorrow, and will bring up the rear unless some teamster, through indolence or negligence, has lost his place in the line, and is condemned to that uncomfortable post. It is within ten minutes of seven; the corral but now a strong barricade is everywhere broken, the teams being attached to the wagons. The women and children have taken their places in them. The pilot (a borderer who has passed his life on the verge of civilization and has been chosen to the post of leader from his knowledge of the savage and his experience in travel through roadless wastes), stands ready, in the midst of his pioneers and aids, to mount and lead the way. Ten or fifteen young men, not today on duty, form another cluster. They are ready to start on a buffalo hunt, are well mounted and well armed, as they need be, for the unfriendly Sioux have driven the buffalo out of the Platte, and the hunters must ride fifteen or twenty miles to reach them. The cow drivers are hastening, as they get ready, to the rear of their charge, to collect and prepare them for the day's march.

It is on the stroke of seven; the rush to and fro, the cracking of whips, the loud command to oxen, and what seemed to be the inextricable confusion of the last ten minutes has ceased. Fortunately every one has been found and every teamster is at his post. The clear notes of a trumpet sound in the front; the pilot and his guards mount their horses; the leading divisions of the wagons move out of the encampment, and take up the line of march; the rest fall into their places with the precision of clock work, until the spot so lately full of life sinks back into that solitude that seems to reign over the broad plain and rushing river as the caravan draws its lazy length towards the distant El Dorado. It is with the hunters we shall briskly canter towards the bold but smooth and grassy bluffs that bound the broad valley, for we are not yet in sight of the grander but less beautiful scenery (of Chimney Rock, Court House and other bluffs, so nearly resembling giant castles and palaces), made by the passage of the Platte through the highlands near Laramie. We have been traveling briskly for more than an hour. We have reached the top of the bluff, and now have turned to view the wonderful panorama spread before us. To those who have not been on the Platte, my powers of description are wholly inadequate to convey an idea of the vast extent and grandeur of the picture, and the rare beauty and distinctness of the detail. . . .

We are full six miles away from the line of march; though everything is dwarfed by distance, it is seen distinctly. The caravan has been about two hours in motion and is now as widely extended as a prudent regard for safety will permit. First, near the bank of the shining river is a company of horsemen; they seem to have found an obstruction, for the main body has halted while three or four ride rapidly along the bank of the creek or slough. They are hunting a favorable crossing for the wagons; while we look they have succeeded; it has apparently required no work to make it passable, for all but one of the party have passed on, and he has raised a flag, no doubt a signal to the wag-

ons to steer their course to where he stands. The leading teamster sees him, though he is yet two miles off, and steers his course
directly towards him, all the wagons following in his track. They
(the wagons) form a line three-quarters of a mile in length;
some of the teamsters ride upon the front of the wagons, some
march beside their teams; scattered along the line companies of
women are taking exercise on foot; they gather bouquets of rare
and beautiful flowers that line the way; near them stalks a stately
greyhound, or an Irish wolf dog, apparently proud of keeping
watch and ward over his master's wife and children. Next comes
a band of horses; two or three men or boys follow them, the
docile and sagacious animals scarce needing this attention, for
they have learned to follow in the rear of the wagons, and know
that at noon they will be allowed to graze and rest. Their knowledge of time seems as accurate as of the place they are to occupy
in the line, and even a full-blown thistle will scarce tempt them
to straggle or halt until the dinner hour has arrived. Not so with
the large herd of horned beasts that bring up the rear; lazy, selfish and unsocial. . . . Through all the long day their greed is never
satisfied, nor their thirst quenched, nor is there a moment of re-
laxation of the tedious and vexatious labors of their drivers,
although to all others the march furnishes some reason of relaxa-
tion or enjoyment. For the cow-drivers there is none.

But from the standpoint of the hunters, the vexations are not
apparent; the crack of whips and loud objurgation are lost in the
distance. Nothing of the moving panorama, smooth and orderly
as it appears, has more attractions for the eye than that vast square
column in which all colors are mingled, moving here slowly and
there briskly, as impelled by horsemen riding furiously in front
and rear. . . .

The pilot, by measuring the ground and timing the speed of
the wagons and the walk of his horses, has determined the rate of
each, so as to enable him to select the nooning place, as nearly as
the requisite grass and water can be had at the end of five hours'
travel of the wagons. Today, the ground being favorable, little
time has been lost in preparing the road, so that he and his pioneers are at the nooning place an hour in advance of the wagons,
which time is spent in preparing convenient watering places for
the animals, and digging little wells near the bank of the Platte,
as the teams are not unyoked, but simply turned loose from the

wagons, a corral is not formed at noon, but the wagons are drawn up in columns, four abreast, the leading wagon of each platoon on the left, the platoons being formed with that in view. This brings friends together at noon as well as at night.

Today an extra session of the council is being held, to settle a dispute that does not admit of delay, between a proprietor and a young man who has undertaken to do a man's service on the journey for bed and board. Many such engagements exist, and much interest is taken in the manner in which this high court, from which there is no appeal, will define the rights of each party in such engagements. The council was a high court in the most exalted sense. It was a senate composed of the ablest and most respected fathers of the emigration. It exercised both legislative and judicial powers, and its laws and decisions proved it equal and worthy of the high trust reposed in it. Its sessions were usually held on days when the caravan was not moving. It first took the state of the little commonwealth into consideration; revised or repealed rules defective or obsolete, and enacted such others as the exigencies seemed to require. The common weal being cared for, it next resolved itself into a court to hear and settle private disputes and grievances. The offender and the aggrieved appeared before it; witnesses were examined, and the parties were heard by themselves and sometimes by counsel. The judges being thus made fully acquainted with the case, and being in no way influenced or cramped by technicalities, decided all cases according to their merits. There was but little use for lawyers before this court, for no plea was entertained which was calculated to hinder or defeat the ends of justice. Many of these judges have since won honors in higher spheres. They have aided to establish on the broad basis of right and universal liberty two pillars of our great Republic in the Occident. Some of the young men who appeared before them as advocates have themselves sat upon the highest judicial tribunals, commanded armies, been governors of states and taken high position in the senate of the nation.

It is now one o'clock; the bugle has sounded and the caravan has resumed its westward journey. It is in the same order, but the evening is far less animated than the morning march; a drowsiness has fallen apparently on man and beast; teamsters drop asleep on their perches and even when walking by their teams, and the words of command are now addressed to the slowly creeping oxen in the soft tenor of women or the piping treble of children, while the snores of the teamsters make a droning accompaniment. But a little incident breaks the monotony of the march. An emigrant's wife, whose state of health has caused Doctor Whitman to travel near the wagon for the day, is now taken with violent illness. The Doctor has had the wagon driven out of the line, a tent pitched and a fire kindled. Many conjectures are hazarded in regard to this mysterious proceeding, and as to why this lone wagon is to be left behind. And we too must leave it, hasten to the front and note the proceedings, for the sun is now getting low in the west and at length the painstaking pilot is standing ready to conduct the train in the circle which he has previously measured and marked out, which is to form the invariable fortification for the night. The leading wagons follow him so nearly around the circle that but a wagon length separates them. Each wagon follows in its track, the rear closing on the front, until its tongue and ox-chains will perfectly reach from one to the other, and so accurate the measure and perfect the practice, that the hindmost wagon of the train always precisely closes the gateway, as each wagon is brought into position. It is dropped from its team (the teams being inside the circle), the team unyoked and the yokes and chains are used to connect the wagon strongly with that in its front. Within ten minutes from the time the leading wagon halted, the barricade is formed, the teams unyoked and driven out to pasture. Every one is busy preparing fires of buffalo chips to cook the evening meal, pitching tents and otherwise preparing for the night. There are anxious watchers for the absent wagon, for there are many matrons who may be afflicted like its inmate before the journey is over; and they fear the strange and startling practice of this Oregon doctor will be dangerous. But as the sun goes down the absent wagon rolls into camp, the bright, speaking face and cheery look of the doctor, who rides in advance, declare without words that all is well, and both mother and child are comfortable. . . .

It is not yet 8 o'clock when the first watch is to be set; the evening meal is just over, and the corral now free from the intrusion of cattle or horses, groups of children are scattered over it. . . . Before a tent near the river a violin makes lively music, and some youths and maidens have improvised a dance upon the green; in another quarter a flute gives its mellow and melancholy notes to the still night air, which, as they float away over the quiet river, seem a lament for the past rather than a hope for the future. It has been a prosperous day; more than twenty miles have been accomplished of the great journey. . . .

But time passes; the watch is set for the night; the council of old men has been broken up, and each has returned to his own quarter; the flute has whispered its last lament to the deepening night; the violin is silent, and the dancers have dispersed. . . . All is hushed and repose from the fatigues of the day, save the vigilant guard and the wakeful leader, who still has cares upon his mind that forbid sleep. He hears the 10 o'clock relief taking post and the "all well" report of the returned guard. . . . The last care of the day being removed, and the last duty performed, he too seeks the rest that will enable him to go through the same routine tomorrow.[5]

The cavalcade moved up the South Fork road and crossed to Ash Hollow on North Fork. The dry atmosphere began to shrink the wagons. Tires became loose. Some teamsters drove hoop iron between the fellies and the tires to tighten them. Others pounded in pine wedges crosswise. With such makeshifts they rattled past Chimney Rock and Scotts Bluff to Fort Laramie. The stream was too high to ford. From the forts the emigrants borrowed two small boats. They built a platform over them and the long slow job of unloading the wagons on the east side and reloading them on the west commenced. Most of the wagonmen stayed a day or two at the Sybille, Adams or American Fur Company's fort purchasing supplies, trading horses and fixing their wagons. Many men traded for buckskin shirts and moccasins and strutted around like mountain men. Waugh!

Peter Burnett priced articles in the American Fur Company store and jotted down the amounts: "Coffee and brown sugar, $1.50 per pint; flour, 25 cents per pound; powder, $1.50 per pound; lead, 75 cents per pound, percussion caps, $1.50 per box; calico (inferior quality), $1 per yard."[6]

The Sybille, Adams & Company fort at the forks seemed to be

doing more business than the elaborate American Fur Company establishment. With less money tied up in equipment, Bisonette's Indian ways brought in the trade. Then, too, Sir William Stewart, the indefatigable sportsman, was camped near by with a party of ninety-three pleasure seekers and their forty carts and three wagons well provisioned with food, wine and liquor. Among his guests were the son and the nephew of the great William Clark, who had died five years ago. Some of the old chiefs recognized young Clark from his resemblance to the "Redhead Chief." They gave a dog feast in his honor. Mr. Charbonneau, son of Sacagawea, Bird Woman, was also in the party, along with a group of Catholic missionaries. William Sublette, builder of the first fort here on the Laramie, had come with the tourists for his health. Tuberculosis was drawing away his vitality. Sir William made him honorary leader of the excursion. A prominent actor and newspaperman, Matt Field, scribbled in a notebook and recited *Hamlet* around the campfire. Stewart had also brought an artist to paint the Indians. In the center of the wagon square a flagpole had been erected. The Stars and Stripes were raised each morning with military formality. William Sublette recorded in his journal that the company consisted of "Individual gentlemen, Some of the armey, Some professional Gentlemen, Come on the trip for pleasure, Some for Health, etc. etc. So we had doctors, Lawyers, botanists, Bugg Ketchers, Hunters and men of nearly all professions, etc. etc. One half or rather more was hired men Belonging to Sir William, which he had employed on the trip."[7]

In addition to the regular traders at the two forts, others came in each summer from Taos with kegs of alcohol. To sell liquor to the Indians was against the law but the forts had to resort to it or be outtraded by the peddlers. Alcohol was diluted three to one and the emigrants noted that three cups of grog cost a buffalo robe. Even this price yielded unsatisfactory profits and rum sellers resorted to tricks to cheat the Indians. Some traders had two sizes of whisky cups, one for display and one for measuring out the liquor. Another trick of the trade was to dip up the drink in a cup half-filled with tallow. Then, too, as the purchaser became intoxicated the liquor seller invariably substituted Laramie Creek water for whisky at the same price.

Cheating, faulty scales, counterfeit money were all the order of the day back east in the States as well as out in the Indian country. Regulation would have been resented as socialistic. Men felt a pleasurable conceit in knowing that they were superior to traders' wiles. They enjoyed writing exposures of dishonest trade practices in their journals.

The long columns of emigrant wagons pulled out of Fort Laramie across the high uplands to the well-known crossing. At Independence Rock all danger of Indians was considered past. The powerful plains tribes seldom went west of here. The emigrants broke into dozens of parties, each setting its own pace, rising at will in the morning, dropping behind to rest, hunt or fix a wagon.

Near Devil's Gate on August 9, 1843, Frémont, in the West on his second expedition, rode over the southern divide to Sweetwater.[8] The great migration had passed. Not a wagon was in sight but when Frémont saw the well-traveled road he pulled up his horse with amazement. The second Frémont expedition contained thirty-nine men, many of them Creoles from his previous expedition. Charles Preuss was assistant once more. Thomas Fitzpatrick, or Broken Hand, and Kit Carson acted as his guides. L. Maxwell and two Delaware Indians, father and son, hunted game for the party. A free colored man, Jacob Dodson, attended Frémont as body servant. The lieutenant's equipment represented the latest improvements in frontier gear. Water buckets—then as now—aggravated careful packers. Frémont carried folding rubber pails. Again he had brought a pneumatic boat and this time a small howitzer. His orders specified that he find, if possible, a new and better road to the Pacific. From Westport he traveled up the Kansas and Arkansas to the mountains, prowled through the mountain parks in what would later be Colorado and found high snow-covered peaks barring his route. Back on the plains again, he traversed the open country of southern Wyoming which William Ashley crossed on his daring winter trip in 1824-1825 to the rendezvous.

Frémont could hardly believe the change which one year had made in the Overland Road. The sagebrush was broken, crushed and worn off at the stumps by hundreds of passing wheels. He turned into the wagon ruts. His carriages and little cannon rolled along the highway at a fast rate of speed. In South Pass, Frémont noticed that the emigrants had made several roads across the twenty-mile gap. Instead of turning north as he had done last year, he followed the wagon tracks down to Green River, forded on August 16, 1843, rested under the great cottonwoods, then climbed out on the western sage flats and crossed to Blacks Fork—a sluggish willow-bordered stream in the desert with the wall of the Uintah Mountains blue in the south. The party crossed to Hams Fork, a tributary to the Black, with scarcely enough water to wet the wagon wheels.

Jim Bridger and Louis Vasquez, a St. Louis trader, had recently built a fort a mile or two above the place where Blacks Fork spread out in many channels through broad meadows. Bridger and Vasquez had figured, wisely, that emigrants would come down this way where water was plentiful instead of using the Sublette Cutoff, which, although shorter, was bone-dry. A store and a blacksmith shop were sure to be highly profitable. The only thing to mar the venture was that neither of the partners liked to stay on the job. Both preferred to be off on long hunting trips with Indian associates. Their first year's business had been further interfered with by an adventurous Frenchman and a half-breed who had organized a band of Cheyenne to come over to this distant country and steal all the fort's horses. The raid had been only partially successful. A few men had been killed in a running fight and the episode was the talk of the wagon travelers.

Frémont did not go over to the fort. Kit Carson pointed out the location. The grass was scarce and the horses were falling off daily in flesh. Frémont was anxious to hurry on to better feed while the animals had the strength to pull his covered carriages. On August 20 he crossed the divide to Bear River. His men found a cow and calf left behind by the emigrants, milk for the lieutenant's coffee. Still the grass was poor. The emigrants' cattle had eaten it so short that there was little left for Frémont's horses. Next morning the road led the company down to the meadows of Bear River. Here in the green wilderness, Frémont came to a family of emigrants—two men, two women and several children—the tail end of the great migration. The travelers were resting beside their wagon. They said that they were not afraid of Indians since the Blackfeet had left this country.

Next day Frémont came to large groups of whitetop wagons scattered in friendly encampments along the road. The people were cooking, washing, letting their livestock recuperate on the green meadows after the long pull across the Green River sage flats. Women bent busily above cooking fires. Children scampered over wagon tongues and around the wheels.

Frémont traveled leisurely northward down the Bear to Soda or what he called Beer Springs. Emigrant wagons were in sight practically all the way. At Soda Springs he camped on August 25. Covered wagons were here too. Children romped around the cones and splashed in the gurgling carbonated water. Frémont unpacked his thermometers and notebook. He discovered that some of the springs registered over eighty degrees Fahrenheit. Emigrant wagons rumbled past all day and part of the next morning. Then for the first time after many days the Pathfinder and his party were in the silent wilderness again. The great migration of 1843 had passed them.

Beyond Soda Springs, Bear River loops back in a great U and runs due south into Great Salt Lake. Frémont decided to follow it and map the lake. His supplies were used up, so he sent ahead to Fort Hall for flour and started slowly down the river.

Frémont spent twenty-four days on his side trip to Salt Lake. The lake was known to have no outlet and some trappers said that the water drained away in a great subterranean whirlpool. The lake looked calm enough to Frémont when he reached it. He inflated the rubber boat and set off for the nearest island. Before long some of the vulcanized seams gave way and the party envisioned themselves in the middle of the inland sea with no floating support. One man worked constantly at the bellows, pumping air in the pontoons. Frémont sighed with relief, but it was short-lived. He noticed that the boat was moving across the water in a current of water. Could this be the edge of the whirlpool? The men paddled lustily and saw that they could navigate against the stream. At last they reached without further accidents what would be known as Frémont Island.

The party clambered over the barren island. They found no sign of life except one magpie that flew across from the mainland to examine their camp. Driftwood was plentiful. The men built great cheery fires and sat around them in the evening. For once they had no fear of an arrow from the dark. The burning logs, highly impregnated with salt, crackled with brilliant spectroscopic rays. Frémont wondered what some superstitious Indian over on the Wasatch Mountains might think if he happened to see these beacons in the lake.

Next morning a gale whipped the water into a choppy sea. The men had learned that a person will not sink in Great Salt Lake, but the waves of brine, potent as lye, could strangle the strongest swimmer by slapping him in the face. They knew the danger of attempting the crossing but they could not stay where they were without food or water. They shoved off and, with paddles and bellows, reached Little Mountain, a butte in the quaking salt flats across from Promontory Point. With a shout of thanksgiving they hauled the boat out of the syrupy water onto land. Frémont noticed that his bare arms were white with crystals. The water, splashing on him, had evaporated in the dry air and left salt, thick and white as snow, on every hair.

Fort Hall, when Frémont got back, was practically out of supplies. The great migration had bought almost everything. Frémont reorganized his men, sent some back to St. Louis and with the others set off on September 22, 1843, down the Oregon Trail, a month behind the emigrants. An early fall snowstorm beat in his men's faces. On September 26 they came to a road swinging off to the southwest—the route taken by a party of emigrants bound for California under the guidance of Joseph Walker. Frémont, the Pathfinder, followed the road for several miles before he discovered that it was not the Oregon Trail and turned back.

On October 1, he came to the salmon-eating Indians. Frémont was surprised to find them a jolly crew, very different from plains warriors. He noticed, too, that these men dressed in ragged clothes, trousers, old coats and vests—anything that they had been able to trade from the emigrants. Gone completely were the grim red men of beads and feathers, tinkling hawks' bells and vermilion.

Three days later, Frémont came to the Snake River ford. The weather was fine but storms had raised the river. Indians said that the emigrants had crossed by lashing their wagons together, two abreast, to keep them from tipping over. One man piloting the cattle had drowned. The ford followed an irregular route between the two islands. Above, the channel was narrow, only a thousand feet. Kit Carson was not a waterman. Frémont decided to hire an Indian to lead the way.

Trouble started with the howitzer. The current snatched the little gun and upset the mules. Both animals had to be cut out of the harness to save themselves. The gun was dragged out on the south bank, loaded in the rubber boat and taken across. Finally everyone reached the north bank. They encamped by a village of Indians there. On October 8, 1843, Frémont came to Fort Boise, a simple dwelling house on the right bank of the river. The garrison consisted of one *engagé*. The British factor saluted the Americans and offered to give them any help he could.

To cross the Snake and follow along the Oregon Trail, Frémont used his rubber boat and the Fort Boise canoes. On the west side, a few miles from the crossing, the column met two Irishmen walking down the road. They had lost their horses—stolen by Indians, perhaps. Frémont gave them a meal.

The road up Burnt Fork was the worst so-called wagon road Frémont had ever seen. No wonder that Dr. White had left his vehicles at Fort Hall last year and used packs through here! Twice Frémont saw places where a wagon had upset and he realized that it was an advantage to be on the head of a wagon train with restless men behind to help a man reload. He wondered how the last man, with no help behind, ever got through.

At last the explorers reached the head of Burnt Fork. The

high country from here across Powder River made an excellent road. Frémont's carriages rolled along the ruts. To the west they noticed the spruces that feathered the mountain sky line like an Indian's headdress. A little after noon on October 17 Frémont came to Grande Ronde. Twenty miles away he saw the level ridge of the Blue Mountains with their dark icing of conifers. The emigrant road climbed the steep ridge west of Five Points Creek to the cap of pines. Frémont decided to take another route. The agent back at Fort Hall had told him to go on down to the northeast of the Ronde and follow an Indian trail over the mountains from there.

The weather was cold but fine. In the morning a white frost tinted the dark earth but the sun brought warmth. Frémont noted that some of the trees were twelve feet in circumference and 200 feet tall. Down timber blocked the road. Many hours were spent clearing the way. From the dark forest the men looked through the trees at sunny parks brilliant with autumn foliage. The tall tree trunks made zebra stripes on russet mountainsides.

The party came out on the north side of the mountains on October 23, 1843, and looked down on the Walla Walla, a line across the plain. Far in the distance Frémont could see snow-capped Mount Hood. As the party descended they saw many bands of horses in charge of Indian herders. The fort must be near. The men pushed ahead eagerly. They passed several unfinished houses and deserted garden spots. Finally they came to the Whitman adobe house. The doctor was not at home. Although he had come in with the overland wagon train, he was already off again down to The Dalles. A family of emigrants were encamped at the mission and a number of Nez Percé lodges in the dooryard gave the impression of a little village. Frémont halted for a short time, found that he could get no flour and went on to the Hudson's Bay post.

The old fort was the scene of great activity. Jesse Applegate had split his Cow Column near here. Part of his people had gone on overland with their stock. Applegate and others had traded their cattle for California animals to be delivered to them at Vancouver. They were now building boats and intended to float the rest of the journey. Frémont remarked that this was the normal end of the Overland Trail, but he himself intended to ride down the river with carts and howitzer at least as far as The Dalles. He hired an Indian boy as guide and set off with Kit Carson riding beside him. Out on the sandy desert Frémont found the road heavy and the traveling slow. He was a little dismayed when he saw a flotilla of mackinaw boats come around the bend and glide past with disdain. He recognized energetic Jesse Applegate, lucky fellow, and felt self-pity for his own pedestrianism, but a few mornings later the sight of Mount Hood glowing in the dawn sunlight made him forget the drudgery of his path.

Next day Frémont crossed John Day River. He soon reached The Dalles and the near-by Methodist and Catholic missions, established there in 1838 and 1841 respectively. Many emigrants were encamped here. They were all talking about the new Territory of Oregon that had been organized last summer. The Hudson's Bay Company was no longer the law of the land. The settlers had formed a compact of their own, with Joe Meek, a rollicking mountain man whooping things along. The French population had opposed the change and the Indians remained passive.

Frémont walked through the crowded streets of tents, slab houses and mission buildings. The fish Indians seemed very dirty to him. He noticed that they lacked the pride and hauteur of the plains red men. With Preuss he walked into several of their slab houses and found the air foul. Once their entrance caused the children to scurry like young quail. One woman, naked in the hot interior, rushed out using, to Frémont's amusement, "a child for a fig leaf."[9]

At the mission, Frémont learned that Applegate had had bad luck. One of his boats had swamped in The Dalles and two of his children and a man had drowned. Frémont learned, too, that Peter Burnett had left his family here while he went below to inspect the Willamette settlements. In fact The Dalles and the mission had become large emigrant settlements. Frémont decided to leave his own party, too, in charge of Kit Carson. With seven men in a canoe he intended to go down through the Cascade Mountain gorge to Vancouver. He selected three Indian guides, his colored servant, Preuss, the German, and a French Creole. Frémont delighted in the cosmopolitan assemblage—a weakness of his that would crop out and hurt him twenty years later in America's Civil War.

The party went through the mountain gorge without mishap, noting emigrants' camps along the shore. The big migration was scattered all the way from Walla Walla to Fort Vancouver.

West of the mountains, Frémont's party ran into the rain and fog of Oregon's winter season. Dr. McLoughlin showed him his usual courtesy and Frémont noted that this Hudson's Bay official was supplying food and clothing to many poor arrivals, giving them credit until they raised a crop. The Canadians, in fact, were doing much more to help American settlers than was being done by the United States, even though the settlers had chosen the United States government.

At Fort Vancouver Frémont turned back. He did not go on to the Pacific. The American naval explorer, Charles Wilkes, had come up the river as far as the Willamette Valley last summer. Frémont's and Wilkes's surveys had thus been tied together. The Pathfinder returned to The Dalles. Here with Kit Carson he reorganized his party. He stated that he was going south to explore the Great Basin and return to the States by way of the Arkansas. He abandoned all his wheeled vehicles except the cannon. People suspected that it was for somebody more civilized than red Indians.

Frémont returned to the United States in August 1844. Peter Burnett, meanwhile, had sent the journal of his trip in letter form to the New York *Herald*. He pronounced the road to Oregon an easy one to travel, not so expensive as moving from Kentucky to Missouri. The overland trip seemed to be a great lark. People read that they could actually make money on the route. Wagons and cattle both sold for nice profits in the new country. Other newspapers copied Burnett's stories and spread them throughout the United States.

This propaganda aggravated "Oregon fever" on the eve of the

election of 1844. Candidate James K. Polk selected for a campaign cry, "All of Oregon or None—Fifty-four Forty or Fight."

1 "Letters of Peter H. Burnett," *Quarterly of the Oregon Historical Society* (December, 1902), III, No. 4, 406. These letters are reprinted from the New York *Herald.*

2 *Ibid.* The origin of these stories is discussed in this article.

3 *Ibid.,* 402.

4 Joseph Schafer, *A History of the Pacific Northwest* (New York, 1918), 148.

5 Jesse Applegate, "A Day with the Cow Column in 1843," *Quarterly of the Oregon Historical Society* (December, 1900), I, No. 4, 372-83.

6 LeRoy R. Hafen and Francis Marion Young, *Fort Laramie and the Pageant of the West, 1834-1890* (Glendale, Calif., 1938), 101.

7 Harrison C. Dale, "A Fragmentary Journal of William L. Sublette," *Mississippi Valley Historical Review* (June, 1919), VI, No. 1, 108.

8 The balance of this chapter is based chiefly on John Charles Frémont, *Report of the Exploring Expedition to the Rocky Mountains in the Year 1842, and to Oregon and North California in the Years 1843-'44* (U. S. Senate Report No. 174, 28th Cong., 2d Sess., Washington, 1845), 128ff.

9 *Ibid.,* 187.

Chapter 11

Tamsen Donner: 1846

THE Donner party has been exposed to the most minute historical investigation. The fact that some of its members turned cannibal subjected the others to legal examinations. Historians have probed the members' characters, inheritance and environment to explain their depravity. The horror of their predicament and the magnitude of the disaster have kept their experience alive as the greatest overland calamity. As a matter of fact, they were not the only emigrants driven by hunger to eating their fellow travelers. The reader will recall that Robert Stuart's Frenchmen almost stooped to cannibalism on their eastern trip in 1812. Nor is the Donner tragedy outstanding in the number of fatalities. Of the eighty-seven who started, forty-seven survived. Many accidents have killed more.

Perhaps the most revealing thing about the unpleasant story is the number of women and children in the train—even nursing babies. The Overland Trail in 1846—only ten years after Narcissa Whitman's journey—had become as much a woman's as a man's roadway.

Tamsen Donner was the third wife of George Donner, a well-to-do farmer in Sangamon County, Illinois. Born in North Carolina, George had spent many of his years moving in a covered wagon from one new country to another before he settled near Springfield, Illinois. Success and increased land values had rewarded him. Rich in land, he had settled the children by his first wife on their own farms. Two daughters by his second marriage, aged fourteen and twelve, still lived with him. By Tamsen, a whiffet of a woman only five feet tall, he had three more children, aged six, four and three. Altogether his three wives had given him thirteen children.

George Donner had talked all winter about moving to California—the new promised land. He had followed the mirage to new land all his life. His older brother Jacob, aged sixty-five, also well-to-do, decided to go along. He was living with his second wife and seven children, all under fourteen.

Tamsen helped her husband plan and pack three wagons for the trip—two for goods and supplies, one to serve as a house with stove, table and beds. In addition to groceries and bedding, George Donner purchased a goodly supply of gewgaws to trade the Indians and bolts of lace, silks and satins to sell in California. He sold enough of his Illinois property to furnish ready cash for traveling expenses. Tradition says Tamsen stitched $10,000 in bills into a quilt. She was a New Englander, brave but cautious. For her own and her daughters' amusement she stowed away water colors and oil paints, many volumes of books and school supplies. She hoped to open a young ladies' seminary on the Pacific. To pull the wagons, George Donner selected twelve yoke of oxen. Milk and beef cattle were also taken to furnish supplies en route. Five saddle horses and, of course, a dog completed the outfit. Hired men and girls were necessary to take care of the retinue. His brother Jacob prepared a similar outfit.

Another well-to-do family in Sangamon County, the James Frazier Reeds, enlisted in the overland adventure. Reed was a younger man than the Donners, only forty-six, a much more active and versatile fellow. Born in Ireland, he had come to America as a youth and had spent much of his life in Sangamon County. Not a farmer by tradition like the Donners, Reed had prospered as a merchant, railroad contractor and manufacturer of furniture. The lure of California and some recent business reverses seem to have influenced him to emigrate. Besides, he had an invalid wife and a sickly mother-in-law. California might be good for them.

Reed was high-powered, nervous, active. Everything he had must be better than his neighbor's. He prepared three wagons like the Donners but his living wagon was a veritable ark, with two decks or floors, built-in beds and a stove. Reed also bought the fastest horse he could find, a gray mare he named Glaucus with reckless disregard for sex.[1] Reed had three children and a stepdaughter Virginia, aged thirteen. He bought her a special pony to ride. He stored fancy liquors in his supply wagons. Yet he was a man with practical experience in roughing it. In the Black Hawk War he had served in the same company with a gaunt youth named Abraham Lincoln who was now running for Congress. Both men had learned what it was to be hungry and sleep in the rain.

On April 16, 1846, the nine wagons assembled in the Springfield square to show off and say good-by to admiring friends. The entire troop of emigrants numbered thirty-two. They spent almost a month reaching Independence, Missouri. On the way they met many other travelers in covered wagons bound for Oregon and California. A recent guidebook by Lansford Hastings described a new cutoff. Many travelers carried this book.

One day the Reed-Donner party met a wagon traveler from Quincy, Illinois, also on the way to California. Jessy Quinn Thornton suffered from asthma. His wife was delicate also. They hoped to find health in the West. Jessy Quinn Thornton was a much traveled man. He had lived in Virginia, Kentucky and Ohio, had studied law in London, could cite Latin or poetry for every situation and explained his overland journey by quoting:

> If thou art sorrowful and sad,
>   And thought no comfort yields;
> Go, leave the breathing world,
>   And ramble in the fields.[2]

Farmer folk like the Donners—especially Yankee Tamsen—must have been impressed. Thornton wheezed the information that a great party was to organize on the border under Colonel William Henry Russell. Better join and have protection from Indians on the plains. Out there also the Mormons might be as dangerous as the red men. The fanatic Saints were known to be strung out all across Iowa, headed for Council Bluffs.

The new friends moved along toward Independence, Missouri, together. They met another party of three wagons from Keokuk, Iowa. Patrick Breen and his wife Peggy, boss of the roost, had seven children ranging in age from fourteen to one year old. The Breens had come from Ireland and had already been successful Iowa farmers. A friend Patrick Dolan traveled with them.

On the edge of the prairie the friends met the Russell party, seventy wagons. Everybody was anxious to be off, for the grass was getting scarce, but more wagons rolled in daily. At last the men could wait no longer. In the usual election Russell was chosen captain. William Henry Russell was a tall man, very gracious and kindly in manner, but he also had the air of a man set to a hair trigger for duel fighting. He wore a Panama hat with an oiled silk cover. Russell liked politics, bluster and command. He was called "Colonel"—a Kentucky Colonel. Some called him "Owl" Russell. Gossips said that he had once heard owls in the woods who-whooing. He had mistaken the hoots for inquiries and had roared back at them: "Colonel William H. Russell of Kentucky—a bosom friend of Henry Clay."[3]

The emigrants set off under their new chief. Although moving cheered everybody's spirits, dissatisfaction diverted the travelers from the first. A Mr. Gordon decided that Owl Russell was setting too slow a pace. He persuaded thirteen wagons to strike ahead with him. On the Big Blue a party convened to discuss current disorders. Among them were James Reed, George Donner, Jessy Quinn Thornton, Lillburn W. Boggs, ex-governor of Missouri, who had married a granddaughter of Daniel Boone, operated a store at Independence, barely missed assassination from a Mormon bullet and defeated William Ashley at the polls. The malcontents were also joined by Edwin Bryant, a Louisville newspaperman, who would one day be alcalde of a city to be named San Francisco. All got relief, no doubt, by discussing what was wrong with their world. Owl Russell resigned. A debate followed and he was re-elected.

The plains of Kansas and Nebraska were lush after the rains—matted with wild flowers. At noon and night camps Mrs. Thornton and Tamsen both botanized. Tamsen pressed specimens in her album. The children raced to hilltops, then down again, with shrill screams. On May 29, 1846, just two weeks out from Independence, Sarah Keyes, mother-in-law of James Reed, died. Already the travelers saw many mounds along the road. Babies' and little children's graves seemed most common.

Owl Russell brooded over his unpopularity. Claiming illness, he resigned again. This time Lillburn Boggs won the captaincy but the train did not keep its organization long. Members were continually seceding, pulling ahead or dropping behind, catching up with another train or being picked up by the wagons behind. Many wagon trains were also coming down the road from the west, telling discouraging stories and collecting letters from the outgoing women to be mailed in the Missouri towns.

At night the men sat on their wagon tongues, read and reread Lansford Hastings' guidebook, memorized the points of interest they would see next day and noted that they were falling behind schedule. They checked the groceries and divided them by the days ahead. They remembered that the snow was deep in the Rockies and that the worst mountains were at the end of the trip. Bryant and a few friends pushed ahead with their light wagons to Fort Laramie. They were considering abandoning the wagons and going forward with pack horses. The Reeds and Donners rumbled along behind in their luxurious wagons. Grass was scarce around Scotts Bluff and the livestock did not do so well. The long train came at last to Fort Bernard, a new trading post six or eight miles downstream from Fort Laramie. Some Frenchmen, the Richard brothers, operated it to compete with the elaborate fort above. The flat from Fort Bernard to Laramie was a veritable rendezvous of wagons.

A party clattered in from the west, drew rein and dismounted among the throng. The leader Jim Clyman, mountain man, had come across from California with Lansford Hastings himself, author of the emigrant guide that Jacob Donner had purchased back in Springfield. Clyman knew that Hastings did not know what he was writing about; that he was no mountain man but a promoter who wanted to inveigle emigrants to California. Clyman knew, too, that Lansford Hastings was waiting up the trail at South Pass to direct all travelers to California instead of Oregon. Hastings would get the last word but Clyman determined to give the travelers plenty of warning. He moved from fire to fire between the wagons. They were scarcely started on the road to California, he said, yet the summer was half over. Snow on the western slope might block the passes before they got there. Don't try any short cuts and get lost. Stay on the main traveled roads.

At the Reed fire, Clyman met an old friend. Clyman too had been a private in that company with James F. Reed and Abraham Lincoln in the Black Hawk War back in Illinois fourteen years ago. Reed, proud and successful since that day, did not heed his old comrade's advice. He argued with Clyman and referred to Jacob Donner's copy of the Hastings book which described a cutoff by which they could make up some of their lost time.

Clyman reiterated that they must stay on the old road to Fort Hall.

"There is a nigher route," Reed replied stubbornly, "and it is no use to take so much of a roundabout course."[4] Hastings' guidebook said so. The men argued late into the night.

Next morning Clyman again warned the emigrants but they had made up their minds. Tamsen learned that all her friends except her own relatives and the Reeds and Breens planned to avoid the cutoffs. Edwin Bryant had traded for pack animals. He intended to hurry, without any wagons to hold him back. Owl Russell, sobered after drowning his sorrows in rum, decided to go with Bryant. Ex-Governor Boggs and others decided that Clyman was right. They would take the roundabout route through Fort Hall.

The Reeds and the Donners in their palatial wagons plodded up the Platte with the others. Their friends still pleaded with them, but they were determined to take the cutoff recommended in Hastings' guide.

The wagon train crossed South Pass on July 18 and camped at Pacific Springs five miles west of the Divide. Edwin Bryant with his pack horses had stopped here six days before. On July 20 the travelers came to the Sublette Cutoff. It was the shortest route to Fort Hall but fifty miles of the way was without water. Thornton, Boggs and their companions turned. The Reeds and Donners kept on going toward Fort Bridger and the Hastings' Cutoff—the route Clyman warned them not to take. At first the road was good and well watered. All of them seemed happy over their choice except plump little Tamsen. Jessy Quinn Thornton remembered later, after he had heard her horrible fate, that she alone seemed gloomy and dispirited, resigned but reproachful that her people "could think for a moment of leaving the old road, and confide in the statement of a man of whom they knew nothing, but who was probably some selfish adventurer."[5]

The Donners rolled down toward Fort Bridger. George Donner was elected captain of the new party. It consisted of himself, Tamsen, his brother Jacob and his wife, their families, the Reeds, their employees, Patrick Breen and his domineering wife, seven children and the family friend Patrick Dolan. Many other families including several Germans from Cincinnati were in the party. In the weeks ahead Tamsen Donner would learn to know them all and study their characters. At Little Sandy, Tamsen picked up a lonely wretch named Luke Halloran, who was dying of consumption.

At the Green River ford they found the river low. Water scarcely splashed the wagon boxes. The season had been dry here, as well as around Scotts Bluff. The wagons pulled up the west bank and crossed the flats to Hams and Blacks forks. On July 28, 1846, the train rolled into the meadows around Fort Bridger. Water gurgled pleasantly down a half-dozen channels of Blacks Fork. The fort consisted of two double log cabins joined by parallel walls in the form of palisades. Tents were pitched around the fort and under the groves of trees along the streams. Tamsen heard the familiar ring of an anvil.

The post had never been so successful as its founders, Bridger and Vasquez, had hoped. The Sublette Cutoff to Bear River had diverted many travelers. The nomadic habits of the proprietors discouraged others. Both men were prone to shut up shop and ride off on a hunting trip of a week or two. Strangely enough, the two owners were at the fort when the Donner party arrived.

Twenty-two years had changed Old Gabe Bridger since that distant day when he answered William Ashley's advertisement for trappers. His eyes had a fixed, far-off stare. When he looked at writing or a printed page, he squinted as outdoor men often do. He also had the outdoor man's lack of understanding of the value of written messages. Edwin Bryant had left a letter for the Donners and Old Gabe forgot to deliver it. Had he done so, the Donner tragedy might have been averted.

Edwin Bryant, with his pack horses, had tried to follow the Hastings Cutoff. He found it impossible for wagon travelers. To save his onetime friends from being landlocked in the wilderness, he had ridden back to the fort and written them a letter warning them not to attempt crossing the Wasatch Mountains in wagons. Old Gabe not only did not deliver the letter but he told the Donners, with a horseback rider's optimism, that the mountain crossing was all right and much shorter. Hastings himself had pulled out along his own cutoff with a big wagon train, the Harlan-Young party. To follow their wagon ruts should be easy.

The Reed-Donner party stopped four days at Fort Bridger. They fixed their wagons and rested the stock. Reed bought two yoke of oxen to replace those he had lost and George Donner hired an extra driver, Jean Baptiste Trubode. A family of Mc-Cutchens, man, woman and child, asked to join the train and they were welcomed. Thirteen-year-old Eddie Breen fell from his horse and broke his leg. Splints were fixed for him. On July 31, 1846, the party set off—Eddie in a wagon, protecting his leg, a thing that became more and more difficult when the wagon jolted in the mountains.

Edwin Bryant was eleven days ahead now.

A few miles from the fort the new road branched from the Fort Hall trace. Many wheels had looped back down the Bear River from this place during the last four years. Only one outfit had crossed by the new route. The Reeds and then the Donners turned their arks into the unknown way. Ten or twelve miles a day was all the distance that they could make. Sometimes they followed the wheel marks around hillsides that seemed impassable—especially for the great wobbling houses on wheels.

On the fourth day the party reached the valley of the Bear far below the Oregon Trail. They forded the river, went over another ridge and entered Echo Canyon, which led to the Weber. This river they knew flowed into Great Salt Lake, their destination. They followed the wheel tracks down the stream four miles to the crossing and stopped. A letter was stuck in the top of a bush beside the road. One of the men reached up and got it. It was from Hastings. He warned any travelers who might be coming by this route not to follow the tracks down the canyon. It was practically impassable. Before moving another step forward they should send a messenger down to him. He would come back and show them a better way around through the hills.

The Donners stared in amazement. What kind of man was this Hastings to write a guidebook, then lead a party of sixty wagons into a canyon that was impassable? Tamsen Donner's intuition had been justified. However, it was now too late to go back. At Fort Bridger they had been practically on the tail end of the western migration. If they retraced their road they would find themselves far behind the last traveler and there would be no hope of ever getting across the mountains before snow came. They decided to send three men on horseback to find Hastings. Reed, proud and vigorous, little Charles Stanton, an Illinois bachelor, and a man named William Pike rode off.

The emigrants rested in camp. The water was good and the women washed their families' clothes and draped the service-berry bushes. Several days passed and nobody came back. The leaders worried. They knew that every day wasted now might mean that the snow would stop them in the California sierras. Could the couriers have been ambushed by Indians? On the fifth day Reed rode into camp alone and on a new horse. The men crowded around him. Where were the others? Reed said that he had left them in Hastings' camp on Great Salt Lake. All three had ridden along the wagon trail down the Weber. It was terrible. At places the Harlan-Young party had hauled their wagons with ropes up the steep sides of the ridges. One had crashed and now lay at the foot of a seventy-five-foot bluff. That party was better manned than the Reed-Donner, yet they barely got through. It was only twenty-five miles as the crow flew to Great Salt Lake—perhaps thirty-five as the wagons would have to go. Surely they could cross this rough country by some other route.

In the morning they started. For three days they pushed slowly into the brush-covered mountains. Each morning the men went ahead to build road. In the afternoon the wagons moved after them as far as they could—sometimes a very short distance. The men grumbled. They were wagonmen, used to swinging down the road beside their lurching wheels. Working with a pick and shovel was a new life to them. That was not what they came west to do. Reed was blamed for leading them into such a tangle of brushy hillsides.

On the third day three new wagons joined their camp. Franklin Graves was an elderly Illinois farmer. With his wife, married daughter and her husband Jay Fosdick, their children—the youngest a babe in arms—and a teamster John Snyder, they had left the Missouri last spring and worked along with an emigrant train to Fort Laramie. Once past the Indian danger, they had pushed on as fast as they could. At Fort Bridger they were told that the Donners were only a few days ahead and set out to overtake them.

The Donners were glad to add four able-bodied men to their road gang. There were now seventy-eight in all, counting the children. They moved ahead but it seemed hopeless. One day they met poor Pike and Stanton all but starved to death and on the point of eating their horses. The giant and his little companion had attempted to cut across from Great Salt Lake to the wagons and had become hopelessly lost in the Wasatch Mountains. Only by luck had a scouting party from the wagons found them.

At last from a mountaintop they spied the broad valley of Great Salt Lake. It did not seem far away but they soon learned that many deep canyons must be crossed before they came to it. Both Donners were too old to do a day's work. Soon the employers were complaining that their men were not working as much as they could. Next, one family blamed the men in other families for shirking. Desperate with the knowledge that the summer was passing and that they were far from California, they grew short-tempered. The poorer families were running low on grub. Fear for themselves and envy of their richer associates engendered hatreds. A sudden realization that the mountains here would keep them from crossing the sierras farther along threw the party into an unaccountable agitation—claustrophobia of prairie people in deep defiles.

Elderly George Donner, kindly, prosperous, a bit stubborn and never conspicuous as a leader, was confronted with a panic. Time to test the man's metal had come and "Uncle George" met the requirements of a wagon captain. He quieted the desperate people.[6] His wealth and continued success through life seemed to give his words prestige. Tamsen Donner could write a complimentary page concerning her husband in the book she dreamed about writing sometime.

Down a deep valley—historians contest its identity—the wagon people toiled, chopping every foot of the way through willows and alder thickets. Five miles from the plain they quitted. A scout had reported that the next canyon north was open all the way to the lake basin. The pull over the ridge was very steep but anything was better than chopping more brush. The emigrants "double-teamed" and pulled to the opposite side. On August 27 they came out on the plains and looked across the basin of Great Salt Lake. Below them lay the blue inland sea with barren islands. Far away they could see the desert stretching out of sight to the west. Beyond that, below the horizon, they knew they should find the California mountains. Would they get there before the snow blocked the passes? They had spent twenty-one days going the last thirty-six miles. They could never make up this time. Edwin Bryant with his pack animals was already topping the passes to California. Jessy Quinn Thornton and ex-Governor Boggs, who had gone the extra 400 miles via Fort Hall, were now well down the Humboldt, out of sight yonder across the distant salt desert. Hastings and his big wagon train were several days in advance and also out of sight, although the travelers could see nearly fifty miles west across the wasteland.

Truly they were the last people in a deserted world. This alone was enough to discourage them, and in addition they had lost confidence in one another. Unpleasant relations when they were frightened and desperate in the mountains had started gnawing dislikes, festers that broke out at the least road trouble. There was no town between here and California where they could re-group and get new blood. Rest they dared not. So far they had been just emigrants; from now on they were to go through an ordeal that would sift the character of each one of them. In the party there were some real heroes and many cravens. Exter-nally, there was no way to judge who would and who would not meet the test.

The party did not take a single day to rest from the mountain trip. Time was too important. They found Hastings' wagon tracks and followed them. In one day they covered more miles than they had in the last ten. They knew that ahead of them was what was known as the Dry Drive. They must watch out for this but did not know where it started. Hastings' wagon tracks might be some help to them. However, to start off in the morn-ing expecting water within ten miles and not find it for fifty miles might spell disaster. Then a man died, Luke Halloran, the waif who had been picked up by the sympathetic Donners. To everyone's surprise he left his benefactors $1,500 in coin.[7] The train stopped a day to bury him. Eighty-six people remained now in twenty-three wagons.

On the following morning the whitetops crept around the south of Salt Lake and out into the desert. When would they come to the long drive? The Harlan-Young wagon tracks led across a salt creek flowing toward the lake. Then they came to a meadow with good water, the last oasis east of Skull Valley. The lead drivers saw a board. A paper had been fastened to it but either the birds or Indians had torn it off. Tamsen was asked to decipher the writing that was found on a few scattered pieces. She knelt on the ground and put the pieces in place on the board. Men helped her retrieve the bits and watched quietly as she placed them. At last enough of the puzzle was assembled to decipher. It was a note left by Hastings. Two days and two nights of hard driving, he said, would be necessary to reach the next water. They had been told that the dry drive was thirty-five to forty miles. This note indicated that it might be fifty or more.

The emigrants spent the next day resting their cattle and filling all their receptacles with water. They cut some grass in the meadow to take along. The women cooked food for the passage. On Thursday morning, they left at daybreak. They hoped to get across by Saturday morning.

Hastings' wagon tracks led out across a sagebrush flat toward a rocky ridge ten miles away. The Donner train plodded along them. Would they cross or skirt that ridge? Hours later the teamsters saw a road ahead going over the mountains, a climb of at least a thousand feet. In the heat of the day they reached the pass, tired out, and on the other side they looked into the blazing sun. Below them stretched another dry plain and at its far edge another rocky ridge with no promise of water. From this second ridge, when they reached it, the plain stretched to the horizon. There was no sage here. The plain was glittering white—salt. Clearly there were still at least forty miles of desert to the next mountains where they could expect water. Already the emigrants had traveled until they were tired and their animals were choking.

The moon was full—good for night driving. In the dark, too, it was cooler. The great wagons lurched along. The tired men looked forward to the fresh breeze that came with dawn, though they knew that a few minutes later the sun would beat down with full force as another summer day came to the desert.

Well along in the second day the emigrants entered the worst part of the journey. The wagon wheels sank into hot dunes of ashlike sand. The distraught travelers were plagued by mirages. Every man forgot his neighbor and thought only of himself. Drivers with the strongest teams pulled ahead. Others stopped to rest their panting oxen. Men behind them passed without asking if they were all right. The train ceased to be a train. Wagons were scattered along the road for miles, every family for itself, the Donners and Reeds with their palace-wagons at the rear.

In the middle of the desert the hot sand changed to brittle salt sinks. Here the wagons broke through the thin crust and sloshed through sandy brine, bitter as lye. Drinking water in the kegs was giving out. There was scarcely enough for the children. Tamsen Donner gave her brood small lumps of sugar moistened with peppermint, to quiet them and keep their minds off the heat. All day Friday the Donners and Reeds struggled through the slush. Would the morning bring them to water as Hastings had promised?

Saturday dawned, the day of promise. The desert lay ahead with no sign of water. For another twenty-four hours they struggled along. Tamsen gave her little ones flattened bullets to suck. The hard lead drew saliva and kept tender throats from parching. The Donner cattle began to falter. Although they often had to rest, the cool of evening came before any gave up. The fresh night air renewed the animals' courage.

Sunday dawned and still no relief. At daylight Tamsen noticed that the wagons ahead were out of sight. Had they found water? Surely they would come back if they had. At noon Reed decided that he must do something drastic. He said that he would ride ahead, find water and the other wagons. He told his drivers to follow as long as the oxen would pull, then unyoke, abandon the wagons, the women and children, and drive the stock toward water. Once refreshed the animals could be returned to bring in the family and goods.

Reed mounted his mare and followed the wagon tracks. They swung to the left toward a volcanic crag. Could that mean a spring? No, but beyond the ground was covered with a rich green. A meadow! Again Reed was disappointed. An acre of salty greasewood had looked verdant from a distance. He passed the travelers who had gone ahead, found them in all stages of disaster. In wagons deserted along the way, he saw frightened but resigned women comforting their children, waiting for their husbands to come back from the water they hoped to find. Here and there a dead steer lay bloating by the tracks. Finally Reed came to a rocky promontory. His mare labored up the trail to the top but no spring showed from the summit. Instead he saw only the desolate plain stretching at least a dozen miles to brittle mountains against the sky. No use now to go back to his family. His horse would die before he got there. Reed kept on. He came to a wagon containing a woman and two children. William Eddy had left them and gone on to water with the stock.

In the evening Reed reached the springs and meadows at the foot of Pilot Peak. His own wagons must be at least thirty miles back through that inferno. Many of the emigrants were here with their animals, resting, letting them drink, planning to go back and bring in their families. Eddy had been at the water since ten o'clock in the morning. Reed rested an hour with him, then started back. Eddy carried a bucket of water. One of his oxen had lain down exhausted. He hoped to save it. At eleven o'clock at night Reed met two of his hired men driving his oxen without the wagons. He showed them the way and said that he would wait for them with his family back on the desert. The boss and his employees parted. Near midnight—the moon was overhead—Reed passed the Donners. They still drove one wagon. Finally Reed reached his own three deserted whitetops, the last in the line. It was almost daylight. The five family dogs greeted him. His womenfolk were all right and two men were with them. Reed dismounted and gave the bridle reins to one of his "hands," telling him to ride the mare down the road to water.

Reed and his family sat under the wagon all day watching the western horizon. At dark Reed decided that his family must walk down the road in the cool of the evening. They could not possibly go all the thirty miles, for Mrs. Reed was an invalid at best, but they could start. Anything was better than waiting. Reed collected what water was left and also a little bread. The two girls, thirteen and eight, and little Jim, aged five, must walk. Reed carried Tommy, a baby of three. The night was cold. They walked slowly, rested and shivered. At daylight they came to Jacob Donner's wagons with the family asleep in them. The Donners got up, struck a light and told Reed why his teamsters had not come back. The cattle, crazed for thirst, had strayed off in the dark.

Reed left his family with the Donners. Without cattle he could not pull his fine wagons with their precious loads. Perhaps his wealth and property would have to be left in the desert. Reed was anxious to learn the magnitude of his disaster. Many people were abroad now. Some were hunting cattle that had stampeded like his, seeking water. Others were coming back with their oxen to pull in their wagons. Reed reached the meadows, found his hired men and checked his livestock. He had one cow and one ox left to pull three large wagons and all his goods. Unless his men could find his work animals he was financially ruined. During the day Jacob Donner came in with his and Reed's families. All had got across Salt Desert at last. Though no person's life was lost, a quarter of all the oxen were gone. The trip had taken six days instead of two days and nights.

Obviously part of the loads must be left behind. Reed was the greatest loser. Men went back to his wagons with mules and horses, put the most precious material in one family wagon and abandoned his other two. When this load of salvaged property reached the spring, Reed borrowed two oxen. These with the one he had left and the cow made two yoke. They could pull his wagon though not easily.

George Donner and the German, Lewis Keseberg, two other wealthy travelers, had each abandoned one wagon and were reduced to two. Poor emigrants drove hard bargains with the discomfited aristocrats, charging exorbitant prices for the loan of cattle or for hauling extra supplies. With much bickering and haggling the train started again, this time with only nineteen wagons. They traveled along the foot of the mountain that beached on the desert, weary, shaken and disspirited—Hastings' wagon tracks their only guide in a country barren as the moon. Then the weather changed. An iron cold gripped the desert. Next, a sudden snowstorm burst upon them—in September, before the mountains were in sight. What was it doing in the high country that separated them from California? That night they camped early. Ahead of them was another dry drive. The memory of the last one clung like a nightmare to the travelers' tortured minds.

At dawn they started, trudging along all day. At dusk they stopped to feed the animals a little hay that they had brought.

Then they pushed on in the darkness. Weak oxen stumbled and fell. New yokemates took their places and the train staggered on. At daybreak they found water and meadows.

The animals—wrecks with hair dead on hides draped over bones—were turned loose for a twenty-four-hour rest. Everyone knew that a day or two would not restore gloss to the coats of cattle so far gone nor revive the strength that came from good feed and water, but no more time could be allowed. To the fear of being shut off by snow in the mountains was added the realization that all food was running low.

The men held a meeting. Someone would have to go ahead, get supplies in California and come back to meet the party. Who should be sent? The tired men looked at one another. Everyone distrusted his neighbor. Too many disagreements had marred their relations since the Wasatch. If an unmarried man ever got out of this hell into California surely he would not risk his life to come back. A married man would not be apt to desert his family. At last the emigrants selected giant McCutchen and little Charles Stanton, who had followed Hastings' wheel tracks through the Wasatch and got lost coming back. Stanton had no family but he seemed to be a man of honor. McCutchen left a wife and baby. The two rode away together, the giant on a horse, little Stanton on a jigging mule. The men who stayed behind reorganized their loads.

On the last day of September they came to a westward flowing river—the Humboldt—and Hastings' tattered guidebook told only too truly how far they were from California. To make better time and have more feed for the cattle the train split in two sections. The Donners, with their five wagons, went ahead. Reed's teamsters went with them. Reed no longer needed hired men. The separation let the travelers make better time but it exposed them to a new danger, Indians. Night after night the savages peppered the oxen with arrows, killing a few, crippling others. Then one day James Reed rode up from the rear section, his head bandaged, his face unshaved. The once proud man had been expelled from the second train for killing a teamster in a quarrel, striking him down to protect a friend. The dead teamster had been popular, Reed was not. The Germans had wanted to hang him from a wagon tongue. He was lucky to get away with his life.

Tamsen fed the haggard man. That night her husband wrote a letter to Sutter's Fort stating that he would pay all expenses of a relief party sent to save the train. In the morning, after breakfast, Reed set off for California with this letter and one of his former hired men, Walter Herron. Both had food for a few days but they hoped to live chiefly on game. Two parties—not counting Edwin Bryant—had now gone ahead of the doomed train seeking relief in California. Surely they would bring help.

The Humboldt became smaller each day as the travelers approached the sink. This was crazy for a river but not so crazy as the minds of the tortured travelers. Shortly beyond where Applegate's Cutoff to Oregon left the main road, the Donners camped one night after an unusually hard pull across a sandy strip. Here they found the body of a man out of the Hastings party—killed by an arrow. The pioneers had buried him but the Indians had dug him up, stripped off his clothes and left his body to the coyotes. At four o'clock next morning the rear section of the train caught up with the Donners. The meeting was not friendly. A tension of fear irritated everyone. Each person's true character had come to the surface. People told ugly tales on one another. They cursed Keseberg, the German. He had ordered an old man out of his wagon to lighten the load and had driven off, leaving him to the Indians.

On the second night after the reunion, grass was very scarce. The cattle scattered badly and Indians stole nineteen. One of the Germans and the Donners were the principal losers. Tamsen watched her menfolk yoke milk cows to the wagons. The Donner wealth was dwindling like the Reed's. On October 12, 1846, the travelers reached the sink of the Humboldt. In the morning the oxen were turned out to graze and Indians killed twenty-one of them. All in all, 100 head had been lost along the Humboldt.

This disaster made paupers out of many more travelers. William Eddy, who had hauled the remnant of the Reed property, now had but one ox left. One of the Germans, named Wolfinger, had but one. He was believed to be wealthy. His wife had worn handsome jewelry during the early days of the trip. Wolfinger said that he would cache his property and catch up. Two other Germans, Joseph Reinhardt and Augustus Spitzer, offered to stay and help bury it. Mrs. Wolfinger joined the women who were walking with the train. William Eddy was compelled to desert his wagon. Mrs. Reed took out the most precious of her belongings and put the package in Breen's wagon. She got a ride with the Donners. Eddy took his baby in his arms. His three-year-old son toddled with his wife. Together they set off after the train. On the hills Indians laughed at their predicament.

Ahead lay the stretch between the sinks and the Truckee, called by many the worst part of the trail. On October 13 the travelers tackled it. Only about fifteen wagons hauled by cows and oxen were left. Footmen carried packages, kettles of water. The day was a delirium. Shimmering heat, baked rock, brown, red, yellow, dry and deadly. Dust in places was so thick the horses sank in it almost to their knees. Night found the Eddys alone on the desert, all wagons out of sight. Their entire supply of food was a few pounds of brown sugar which they fed to the children. The old moon rose near daybreak and in the distance they saw the wagons standing high like tombstones at some springs.

The water at the Geyser Spring was hot and unpalatable. The emigrants cooled it in their buckets and tried to drink it in spite of the taste. The Eddys sat apart, stoical and starving. One of the Donner women gave them some coffee. Eddy gave it all to his wife and children. He'd get along all right somehow.

Another twenty miles separated them from the Truckee. At sunset the troupe straggled up to the sparkling waters, rested and drank. All deserts were behind them now—but not the crossing of the cool mountains ahead. Going would be good now if the snows held off. Only Wolfinger and the two Germans who had remained to help him build the cache had not come across.

The Truckee cottonwoods were the first real trees the travelers had seen for 500 miles. The emigrants rested for a day to let their animals recuperate.

With lightened loads the oxen that had survived pulled the wagons up a long canyon. Reinhardt and Spitzer caught up. Wolfinger was not with them. They said that Indians had killed him and burned all his property. The news prostrated his widow. The travelers trudged on and said nothing but they suspected that Wolfinger had been murdered.

For three days the train plodded along—slow as oxen. At camp the emigrants scraped the bottom of flour barrels for food. Then they heard the unmistakable click of iron muleshoes ahead on the road. A pack train came down the canyon trail and stopped. Little Stanton, with two Indian packers from Sutter's Fort, had come with seven pack mules loaded with grub. Where was Mc-Cutchen? Sick in Sutter's. Unable to come back. Stanton had seen Reed, and Herron too, four days ago. Almost starved they had caught up with the tail end of the Hastings train in Bear Valley, California. They were safe now in the Promised Land.

Stanton distributed the food. As a single man he might now return to California and save himself. He had already performed his duty but he decided to stay. The Truckee meadows were close, he said. Good grass there would revive the oxen. He and the Indians would lead the way. Stanton noticed the luckless Reed women and children. These people from his own Illinois were afoot and alone, their great wagons, fine food and wines, horses, cattle and supplies all gone. Stanton gave one of his pack mules to Mrs. Reed and Tommy to ride. On another he mounted Patty and Jim behind the Indian rider. Virginia, once proud owner of a race pony, climbed up behind Stanton.

The meadow proved to be all and more than Stanton promised—good grass, clear water, cool air after the furnace heat and hardship of the desert. The oxen were weak. They needed rest and food but could the necessary time be spared? If not, could the emaciated animals pull the wagons over the steep forest roads that lay between them and the pass? October 20 had come—late to be in the high mountains. However, people at Sutter's had told Stanton that the pass was seldom closed before the middle of November. Hastings had come through on horseback the year before late in December. To be sure, there was already snow in the pass but it was not deep. Early snows always looked bad but they settled and fine weather often followed. Stanton advised the emigrants to wait and rest their cattle. They took his advice.

The emigrants left the Truckee meadows when they thought their oxen able. The last dangerous pass was only fifty miles ahead. The Breens went first. By luck the Keokuk Irish had lost fewest cattle to the Indians. Domineering Mrs. Breen had fretted and scolded at the meadow layover. It might cost them all their lives if a snowstorm closed the pass. With them went their friend Dolan and the impoverished and the wagonless Eddys, also the Kesebergs, who were now probably the richest of all the emigrants. Behind the eager, struggling first section came the second group, the less efficient, less strong. The second group was made up of Reeds, all women and hired men; the Murphys, all women and children but one; the Graves; and plucky little Stanton, the bachelor who felt responsibility for so many womenfolk.

The Donners, solid folk, were not stampeded by the others' fears. With cows in many of the dead oxen's yokes, they took their time. The train pulled ahead of them, out of sight. In the forest it snowed, just a flurry, then stopped, but the sky looked gloomy and cold. One evening, probably November 3, 1846, Tamsen could see plainly that a storm threatened. During the night a blizzard whipped around the wagons. In the morning the men looked out from under the wagon covers at a white world. They stepped down into snow up to their knees. It was hopeless to hook up and try to pull. George and Jacob waded back and forth between one another's wagons, stamped off the snow on the wagon tongues and climbed in under the canvas covers. There was nothing to do but make camp. "Uncle George" selected a large pine tree. His hired men scooped away the snow and pitched his tent. Beside it he built a lean-to and covered it with old quilts, rubber coats and buffalo robes. In these fragile caves Tamsen Donner set up housekeeping with her family. She took in, also, the widow Wolfinger. Jacob Donner built a similar habitation for his family near by. Across Alder Creek the hired men and the Germans, four in all, constructed what might be called an Indian lodge. Fires were kindled in all the hovels. The ground underfoot became a quagmire; water dripped from the roof but the people were warm. Beds were constructed on poles above the mud. The little settlement consisted of twenty-one people—six men, three women and twelve children.

As soon as the Donners were settled, some of the men went up the trail to see how the rest of the wagon train had fared. They came back to report that the main party was camped in three groups about five miles above, on Lake Truckee. Tamsen heard, too, that some of the party had almost got over the divide before the storm broke. All had passed beyond the lake but the snow was too deep to pull the wagons farther. Ahead, the pass—and safety—loomed in the afternoon light. A panic had gone through the people. They decided to abandon their wagons, pack what they could on the cattle and get across. Then they lost time deciding what to discard and what to take. The cattle objected to being packed, bucked off their loads or wallowed with them in the snow and turned their packs and kicked them to pieces. Keseberg had hurt his foot and could not walk. A horse had been provided for him to ride.

At last they started. The road was buried, too deep to show. The travelers got off it and floundered in snow above their waists. Stanton, on one of the mules, offered to scout ahead, locate and break a trail to the top. One of the Indians went with him. They plunged through deep drifts, sometimes head first, but they reached the top. Stanton looked west across the dark ridges below. Another storm was in the air. With one more blizzard this pass would be closed completely. The two men, the red and the white, paused on the threshold. It was their last chance to save themselves. They turned their mules around and went back to the sixty miserable people they had left in the snow below: nineteen men over eighteen, twelve women and twenty-nine children. Stanton, with the Indian, got back by twilight. He urged the emigrants to come on, get across if it took all night. The poor wretches were tired out. They had built a big fire, were spreading quilts and buffalo robes. Breen was playing his fiddle: "Jimmy Crack Corn and I Don't Care." They said that they would try in the morning.

That night the snow came which entrapped the Donners ten miles below on Alder Creek. At the pass in the morning the drifts were ten feet deep. The emigrants could not go ahead on foot. They spent almost all day (while the Donners were building the lean-tos) getting back to the lake, where they built cabins.

The only immediate problem confronting them now was food. They had some coffee, tea and sugar, a few thin cattle and horses, Sutter's mules and a few dogs. Big game left the mountains with the snow. The marooned emigrants tried fishing without success. The 100 cattle that had been lost in the desert would have supplied them with meat until spring. Friends in California knew that the train had this large herd of cattle. Would they believe them safe from starvation and not send help? Where were Reed, his hired man Herron? And the giant McCutchen?

Twice in November parties started over the pass on foot. The strongest wanted to go so as to save food for those left behind. Both efforts failed. By the first of December snow had piled up even with the cabin roofs. Little Stanton and Graves decided to make snowshoes. Hickory oxbows served their purpose admirably. On December 9 Milt Elliott and one companion, Noah James, went down to Alder Creek to see the Donners. The two families had not been heard from for weeks. As soon as the pair left, snow fell for five days without stopping. The snowshoe makers completed their work. On December 16 a party of fifteen of the strongest adults, five of them women, crossed the pass and entered the gloomy forest on the western slope. Some husbands and wives were leaving all their children behind. The little party carried six days' rations[8] but they spent thirty-three days wandering toward safety in the valley of California. Of the ten men Eddy and one other survived. All the five women reached Sutter's Fort. Game little Stanton, who had gone back when he could have saved himself, gave out. He asked the others to go on, said he would follow. That was the end of Stanton. The two Indians were killed and eaten.

Back in the cabins on the lake, the snow drifted deeper on the flat roofs. The people spent much of their time in bed. The dark rooms became infested with vermin. Practically everybody was ill. The fires burned and the kettles of bones, hide and lean meat steamed. Smells of unwashed babies, sickness, filth! Through it all Breen kept a diary that was optimistic—the natural product, perhaps, of a man who could get along with a domineering wife. At Christmas there was still a little flour to make gruel for the babies. Breen's dog Towser and Mrs. Reed's little Cash were both alive but most of the dogs had been eaten. Oxhides formed the main ration. The emigrants had learned how to cook them. First the hair was singed off. Then the hide was soaked soft and boiled. Glue came to the surface of the kettle. When the water cooled the glue hardened. This was eaten like cheese.[9]

The people visited one another very little. Nothing was known about the Donners or the two men who had gone back to see them. Then on the night of December 20, 1846, Milt Elliott stamped in out of the darkness. He was alone. Things were so bad down there, he said, Noah James had remained to do what he could. The Donners were not frontiersmen. They did not know how to survive in the mountains. They were shorthanded. Tamsen, like the rest of the party, did not know what to do but she had retained calm courage. The lean-to and the tent dripped continually. She ventured out of doors and brushed the snow off the roof. Constantly she feared that the whole clammy edifice would collapse on them. Most of the few cattle left to the Donners had strayed off in the first storm. Not even the hides and bones were available to eat. Little wood mice in their provisions served as the choicest meat for the table. Uncle Jake, sickly most of the way across the plains, had died. George Donner had hurt his hand with the ax. The wound was festering and did not heal. In the lodge across the creek Sam Shoemaker, James Smith and the Dutchman Reinhardt had died. Reinhardt, before the end, had confessed the murder of Wolfinger for his money, back in the Humboldt Sink. Some days the survivors lay in bed all day long without making a fire. Uncle Jake Donner's young stepsons and Jean Baptiste were the only men able to do the chores. So Noah James had stayed to help them.

Christmas came. Mrs. Reed prepared a party for the children.

January dragged along. Then on February 18, 1847, relief came.

Seven men staggered into the upper cabins, almost exhausted themselves. They had left the nearest ranch, Johnson's, down in the valley with fourteen companions, two weeks ago. They had started with ample provisions but had consumed the greater part of them before arriving. The emigrants' only hope was for those with sufficient strength to follow these rescuers out. The seven men did not tell the fate of the first party over the pass lest they frighten those who had remained. Four of the seven rescuers selected the strongest people from the upper cabins, three went down to Donners'. They were in a hurry as another storm might shut them in with the hapless emigrants.

At the Donner camp the rescuers found George alive but his arm infection worse. There was no hope for him. The men urged Tamsen to save herself and children. The little New Englander refused. So did her sister-in-law Elizabeth, who was delicate. Tamsen dressed the four older children in warm clothes and sent them. Noah James went, too, and so did Mrs. Wolfinger. Jean Baptiste Trubode wanted to go also but the rescuers would not let him. He was the only able-bodied man left among the twelve at the Donner camp. Before starting, the rescuers chopped down two trees for firewood, then they hurried away—men, women and children. Tamsen looked at her own toddlers. She had just one hide left to feed twelve people. Grimly she said that when this was gone they would have to dig up the dead and eat them.

Back at the lake the second exodus was organized. Besides the six from the Donner tents, twelve more were mustered—all the Reeds but two tots, Reed's hired girl Eliza Williams, who was out of her mind, the several motherless children, Mrs. Keseberg and her little daughter. Old Keseberg, her husband, seemed too ill to attempt the crossing. Some said later that he stayed to rob the dead of their property. The only other man who did not go was Patrick Breen with his fiddle, his diary and a good supply of hides. Three women and twelve children were left, including Mrs. Graves, old Mrs. Murphy and Mrs. Breen. On February 22, 1847, twenty-five started. Eighteen of them survived. On the way they met Reed and giant McCutchen coming in with an-

PROMINENT POINTS AND REMARKS.	DIST. miles.	From W. QRS miles.	From C of G S L miles.
Junction of California and Oregon roads. Take the left hand road. Good road a few miles, afterwards sandy and heavy.	6	819	212
Little Sandy, 20 feet wide, $2\frac{1}{2}$ feet deep. Muddy water—swift current. Plenty of willows and wild sage. Abundance of grass down the stream. After this, barren and sandy land.	$7\frac{3}{4}$	$826\frac{3}{4}$	$204\frac{1}{4}$
Big Sandy, 7 rods wide, 2 feet deep: Lat. 42° 6′ 42″. - - - - - Good chance to camp. A few miles further, you will find a short piece of rough road, over rocks and cobble stones. No grass or water after this for near 17 miles.	$8\frac{1}{4}$	835	196
Big Sandy. - - - - - - Good chance to camp. After this, barren, sandy land and heavy road till you arrive at Green river.	17	852	179
Green river ford, 16 rods wide. - - Good camping any where on the banks, and plenty of timber. It is not difficult fording in low water, but if too high to ford, the best crossing place is up stream. Latitude—2 miles above—41° 52′ 37″; Long. 109° 30′. Alt. 6,000 feet.	10	862	169
Good camping place on Green river. - Plenty of grass here. But no other very good chance to camp on this side the river.	$1\frac{1}{2}$	$863\frac{1}{2}$	$167\frac{1}{2}$
Road leaves Green river. - - - No grass nor water after this for fifteen and a half miles. Land rolling, barren—mostly sandy, and several steep places to pass.	$3\frac{1}{2}$	867	164
Black's fork, 6 rods wide, 2 feet deep. - Good chance to camp, and a nice place, though not much timber.	$15\frac{1}{2}$	$882\frac{1}{2}$	$148\frac{1}{2}$
Ham's fork, 3 rods wide, 2 feet deep. - Rapid current, cold water, plenty of bunch grass and willows, and is a good camp ground.	$3\frac{3}{4}$	$886\frac{1}{4}$	$144\frac{3}{4}$
Black's fork again. - - - - Not much grass, but plenty of willows. You will now have some uneven road, with many ravines.	$1\frac{3}{4}$	888	143
Small creek, 2 feet wide. - - - No grass, and probably no water.	$10\frac{3}{4}$	$898\frac{3}{4}$	$132\frac{1}{4}$
Black's fork, third time. - - - After crossing you will find a good camping place. Plenty of bunch grass; also, wild flax.	2	$900\frac{3}{4}$	$130\frac{1}{4}$
Black's fork, fourth time. - - - You ford again at a good camping place.	$2\frac{1}{4}$	903	128
Stream 2 rods wide, 2 feet deep. - Very swift current, and plenty of bunch grass. Road pretty rough after this.	$2\frac{3}{4}$	$905\frac{3}{4}$	$125\frac{1}{4}$
Stream—good camping place at a bend. You do not cross the stream, but there is a good camping place, where the road passes a bend of the creek.	$3\frac{1}{2}$	$909\frac{1}{4}$	$121\frac{3}{4}$
"Fort Bridger:" Lat. 41° 19′ 13″; Long. 110° 5′; Altitude, 6,665 feet. You cross four rushing creeks, within half a mile, before you reach the Fort, and by traveling half a mile beyond the Fort, you will cross three others, and then find a good place to camp. The Fort is composed of four log houses and a small enclosure for horses. Land exceeding rich— water cold and good, and considerable timber.	$8\frac{1}{4}$	$917\frac{1}{2}$	$113\frac{1}{2}$

2

Courtesy, Illinois State Historical Library

PAGE FROM WILLIAM CLAYTON'S EMIGRANT'S GUIDE, 1848

other relief party of nine men. Reed passed his wife and Virginia and went on to get the two children left behind.

The second relief party arrived a week after the first had departed. Horrible things had happened in that time but Reed found his children alive. In the Breen cabin conditions seemed the best. Down at the Murphy cabin old Mrs. Murphy was out of her head. Children cried for food. Keseberg lay in appalling filth. The dismembered body of Reed's faithful hired man Milt Elliott was on the floor by the door. The men cleaned the cabin, washed the children. Keseberg protested at being bathed by Reed, the man he had wanted to hang on his wagon tongue.

Two of the rescuers, Cady and Clark, went on down to the Donner camp. Next day, March 2, 1847, Reed and the three others followed their tracks. Cady and Clark walked in on Jean Baptiste carrying a human leg. In front of the Jacob Donner tent some children sat on a log. Their faces and clothes were smeared with blood. They were eating the partly roasted heart and liver of their father. The children did not look up at the strangers or even notice that they were present, even when the men stood beside them. Inside the tent lay invalid Elizabeth, far gone with starvation. Weakly she said that she would die before eating the flesh of her husband but she had permitted her five children to eat their father—anything to save their lives.

When Reed arrived he cleared away the snow and moved the tent to a cleaner location. The rescuers found four open graves. In one was the dismembered body of Jacob Donner. Reed looked at the bearded head severed from the body. In the other graves nothing remained but a few fragments. Reed stepped in George Donner's tent. Tamsen appeared healthy and apparently strong. Three little daughters, the oldest six, still survived. Kindhearted George Donner lay in bed, emaciated and prostrate. The infection in his hand had reached the shoulder. His eyes shone unnaturally bright in sunken sockets. Only a year ago he and Reed, at their homes back in Sangamon County, Illinois, had planned this trip.

Tamsen explained that the family were on their last hide when the first relief left. It was soon eaten. Then they stooped to the extremity. Finally Elizabeth had lent them meat from Uncle Jacob's body. Jean Baptiste had been a help to them. At first he had sulked when forced to stay but he overcame his bad humor, chopped wood for both tents and was kind to the children. He took them out in the snow with him for fresh air. When it was cold he spread his Navaho blanket on the snow with a child in each end, then rolled them together until they met. This amused the children. Then Jean Baptiste propped them against a tree to watch him chop limbs from the trees which the relief party had cut down for them. Sometimes Tamsen, almost as small as a child herself, came out, too, and sat with the children. She told them stories about Joseph and Daniel and Elijah. She wrote entries in her diary—the book she had hoped to write some day. Occasionally she brought out her sketch box and drew pictures of the mountains, the snow and pine trees draped with drifts. She taught her little ones to say over and over that they were the children of Mr. and Mrs. George Donner. They must always remember this—just in case. . . .

George urged Tamsen to go out with the rescuers but she refused. She would stay with him to the end. Reed ordered Cady and Clark to guard the camp. Another relief expedition was expected daily. With the three older Donner children, Reed returned to the upper cabins. Only George, Tamsen, Jacob's wife Elizabeth, five children, the guards and Jean Baptiste remained on Alder Creek—alive.

Up at the lake, preparations for the next exodus were hurried. Everybody who could be moved or carried was to go. They would surely meet the big rescue company on the way. Reed's party consisted of fourteen children and three adults, Patrick and Peggy Breen and Mrs. Graves. The Breens had become the richest—in hides—of all the stranded emigrants. But before leaving, Mrs. Graves surprised everybody by asking to have a cleat removed from their wagon. This innocent piece of wood had apparently been used as a brace for a table but underneath it the astonished rescuers found auger holes containing several hundred dollars in coin.[10] Mrs. Graves took this and also her son-in-law's violin. He had gone out in the first party and she did not know that he was dead. Patrick Breen also took his fiddle. The party seemed confident of survival.

Reed left one man named Stone in charge of the upper camp until the big rescue party came in. Only two adults, Keseberg and insane Mrs. Murphy, remained. With them were three children, Mrs. Murphy's Simon and the two waifs, little Jimmy Eddy and George Foster. On March 3, 1847, Reed led his party toward the pass.

The people were too far gone to hurry. They plodded listlessly. The children wandered, repeatedly sat down in the snow. Around the fire at night Patrick Breen played his fiddle optimistically—or was it habit? After three days they reached the pass—only a short way above the lake—and their food was gone. That night a storm swirled over the travelers. They built a platform of logs on the snow, lighted a fire on it and covered themselves with the blankets. The wind and snow continued all next day and the next night. Little Isaac Donner died. At noon on the third day the snow stopped. The starving people threw back the covers, looked around at the great drifts of snow. A fire was started. The seven Breens and five Graveses announced that they would stay at the camp. The other eight, four men and four children, started away. Soon they were out of sight and Peggy Breen, boss to the last, produced some food that she had hidden in her clothes, seeds, tea and a pound of sugar. Then one of the men who had gone staggered back with Mary Donner. She had given out.

Back at the filthy cabins on the lake, Stone, the rescuer, left his charges and went down to the Donner camp. He knew that they were wealthy. Clark was hunting when he arrived, so he whispered to Cady. Then the two confederates made a deal with Tamsen to take out six-year-old Frances, five-year-old Georgia, and little Eliza, almost four, if Tamsen would pay them $500. Tamsen accepted the offer. She combed the children's hair and dressed them for the journey. From the trunk she brought out quilted petticoats, woolen stockings and linsey dresses. The two littlest tots had fine garnet-red coats, twilled with an interwoven white thread. Tamsen herded the three little ones to their father's bedside for them to say good-by. She wrapped up a bundle of fine clothes and some silver spoons to go with them, as keepsakes or to help pay for anything that they might need. She gave the bundle to the men and climbed up the steps to the surface of the snow and watched the little red figures going up the trail. She was glad now that she had drilled them so carefully to repeat that they were the children of Mr. and Mrs. George Donner.

Stone and Cady left the children at insane Mrs. Murphy's cabin up at the lake, shouldered the rich booty and struck off for civilization. During the blizzard that overtook the last refugees west of the pass the unfortunate Donner children trembled with terror in the Murphy cabin. Keseberg's health had improved. He was eating food that revived his strength. Frances Donner was old enough to understand what it was. Once when Eliza was sleeping Keseberg stood looking at her. He made a remark that set the little ones all in a frenzy of fear. Outside the blizzard howled.

West of the divide another relief under William Eddy was coming in. Eddy's wife and daughter were dead but he still had little Jimmy. His party came to the Breen encampment. The fire had burned a hole in the snow twenty-five feet deep. At the bottom of the pit the Breens sat stupidly around a steaming kettle. The mutilated bodies of two children lay beside the family and there were the partly eaten remains of Mrs. Graves. The Breens had been here five days.[11]

The relief party divided. Some of them started out with the Breens. The rest went on. Eddy was eager to rescue his little Jimmy—but he was too late. In the Murphy cabin, five-year-old Georgia Donner told the men that Jimmy was gone. Keseberg had taken him to bed one night and in the morning the lad was dead. Grandma Murphy had taken the little body in her arms and turned on Keseberg, calling him a murderer and cannibal. The crazed German had snatched the body from her and hung it on the cabin wall.

Keseberg himself faced William Eddy and admitted that he had eaten the little boy. Eddy sprang forward to kill him, then stopped, ashamed to kill a demented scarecrow, but if the fiend ever reached California and regained his mind, Eddy would get him.

To Eddy's surprise Tamsen Donner was at the Murphy cabin. The sturdy little whiffet of a woman had worried when the storm came so soon after her children left with Stone and Cady. Now she knew what the treacherous fellows had done to her. She offered Eddy $1,500 to get the youngsters out.

Eddy refused to take even $100. He would save them or die on the trail. He urged Tamsen to come also. She asked for a little time to consider. Back on Adler Creek her sister-in-law Elizabeth had died. Only her little nephew Sammie and her husband George were alive. George was sinking fast. He had asked her to go with the last rescue party and she had refused. To go now would be to desert Clark and Jean Baptiste who were down there caring for George in her absence. She could not leave without consulting them.

Eddy and his companions would not wait for her to go down to Alder Creek and back again. They knew what it meant to be caught east of the pass if another storm came. They had no extra food. Tamsen must make up her mind. Her older children had gone out. These tots now faced the ordeal. Tamsen decided that her duty lay back with her dying husband. She would stay with him to the end.

The relief party remained at the cabins only two hours, always watching the sky for a storm. They started back with four children. Tamsen turned down the creek trail to her dripping tent and dying husband. Eddy and his party had no food to leave the stranded emigrants. They cut them some wood. That was all. The ancient, doddering widow Murphy and crazy Keseberg were left together in the cabin. At the foot of the pass the retreating rescuers met Clark and Jean Baptiste with forty pounds of loot and two guns. They had deserted George Donner in Tamsen's absence. Only old George, his New England wife and little Sammy were left below.

In April the last relief expedition entered the mountains with W. O. Fallon, a mountain man known as "Le Gros." Most of his party had been over the divide before. Keseberg and Tam-

sen Donner might still be alive but the main incentive of the
party was to get treasure. At the lower end of Bear Valley they
left their horses and started in on foot with packs as the other
parties had done. In the pass they looked down on rotting ice in
the lake, dirty snow, the sodden mountain earth of early spring.
Bare ground showed in patches. After midday they reached the
cabins. The men stood in horror before the filth, the mutilated
bodies. A shout aroused them. They ran toward it and saw three
Indians scampering away. The savages had dropped their bows
and arrows in their haste. All hope of finding anyone alive vanished now.

The seven men searched around the lake cabins for two hours,
then started for the Donner camp. The treasure should be there.
On the way they saw the tracks of a man in the trail and wondered if some party had beaten them to the loot. The tracks went
straight to the Donner tents but no one was at camp. Fallon, a
mountain man, understood tracks and trailing. He said that the
man must have left Donners that very morning. Perhaps he had
heard them coming and evaded them on the trail.

The rich property of the Donners lay scattered under the
trees in the mud, books, bolts of cloth, tea, coffee, shoes, percussion caps, pots and pans. At the entrance to the tent a large iron
kettle contained human flesh, cut up. Near by, on a chair, were
three legs of an ox that had been buried under the snow all winter. A melting drift disclosed a dead horse. The men found
George Donner carefully wrapped in a sheet. His head had been
split open and the brains removed. Flesh had been cut from his
body for the pot. They judged that he had been dead about four
days. The seven men camped near by that night. Next day they
searched more carefully. Where was the Donner money? In
addition to their own wealth, Halloran, when he died back by
Salt Lake, had left the Donners $1,500. Also Tamsen had offered
that amount to Eddy to take out her children. It must be hidden
somewhere. Three remained to search further. Four followed the
mysterious tracks to find the man. The snow was melting fast.
The trail disappeared in the wet woods. The men gave up and
went straight to the lake cabins. Here they found their quarry.

Keseberg lay amid human bones in one of the cabins. Beside him was a large pan of liver and lungs recently taken from a human body. They roused him and asked for Mrs. Donner and the others. "All dead," he replied. Mrs. Murphy, he said, had lingered about a week after Eddy's party left. Then she died. After that, about another week—he was vague—Tamsen Donner came to his cabin at midnight. Her husband had died the evening before, she said. She wanted to go now to her children, even cross the pass that very night. Keseberg said that she seemed a little crazed. Her clothes were wet as though she had fallen into the creek. He rolled the little woman in blankets to warm her and in the morning she was dead. Keseberg said he ate her, "the best he had ever tasted."[12] From her body he had obtained four pounds of fat.

The men believed that Keseberg had killed her. A month before she was in surprisingly good physical condition. They rummaged his cabin and found two kettles of human blood. Where did that come from? "There is blood in dead bodies," Keseberg replied. The men said that blood flowed only from live or dying bodies. They asked further questions. Where was Donner's money? Keseberg said that he knew nothing about it. Tamsen must have cached it before she left. The men searched his cabin. They found silks and jewelry belonging to the Donners worth about $200, and also two of George Donner's pistols. In Keseberg's waistcoat they found $225 in gold. Fallon bent a rope around the German's neck and told him that he would hang him if he did not tell where the Donner money was hidden. Keseberg took them to a spot where an additional $273 was buried. This was all that they got.

When asked why he ate human flesh when other meat was available, he said he had not seen it. They told him he lied. It was in plain sight. Keseberg replied, "Oh, it's too dry eating." The liver and lights, he said, were better and brains made good soup. The disgusted men commanded him to follow them. Before he left, Keseberg put all the bones in a box, blessed them and said, "I hope God will forgive me what I have done; I couldn't help it! and I hope I may get to heaven yet!"[13]

1 George R. Stewart, Jr., *Ordeal by Hunger: The Story of the Donner Party* (New York, 1936) , 17.

2 J. Quinn Thornton, *Oregon and California in 1848* (New York, 1849) , I, 53.

3 Bernard DeVoto, *The Year of Decision, 1846* (Boston, 1943) , 122.

4 Charles L. Camp, *James Clyman, American Frontiersman, 1792-1881* (San Francisco, 1928) , 229.

5 Thornton, *Oregon and California in 1848,*

6 DeVoto, *Year of Decision, 1846,* 344.

7 *Ibid.*

8 Stewart, *Ordeal by Hunger,* 120-23.

9 *Ibid.,* 163.

10 *Ibid.,* 220.

11 Thornton, *Oregon and California in 1848,* II, 221.

12 Stewart, *Ordeal by Hunger,* 262.

13 Thornton, *Oregon and California in 1848,* II, 238.

Chapter 12

Francis Parkman: 1846

FRANCIS PARKMAN wanted to write history. Also, according to one of his classmates, he had "injuns' on the brain." As a boy he liked to prowl through the woods, hunt and trap. During his vacations he took canoe trips in the White Mountains, on Lake George and Lake Champlain. At Harvard he received good marks in subjects that interested him but neglected other courses. He liked amateur dramatics—a preference reflected in his later writings. Parkman was especially anxious to write the story of an Indian chieftain named Pontiac who led a great rebellion to expel the British colonists from the country west of the Alleghenies, and, having failed, remained thenceforth a staunch friend of the redcoats.

In order that he might understand Indian character in all its moods he decided to visit the Rocky Mountains. Scion of a family of means and refinement, descendant of a long line of scholars and just back from finishing his own education with a tour of Europe, he saw the promise of a new experience on the frontier. With Quincy Adams Shaw, a friend and relative (most New Englanders who were anybody were both), and sufficient money for equipment, Francis Parkman arrived in St. Louis in April 1846. The hotels were crowded and gunsmiths and harness makers were doing a big business. Steamboats along the levee were jammed with passengers headed up the Missouri for the frontier.

Parkman and his friend presented letters of introduction to wealthy fur traders. They met Colonel Stephen Watts Kearny, commander of Fort Leavenworth on the far frontier, and also a Britisher, Captain William Chandler, who was planning a big game hunting vacation. Young Parkman, twenty-three years old, told the St. Louis fur men his plan. Could they recommend a suitable guide for a trip to the Rocky Mountains? The traders suggested Henry Chatillon, a mountain man who had just arrived in town. They offered to call him to the office. Parkman was surprised to meet a tall, exceedingly well-dressed man. The New Englanders could not believe that this was a mountain man. They employed him at once.

On April 28, 1846, they left St. Louis on the steamboat *Radnor.* Her upper deck was loaded with wagons for the Santa Fe trade. Oregon emigrants were also on board with horses, mules, saddles and camp equipment. The Santa Fe traders lounged in the ship's cabin along with gamblers and speculators. In steerage, Parkman saw Negroes, mountain men, Oregon emigrants and a party of Kansas Indians coming back from a visit to St. Louis. The sky was overcast. The heavily laden vessel pushed up against the current and the water broke threateningly over her guards. The steamboat neared the mouth of the Missouri and a drizzle of rain peppered the water. Soon the storm lifted and Parkman looked out across the turbulent coffee-colored stream. Spring freshets were cutting the banks. Undermined trees crashed into the river, then came churning down the flood. From the deck Parkman noticed the water's surface, the colors which told pilots where the channel was deep and where sand bars were forming. Occasionally the *Radnor* ran aground. Sometimes an hour was spent backing off. At other times the spiked limbs of a submerged tree rattled along the ship's side. The passengers realized that a square hit on such an abatis would puncture the hull and sink them in midstream.

The *Radnor* puffed upriver for five or six days. Then the passengers began to notice signs of the great migration on the banks. Covered wagons were everywhere. They plodded along the roads. Fires burned by their sides in every clearing on the riverbank. At sunset, on a rainy day, the *Radnor* paddled into the old Independence landing. Parkman looked over the ship's rail at the muddy shore. Some thirty or forty broad-hatted Mexicans—employees of the Santa Fe companies—stared back at him. One or two French hunters, with long hair and buckskin shirts, leaned on their rifles and watched the incoming steamboat. Parkman felt close to the frontier indeed.

Next morning the *Radnor* arrived in Kansas and the Bostonians landed. They left their equipment at a log tavern and set off in a wagon for Westport where they hoped to buy horses and mules for the trip. The day was fresh and beautiful. The wagon track—it could not be called a road—wound through the woods in sunshine and shadows. Around them a multitude of birds sang and flitted through the leaves. Before long the Easterners overtook their late fellow travelers, the Kansas Indians. On the boat they had appeared drab and squalid. Here in the forest, fluttering with gaudy finery, they appeared strikingly picturesque.

Westport was full of Indians, with shaggy ponies tied along the fences and in front of the houses. Parkman learned to recognize the Sauk and Foxes by their shaved heads and painted faces. The Shawnee and Delaware preferred calico frocks and turbans. The Wyandot dressed like white men. These all were eastern Indians who had been removed to this edge of civilization. Parkman stood at the tavern door watching the play of colors in the dirt street. Then he saw a strange figure. He had a ruddy face and several days' growth of red beard. On his head was a round cap with a nob on top. He wore a coat of gray Scotch plaid and his trousers were of homespun. A little black pipe was in one corner of his mouth and hobnailed shoes on his feet. Parkman recognized Captain Chandler, the Britisher who, with his brother Jack and a Mr. Romaine—De Smet's companion—planned a big game hunting excursion to the Rockies. The captain's party was too small to go into the mountains alone. He suggested that Parkman and Shaw join him. With their guides and drivers they would have enough of a group to protect themselves. Captain Chandler had considered going with some of the emigrants but did not like the looks of the "Kentucky fellows." The emigrants with their oxen, dusty wagons, slattern women and grimy-faced children did not attract Parkman either. He decided to go with the British party but he must purchase his horses first.

To get the saddle and draft animals he wanted, Parkman rode over to Independence. He found the old town crowded like Westport, the street filled with horses and mules. There was an incessant hammering and banging from a dozen blacksmith shops, the hiss of steam as tires on the great wheels for Santa Fe wagons were reset, the smell of the burning hoofs of horses and cattle being shod. A train of emigrant wagons rumbled into town and stopped in the dirt street, travelers from Illinois. Parkman noticed a multitude of healthy children's faces peeping from the wagon covers. Beside the train a buxom damsel sat on horseback with a parasol over her sunburned face. The men, sober-looking farmers, stood in the dust by their oxen. Could this have been the Reed-Donner train? Parkman did not ask their names, but he noticed three elderly men with whips in their hands. He edged closer to hear their conversation. They were discussing the doctrine of regeneration. The Boston Brahmin was surprised. Surely this was not typical of such uncouth fellows. Many of them, Parkman mused, appeared to be "the vilest outcasts in the country."[1] He wondered why they were going west. Was it an insane impulse to better their condition in life, a desire to shake off the restraints of law and society or only restlessness? The men shouted to their oxen. Parkman watched the great wagons lurch forward and pass out into the prairie to join the rendezvous under Owl Russell.

Parkman and Quincy Adams Shaw spent a week purchasing animals and hiring a teamster. The Englishmen became restless, said that they would move out on the prairie and wait at the Kansas crossing. Next day Captain Chandler sent back word that they had decided to go to Fort Leavenworth and follow the tracks of some dragoons who had ridden from there across to the Oregon Trail. The New Englanders did not like the presumption of the old Englanders thus to change plans without a consultation. However, they accepted the situation and prepared to drive to Fort Leavenworth.

Parkman looked at his outfit. He and Shaw were both equipped alike with pistol holsters on Spanish saddles. A picket rope was tied to the neck of each mount and coiled on the waiting saddles. Shaw planned to carry a double-barreled shotgun. Parkman, on a horse he had named Pontiac, intended to labor under the weight of a fifteen-pound rifle. Henry Chatillon stood near by in a costume completely different from his St. Louis clothes, a white blanket coat, a broad felt hat, fringed buckskin leggings and moccasins. Around his shoulder hung a bullet pouch and powder horn. A sheath knife was stuck in his belt. On his horse, a gray Wyandot pony called Five Hundred Dollar, he had a saddle cushioned with a woolly buffalo hide. For baggage, Parkman had purchased a cart and hired a French teamster, Deslauriers. All in all, the outfit contained four men with eight horses and mules.

Everything was packed ready to go. Parkman, like any Bostonian of good family, was familiar with horses, but he had yet to learn that horses were different out west. He ordered the little cavalcade to start. The shaft mule in the cart refused to pull. Deslauriers whipped and swore. The mule reared and plunged. Bystanders offered advice. Finally a Mr. Boone, grandson of the great pioneer, offered to trade her for another. Parkman swapped and the cavalcade set off proudly. Westport was scarcely out of sight when a second mishap occurred. The trail crossed a muddy gulley. Deslauriers drove in. The wheels sank suddenly and the cart stuck. The men spent an hour getting it out. They were beginning to look bedraggled like the despised emigrants, and they had not even got to the Oregon Trail yet.

At noon they left the woods behind and crawled out on the prairie, flat all the way to the horizon. The day was mild and balmy. They stopped to rest at a little creek full of frogs and turtles. Indians had camped here and the travelers spread their blankets over the deserted lodge poles for shade. The horses were turned into the oozy meadow. Deslauriers began cooking, huddled over the frying pan with a sharpened stick to turn the sizzling bacon. Shaw lay back on a roll of bedding and experimented with smoking an Indian pipe. A drowsy, springlike sultriness pervaded the air, the voices of insects and young frogs piped in a chorus from the creek and meadow. Before long a ragamuffin horde of Kansas Indians straggled by, some on foot and some on horseback. The squaws were mounted on wretched little ponies with one or two snake-eyed children on behind. The young men strode along with bows and arrows in their hands. They were the dregs of the Kansas nation coming back from a begging expedition to Westport while their more savage brethren were off hunting buffalo. After they were gone the New Englanders caught their own animals and followed down the road. To Francis Parkman every party but his own looked wretched.

That night, on the Kansas River, they camped at the Lower Delaware Crossing. In a meadow the tent was erected for the first time and the horses were hobbled in the grass. It grew dark. The voices of the whippoorwills succeeded the whistles of the quail. The men took their saddles into the tent for pillows. Deslauriers crawled into a snug cubbyhole in the covered cart and soon all were asleep on the first night in the open.

In the morning the vacationists took the old military road to Fort Leavenworth. The day was warm, bright and perfectly still. For miles the wagon trail led between the farms and cabins of the Delaware. Next day in the afternoon they saw in the distance the whitewashed walls of Fort Leavenworth. In a short time they came to a tent beside the timber. Horses grazed around it. Their British friends were camped here. Parkman's cart came closer. Wright, the Britishers' teamster, was seated on the tongue of a big six-team wagon, repairing harness. Boisverd, a French hunter, stood at the door of the tent cleaning a rifle. Sorel, another Frenchman, lounged idly about. The captain's brother was sitting in the tent splicing trail ropes. With a rich Irish brogue he said that the captain was down on the river fishing and Romaine had gone to the garrison.

Parkman ordered his tent pitched near by. Supper was prepared. The Britishers came in and, after eating, all sat around the campfire. They decided to stop one day at Leavenworth—Colonel Kearny had come back from St. Louis and had excellent wine—then they would "jump off" for the Rocky Mountains. At the fort Colonel Kearny greeted them cordially in his quarters, set out the glasses, and Captain Chandler talked about past steeplechases and future buffalo hunts. The travelers also rode over to the Kickapoo village and called on the trader in a little green and white cottage furnished with carpets, sofas, chairs and a well-filled bookcase that surprised the Bostonians. His merry Creole wife set out iced water and a bottle of excellent claret. The taste of luxuries on the edge of civilization sharpened the drama of their impending journey. They all galloped back to camp, anticipation and regret mingling with alcoholic fumes in their brains.

On May 23, 1846, they saddled up for the great adventure. Over a month had passed since Parkman came first to St. Louis. They were still many miles from the Oregon Trail. Captain Chandler was sure that they would find it in a few days by following Colonel Kearny's horse tracks made the previous summer across the prairie. The Britishers' six-mule team, the Americans' cart and the lead saddle horses made quite a cavalcade. Mr. Romaine, the veteran of a previous trip, was sure that he knew the way across the ocean of grass. They all rode with him confidently for a couple of hours. A cluster of buildings appeared ahead. Strange, wasn't it! Presumably they had left the last settlement. They rode closer and noticed something familiar about the houses. The buildings looked exactly like the Kickapoo trader's establishment where they had visited yesterday except that they were on the wrong side of the road. Soon it dawned on the travelers that this was the trader's post and that they, not the post buildings, were turned around. Instead of riding west they had described a great circle and the willing horses were leading their masters back to Leavenworth. Almost a half-day of travel had taken them nowhere. The kindly trader pointed the way and reminded them that the sun went down in the west—a sure indication of the points of the compass. The travelers turned around foolishly and started again on a beeline across the untracked prairie. Traveling across the natural sod was slow but beautiful. They waded brooks, pushed through lines of brush and plodded mile after mile across the emerald ocean.

"Here we are at last!" the captain shouted. The men looked

down at tracks in the turf made by a large body of horse. Nothing now to do but follow these to the Oregon Trail. Parkman's spirits brightened. Everyone felt better now that they had found the way. Toward sunset they camped on the bank of a lazy stream that soaked through tufts of grass.

"Drive down the tent pickets hard," Chatillon warned. "It is going to blow." The mountain man knew the sky. The men worked hard as the sky darkened with great suddenness. A fresh, damp smell in the wind warned them that a storm was near. The prairie that had glowed in daytime with yellow-green light became black and somber. Thunder growled in the distance. The men took the horses into a meadow and hobbled them. Rain began to fall as they reached the tents.

Next morning the sky had cleared. They traveled a mile or two and came to a belt of woods skirting a muddy stream. The trail crossed it. Deslauriers looked at the mudhole, took the pipe from his mouth and began to whip his mules. The cart plunged in and stuck fast. He leaped into the stream knee-deep and let loose a torrent of French oaths. The mules bent their backs and pulled out the cart. The Britishers' wagon came next. Wright stopped and looked ahead at the quagmire. The captain began to give orders. His brother gave conflicting orders. Mr. Romaine shouted, "Drive on! Drive on!" The teamster sat quietly, then made up his mind. With his whip he lashed the back of his six mules and with a volley of American oaths he made Deslauriers' French sound weak as Chinese firecrackers beside heavy artillery. The mules scampered forward in panic. The great wagon settled hub-deep in the mud with the frantic mules huddled in tangled confusion on the far bank. Nothing to do now but unload, dig out the wheels and get the wagon bed back on dry land—a long hard job but they did it. The men reloaded the wagon and set off—everyone tired and caked with mud. A few miles farther they nooned. Here the greenhorns had more trouble. Parkman took his two saddle horses, Pontiac and Hendrick, down to drink. Pontiac bolted for home with his lead rope trailing. Parkman started after him on Hendrick. Wise old Pontiac kept just far enough ahead to prevent the man from getting hold of that rope. Parkman realized that he would have to match wits with the animal's—a challenge for a Bostonian. He dropped behind and circled out across the prairie to get ahead of Pontiac. The old horse was too smart for such tactics. When he saw his master circling ahead of him he thundered down the road until he again had a safe lead. Young Parkman feared that he might have to follow his horse to Leavenworth, forty miles away, before he could catch him. If so, so be it. Parkman had a New England heritage—like Tamsen Donner's.

Finally Pontiac came to the creek where the wagon had stuck. Here was Parkman's chance. Pontiac had become thirsty after his run. He stopped to drink and promptly forgot his pursuer. Parkman slipped off Hendrick and picked up the dragging trail rope. The fugitive was a prisoner once more. Parkman remounted and headed back to camp with Pontiac in tow. Old Hendrick had been as intent as Pontiac on getting back to civilization. He returned reluctantly, grumbling inside, like a submissive but disappointed horse. Parkman's temper was aroused. He gave Hendrick a sharp cut with the whip and "restored his cheerfulness." Then, dragging Pontiac, he set off for camp. Near sunset he reached his companions.

Days followed. The party trailed the horses' tracks. One day some dragoons caught up with them—deserters from Fort Leavenworth. They told the travelers that the horse tracks did not lead to the Oregon Trail but to a village of Iowa Indians, instead. The deserters suggested that the travelers change their course, strike straight north and come to a feeder to the Oregon Trail that crossed from the new town of St. Joseph, Missouri (laid out in 1842), then follow it west. The deserters galloped away and the tourists encamped in a bad humor. After all these hard days, they had not yet found the Oregon Trail. Next day they came to the St. Joe branch and turned their horses' heads west. Fort Laramie was, according to their figures, only 700 miles away, provided they did not get lost again.

The St. Joseph trail showed plainly that a large number of emigrants were ahead. Parkman supposed them to be Mormons and in consequence feared that they might be hostile. Day after day his party traveled across the flat greensward watching and wondering. Wood for camp became increasingly scarce.

Early each afternoon they saw thunderclouds piling up. Day after day a deluge drenched them. Between showers the sun beat down with sultry fury. The world steamed. The horses plodded along dejectedly, splashing in hot mud fetlock-deep. At night storms pounded the tent like a cataract. Water dripped from the seams and filled the tent with spray. Parkman noted that western thunder was more terrific than the Atlantic seaboard variety. He wanted to remember the night's fury of the elements for one of his proposed books. He noted:

Bursting with a terrific crash directly above our heads, it roared over the boundless waste of prairie, seeming to roll around the whole circle of the firmament with a peculiar and awful reverberation. The lightning flashed all night, playing with its livid glare upon the neighboring groves, revealing the vast expanse of the plain, and then leaving us shut in as if by a palpable wall of darkness.[2]

In the morning Parkman looked out from under the tent flap to see a leaden sky and no prospect of clearing. Through the vertical lines of falling rain he saw the dim figure of Captain Chandler wrapped in his Scotch tweed coming back from inspecting the horses with Brother Jack at his heels.

The sky cleared at noon and they set off again. In the afternoon they came to a cow standing beside the trail. For a fortnight the huntsmen had seen no game. Biscuits and bacon had become a monotonous diet. The Englishmen looked hungrily at the cow, then uncoiled their ropes and tried to lasso her. They were unsuccessful. Next they decided to drive her along with the party. She could be butchered at camp. During the afternoon the usual storm came up. The horses turned tail to it and stood dejectedly. The cow wandered back down the road. Captain Chandler pulled his cap down tight on his head, drew out his large buffalo pistol and splashed off after her, brought her back and shouted to Parkman and Shaw to head the brute. The

New Englanders, humped on their saddles in the rain, did not feel like moving. They watched dumbly through the veil of rain. The captain became desperate. He shot the cow through the body. She turned meekly and came back, unable to run farther. Soon the storm moderated and the men continued their journey. The captain put the cow in his brother's charge and she followed along painfully. The captain himself rode ahead, playing the part of a vedette.

A long line of trees appeared across the prairie. The vedette approached them, then turned and galloped back to the train. "Let that cow drop behind," he shouted with a grin. "Here's her owners." Ahead in the trees a white object could be seen that resembled a covered wagon. The men came up to it and found a large white rock instead of the Mormon encampment they expected. Jack went back for the cow and she again took her place in the procession. That night in camp she was butchered and divided between the two messes.

More days passed. Finally, the men came to the crossing of the Blue—the last big stream before the Platte. Swollen by the rains, it had overflowed its banks. Only the tops of occasional willows showed the margin of the stream bed. The treacherous water swirled like a millrace. Mr. Romaine did not pause. He flung off his clothes and with a rope in his teeth splashed and swam to the far shore. Parkman admired his audacity and wondered what he planned to do. The Britisher shouted orders continually. No one paid him the slightest attention but he did not stop.

Henry Chatillon understood this kind of crossing. He gathered some logs and built a raft. The wagons' loads were placed aboard and, with one man swimming at each corner, the raft was towed across. Then the empty wagon boxes were ferried over. Next, each man mounted his saddle horse and rode through the stream. On the far side they came to the Oregon Trail proper, and camped on the edge of a pool in the bottom of a grassy hollow. After supper they lolled around the campfire. In the distance they heard a strange sound—the voices of men and women.

Just before dark two men came down the road toward the

camp. They splashed through the pool and dismounted. One was a sallow-faced fellow with a wet broad-brimmed hat weeping around his face. Parkman noticed that his companion was heavy-set and intelligent. He said that he was captain of the train ahead—twenty wagons. Part of the outfit was still back at the crossing of the Blue. They had stopped for one of the women to have a baby. The emigrants looked at the New England tourists curiously and rode away.

Next morning the Bostonians were late as usual in getting away from camp. Finally they had packed. Out on the prairie they overtook the emigrants. Parkman looked at his first overland wagon train with an artist's eye. Later he wrote:

We saw close before us the emigrant caravan, with its heavy white wagons creeping on in their slow procession, and a large drove of cattle following behind. Half a dozen yellow-visaged Missourians, mounted on horseback, were cursing and shouting among them, their lank angular proportions, enveloped in brown homespun, evidently cut and adjusted by the hands of a domestic female tailor. As we approached, they greeted us with the polished salutation: "How are ye, boys? Are ye for Oregon or California?"[3]

The Bostonians did not feel so friendly as the emigrants. With their lighter mule-drawn wagons, they quickly passed by. Urchins peeped at the "rich fellahs" as they passed. Parkman thought that the women looked careworn but the girls were plump and rosy. All the women he saw were sitting in the front of the wagons knitting, but they dropped their work in their laps to stare at the British-Boston cavalcade. Each covered wagon's proprietor walked beside his oxen. Every driver's first words to Parkman were complaints about the wagon train's managament, details of the quarrel over leadership. Some wanted to wait for the woman in the party and her baby. Others criticized the train's captain on general principles. Parkman suspected that these chaps were jealous. He was glad to leave them and be surrounded once more by the wilderness.

The vacationists rattled away cheerfully. Then they came to a mudhole. The Britishers' heavy wagon stuck. The Bostonians stopped to help them. At last they were out and loaded again. It was almost dinnertime and over the swell of the prairie came the leading covered wagon. In no time the emigrants arrived. Each plunged through the mudhole and came out. None stuck. Oxen were better than mules in mud. There was shade on the north bank and Parkman noticed with satisfaction that the emigrants were preparing to encamp for noon. With his own party, he kept going, anxious to be rid of them, but Romaine, always friendly and willing to mix with overland travelers, remained behind to get his horse shod by one of the emigrants. Parkman camped at the next water, prepared dinner and wondered why Romaine did not catch up. Surely he had not got involved in the emigrants' quarrels. Before dinner was finished, Romaine appeared on the sky line. Behind him rose slowly the arched bow of a covered wagon.

"What is that blockhead bringing with him now?" Parkman mumbled. A moment later he saw plainly enough. Slowly and solemnly, one behind the other, four ox-drawn covered wagons rolled over the crest and gravely descended toward camp. Romaine rode in the lead guiding the way with the majesty of a king. The "go-ahead faction" had made friends with the Britisher. An alliance had been concluded and Parkman, against his inclination, found himself part of an odious wagon train. The Bostonian could not refuse to go with them and help guard against Indians, but he told the leader that the oxen would have to keep up with the horses or be left behind. The emigrants' leader assured the Brahmin that the oxen would do so. Parkman did not know how ridiculous was his demand. Next day the Britishers broke the axletree in their wagon. The oxmen went on. That night the Bostonians did not overtake them.

This was Pawnee country, the range traversed each spring by the Indians on their way from the lower Platte River villages to the buffalo range. The savages were not apt to attack an armed man but they were sure to rob an unarmed one. Any night now Indians might skulk around camp and steal horses. Henry Chatil-

lon was in his element at last. He ordered the travelers to take
turns standing guard. Too bad that the ten wagonmen were not
here to help but the tourists would soon overtake them, no
doubt.

Days passed without more excitement. Parkman's party came
to the Platte and turned up its treeless course. At the end of a
week they caught up with the ox teams that Parkman had said
were too slow. The four wagons were crawling patiently along
the sandy brink of the Platte. The emigrants had had an adventure with the passing Pawnee. One day they had seen many
black spots on a distant hill. They believed them buffalo and
set off with their rifles, some on foot, some on horseback. Suddenly they topped a swell and found themselves face to face
with thirty warriors. The Indians were as much surprised as the
white men. They were armed only with bows and arrows and
saw that each white man had a gun. Although three to one they
instantly shouted their friendship and came forward to shake
hands. The whites then went back to their wagons wiser and
more cautious men.

On the Platte everyone felt cheerful. Fort Laramie was still
400 miles away but the endless days of getting lost on the
prairie were over and the men would soon feast among the
buffalo herds. Around the feeble and lonely line of wagons the
vast solitude stretched interminably. Its size awed the Bostonians. They reasoned with themselves that there was no beauty in
such monotonous land wastes. Mile after mile of shallow river
lay before them, the sandy channel traversed with a dozen thread-
like sluices. Francis Parkman, with crude companions in this raw
land, found one consolation. The ten additional men in camp
made guard duty lighter. Almost was Parkman becoming a
democrat.

West of the forks of the Platte they came to the buffalo range.
Parkman with Shaw and Chatillon rode off for a chase. The two
New Englanders took only their pistols. On the plains back
from the river bottoms they found the herds. Parkman had trouble getting Pontiac to run in for a shot. The hard-mouthed
charger got excited and ran away. Parkman finally stopped him,

turned around and rode back toward the place where he thought he had left his companions. He rode over the swell of the plains and saw before him nothing but more monotonous plains. He was lost!

Parkman knew that the Platte ran east and west. He looked at the compass hanging around his neck, plotted a course north and touched Pontiac with the spur. He rode for two hours and did not come to the river. Something must be wrong. Parkman had forgotten that the South Platte turns southwest. He noticed that the buffalo paths all lay at right angles to his route. He turned his horse into one of them. Pontiac pricked up his ears at once. Before long, horse and horseman came to the river.

On June 8, 1846, a little before noon the travelers came to the usual fording place on the South Platte. No stick of wood for a fire was visible on the glaring white sand. The men gathered buffalo chips and cooked a meal—charcoal-grilled steak. As they crouched around the sizzling meat they saw the whitetops of an emigrant camp across the Platte. Four or five horsemen entered the water and splashed across to call on them. The visitors were ill-looking fellows—so Parkman thought—thin and swarthy. Their faces were thin and careworn and they had good cause. They had been encamped for three days hunting twenty-three lost cattle. The animals had got away when a guard fell asleep. Moreover, they had been raided by the Sioux and all their best horses were lost. The animals left them were crowbaits that had not been able to run when the Indians had whooped down on the horse herd one evening.

With most of their stock gone, they would be obliged to leave behind a great quantity of their goods. Parkman had noticed many pieces of furniture that had been cast out of the wagons of other travelers as they moved along. Some of it was handsome, probably brought from the seaboard to Kentucky or Illinois, but at last it had been thrown out to bleach in the sun because its owner could not move it farther. Parkman was sorry for people whose ancient prosperity had degenerated to a standard of living that forced them into the hazards of this overland journey. What the emigrants thought of an artistic Boston boy who did not get along well with people on the plains has not been recorded.

After dinner the mess boxes were put back in the wagons. First the heavy ox-drawn wagons plunged down the bank into the shallow Platte and dragged slowly across the sands. Parkman stood on the bank and watched. In places the water was so shallow it did not cover the hoofs of the cattle. The next moment the train dipped into a pool—water boiled against the wagon sides and eddied around the revolving wheels. Slowly the wagons receded from Parkman's view until they seemed to be floating far out in the middle of the river.

Parkman had learned that cattle were better in mud and sand than mules. He waited with concern to see how his mule cart would make the crossing. Deslauriers clucked to the long-eared animals. The cart entered the sandy stream and receded from the shore, dwindling in size every moment. At last it appeared to be only a motionless speck in the middle of the Platte. It was motionless sure enough, for it had stuck in the quicksand. The men beside Parkman on the south bank galloped with a great splashing of water to the helpless cart. All jumped into the shallow water, tugged at the sinking wheels and sloshed water on the hard sand that imprisoned the spokes and fellies. With much effort the cart was moved forward and at last came dripping and muddy from the stream. The teamster and his rescuers rested, dried out, then started forward. At the end of a mile Mr. Romaine shouted, "We'll camp here."

Parkman had been annoyed for a long time by what he called the Britishers' dictatorial attitude. Often they had ordered a camp without consulting the rest of the party. Parkman was fed up with it. "Why do you want to camp? Look at the sun. It is not three o'clock yet."

"We'll camp here!" Wright swung the mule wagon from the track. Deslauriers was at the head of the line but he saw the movement and turned his mules, too.

"Go on, Deslauriers," Parkman said determinedly. The Frenchman turned again into the road. None of Parkman's party looked back but in a few minutes they heard the rumble of wagons and jingle of harness chains. Wright was swearing at his mules furiously. Parkman suspected that the oaths were aimed at shorter-eared animals farther ahead but said nothing.

Relations between the two parties had been getting tense lately. Parkman deplored the inability of the emigrants to get along among themselves. In his own case, he thought that the fault was with the Britishers. More than once Parkman had taken it on himself to pitch camp without discussing it with his neighbors. He had noticed that they always camped, however, and pitched their tents with sullen and wrathful faces. Parkman resolved to put up with the discord no more. In the morning he would get up early and go. Let the rest keep up if they could. Parkman told his resolve to Captain Chandler.

"A very extraordinary proceeding, upon my word," said the Englishman.

Parkman reassured him that they were not deserting him in dangerous Indian country. Instead, the party that would be left behind had sixteen men while Parkman's group had but four.

"A very extraordinary proceeding, gentlemen," the captain repeated and went back to consult with his comrades.

Parkman got his men up before sunrise and struck the tent. This was something new for the outfit that sometimes did not move until noon. Hendrick was hitched to the cart. Mules were too slow for the forced march Parkman determined to make to get away from his annoying companions. Four days, he figured, should put him at Fort Laramie. In the morning twilight the Bostonian went to the emigrants' wagons and shook hands. The British were not at their tent. Parkman saw them on the top of a knoll wrapped in their plaids, watching the horse herd. The Brahmin waved adieu. Captain Chandler returned the salutation with dignity; Brother Jack tried to imitate him and was awkward as usual.

In five minutes the New Englanders were on their way. They came to the sand hills. Hendrick balked in the shafts. He kicked, pitched, plunged and refused to go farther. Parkman tried whipping him on one side, then on the other. At last Deslauriers and Shaw tried whipping him on both sides at once. It was no use.

Back at the camp the deserted party packed up. Perhaps the Bostonians, not the wagonmen, would be left behind again, as they had been before back on the Blue. Parkman was furious. He jumped off Pontiac, ordered the harness taken from Hendrick and put his saddle animal in the shafts. The change was made and the cart moved away but their comrades' wagons were already in motion. Parkman ordered Deslauriers to leave the road, take a straight cut for the North Platte. A cart could go where wagons could not follow. He would lead his party by the straightest course to Fort Laramie.

In due time they came to the edge of the deep gulch known as Ash Hollow. At a pool of rain water they stopped for a short noon rest. They were compelled to skirt the rim of the hollow to find a passage that they could drive down but at last found one. At the river they turned west and drove four or five miles. Ahead in a meadow they saw a big encampment of wagons, fifty at least, in a great circle. Parkman noticed a party of horsemen coming toward him from the wagons. The strangers rode up, stopped suspiciously and asked impertinent questions. The New Englanders were perplexed. Then it dawned on them that the emigrants suspected them of being the advance of the dreaded Mormons.

The men accompanied Parkman's cart to their own camp. Here the entire population surrounded them, even the women and children. The scene appealed to Parkman's artistic eye but he wanted to get away as soon as possible. For one thing he could not give a satisfactory answer to their inquiries. These poor people would never believe that a man had come out into this country for the sole purpose of attaining knowledge for a book.

Parkman moved ahead a mile to get away from this crowd, then pitched his own camp. The four men could not stand guard without excessive fatigue, so they extinguished the fire and lay down in the dark close to their horses.

Three days' more travel put them at the well-known spring at Scotts Bluff. Next morning Henry Chatillon and Parkman rode ahead together. In the distance they spied something. Parkman thought it a file of buffalo. Chatillon's eyes were better trained. He could tell by the movement of the distant line that it was Indians. "Old Smoke's lodges, I b'lieve," he said. The two men galloped toward the distant objects. Before long they saw a black speck approaching them on the plain. It grew larger and assumed the form of a man on horseback, a naked Indian careening toward them. Suddenly the savage wheeled in a wide circle and made his horse describe various mystic figures on the prairie. Henry immediately compelled Five Hundred Dollar to execute similar movements. "It *is* Old Smoke's village," he said. "Didn't I say so?"

The whites waited for the Indian to come up to them. Instead he vanished, sinking, as it were, into the earth. He had gone down into one of the deep, invisible gullies that crossed the level plain. A moment later the rough head of the Indian's horse appeared, then horse and rider scrambled out, bounded up to them and stopped with a sudden jerk in a shower of sand. The formality of handshaking followed. Parkman noted every item of this wild man's costume and remembered it with a photographic brain. Later he described the Indian:

He was a rough fellow, of no note in his nation; yet in his person and equipments he was a good specimen of a Sioux warrior in his ordinary travelling dress. Like most of his people, he was nearly six feet high; lithely and gracefully, yet strongly proportioned; and with a skin singularly clear and delicate. He wore no paint; his head was bare; and his long hair was gathered in a clump behind, to the top of which was attached transversely, both by way of ornament and of talisman, the mystic whistle, made of the wing-bone of the war eagle, and endowed with various magic virtues. From the back of his head descended a line of glittering brass plates, tapering from the size of a doubloon to that of a half dime; a cumbrous ornament, in high vogue among the Sioux, and for which they pay the traders a most extravagant price; his chest and arms were naked; the buffalo robe, worn over them when at rest, had fallen about his waist, and was confined there by a belt. This, with the gay moccasins on his feet, completed his attire. For arms he carried a quiver of dog-skin at his back, and a rude but powerful bow in his hand. His horse had no bridle: a cord of hair, lashed around his jaw, served in place of one. The saddle was of most singular construction; it was made of wood covered with raw-hide, and both pommel and cantle rose perpendicularly full eighteen inches, so that the warrior was wedged firmly in his seat.[4]

Parkman and Henry Chatillon went with the Indian to the village, which was on the move. They all nooned on Horse Creek. Part of the village had arrived there ahead of them. Across the creek Parkman saw a powerful man nearly naked standing with a rope around a white horse. Behind him his youngest and favorite wife sat astride a fine mule caparisoned with whitened skins garnished with blue and white beads. The girl had a light, clear complexion and a spot of vermilion on each cheek. Henry Chatillon said that the great man was Old Smoke. Parkman was now seeing real Indians in their home.

That night the whites returned to their camp on the Platte. Next morning Parkman's party crossed a sun-scorched plain. On the horizon the Platte was edged with cottonwood trees. Nestled under the foliage Parkman saw a log structure—Fort Bernard. Chatillon said that it was a trading post operated by free trappers. The fort, only seven miles from the great Fort Laramie, had never been completed. The Americans jogged forward. They noticed two skin lodges pitched near the cabin but no one seemed to be at home. The men drew rein at the door. The scorching June sun beat down on the logs. An old squaw thrust her round head from the lodge flap, as a line of stout young puppies stuck inquiring noses from under the tent; there was no other sign of life. Then the door opened and out stepped a swarthy little Frenchman. His black curly hair was parted in the middle and fell below his shoulders. He wore a frock of smoked deerskin embroidered like his moccasins and fringed leggings with dyed porcupine quills.

Henry Chatillon introduced the Frenchman as Mr. Richard. The trader nodded, called a Navaho slave to take the horses. Richard took their rifles and led the way into the cool, cellarlike cabin. The mud-daubed room was ten feet square with a fireplace at one end. On a settle covered with a buffalo robe lolled a tall half-breed, his hair saturated with vermilion and glued to his temples. Some mountain men dressed like Richard squatted cross-legged on the floor. A naked Indian boy about sixteen years old caught Parkman's eye. He had a handsome face and sat in an easy posture in the corner by the door. His eye was fixed immovably on the corner of the fireplace opposite him. The lad did not move a muscle or show any indication that anyone had come into the cool interior.

Parkman and Chatillon got out the pipe. All smoked Indian fashion, each man inhaling a few puffs and passing the pipe to his neighbor. The white men rested half an hour, made some purchases of moccasins and other savage haberdashery, then invited all the men to come to their camp and drink a cup of coffee. This formality completed, Parkman's men stepped out into the brilliant sunshine and rode away. They camped a mile up the stream. Here they hung up mirrors and stropped their razors, bathed in the muddy Platte and tried on the mountain clothing they had bought. Before long their guests arrived, drank their coffee, smoked more of their tobacco and the entertainment was over.

Parkman and his men rode on toward the fort. An hour later they saw the ruins of a building at the junction of the Laramie and the Platte. This was an old fort, Sybille, Adams & Company's post. New as the country seemed to be, it already had a past. A few minutes later, Parkman saw Fort Laramie proper. His men came to the river but could not find a ford. They rode along hunting a good crossing. Above the walls of the fort they saw men looking at them. "There's Bordeau!" Henry Chatillon called. "Him there with the spyglass."

Henry found a crossing. He spurred his pony to the bank's rim. Five Hundred Dollar set his feet and slid into the water. Parkman and Shaw followed, the water swirling around the horses. Behind them the mules and cart splashed in and were almost swept downstream but finally came out dripping. The little cavalcade crossed the river flat, rode up a steep bank and stood under the beetling blockhouse erected to defend the entrance. For Parkman this was the end of the Oregon Trail.

To complete his study of savage character Parkman tried to find some Indians on the warpath. He learned that Whirlwind, an Oglala Sioux, was planning a coalition of his people to make war on the Shoshoni, a counterpart of Pontiac's conspiracy. The traders were working to prevent hostilities. War hurt trade but Bisonette, still loafing around Fort Laramie with his Indian family, offered to help Parkman with his studies. A warrior rendezvous had been called on Labonté Creek. The Bostonian rode to the muster ground and found nobody there. Whirlwind, impulsive and fickle savage, had given up his war. Back at Fort Laramie on June 27 he met Paul Dorion, son of Pierre, the half-breed who had served Lewis and Clark and the Astorians. Paul Dorion, grandson of the old French rascal, was more Indian than white man. In broken French and English he told Parkman that Old Smoke, the Oglala, and two villages of Miniconjou Sioux were gathering at Fort Bernard eager for war regardless of Whirlwind.

Parkman rode down the Platte to see for himself. The flat around the cabin where he had stopped with Chatillon on his way up could hardly be recognized as the same place. Not only was it covered with the conical lodges of three bands of Indians, but dozens of prairie schooners were parked in a village of their own. Parkman had been ahead of the big migration which was just now coming up the Oregon Trail. Whites and Indians were beginning to carouse. The Miniconjou were drinking Taos Lightning and some of the emigrants had rolled out kegs of their own to sell drinks at a handsome profit. Lank bullwhackers, gaunt women in calico and sunbonnets tripped curiously among the tepees, traded horses, pointed to beadwork and asked, "How much?" Both the Donners and the Reeds were encamped among the emigrants; so were Patrick Breen, the fiddling farmer, and Jessy Quinn Thornton quoting poetry. Indians reeled in and out of skin lodges. Bleary-eyed mountain men whooped past the wagons hell-bent on important errands that they soon forgot. Parkman noticed "a tall, lank man with a dingy broadcloth coat" and a jug of whisky. The man twitched the fringe on the Bostonian's hunting shirt, hiccupped and confided that he had been captain of the train until deposed by lesser, jealous men.[5] Thus Francis Parkman, who had come west to study wild Indians, was buttonholed by Owl Russell, the bosom friend of Henry Clay.

Less than a year later Francis Parkman wrote a series of articles for *Knickerbocker Magazine* entitled "The Oregon Trail." The emigrants he described were bound for California as much as they were for Oregon but his narrative answered the craving of readers suffering from "Oregon fever." The charm, strength and drama of the young man's prose fixed an aura of romance on the name Oregon Trail that has survived a hundred years. Reprinted in book form, Parkman's *Oregon Trail* became one of the nation's classics.

Of the Fort Laramie he saw on his trip Parkman wrote:

Looking back, after the expiration of a year, upon Fort Laramie and its inmates, they seem less like a reality than like some fanciful picture of the olden time; so different was the scene from any which this tamer side of the world can present. Tall Indians, enveloped in their white buffalo-robes, were riding across the area or reclining at full length on the low roofs of the buildings which enclosed it. Numerous squaws, gaily bedizened, sat grouped in front of the apartments they occupied; their mongrel offspring, restless and vociferous, rambled in every direction through the fort; and the trappers, traders and *engagés* of the establishment were busy at their labor or their amusements.[6]

[1] Francis Parkman, "The Oregon Trail," *The Knickerbocker* (February, 1847), XXIX, No. 2, 163.
[2] *Ibid.* (June, 1847), XXIX, No. 6, 504.
[3] *Ibid.* (July, 1847), XXX, No. 1, 20.
[4] *Ibid.* (September, 1847), XXX, No. 3, 232-33.
[5] Bernard DeVoto, *The Year of Decision, 1846* (Boston, 1943), 179.
[6] Parkman, "Oregon Trail," *Knickerbocker* (October, 1847), XXX, No. 4, 283.

Chapter 13

The Mormon Pioneers: 1847

IN APRIL 1847, a year later than people expected, Brigham Young led his pioneers to the Rocky Mountains. He was an old hand at the game. His people had been movers, wagon travelers, driven from settlement to settlement, almost since the beginning. At Nauvoo in Illinois the Mormons had built a city. The state gave them a charter to govern themselves but this had brought no peace. Fugitives from the law made a haven of the brick village where the county sheriff dared not come. In the spring of 1846, before the Reeds and Donners had assembled on the public square in Springfield preparatory to starting west, the Mormons had crossed the Mississippi and in their wagons moved slowly toward Council Bluffs. They had not gone as a body but as a steadily flowing stream. Some reached their destination before the last left Nauvoo. Along the way Brigham Young established stations where livestock could rest and wagons be repaired.

Across the Missouri from Council Bluffs, Young built what he called Winter Quarters. In the spring of 1847 he intended to move a little group of pioneers west. He knew the time that was eaten up in crossing rivers and decided to be ready on the west bank to start with the grass. His men were not sure where he intended to lead them—to California, if California would permit, or to some isolated valley in the Rocky Mountains.

Father De Smet had stopped at Winter Quarters and discussed the possibilities of a settlement in Great Salt Lake Valley with

OVERLAND STAGE PHOTOGRAPHED ABOUT 1906

Similar Vehicles Connected Inland Towns with the Railroad Until World War I.

COACHING DOWN THE SIERRAS

the church leader. On April 7, 1847, Young set off with seventy-three carriages and wagons, 143 men, three women and two children. The women were wives of Brigham Young, his brother Lorenzo and his best friend Heber C. Kimball, an Apostle. Polygamy was not yet recognized in the church and the consorts of Brothers Brigham and Heber traveled under their maiden names.[1] As secretary and historian, or Clerk of the Camp of Israel, Brigham Young took William Clayton, a Lancashireman who had been converted in England and had come to Nauvoo, Illinois, with an immigrant party. Most of the men in Brigham Young's pioneer expedition were brethren but not all, and at least three were Negroes. Young organized his expedition carefully. He appointed what he called two Captains of Hundreds; five Captains of Fifties; fourteen Captains of Tens. He knew the value of giving many people high-sounding ranks.

The wagons were hauled by horses, mules and oxen. Nineteen cows provided milk, and crates of chickens hung from the end-gates of many wagons. Dogs trotted between the wheels. The pioneers took household goods, blacksmith tools, looms, spinning wheels, cobbling outfits as well as a supply of corn for the animals. The Saints had a cannon and a leather boat on wheels that they called the *Revenue Cutter*. The party followed the route along the north bank of the Platte. A plain road went out to the missionaries' and agents' houses at the Pawnee villages. Young ordered the wagons to proceed in double file. Spring was late in 1847 and the grass had not started. The group camped near groves, where they cut down hundreds of trees and turned the livestock into the fallen tops. Plainsmen had long since learned that the bark of the round-leafed cottonwood was as good as hay for horses and cattle.

Brigham Young conducted prayers both morning and evening. Always practical, he gave advice and marching orders at these meetings. The men must not stroll along arguing, he said. Each man must walk beside his wagon and leave only with permission. At night they might visit one another's fires, fiddle and dance on the hard earth. A few days out they met a trader's wagon coming in from the Pawnee villages loaded with pelts. Brother

Ellis Eames decided that he had had enough of pioneer life and went back with it. He was in poor health, spitting blood.

On April 20, 1847, the Mormons arrived at Shell Creek. Five miles beyond they spied three deer. Two of the Saints set off after them on horseback, chased them four or five miles but came back empty-handed. Other brethren unlashed the leather boat and fished in the sloughs along the way.

At the Pawnee village Indians ran out to look at the Mormons and shake hands. The chief wanted a powwow. Heber Kimball and Brigham Young gave him a little powder, lead, tobacco and salt. The chief was disappointed, said it was not enough. Brigham assured him that it was. The chief replied that the Saints would kill more buffalo on his territory than the few presents were worth. Brigham answered that Mormons did not kill buffalo. That ended the argument. A Pawnee chief had no business arguing with Brigham Young. The churchman always had the last word, and he knew, too, that although the Pawnee Indians might be tough with a stray teamster whom they found unarmed, they would be helpless before his well-armed caravan.

The Saints drove off and the red men accepted the situation. At the Loup some of the brethren went ahead and dug down the banks for a ford. The quicksand was bad and the Saints experimented by sending over empty wagons. Finally they doubled teams and pulled loads across. Three miles beyond the Loup the Saints camped to let the stock rest. In a near-by slough the men caught sunfish. Some Indian tracks made them suspect that they were being spied upon—disconcerting in a country where a Sioux war party might be skulking after unwary Pawnee. That night Brigham Young ordered the Saints to drill around the cannon.

After assembly on April 25, 1847, the Twelve Apostles met before Brigham Young's wagon and discussed appointments for hunting buffalo. Eight were nominated to hunt on horseback and twelve on foot. It was moved, seconded and passed that the second group "have the privilege of hunting when they have a mind to."[2] The next morning at 3:30 two shots in the dark aroused the camp. The guard reported that they had seen what they supposed to be wolves among the horses. Two sentries had fired and a half-dozen Indians jumped up and ran away. After daylight the Saints went to the spot and found moccasin tracks, but the Mormons never learned the identity of the thieves.

Each day Brigham Young, with Heber Kimball and other elders, rode ahead to select the road and pick camp sites. He warned all the brethren to keep their guns ready for Indians, either to carry them or have them handy in the wagons. All must be loaded. Cap-and-ball guns should not have the caps attached and flintlocks should have cotton in the pans. Thus all firearms could be primed instantly.

By the last of April, near Grand Island, the Saints entered the upland climate, the dry air of the plains. The men, especially those with red or blond hair, were troubled with chapped and cracked lips. When they licked their lips, the moisture collected alkali dust and increased the irritation. Dust from the wagons choked the drivers. The wagon wheels began to shrink so that spokes rattled as the wheels turned and the tires loosened. William Clayton noticed that the drought split his writing desk. On the dry sand in the bed of the Platte the men saw a white substance that looked like salt. They tasted it and pronounced it poor seasoning. On the plains back from the river they found buffalo grass, short and curly like buffalo hair—but no buffalo. They passed a deserted Indian camp that covered a number of acres, saw an antelope, shot at it and missed.

The morning of May 1 dawned very cold; water was frozen in the pails. The Mormons broke camp and traveled for six miles with buffalo robes over their overcoats, then halted for breakfast. During the march the men had noticed buffalo all around them. Few of the Saints had ever seen the shaggy monsters before and the whole camp was excited. Telescopes were extended and rested on the corners of wagons. Three hunters cantered away on horseback to make a kill. They came back after breakfast with convincing details describing how the buffalo got away. In a mad chase one man had lost his cap.

Shortly before noon buffalo were sighted again. President Young—his followers used the title though the honor was not formally conferred upon him until fall—ordered the wagons stopped at some lakes while eleven men went out to kill meat for the company. Elder Kimball accompanied the hunters. The Saints perched on their wagons, saw the men come back smiling. Yes, they had killed buffalo and Brother Kimball had nearly been thrown from his horse.

Brigham Young ordered some wagons unloaded and sent out for the meat. That night green buffalo hides were spread on the ground in front of Brigham Young's wagon. The bearded monsters' heads were displayed for the faithful to see and admire in all their hideousness. A mountain of meat was piled on the ground before the President. Later, Brigham Young distributed the buffalo steaks and a great feast was held around the campfires.

The next day Young announced that more buffalo would be killed. He sent a party of hunters off to the hills and ordered a road gang to prepare the way ahead. In camp, blacksmiths were ordered to repair wagons while the two parties were gone. A few hours later the road gang galloped into camp excitedly to report a large party of Indians in a hollow twelve miles away. Young ordered twenty-three men to arm themselves, go out and bring in all the hunters. By six o'clock all were back, safe and sound. Some suspicious objects had been seen in the distance but no Indians had attacked anyone.

In the morning the wagons moved forward in a column of fours with the cannon behind. Solid formations of wagons made a good defense against Indians. During the day the wagonmen spied three vehicles south of the Platte rolling east. They wanted to go across and find out who was traveling east, but since the Platte was two miles wide and its bottom often treacherous quicksand, Brigham Young would not let them go. An hour later a man from the distant wagons came to the train on foot. He said he was one of a party of traders coming down from Fort Laramie.

The Mormons asked if he would take letters back to the States. When he assented, Brigham Young ordered the train stopped. Pencils and quill pens were sharpened. The man left with a sack full of mail.

Young reminded the faithful about his order that no hunters should leave the train without permission. The drivers talked to one another as they trudged along. Some wanted to cross to the south bank of the Platte, where, according to the traders, the road was good. Why break a new trail? At the first halt a meeting was held to discuss crossing. The brothers arose one by one and debated the question. Leaders—or would-be leaders—pointed out that since they were pioneers opening a new road for thousands of Saints to use they should not cross to get an easier way. This doctrine impressed a majority and the Saints voted to stay on the north bank. Brigham Young had not said a word. A wise executive, he knew when to let the people rule.

On May 5, 1847, the prairies ahead were reported to be on fire. The Mormons thought it was the work of Indians. Brigham Young, believing it unsafe to permit the wagons to go ahead, ordered them to cross the sand bars to an island in the Platte—a safe place but without feed for the stock. During the night the Lord sent a shower that put out the fires. In the morning Young ordered the company to move quickly ahead and find grass for the animals. The Saints, unaccustomed to such an early start, had not had time to do their chores and milking. The train started slowly. Some of the faithful even smuggled out precious corn and fed their livestock. "I don't keer about myself so long as my stock gits fed" was a rule of ethics cherished in the backwoods.

On the burned plains the charred grass lay glossy as a black dog's hair. The wagons made a trail across it, stirring up a cloud of black dust, fragrant with the smell of charcoal. The white men's faces soon became as black as those of the Negroes in the party. A few hours' travel brought them to green grass again. They stopped and turned out their cattle.

Buffalo were plentiful here. The grass was cropped by them as by a mower. The men shot dozens of buffalo calves, little saffron-yellow fellows colored like the offspring of Jersey cattle. Brigham Young finally ordered the slaughter stopped. Buffalo were so numerous he rode ahead to drive them from the riverbank lest they stampede and wreck the wagon train in an effort to get back to the open plains. Some of the milch cows watched the wild bulls curiously and strayed away with them. Brigham Young clattered off on their trail, the Apostles at his heels, and in the course of a wild chase lost his spyglass. Next morning he called a meeting and chastised the cow herder, Brother Erastus Snow, for not guarding his charges and thus making him lose his glass. Then in the afternoon the spyglass was found, "a source of joy to all the brethren," Clayton recorded.[3]

The herds of buffalo surpassed all belief. The ground on both sides of the river was black with them. William Clayton wrote in his journal: "No pen nor tongue can give an idea of the multitude now in sight continually."[4] The wagons often moved within 200 yards of the monsters before they galloped away.

Clayton's active and inventive brain played with the idea of measuring the distance traveled each day. He tied a rag on a spoke of Heber Kimball's wagon and counted the revolutions as the train moved along. He was satisfied that this method measured the distance as accurately as a surveyor's chain, but after four days he found the task monotonous. Brother Appleton Harmon was mechanically dexterous. Clayton urged him to make a wheel that would record the revolutions and thus tell the distances. Harmon worked on the contrivance during his spare time.

A quarrel disturbed the Saints at prayer meeting on May 12. Forced association under tension was beginning to tell. The bugle had blown for evening prayers and Brother Aaron Farr had continued to talk loudly. Brother Thomas Tanner was officer of the day. He put Brother Farr under guard and the Saints took sides. In this state of unrest Brother Appleton Harmon began to claim credit for William Clayton's invention of the wheel-meter. Brotherly tolerance weakened under strain.

At the forks of the Platte the buffalo were less plentiful. Hunters reported Indian "sign" and suspected that the red men had driven the buffalo away. Every day or two William Clayton left a note in some prominent place for the Mormons who were expected to follow up this road.

On May 18 Brigham Young called a meeting of the Captains of the Tens for a lecture at his wagon. The brethren were getting careless, he said. The hunters wasted ammunition. With meat abundant, people turned up their noses at the forequarters of buffalo and would eat only the choicest pieces. Such extravagance must stop. Young cited another waste even more serious. He had seen a party of Saints shoot ten times at one rabbit and miss it every time. When wastrels had used up all their ammunition, President Young said, he would give them no more. They would have to carry their guns empty. Moreover, said Young, the Saints spent too much time hunting instead of looking for the best road ahead and improving it with pick and shovel to help the wagoners. He expected everybody to "take an interest in the welfare of the camp, be united, and receive the meat as a blessing from God and not as a stink offering from the devil."[5] To be censured from on high may have made Brothers Tanner and Farr more tolerant of each other but it was plain that a common danger was really needed to reunite the faithful in Christian unity.

Above the forks of the Platte the Mormons continued on the north side, breaking a new road for those behind. They noticed cedars on the bluffs across the river. A few sticks were picked up along the bank. Thus real wood was added to buffalo chips for cooking fires—an advantage not found on the old trail.

On May 20 the Mormons saw a wide gulch in the cedar-stippled bluffs south of the river. They believed this to be Ash Hollow, down which the old road came. A few men took the leather *Revenue Cutter*, went across and back. They had found the road. Perhaps now they might encounter the hated Missourians on the way to Oregon. For two days more they toiled up the North Platte, seeing no sign of life. Then Brother Porter Rockwell came in one day and announced that he had seen Chimney Rock in the distance. The famous landmark cheered the weary travelers.

The train followed the river but continually turned out. The wagons strained up draws behind the cliffs, crossed the flats and jolted with brakes squeaking to the river beyond. Brigham Young led the way and waved his broad hat to indicate the route. Court House Rock and the other buttes impressed the Saints with their "romantic beauty which cannot be described with either tongue or pen."[6] They prowled around natural "ruins of castles, cities, etc.," as represented by Scotts Bluff, and found rattlesnakes annoying. Five or six were killed in one day. Brother Nathaniel Fairbanks was bitten. His leg began to swell. He complained that his tongue and hands felt numb. His friends bound the wound with moist tobacco and turpentine. They gave him a drink of alcohol and water, dosed him with lobelia, then the elders treated him by "laying on of hands." Brother Fairbanks vomited—and got well.

The leaders kept always before their eyes their divine purpose. On May 23 William Clayton remembered that he and Elder Kimball strolled a short way from the wagons, knelt and "poured out our souls." A gust of wind swept down on them and snatched Elder Kimball's hat. The two men concluded their prayer and said "Amen" as quickly as they could without being abrupt, then rose to their feet. Brother Heber's hat was nowhere to be seen. They hurried down-wind and soon saw it in the distance still rolling away. Both men broke into a run. They pounced on the vagrant headpiece at the very edge of the river.

Buffalo gnats troubled the men and the horses. The sun was hot but not oppressive for Illinoisans. Hunters brought in coyote pups for pets. Once they caught a young eagle. On May 24, 1847, some Indians visited the Mormon camp. The savages were clean, handsome people, dressed in embroidered buckskin—indeed, much better dressed than the Mormons.

The wild, free life, the monotony of the traveling broke some of the Saints' piety. At night they danced around their fires. Brigham Young approved of this, but his followers soon indulged in other less harmless pastimes. They played cards, checkers and practical jokes, and finally held mock trials. Brother Davenport was formally arrested by two "box-headed jokers" and arraigned before his peers "for blockading the highway and turning ladies out of their course."[7] Each witness tried to outlie the one before him. Roars of laughter boomed through the camp. On May 28 Heber Kimball exhorted the people to be less boisterous, more sober and wise. The next morning all the men harnessed their animals and waited for the bugle to order the columns to start. Brigham Young climbed into the boat where he could see all his people, and began to preach:

I remarked last Sunday that I had not felt much like preaching to the brethren on this mission. This morning I feel like preaching a little, and shall take for my text, "That as to pursuing our journey with this company with the spirit they possess, I am about to revolt against it." . . . Nobody has told me what has been going on in the camp, but I have known it all the while. . . . If this camp was composed of men who had newly received the Gospel, men who had not received the priesthood, men who had not been through the ordinances in the temple and had not had years of experience . . . I should feel like preaching to them and watching over them and telling them all the time, day by day. But here are the Elders of Israel, men who have had years of experience. . . . I do not mean to bow down to the spirit that is in this camp. . . . I do not mean to bow down to the spirit which causes the brethren to quarrel. When I wake up in the morning, the first thing I hear is some of the brethren jawing each other and quarreling because a horse has got loose in the night. I have let the brethren dance and fiddle and act the nigger night after night to see what they will do. . . . Well, they will play cards, they will play checkers, they will play dominoes, and if they had had the privilege and were where they could get whiskey, they would be drunk half their time, and in one week they would quarrel, get to high words and draw their knives to kill each other. That is what such a course of things would lead to. Don't you know it? Yes. . . . I would rather see in your hands the dirtiest thing you could find on the earth, than a pack of cards. You never read of gambling, playing cards, checkers, dominoes, etc., in the scriptures, but you do read of praising the Lord in the dance, but who ever heard of praising the Lord in a game at cards? . . . Some of you are very fond of passing jokes. . . . If you do not want to take a joke, don't give a joke to your brethren. Joking, nonsense, profane language, trifling conversation and loud laughter do not belong to us. Suppose the angels were witnessing the hoe down the other evening, and listening to the haw haws the other evening, would they not be ashamed of it? I am ashamed of it. . . . I think it will be good for us to have a fast meeting tomorrow and a prayer meeting to humble ourselves and turn to the Lord and he will forgive us.[8]

Brigham Young closed his impressive speech. He asked all the High Priests to stand in line. Behind them he lined up all the bishops, then he formed the Seventies into line, next the elders, then the Quorum of Twelve, then the brethren. Young asked them all to raise their right hands and repent their follies. Every man responded. Brigham retired to his wagon. Elder Kimball arose and gave another lecture. Then Elder Pratt added a few words. Elder Wilford Woodruff combined an experience of his own with a sermon. Others told of their sins. At one-thirty in the afternoon the journey was resumed with no loud laughing, no swearing or hard speeches to man or beast. Brigham Young had spoken.

The following Sunday was observed with fasting, repentance and prayer. Members of the council walked from camp back into the sand hills to dress themselves in their priestly robes and offer a prayer to God. A heavy black cloud threatened rain, but the council did not falter. Two members stood guard at a little distance to prevent any disturbance from the ungodly in the wagon train. The cloud reached out overhead. The men of the council looked up apprehensively, but they robed themselves, performed their service and were dressed again before it began to sprinkle. By the time they got back to the train it was raining hard. The men visited one another's wagons, sat around under the wagon covers and discussed religion.

The next day, May 31, 1847, the Mormon wagon train came to the Overland Trail, which they would follow to Fort Bridger. The following day they sighted Fort Laramie and encamped at the ford two miles below the fort. On the south bank of the Platte they saw some of their fellow Mormons who had wintered on the Arkansas and had come across to join the exodus.

The Platte was 100 yards wide here with a deep channel. Brigham Young crossed in the *Cutter* with a few companions and rode up to the fort. Bordeau met him cordially but said that he had little to sell as his supply wagons had not yet arrived for the summer trading. Brigham Young rested in the fort as Bordeau talked. Across the compound to the west he could see Laramie Peak. Sometimes invisible in the distance, that day it stood boldly, white patches of snow gleaming on the mountain's shoulders. Young asked about suitable places to settle beyond the distant mountains. He learned that Bear Valley along the Oregon Trail had good grass, timber for building and mild winters. The church leader heard, too, that many gentile emigrants were coming up the road behind him. One man claimed to have seen 2,000 wagons of the hated Missourians. Surely the Saints had better get along as fast as they could. Bordeau said they would be obliged to cross the Platte. The country above, on the north bank, was too rough for wagons. The *bourgeois* offered to hire his ferryboat to the Mormons at twenty-five cents per wagon crossed. Young closed a deal with him and the boat was floated down the Laramie and then up the Platte to the ford. The slow process of crossing commenced. On June 4 the Saints started off again along the Oregon Trail. Seventeen new members, including some women, had been added to their number, making a total of 161 in all.

The road from here on was well traveled. Indeed, there were two roads and the way was much more hilly. In several places the teamsters had to unhook and "double" to pull the heavy wagons over some of the pitches. On Sunday June 6 the Mormons rested. They stayed in camp for divine worship. During the morning eleven wagons of gentiles passed. Four men rode over to see the Saints. Mormons and gentiles appeared mutually suspicious but they exchanged civilities, and Brigham Young learned that he would have to travel, Sunday or no Sunday. There was water within six miles but the next stopping place beyond was farther than he could drive in a day.

Early in the afternoon the Mormons hooked up again, passed the gentile camp and stopped a short way beyond them. The Missourians came out to watch the Saints. The roadometer caught their eyes. One man asked bashfully for permission to inspect it. Another learned that the Mormons had a forge along and asked if they could weld his broken wagon spring. Thus bitter enemies back in Missouri forgot their animosity on the plains.

The next morning, June 7, 1847, the Missourians passed the Mormons while they were still at prayers. At the noon camp another party of "pukes" rumbled by with thirteen wagons. On June 8 some mountain men came down the road and stopped at the Mormons' night camp. Here was an opportunity to send mail back to the States. The Saints sat up writing letters by candlelight in their wagons. The mountain men, waiting around the fires, said the water was high at the Platte Crossing seventy miles ahead. To get across they had made a bullboat which the Mormons would find hanging in a tree. After breakfast the two parties separated. Brigham Young saw an opportunity to make some money. He selected nineteen wagons and the *Revenue Cutter*, with fast teams and forty men, ordered them to hurry up the trail, get ahead of the Missourians, take possession of the bullboat, build a raft, kill game and be ready to charge for ferrying travelers across the Platte.

The light column rattled off. Brigham Young and his followers continued their leisurely gait, their religious services and discussions.

Twelve miles below the crossing the Mormons overtook the Missourians. One of them came to the Saints' camp with a snowball. He had got it in the mountains (Casper Mountain?) to the south, he said. He also told the Mormons that his party had killed three bears and a buffalo. The next day the Mormons encamped within half a mile of the ferry. Their advance party had arrived the day before at noon and was now busy ferrying Missourians at $1.50 a trip in cash, or an equivalent value in flour at $2.50 per hundred—the latter a godsend to Saints who had run out of provisions since leaving Fort Laramie. Relations between the traditional enemies were now excellent. The men visited and traded back and forth. Brother Rodney Badger earned the esteem of the Saints by trading off his wagon for another as good except for a loose tire which could be fixed, and getting "to boot" a horse, 100 pounds of flour, twenty-five pounds of bacon and some crackers.

Frenchmen camped at the crossing told the Mormons that Indians must be hunting on the Sweetwater. Buffalo, migrating east along the plains north of the crossing, were no doubt being driven from their range. Mormon hunters went out and killed three bison, a grizzly bear, three cubs and two antelope. They came back with tales of the deceptive atmosphere. Hills and ridges that appeared to be within a mile were in reality eight and ten miles away. Brother Tunis Rappleyee wandered off south to get some snow. Instead he got lost. Young sent the bugler and a party out after him. The Mormon leader did not like such a waste of man power.

On Sunday June 13 divine services were held at the ferry. Brigham Young took for the text of his sermon "The Liberty of the Gospel." He said that the Gospel guaranteed liberty, but not liberty to break the laws of God or the liberty to wander into the mountains and get lost. Young let this truism sink properly into the minds of his followers. Then he suggested that they all get to work on rafts for transporting the baggage across the Platte. The day was very hot and it was pleasant to work in the water.

Monday was cloudy and therefore cool. At this altitude sunshine changed the temperature quickly. Immediately after breakfast the Mormons began to ferry their goods and wagons. They had two rafts and the *Cutter* but only one wagon could be carried on a raft at a time. Brigham Young estimated that the crossing would therefore consume three or four days—much too long. The drivers looked at the gathering clouds and the muddy water and suggested that the wagons be converted into boats. Two were lashed together with poles and attached to a rope on the far side of the river. The men pushed the odd craft into the deep water. The current carried it away at the end of the rope, downstream in a great arc, until it hit the shore on a sand bar. Then one wagon bed rolled over the other, crushed the bows of both and broke one wagon's reach. This would never do. The men tried lashing four wagons together. These were launched in the same manner. All drifted across but the upper one, which turned on its side. Next the men tried ferrying one wagon alone. This rolled over and over, breaking its bows and churning the water like the wheel on a steamboat. The men decided with regret that it was best to cross on the raft, one wagon at a time.

The dark clouds began to sprinkle and thunder rolled across the sky. The swirling surface of the Platte danced with raindrops. The men ran for shelter. Between showers they worked but by ten o'clock at night counted only twenty-three wagons across.

On the fourth day the last wagon crossed at noon. In the meantime the diligent Mormons had constructed another raft and a boat. They were now well equipped for ferrying, and Brigham Young announced that he intended to leave a party here to help all the gentile emigrants who were behind. Ferrymen could make good money for Zion until the next caravan of Mormons came along from Winter Quarters. Then the ferrymen were to quit and come on to the new settlement—wherever it might be.

In the afternoon two trains of Missourians came down to the ford. The first made a deal to be ferried across at $1.50 a load. The second train was anxious to beat its predecessor and offered an additional fifty cents if the Mormons would take it first. This was a temptation, but the original contract had already been made. A Saint could not well break his word. Yet everyone realized that the Lord wanted His children to get as much money from the gentiles as possible. A bit of "high finance" got the Saints out of this predicament to their satisfaction. Secretary Clayton did not record in his diary the author of the scheme but he did say that the ferry foreman "received a hint" that the ferry was in charge of another ferryman when the first party's wagons jolted down the bank to be loaded. The foreman took this "hint," refused to take the $1.50 emigrants and let his colleague transport the second, or $2.00, group. Brigham Young halted his wagons on the north bank until the negotiation was complete. He wanted to revictual his entire flock from the supplies the Missourians would have to pay.

On June 19, 1847, the Mormons started from the ferry with refilled wagons. The Missourians had rumbled on ahead of them but the delay at the ferry had done wonders for the Mormon livestock. The grass was good there. The teamsters said that they hardly knew their animals, they looked so sleek and fat. The road ahead had little forage. West of the Red Buttes, Brother Kimball rode ahead to look for a good place to encamp. He saw six blanketed figures at the side of the road. They motioned the Mormons to go back but the elders stood their ground. The blanketed figures galloped away and disappeared in a draw. Suspecting that they were not Indians, Brother Kimball led the way to a near-by hill where they could watch the Missourians' camp. Sure enough, the Mormons saw the pretended Indians ride into it. The churchmen clattered back to their wagon train no doubt murmuring the expletives "By hell and by damn"—or their 1847 equivalent. They were properly outraged. So the puke gentiles were intimidating them, were they? Scaring them back in order to have all the best grass for themselves! Brigham Young ordered his drivers to move faster on the march and to crowd the Missourians for their insolence.

On June 21 the pioneers sighted Independence Rock and nooned near it. They swarmed like ants over the elephantine boulder, tasted the pools of rain water on top and exclaimed over the hundreds of names carved and painted on the smooth surfaces. Secretary Clayton put up a signboard for the following party of Mormons. He consulted the roadometer and recorded for the later party that they had come 175¼ miles from Fort Laramie. Five miles beyond, the Mormons came to Devil's Gate. President Young, with Elder Kimball, walked over to view the cleft and returned. The Devil would not let them pass through, Young said mirthfully. That night at the camp William Clayton saw a panorama that impressed him greatly, the long translucent purple and white ridge of the Wind River Mountains.

On June 23 the Mormons came to two Missourian camps. They were told that this was the jumping-off place for South Pass, with no water for fourteen miles and the pass about twenty-eight miles ahead. Young ordered an encampment. Brother Frost set up his forge and repaired wagon tires for the Saints and for some of the Missourians. Brigham Young planned to make an early start, beat the puke trains to the road and thus be able to choose the best camping places. The Mormons moved at 6:15 the next morning, an early hour for them—but not early enough. William Clayton recorded in his diary: "They [the Missourians] started out a half an hour before we were ready."[9]

During the day the Mormons passed the famous Ice Spring, a sulphur water hole where ice could be found in midsummer. The brethren broke off chunks which forthwith floated to the surface. On June 25 some of the Saints discovered a snowbank. They led the girls out to see it and pelted them with snowballs. The days were hot but the nights were cold. On June 26 water froze in the pails. Table Rock appeared in the southwest, the southern boundary of South Pass. That night they encamped two miles short of the Divide and crossed it the next morning.

In the great flats of South Pass they met a pack train coming east—"Peg Leg" Smith headed for the States from Oregon. One of "Peg Leg's" traders dropped out with a pack of buckskins and trinkets to sell. He joined the Mormons, promised to show them things they would want to buy when he had time at the evening camp. Also he had newspapers from California and Oregon. The Mormons gave letters to "Peg Leg's" main party to be mailed and they separated.

West of the Divide the Saints had a clear view of the Uintah Mountains. They encamped with the vast panorama spread before them. The trader opened his packs, offered to sell buckskins at $1.50 and $2.00, a pair of pants at $3.00. Brigham objected that the price was too high. He queried the man about the western valleys, especially Bear River and Great Salt Lake. The trader said that he considered Cache Valley near the Salt Lake most likely for a settlement.

Next morning the Mormons "gee-hawed" down the wagon trace. They came to a fork in the road, the Sublette Cutoff. The wagon train took the left-hand road to Fort Bridger. In the afternoon they met Jim Bridger himself, Old Gabe, headed for Fort Laramie. He knew the country in all directions as well as any man. Brigham Young urged him to camp with them and discuss possible locations for Zion. Old Gabe agreed. The wagons wheeled out of the road and formed near Sandy Creek. The grass was good but the mosquitoes were bad. The men built fires and stood in the smoke. Old Gabe talked in a rambling manner that baffled his listeners. He knew the mountains but was hazy about distances. Like a deer he could move by instinct from range to range, could find his way anywhere in the Rockies, but was unable to tell others how to do so. Old Gabe's imperfect and irregular descriptions of the country ahead were of little help to the Saints, but they did learn from him that the Indians were not ferocious around Great Salt Lake and that corn and pumpkins could be raised near Utah Lake.

On June 30, 1847, the Mormons reached Green River a little before noon. The men lighted dinner fires under the cottonwoods. The women brushed dirt off their clothes, climbed down from the wagons using the wagon tongue for a step, careful always, of course, to watch the hems of their calico dresses. The river was much too deep to ford. After eating, the men took their axes and soon the crash of trees could be heard. Rafts would be constructed in no time. As the men worked, a party of horsemen rode up to the wagon camp. Elder Samuel Brannan had come from California to meet the pioneers. He and a party of Mormons had gone to the west coast by the sea route. His colonists were now comfortably settled in the San Joaquin Valley. Brother Brannan distributed copies of a new newspaper, the *California Star*. Coming down from the Sierras, Brannan and his party had ridden past the Donner party's wrecked wagons and filthy cabins in the cold mountain mud. He told the Saints the harrowing story but urged them to come on to California.

Brigham Young was not impressed with Brother Brannan's description of California, nor by the fact that one of his companions was a counterfeiter who had made trouble in Nauvoo. The church leader had made up his mind to settle somewhere else.

The night camp on Green River was almost intolerable because of mosquitoes. For three and a half days the Mormons fought mosquitoes and ferried their wagons. On the west bank the train reassembled and creaked down the riverbank to a flat opposite the mouth of Big Sandy. The worst part of the long journey seemed to be over at last. Brigham Young detailed couriers to go east and guide the second expedition. He warned those who were to go ahead with him to be careful in their trading at Fort Bridger, not to spend money carelessly.

Young and a few others rode back up the river with the couriers as far as the ferry. Later that day they returned to the main party with twelve new men, brethren who had ridden hard from the east to overtake the pioneers. A meeting was called to welcome the newcomers and Brigham Young moved that all the brethren give glory to God.

One day's march from the Green River camp put the Mormons on Blacks Fork. The next day they crossed Hams Fork and at night camped again on Blacks. Across the flats between the streams sego lilies and other highland flowers bobbed and sparkled in the breeze. The men urged the oxen ahead and wondered what kind of place they would find at Fort Bridger.

On July 7 the wagons creaked down off the plains into broad green meadows interlaced with lines of cottonwoods. In the midst of this valley with the Uintahs standing like a wall, lucent and purple against the sky, the Mormons saw two log cabins joined by a palisade. Several Indian lodges stood close by and dusky children scampered hither and yon. The covered wagons jolted across one or two narrow streams of crystal mountain water and encamped on a green pasture. President Young announced that they would stop for a day, let the livestock feed, repair the wagons and reset shrunk tires. No doubt many of the men and the few women, too, walked back to examine the fort. The scanty cabins disappointed them. The trader offered to exchange tanned buckskins for woven clothing and for rifles, two things the Mormons could ill afford to spare. After a trip of 397 miles from Fort Laramie—roadometer measurement—Fort Bridger offered little for diversion.

On July 9, 1847, the Mormons left the fort. Soon they encountered their first real mountain traveling. On the divide between Blacks Fork and Bear River they repeatedly unhooked their cattle to "double" up the hillsides. Chains were necessary to lock one wheel on the downgrades and thus break the descent. On July 10, after camp was set, a mountain man rode into the wagon circle with four Mormons who had been scouting the neighborhood. The stranger wore long sun-bleached yellow hair hanging on his fringed buckskin-clad shoulders. It was Miles Goodyear. He told the Saints that they were only about two miles from Bear River. His own farm, the first white man's in Utah, stood seventy-five miles beyond in Cache Valley to the north. Goodyear described his country in glowing terms. It was much more fertile, he said, and more verdant than Salt Lake Valley.

The Mormons decided that he was overpainting his neighborhood. Perhaps he wanted them to build a road to his farm. No, they would go on to Great Salt Lake, but they were undecided whether they should use the Donner or the Hastings road. President Young called a meeting. The Twelve wanted to take the northern or Hastings road, but the majority decided on the Donner route and Brigham Young ordered that it be taken. The wagon tracks left by the tragic party had already been washed away and could be followed only in places.

On July 12 Brigham Young was struck with a sudden attack of mountain fever. The jolting wagon gave him much pain. Heber Kimball ordered the train to go forward, leaving his wagon and Young's behind until Young was able to travel. The next day Kimball overtook the Saints and reported that President Young was better but that he had been delirious and very ill during the night. Kimball suggested that the train stop and send ahead a few wagons to scout out the Donner road or some other pass so that they could avoid the Weber Canyon. Elder Orson Pratt was chosen for this job. He organized his helpers and Kimball rode back to his suffering chief.

On July 15 President Young, with his companions, joined the train again. He was weak but able to travel. The train started slowly along the trail opened by Brother Pratt's wagons. At noon a messenger came back from Orson Pratt to report that the canyon was about twenty-five miles below and that the scouts had found the Donner road. They expected to camp on the divide that evening. The wagon train pulled out at once along Orson Pratt's route but President Young stayed behind once more.

The road led deeper and deeper into a narrow defile. Sunshine did not penetrate the mountain valley. The rattle of the iron tires on the cobblestones echoed above the travelers like carpenters hammering boards on the highest rocks. A rifle shot cracked like a clap of thunder and reverberated from cliff to cliff. The bugler had a hideous time. The train encamped deep in the gorge. In the morning, reports from Brigham Young announced that he was very ill. The wagons made only a short pull, then halted on the Weber. Young's illness had become worse. Several of the elders went into the mountains, put on their priestly garments and prayed for Brigham Young's recovery. Coming back, they experimented with rolling rocks from the mountains. Two men sitting down could push a huge boulder with their feet and listen to it crash hundreds of feet below.

The next day was Sunday. Heber Kimball conducted the services. He told the congregation that Brigham Young was a very sick man. Everyone should pray for him. Fishing, hunting, mountain climbing must be foregone until their President recovered. The site of Zion was close, but the season for growing crops was also well along. Brother Kimball said that all the wagons but eight or ten must go ahead, select farm land and put in the crops. Then the sacrament was administered and the Saints prepared to move in the morning.

The day dawned clear and warm. Two and a quarter miles below camp the Mormons forded the Weber. Three-quarters of a mile below they turned from the river and started up the steep, circuitous climb to the summit and a route around the canyon. For over two miles the wagons strained and labored before reaching the top. Going down the other side they slipped and skidded on the slopes. The spokes in the wheel of Elder G. A. Smith's wagon had worked loose in the fellies. On a sidehill the wheels dished, then collapsed, scattering the load. The other wagons could not well stop here. They all proceeded for two miles to a good stopping place. Then one wagon was unloaded and sent back to pick up the lost supplies. When it came back the load was distributed among the wagons.

On July 20, 1847, a messenger came back from Orson Pratt's advance company. They were still having very rough traveling, he reported. Brother Pratt had had a touch of claustrophobia like the Reed-Donner party in these same mountains. He had climbed the nearest ridge and from the top had been unable to see the Great Salt Lake, which he supposed to be near. This was discouraging news. The second party rumbled along slowly in the Orson Pratt ruts. The mountainsides were covered with scrub oak and serviceberry bushes. Willows twenty feet tall choked the bottom of the gulch. Limbs scraped along the sides of the wagon covers. On the night of July 21 the second section camped within half a mile of Orson Pratt's company. The road ahead had become more brushy, almost choked with willows. The Saints noticed that the Donner party had done a poor job of cutting brush. They told one another that the gentiles had not been very good workers and had got what was coming to them.

Early the next morning the second section came up with Orson Pratt. Only a mile and three quarters below they came to the place where the Donners had climbed out of the canyon up a terrific grade, rather than cut one more willow. To the Mormons it seemed almost impossible to realize that heavy wagons had been pulled up that slope. Brother Stephen Markham went on down the canyon. A little chopping and some digging, he said when he came back, would open a road to the plains. The men took their tools and went to work at once. Orson Pratt and a few companions mounted horses and went ahead to select a place to plant crops.

William Clayton climbed up the year-old trail made by the Donners. On the ridge he looked across the Great Basin. Salt Lake was twenty-five miles away, with two mountain peaks thrust through the blue, sparkling water. On the east the Wasatch Mountains rose precipitously to snow-capped summits. At the mountains' feet, clusters of green cottonwoods disclosed streams running from deep gorges. South, across a broad plain, stood the Oquirrh, brittle, dry and barren as lunar mountains. Beyond them, westward, glistened salt flats and alkali sinks, with endless azure deserts in the distance. Elsewhere in America or in Europe there was no scene more inspiring and William Clayton was deeply moved.

This great basin was indeed the Promised Land. True, wood for building was not available, but adobe bricks might be used instead of logs. The Pawnee back on the Platte made comfortable house walls with mud and wattle. In any event, Clayton mused, "I have no fears but the Saints can live here and do well while we will do right."[10] Surely it would be better to enjoy "the privileges and blessings of the everlasting priesthood" than to "dwell amongst the gentiles with all their wealth and good things of the earth, to be eternally mobbed, harassed, hunted, our best men murdered and every good man's life continually in danger. . . . Give me the quiet wilderness," Clayton soliloquized, "and my family to associate with, surrounded by the Saints and adieu to the gentile world until God says return and avenge you of your enemies."

That night the wagons came within five and a half miles of the mouth of Emigration Canyon. The next day two brethren went back to tell President Young the good news, while the wagons lurched and struggled across the last few miles. Out on the plain a prayer meeting was held, then the plows were unloaded. Some men prepared the ground for potatoes and turnip seeds, others dammed the streams to get water for irrigation. The next day at noon Brigham Young was driven out of the canyon in a carriage. The farming was well started. One of the pioneers remembered years later that the convalescing President looked across the great basin, to the lake and the Oquirrh, far-off peaks rising from the mauve desert mist, and said, "This is the right place. Drive on."

---

1 Dale L. Morgan, *The Great Salt Lake* (Indianapolis, 1947) , 188.

2 *William Clayton's Journal: A Daily Record of the Journey of the Original Company of "Mormon" Pioneers from Nauvoo, Illinois, to the Valley of the Great Salt Lake* (Salt Lake City, 1921) , 103.

3 *Ibid.*, 135.

4 *Ibid.*, 137.

5 *Ibid.*, 157.

6 *Ibid.*, 175.

7 *Ibid.*, 176.

8 *Ibid.*, 189, 191-94, 197.

9 *Ibid.*, 261.

10 *Ibid.*, 309.

Chapter 14

The Forty-Niners

"GOLD! GOLD! GOLD from the American River!" Sam Brannan waved a container of the precious dust. A newspaperman at heart, he had returned to California after talking with Brigham Young on Green River. Sam Brannan still devoted some thought to the Mormon colony on the San Joaquin, but worldly affairs took more and more of his time.

During the summer of 1848 the discovery of gold had not excited the village of San Francisco until the echo returned from the outside world. The first immigrants came from Hawaii. This island crossroads in the mid-Pacific had been settled by merchants in the wake of the missionaries. The foreign settlement in Hawaii had established schools, newspapers and a social life in many ways more advanced than in California.

News of the discovery reached Oregon by way of a ship from Hawaii. The captain kept the secret, so tradition says, until his ship was loaded for the return trip. By sea and by land the American-Oregonians set off for El Dorado—probably half the population, certainly more than half the male population. The Hudson's Bay employees were practically the only people who remained. Old times had come back again. In September 1848 one party of 150 men with fifty ox-drawn wagons started up the Willamette Valley. The leader was Peter H. Burnett, unsuccessful captain on the Great Migration of 1843. In a little over a year he would be the first governor of the new state of California. The party followed the Applegate road to the lava plains of northern California, then struck south to the Sacramento.

In Mexico the mania also appeared. Gangs of laborers journeyed up from Sonora. Officials tried unsuccessfully to dissuade them with stories of mistreatment in the mines. From four to six thousand persons emigrated to California.

Official news reached Washington, D. C., in the middle of September 1848. This word came by way of Mexico. By the last of September the big metropolitan papers carried amazing stories about picking up nuggets under the oaks, of fortunes made in a few days, of men too lazy to work employing Indians to gather in the glittering dust. President Polk, in his annual message to Congress on December 5, 1848, said:

The accounts of the abundance of gold in that territory are of such an extraordinary character as would scarcely command belief were they not corroborated by the authentic reports of officers in the public service who have visited the mineral district and derived the facts which they detail from personal observation.[1]

The time was ripe for a great California emigration. The close of the Mexican War left many discharged soldiers foot-loose and fancy-free. The failure of the 1848 revolutions in Europe provided another stratum of adventurers eager to leave their countries. Vessels bound for California left from British, French, Dutch, German and Spanish ports. In London five companies were organized with an aggregate capital of over six million dollars. Foreign governments complained about the departure of their populations and prophesied that the increase in gold would cause inflation, depreciate the value of present holdings and throw world finance out of gear. From the Orient 4,000 Chinese crossed the Pacific in the first two years. The Spanish population in the Philippines, the French in the Marquesas Islands, squatters and rogues in Australia felt the fever and came, along with Chileans, Peruvians and other South Americans. People from almost every nation in the world assembled to form the new state of California.

The transportation problem of the vast throng of California

emigrants gave to the Overland Trail its day of greatest prominence. From the eastern seaboard the easiest way for Argonauts to reach California was by boat and muleback across Panama or Mexico. A leading New York capitalist, William Henry Aspinwall, immediately set to work to build the Panama Railroad. With control of the shipping lines to his Atlantic and Pacific terminals, Aspinwall soon had a virtual monopoly on all but overland passage to California. Many gold seekers from the midlands floated down the Mississippi and completed their voyage on Aspinwall's railroad. Others rode wagons and saddle horses west along the Santa Fe Trail. The most logical route, however, for residents of the upper Mississippi Valley was by way of the Oregon Trail.

Saddle shops and hardware stores along the Missouri, Kansas and Iowa frontiers laid in heavy stocks of emigrant supplies. Manufacturers filled the newspapers with advertisements of guns and saddles. Publishers took advantage of the demand for overland guidebooks. Full directions for following the entire route and hints for purchasing necessary equipment were written and printed in handy pocket form. One inventive fellow in New York, Rufus Porter, tried to perfect an "Aerial Steamboat"—a balloon. He believed that passengers might cross to California in two days if winds were favorable, otherwise in five. Less ambitious but equally determined people set off on foot with all their property in bundles on their backs. At least one Scotsman started with his outfit in a wheelbarrow. Most people of means purchased two or three covered wagons. Poor people got jobs with the wagon trains working for wages or for passage.

During the late winter of 1848-1849, some twenty thousand people with hundreds of wagons congregated at Independence, Fort Leavenworth, St. Joseph and Council Bluffs. Among them were gamblers, pickpockets and all the other parasites of a fluid population. The emigrants planned to start in April and reach the plains in time for the May grass. Along the border a few miles out from the towns, they congregated to exchange information about the road and inspect one another's camp outfits. The Argonauts read, reread and discussed the guidebooks and listened attentively to anyone who had heard a man who had heard a man who had heard a man who had heard a mountain man tell the best way across country. New friendships were made, companies organized and, with much oratory, captains were elected, constitutions and bylaws adopted.

Once organized, the wagon governments, like other democracies, were confronted with the unpleasant obligation of majority rule—an obligation that was making trouble in the national government at Washington as civil war loomed. In the halls of Congress, John C. Calhoun was devising unique constitutional amendments to thwart the majority's will. More than once secession had been suggested as an effective veto to a majority vote against the interests of certain sections. It is not surprising that disgruntled minorities of people in wagon camps appealed to this loose school of politics and sought relief by secession—except when Indians threatened. Waggish journalists told about a civic-minded group of Tennessee wagoners, seventy strong, who had a president, a vice-president, a legislature, three judges, a court of appeals, nine sergeants and other petty officers. The plebeian bullwhackers who did most of the work protested, then drafted a petition for an amendment to the constitution. The authorities ruled it out of order and an open rupture followed. Colonel Joseph S. Watkins, a leader of the disaffected group, declaimed on the folly of the existing administration's course and withdrew from the commonwealth with thirteen wagons.

Another wagon government settled its problem without secession. In this case the disagreement arose over the large number of dogs in the wagon train. A proposal was made for a statute to kill all the company's canines. Advocates of the law maintained that dogs ate more food than could be carried across the plains, and at night their barking would expose the emigrants' position to marauding savages. Opponents of the motion stated that the dogs would be able to live on table scraps and wild meat, and their barks would warn emigrants of the approach of hostile Indians. The camp divided on this issue along purely sectional lines. The anti-dog party won the vote by a small majority. Canines had no constitutional protection under wagon law, so the dog-loving minority drew their guns and determined to nullify the enactment. The question of the life or death of individual dogs was no longer considered important. A great principle was involved. The officers of the law were under oath to perform their bounden duty. The defenders of the dogs appealed to the most basic of all American rights, the Declaration of Independence, the right of revolution against tyrants. In this emergency the wagon captain saved the train by calling a special session of the wheeled legislature. By a vote, almost unanimous, the decree was abrogated, all honors and principles upheld.

This, like the previous story, was a favorite campfire tale. Both stories had a modicum of truth. Political dissatisfaction was a characteristic of the overland trains. Most of the wagons left the jumping-off place as part of an organization. Most of the drivers seceded or deposed their leaders before they reached Fort Laramie, and by the time South Pass was reached practically all companies disintegrated and began a race for the Pacific, each family for itself. Fortunately, the dangerous Indian country was then far behind. The Diggers could be cowed by a handful of white men with rifles. A permanent organization was further handicapped by the fact that the great number of wagons on the trail made practically a continuous line, the van of one company touching the rear of another. Constantly one train was driving around another, burying it in dust. Races for the best springs and meadows occurred daily. Fortunately, 1849 was a moist year with grass unusually good. Congestion along the trail got worse instead of better as the emigrants progressed. At the Leavenworth and St. Joe road junctions, additional wagons jostled into the Westport trail and crowded down to the crossing of the Blue. At the Platte, emigrants saw a solid line of wagons from Council Bluffs and the new Mormon town, Kanesville, driving up the north bank. What would happen when they all came together above Ash Hollow?

Amid the scrambling and jostling and complaining there was plenty of laughter and good-natured rivalry as the wagons passed and repassed one another, reversing positions day after day. With a fusillade of whips a wagon might loom out of the dust. Rival wagoners would read on its canvas side: "Live Hoosier." Another wagon called itself the "Wild Yankee," a third the "Elephant," a name particularly amusing in 1849. "See the elephant" was considered quite a witty thing to say, so when the "Elephant" passed everybody laughed.

At noon and in the evening each company of wagons formed a square to serve as a corral. Chicken coops were opened. Cows were milked. Young folks helped old folks down from the wagons. Women cooked meals and children played tag between the wagon wheels. At dark herders brought the livestock inside the circle. People visited from fire to fire. Fiddles began to whine "Ol' Dan Tucka." Young men in homespun courted maidens in calico and led them into the gloom where they could see campfires ahead and behind, like stars—a red Milky Way—across the plains. With the white cover of a wagon for an altar, weddings were performed. Babies were born. Simple funerals were held. Over all hung the fear of cholera. The dread disease had been raging in the cities for a year or two and it naturally became prevalent in the unclean conditions which arose when thousands of people moved across the wilderness with no sanitary precautions.

It usually struck quickly and victims often died—or got better—within twenty-four hours. The trail of the forty-niners was soon lined with graves. In the following year, 1850, cholera became worse. It is estimated that some five thousand died of the disease crossing the plains.[2] Fear brought out heroism as well as depravity in the travelers. Quite often a tent would be seen beside the road where a patient lay in agony. Sometimes his wagon and family camped beside him, waiting. Occasionally a victim was left behind alone. His malady was considered contagious. To protect his family it was best to leave him. Sometimes one woman remained. After the end came she would catch up with the party.

Across what is now Kansas the half-civilized Shawnee and degraded Kansas Indians begged of the emigrants, tried to sell them relics or ignored them. The Frenchman at the Kansas ferry reaped a big harvest. When the Argonauts reached the Platte they found a new settlement, Fort Kearney. Built on the south

side of the river near the head of Grand Island in 1846, the garrison's quarters consisted of barracks with sod walls and brush
roofs. A two-story frame building housed the officers. The fort
was not for defense. Instead, it was merely a place for troops to
live. It had been established to awe the Indians and protect the
emigrants. On June 23, 1849, a count of the wagons that had
passed Fort Kearney on both sides of the Platte during the spring
totaled 5,516. Wilford Woodruff, a Mormon leader, estimated
that 35,000 gold seekers went up the trail in addition to the
Saints, and with them some 60,000 head of livestock.[3]

Three places on the South Platte served as crossings. All were
bad during the high water in June. Wagons would upend in a
treacherous hole, swing around in the current, then be pulled
along. Often one ox would be swimming while a yokemate still
kept his footing. The most popular ford lay sixty miles west of
the forks. During the month of June this crossing was bedlam.
A traveler in 1850 reported 400 wagons on the bank with 3,000
cattle milling up the dust that drifted over the encampment, settled on the wagon covers and in the food.[4] Arriving on the north
bank people said, "Thank God," dried out and repacked.

Many midlanders looked at the bench between the forks of the
Platte and called it a mountain. One poetic fellow wrote: "Alps
on Alps arise."[5] When the prairie farmers drove their wagons
to the brink of Ash Hollow and looked down into the gulch they
marveled at the "defile."

Fairyland for many began with these rocky arroyos and fantastic promontories. The guidebook listed the most conspicuous
buttes by name, and emigrants looked forward to seeing Court
House and Chimney rocks and Scotts Bluff beyond. Those who
could wrote their own impression of these wonders. Some letters were designed for members of the family who had remained
behind. Others were sent to the home town newspaper. "It is
vain to attempt a description of those enchanting wonders," one
traveler wrote.

Even the strange creations of fancy which gives to Alladdin's
Lamp such wonder-working powers could never display to the

dreamy mind a tenth of such astonishing grandeur as is displayed on those places where nature has made such mocking of the works of Art.[6]

This writer also wrote:

The whole country seems overspread by the ruins of some of the loftiest and most magnificent pallaces the imagination of man can reach in its most extravagant conceptions. Here lays the ruins of a lofty Pyramid, there a splendid castle. On one hand is a tremendous citidal, on the other the grand hall of legislation. Yonder is the facsimile of our nations' capitol at Washington and there again is the City Hall at N. Y., only enlarged perhaps a dozen times or more.

The scenery of Kansas and Nebraska produced these raptures. Think what this man was destined to see and feel when he reached the Rockies! Here is more of it:

On all sides lay the ruins of more grandeur than man has ever had a conception of. Even the ruins of Rome, Athens, Bagdad and Petria fall into perfect insignificance by the side of these apparent ruins of a city that must have been inhabited by Giants.[7]

Above Scotts Bluff this traveler reported that his party came to a beautiful plain where a blacksmith named Thibbadoux lived with three squaws and numerous progeny. "This man is evidently of French descent and a desperado,"[8] he recorded. Above Scotts Bluff the forty-niners entered Sioux country. The Indians visited their camps. Some of the emigrants admired the red men— and the red women, too. The whites told one another that these people were finer specimens than the treacherous Pawnee down the Platte. They told one another, too, that the Sioux never made war on the white men, but of course no one took that seriously. After all, the Sioux were one of the most powerful nations west of the Mississippi. In the distance the emigrants saw Laramie Peak. The famous fort stood twenty miles this side. Hurrah!

From Ash Hollow, where all the roads joined, to Scotts Bluff the way resembled the rear of a retreating army—broken wagon wheels, old shoes, worn-out clothes, battered sheet-iron stoves with telescoping pipes that had looked good in the outfitters' store but didn't work on the plains, bookcases and furniture whose weight retarded the oxen, supplies that the Argonauts considered superfluous. Men eager to beat their comrades to the best grass and water—and to the gold fields—were lightening their loads. Others were compelled to throw away heavy articles on account of the accidental loss of part of their livestock. Also, the dry air was shrinking wagon spokes, making wheels rattle and break down, forcing the drivers to leave more impedimenta by the side of the road. Much of the discarded material was burned to keep others from using it—a revealing commentary on the character of men who seek for gold. Occasionally a forty-niner with a different disposition posted a sign on his abandoned goods telling anyone who followed to help himself.

Seventy miles above Scotts Bluff the gold seekers came to Fort Bernard. A few more cabins had been added to it since Parkman had stopped there. Outside, two piles of buffalo robes loomed as large as haystacks. The forty-niners left their teams and wagons, walked through and around the cabins, found little of interest and went on. Eight miles beyond they came to Laramie Creek. On the other side they could see the fort. Men with wagons and the "know-how" offered to pilot timid Argonauts across.

Fort Laramie had been taken over by the Army on June 26, 1849.[9] Two companies of soldiers were garrisoned where the French *bourgeois* and his Indians used to live and trade. The adobe walls, sagging with age, had been reinforced with props. The army had a bakery for the soldiers, but travelers could purchase supplies only from the sutler. He offered sugar, tea, coffee, salt and a few medicines, all at prices which made the emigrants whistle. But practically everybody stopped and many bought something.

While at Fort Laramie forty-niners asked about friends who had gone ahead and left word for those behind. Wagons were greased and repaired. Trunks were left in storage. All knew that the worst was ahead. Grass became thinner from here on, and the water in alkali springs did unpleasant things to the insides of men who were not to the manner born. Some gave up and turned back.

Between Fort Laramie and the Upper Crossing the forty-niners traveled by several interlacing roads. They shot antelope on the rolling sagebrush swells and fished in the Platte. Like emigrants before them, they noted the horned toads and laughed at them. "They are smaller than the common toads seen in the Eastern States and are of a light grey colour with frequent dark brown spots. They are harmless," one traveler recorded.

A few miles east of the Upper Crossing, Mormon ferrymen met travelers on the road. Keen for more profits like those of 1847, they now operated a boat below the crossing and told credulous emigrants that their new road was best.[10] A few Argonauts may have taken their advice and turned off, but most of them drove on to the usual ford. Several boats were operating and travelers had to wait their turn. By the next year, 1850, four cable ferries carried emigrants and their wagons across. Travelers registered and waited, sometimes a week, to take their places.

The Upper Crossing was out West, no mistake. Waiting travelers with time on their hands killed buffalo, deer and bear. At the crossing travelers suffered from alkali chapping. The Platte bottoms, dry since the spring freshets, were white as new snow with precipitated mineral. The alkali, fine as flour, blew in the dry winds against men's faces, chapped their hands. Ugly sores appeared around their mouths and across their knuckles. Sufferers said that chewing tobacco kept their lips soft and healed the ulcers. Licking sore lips, giving medical advice, the Argonauts passed Red Buttes, saw the Fiery Narrows south of them, crossed dry lakes, white and shimmering. The dust, light as ashes, smarted on their tender mouths and reddened the rims of their eyes. At last they came to the Sweetwater—and all the name implied. At Independence Rock they searched for familiar names and added more. They knew that Devil's Gate came next. The grass was good here and the stream was lined with wood suitable for campfires. People's faces appeared more cheerful. Dangerous Indians seldom came this far west. Emigrants could scatter out, each at his own pace, and no longer submit to the

UNION PACIFIC CONSTRUCTION TRAIN, 1868

"overbearing insolence of the tyranical captain." Some raced ahead for the gold fields, others decided to enjoy life on the way. When the wagons stopped, the women put away their knitting and turned their hands and thoughts to more complicated things. Cherished strips of cloth were unfolded. Patterns were cut. Mothers with mouths full of pins fitted dresses on their girls around the campfire. Fathers, free from discipline, pegged boots for their boys. The older generation was planning to begin a new life in California.

Before long the forty-niners saw, far in the northwest, the Wind River Mountains. Two more days brought them to South Pass. Before they knew it, the wagons rolled into Pacific Springs, but the worst of the road lay ahead. From here on, several routes could be taken to the Humboldt. The road down to Fort Bridger and then up Bear River to Soda Springs was the best for water. Though fifty-three miles longer than the old Sublette Cutoff, it had been traveled heavily during the past two years.

Travelers taking the Sublette route tackled the dry pull to Green River by one of two methods. Some nooned on Big Sandy, filled their kegs, cooked a mess of bread and rested. In the cool of the evening they started out over the forty-three waterless miles to Green River. In the heat of the next day the animals pulled desperately for water and often reached it before noon. The other procedure was to wait until three in the morning, cook breakfast in the dark and pull out with the morning star rising above the horizon at the tail end of the train. For three miles the road was fair. As the eastern sky paled with dawn the wagon ruts entered a flat of bitter black weeds sugared with alkali. The mules' little feet sank in the treacherous ground, stirred up the powdery mineral and floured the men and the wagons with dust. Greenhorns swore, wished they had taken the longer route, feared the worst when the hot rays of the sun hit them, stopped to discuss going back. Old-timers rumbled past them with a grim joke and the crack of a whip. They knew that the road became better soon. A twenty-five-mile stretch of it was hard and springy, ideal for wagons, but there was no water and no time to stop for lunch.

Emigrants with good luck and fast teams neared Green River when the sun was low, shining hot in their faces. The road crossed the heads of many gulches. Wagons jolted to the bottoms with braked wheels. The horses and mules tugged on their bits, scrambled and strained up the steep pitches. Some teams balked. Doubling was necessary. Men were tired and in a bad humor. Worst of all, it usually got dark in this rough bit of road. Hungry men wanted to leave their unfortunate companions, thought up excuses for going ahead. The stouthearted cheered the laggards, said that Green River was near at hand. At last the road came out on the bluff. With chain-locked wheels the wagons skidded down to the cottonwoods and water. Supper fires lighted the wagons and enabled the men to see their mess boxes and prepare a meal.

In the morning the forty-niners drove ten miles down Green River to the ferry. Wagons were always congregated here, waiting their turn to cross. The ferryman, with little capital, made good money. For a boat he had calked a wagon box with rags. The animals had to swim across. Wagons were taken apart and ferried. The forty-niners told one another that a man or two drowned here every day.

West of the Green River the Sublette road climbed fast. Feed was good in the high, rolling country but the hills made the draft animals tug. Three days out the Argonauts crossed Hams Fork. Recent rains had filled the stream to the banks. At the ford the water was obviously above the wagon beds. The emigrants had a solution for this predicament. They raised the loaded wagon boxes in the standards, thrust logs over the bolsters to hold the boxes up, then lashed them tight to the running gears. In this manner the load was lifted eight or ten inches, and in a ford the load held the wheels to the bottom in water that sometimes swam the stock.

West of Hams Fork the road wound its way up into high country. The feed became lush with wild parsnips and pennyroyal bushes whipping the axletrees. Icy water gurgled down all the gulches and quaking aspen leaves danced in the brilliant sunshine. On muddy hillsides, snowbanks were found with marsh marigolds blooming in the ice water at their feet. Mosquitoes swarmed in numbers beyond belief. Some teamsters said that bacon stewed with vile-smelling herbs would keep away the insects. At least it diverted the men's attention. Certainly cold nights and camps near snowdrifts affected their winged tormentors not at all. The forty-niners learned that Rocky Mountain mosquitoes could withstand as wide a range of temperatures as midland farmers.

The high altitude seemed very strange to Mississippi Valley men. They had not yet got used to cold nights and hot days, a blistering sun and a cool breeze with every passing cloud. Added to these phenomena was the peculiar action of water that boiled at a low temperature. Beans cooked endlessly without becoming tender. A man lost his breath quickly when he ran. A few suffered from nosebleed.

From the mountains down to Bear River, where the Sublette Cutoff joined the Bridger-Fort Hall road, the pitch was steep. With "rough-locked" wheels and ropes around axletrees, the men held back the wagons on the descent. The meadows at the bottom and the well-traveled road came as a relief to them. They had the comforting knowledge that they had saved fifty-three miles on the road to California.

In Bear River Valley, "Peg Leg" Smith—the man who had met Brigham Young in South Pass—kept a store. Yes, the country was beginning to settle. His stock was not large, mainly buckskin shirts and pantaloons similar to the kind his partner had tried to sell the Mormons two years before, but he also took broken-down horses and traded travelers sound animals. This exchange was profitable, for he bought cheap and sold high; and a little rest restored the used-up animals. The worst angle of his business was the shortness of the season, which lasted only thirty days.

At Soda Springs, Frémont's Beer Springs, where the road left Bear River for Fort Hall, the forty-niners tarried to see the sights. Men, women and children walked down below the road to see Steamboat Spring. On the hillside above the river, water gushed out of a hole a foot across with a chugging sound like a steamboat. The first puff threw up water about twelve inches.

The next puff threw the water higher, the third still higher, perhaps four feet. Then the performance began over again. Hundreds of forty-niners stood every day and watched Steamboat Spring until they were tired. Why not? The women and children might never have an opportunity to see anything like it again, and there was plenty of gold for everybody in California.

The Soda Springs were equally attractive. Mothers filled drinking cups with the carbonated water and dropped lemon syrup into it. Sugar or peppermint also tasted good. The charged water tingled refreshingly in the mouth. Children loved it.

Beyond Soda Springs most of the forty-niners took the old road to Fort Hall. Looking back from under the covered-wagon canvas, travelers could see the magnificent valley of the Bear receding among the distant mountains. Down the north slope the country opened quickly into the lava hillsides of the Port Neuf. Grass was good, but everybody began to talk about the terrible deserts ahead. Close to Snake River the mosquitoes came in clouds to meet the gold seekers. Word was passed along the wagons that mosquitoes were still worse in the sloughs around Fort Hall. Moreover, the grass there was said to be eaten out. Many Argonauts camped before they reached the place in order to assure feed for their animals.

Fort Hall in 1849 was described by travelers as resembling Fort Laramie on a smaller scale. The Hudson's Bay Company still operated the post, having been granted a number of years to close out its business by the treaty of 1846, which set the Oregon boundary approximately at its final location. James K. Polk had been right. The Great Migration of 1843 and his own election on an expansionist platform in 1844 had won the Columbia River for Americans.

The forty-niners were not attracted to Fort Hall. Its situation in the center of a great flat was forbidding after the beautiful Bear River Valley. The store was poorly stocked. In fact, some of the emigrants sold their excess supplies to the traders. A few dirty Indians were encamped near by. The Shoshoni of the neighborhood were reported to be entirely harmless. Guards over the livestock were no longer considered necessary.

The road from Fort Hall to Oregon was said to be 800 miles long, the road to Sutter's Fort, California, only 700. Both distances seemed farther when the forty-niners turned their oxen into the desert west of the fort and trudged across the sage and greasewood. Suffocating clouds of dust enveloped them. The oxen plodded along with their mouths open. The mules coughed. At night the Argonauts camped on the rim of the canyon above the Snake. Grass was good but water, in plain sight below the rim, was hard to reach. At American Falls most of the forty-niners stopped. One man reported in his journal that the water fell perpendicularly over black traprock. At the Raft River the forty-niners left the Oregon Road—the Fort Boise-Blue Mountain route. The gold seekers went up the Raft and over the divide to what was known as the City of Rocks where the state lines of Nevada, Idaho and Utah would corner a half-century later. From here the road dropped southwest until it joined the Hastings' Cutoff on the Humboldt.

Most of the forty-niners took the Fort Hall road, but late in July 1849 a party led by James Hudspeth opened a new cutoff from Soda Springs to City of Rocks. Hudspeth was a mountain man. Like many of his fellows he had turned guide for emigrant trains. Back in 1842 Frémont had used Hudspeth's knowledge to guide him across the Great Basin. Hudspeth realized that the road north to Fort Hall and back to the City of Rocks was a long detour. He reckoned that he could save 134 miles by going straight west from Soda Springs. And he could have, sure enough, as the crow flew, but on the ground the way proved very rough. The road which Hudspeth charted led first through a waterless volcanic area, then into high country where snowy peaks towered above the wagon train. Continual work was required to build the road, fill gulches with logs for crossing, cut out trees in order that wagons could get through the forests. Fort Hall travelers had dust and heat and more miles, but the road was good. Men who followed the cutoff found a better climate but more work, more upsets and more broken axles. In the years that followed both routes were used, but Hudspeth's was never popular. J. Goldsborough Bruff, who crossed in 1849, estimated that there was not five miles' difference in the two routes.[11]

Below City of Rocks, where the new road joined the old Hastings route, the way became as congested as it had been back on the long stretch between Fort Laramie and South Pass. The new wagons joining the continuous throng here came by way of Fort Bridger and the Mormon road to Salt Lake City.

Through the Wasatch Mountains, rough but cool in summer, the Mormons had hewed out a road that they used constantly. A United States mail route traveled it first in 1848. In the same year a man by the name of Ben Holladay—a name to remember in stagecoach history—hauled $75,000 worth of goods to Salt Lake City. In 1849 he brought out $150,000 worth. In two years Brigham Young had built a tidy settlement on the edge of Great Salt Lake. Fresh water from the Wasatch canyons babbled through ditches across the desert, and many little farms had appeared. In the town proper, irrigation water flowed down the gutters. Shade and fruit trees had been planted. Brigham Young kept indigent Saints busy on community buildings—a vast public works program.

From Salt Lake City, travelers bound for California could go around the north end of the lake to the Humboldt. This was the long and the easy way. The Hastings' Cutoff south of the lake and across the desert was much shorter. It had a bad name since the Donner disaster but men in a hurry to get gold in California tried it. Six days after leaving Salt Lake City, travelers came to a desert, the first of three bad ones—the Salt Lake desert, the Humboldt and the Truckee Crossing.

At the jumping-off places all grass had been mowed and taken along for feed. Late-comers must bring hay crammed in their wagons from meadows far back on the trail, sometimes a day or two's drive away. At the last water many wagons congregated, often fifty at a time. Bread and meat were cooked for the jump to Pilot Peak. A hundred men waited in line to fill kegs at the springs. The water was brackish, stinking with sulphur. Some cattle would not drink. The owners could not make them, though they knew how important this last drink would be to the animals in the next twenty-four hours. Parties started in the afternoon, stopped for a rest at dark, then traveled all night. Grass disappeared from the ground, then sagebrush disappeared. In the dark the wagons crossed barren ridges so steep the men had to put their shoulders to the wheels. In the morning the travelers stopped again, gave the animals a little water—about a quart each—and some hay. A few of the oxen were too thirsty to eat—sure sign that they might soon drop out. At daylight, too, a few travelers were always out of water. The next water should be found at nightfall—if the cattle could travel that long.

For many, night came and no water, the old story that Hastings and the Donners knew so well. Some men, foreseeing the emigrants' predicament, had hauled out water and offered it for sale at $1.00 per gallon. Cattle dropped out constantly during the second night. Drovers stopped only a moment to turn them loose, and plodded on. Dead and dying animals were almost constantly in sight. Drivers picked their way through the carcasses and noticed that their own animals no longer flinched when the lash snapped on their hides. They walked stupidly, mechanically, mouths wide open, saliva drooling like a silver net onto the parched ground. Each slow step might be the last. Some men gave up and camped, knowing, but not caring, that every hour wasted now made the trip harder in the end.

A few of the faster teams reached water on the second night. The cattle smelled it several miles away. Drovers had to prance in front of the teams, whipping right and left, to hold back the oxen. Crazed for water, the animals wanted to run and would have become exhausted. In the springs they stuck their noses deep under water, waded to their bellies to absorb moisture through the hide. Waterlogged at last, they began to eat, and the men crawled under their wagons to sleep, tired out. A few filled kegs and went back to help their suffering friends. Hour after hour, wretched men and women staggered in. Some had tongues swollen until they could not talk. Others were hysterical. The specter of the Donner party haunted everybody and the worst was ahead. Many regretted coming by the shorter route. They would gladly have gone back, but now it was too late. They could do nothing but go ahead. Loads were reduced, supplies thrown away. Wagons were cut in half and changed into carts. Some were simply abandoned. The owners made packsaddles by stuffing hay in wagon covers and took what goods they could. Ten more days' travel put Argonauts at the junction with the Fort Hall road. This was the country where the Donners had split into two parties to get more feed.

Argonauts coming to the junction via Fort Hall were also worn out. All livestock was usually exhausted by the time it reached the Humboldt. The smell of dead animals hung heavy in the air. Carcasses clogged the streams, yet people were obliged to drink the water.

Swamps lined the lower Humboldt. Men waded in them to cut rushes for the livestock. They dared not let the animals graze or even go to drink in the swamps lest they stick in the bogs. At many camps the horses and cattle had to be watered in buckets dipped from the marsh. Each wagon train had a crazy mule, it seemed, that would not drink from a bucket. Some of these long-eared eccentrics learned, some died. On the lower Humboldt, too, groceries began to run low. Sugar, coffee and flour never came out even. At camp someone was always making the round of the fires offering to trade one staple for another, asking to buy a little coffee, sugar or flour, and seldom succeeding. Men offered $2.00 a pound for bacon, but could not get it. Most people needed what they had for themselves, yet hundreds of pounds had been thrown away east of Fort Laramie. Argonauts liked to tell a joke about bacon, a joke that was old even in 1849. Wise hog raisers, they said, fed a hog for a spell, then starved him for a spell, so the bacon would have a strip of fat and a strip of lean. The Humboldt, these jokers thought, was a good place to put on the strip of lean. They said their cattle, fat and "sassy" when they started from Missouri, had become so thin at the Humboldt Sink that "it takes two to make a shadow."[12]

Fifty miles above the sink the road turned southwest. A short way below the turn a road branched off to the north. This was Applegate's Cutoff to Oregon, a road opened in 1846. Some travelers went up it as far as Goose Lake on the Oregon-California line and then turned south to Lassen's trading station on the upper Sacramento. This route was longer than the other trails to California that left the Humboldt and it was not a better road. Some Argonauts maintained that its chief advantage was to Lassen, who profited by having emigrants reach his establishment at a time when they had run out of supplies.

West from the Humboldt Sink, Argonauts took their choice of several roads. To evade the dry Truckee Crossing some went from the Humboldt Sink to the Carson Sink. The two were one in wet seasons. From the Carson Sink, wagons went up the Carson and Walker rivers and over the high Sierras into the valley of California. Better roads went through Beckwith, Henness and Donner passes. Of them all, Donner Pass was the best, except for the horrible memories of that route. The road to all three crossed a desert to the Truckee, a twenty-four-hour hike. Travelers usually left in the cool of the evening. A hot spring halfway across served as a resting place at dawn. The water was dipped out in buckets and cooled. For the oxen it was poured into pans. Buckets would not do for thirsty cattle. A dry steer with his head in a bucket would guzzle it all before his yokemate got a drink. A little hay was also fed at the hot spring. Then the Argonauts threw their discards into the water so the next party could not use it. Mrs. Helen M. Carpenter, who crossed the plains in 1857, wrote in her journal: "It seemed to be quite full of wagon tires & all kinds of irons belonging to the outfits."[13]

The day's drive on to the Truckee was a nightmare. Dead animals lined the entire way. Mirages tortured travelers and tempted them to leave the road and trail away to sure disaster. Deep sand made heavy pulling for the mules and oxen. In places the wagons sank in sand holes almost to the beds. When the mules sweat profusely the drivers stopped and unhitched their teams. A good roll refreshed a horse or mule almost as much as a drink of water. At last the animals smelled the Truckee. Sometimes they began to bawl and bray four miles from the stream. Teamsters could hardly hold them back. At the riverbank they ran out into the stream as though they, too, knew that they had crossed the last desert on the road to California. The Truckee was cool mountain water and drovers were often a little fearful that their animals might founder. They told one another that the only sure preventive was for the animals to stand in water up to their knees when they drank.

The cottonwoods along the Truckee were the first shade trees that some Argonauts had seen for a thousand miles. Men embraced the rough trunks and thanked God that they had made it. The trip up the Sierras was not free from trouble, but there was wood and grass. In the high mountains, some four or five days from the Valley of California, horsemen pranced into emigrant camps. Their spirited mounts caught the eyes of Argonauts whose own animals were worked down after a summer's hardship. The Californians, like their animals, seemed fresh, not travel-worn. What was more, they greeted the newcomers with enticing business propositions. They offered to pay for options on everything the emigrants had, their draft animals, wagons and supplies. They agreed to prices that seemed fabulous. The Argonauts had indeed reached El Dorado. Everyone began to feel good. Quarrels on the trail were forgotten. Old grudges seemed trivial. The last few miles were downhill through evergreens, then out into the foothills to the rainbow's end. At night fiddles whined a faster jig step, and in daytime, as the wagons rolled along, drivers sang, "Going to California with a gold pan on my knee!"

1 James D. Richardson (comp.), *A Compilation of the Messages and Papers of the Presidents, 1789-1897* ([Washington], 1900), IV, 636.

2 Owen Cochran Coy, *The Great Trek* (Los Angeles, 1931), 318.

3 LeRoy R. Hafen and Francis Marion Young, *Fort Laramie and the Pageant of the West, 1834-1890* (Glendale, Calif., 1938), 150.

4 Coy, *The Great Trek*, 133.

5 *Ibid.*, 134.

6 *Ibid.*, 135-36.

7 *Ibid.*, 135.

8 *Ibid.*, 136.

9 Hafen and Young, *Fort Laramie*, 153.

10 Georgia Willis Read and Ruth Gaines (eds.), *Gold Rush: The Journals, Drawings, and Other Papers of J. Goldsborough Bruff, Captain, Washington City and California Mining Association, April 2, 1849-July 20, 1851* (New York, 1944), I, 46.

11 *Ibid.*, 528.

12 Coy, *The Great Trek*, 180.

13 *Ibid.*, 198.

Chapter 15

The Pony Express

Pᴇᴏᴘʟᴇ in New York saw the headlines on March 26, 1860, and purchased the New York *Herald*. They read:

The first courier of the Pony Express will leave the Missouri River on Tuesday, April 3d, at 5 o'clock p.m., and will run regularly weekly thereafter, carrying a letter mail only. The point of departure on the Missouri River will be in telegraphic communication with the East and will be announced in due time.[1]

Readers learned from the article that the express would pass through Forts Kearney, Laramie and Bridger, Salt Lake City, Camp Floyd (established south of Salt Lake during the invasion), Carson City (ambitious to be the capital of a new territory), the Washoe Silver Mines, Placerville and Sacramento. Special couriers in New York and Washington would take mail to the jumping-off place. This service would be available in New York at the office of J. B. Simpson, Room 8, Continental Bank Building, Nassau Street, until 6:30 ᴀ.ᴍ., March 31, for the April 3 mail.

Fast horses for relaying news were nothing new. They had been employed years before to meet sailing ships and bring dispatches into New York City. The idea of getting mail across

361

the continent in eight days was said to have started with Senator William McKendree Gwin of California. Mail usually went to the Golden State by way of Panama in twenty-two days or more. A mail service had been opened to Salt Lake City in 1850.[2] A stage line to California was urged but the United States Senate was controlled by Southerners, and a line from the South, not from the North, was favored. Gwin was a Southerner too, but since moving West he had become more interested in himself than in his patrimony. While senator from California, he set off on horseback for the Missouri River in the fall of 1854. He went by way of the Sierra mining towns and Salt Lake City. For traveling companion he had B. F. Ficklin, general superintendent of the pioneer freighting firm of Russell, Majors & Waddell, the giant partnership that had grown to fame and fortune on the Overland Road. William H. Russell and Alexander Majors had both been teamsters with a few wagons. They had made a stake hauling supplies to the army in Utah in 1857. William B. Waddell was a Missourian, rich and religious. He insisted that all employees sign a pledge to drink no liquor. The firm's headquarters were located in Leavenworth. General Superintendent Ficklin was in direct charge of division superintendents from the Missouri to California.

Ficklin and Senator Gwin talked of the future of the great wasteland that separated California from the East. Ficklin had been in the transportation business for years. A forward-looking man, he unfolded to Senator Gwin the possibilities of a pony express across the continent. To Ficklin it meant prestige for his firm, to Gwin a name in the Senate and votes for himself in the Golden State. The men parted. Gwin reached Washington and drafted a bill. In January 1855 he introduced it in the Senate. The bill called for a weekly mail service between St. Louis and San Francisco. The trip was to be made in ten days, and the carrier was to receive a sum not to exceed $500 for each round trip. The bill was referred to the Military Affairs Committee and there it died.[3] The country was concerned mainly about the growing slavery controversy—the prospect of civil war. Only a year before, another senator, Stephen A. Douglas, had hoped to get the government to aid the construction of a railroad to California by a Northern route that would increase land values in Chicago, the chief city of his home state. Douglas knew that Southern senators would favor a railroad via the Southern route. To get their votes he had sold out the territory of Kansas to the slaveholders. The row that followed had aggravated the incipient civil war. It was no time to try similar tactics with a pony express. Gwin dropped the matter.

Then in 1858 a regular mail and stage route was started to California by the southern route from St. Louis and Memphis to El Paso and California. The contract was given to John Butterfield and William Fargo, both from New York State. The war danger became more intense and it was plain to many that in case of conflict this line could be cut off and California would be dependent on the South for its communications. So when William H. Russell was in Washington attending to his firm's business in the winter of 1859, it is not surprising that he met Senator Gwin and again discussed establishing a pony express, but the government was in no more of a mood to inaugurate the line than it had been previously. Russell, however, returned to Leavenworth with a grandiose plan for his company to organize the line as a private enterprise.

William Russell's partners were not enthusiastic about the proposed pony express. They remembered that he had promoted an extravagant Pike's Peak Express and they had taken it over to save him from ruin. The fact that the firm's competitor, John Butterfield, threatened to inaugurate a pony express over the Southern route to California did not move the hardheaded members of the firm. But imaginative and impulsive William Russell was persistent. He knew his partners. It is claimed that he finally told them that he had already pledged the firm's word to organize the fast mail. Both Majors and Waddell were the souls of honor. To uphold their partner's alleged commitment, they agreed to go ahead with the deal.

With vast experience and a trained staff they set to work. Horses must be purchased, riders employed, relay stations equipped with men and horse feed. The freight routes had to be altered to shorten the distance. In places a detour was necessary to bypass points where Indians might shoot a passing rider. As far as Salt Lake there was already a line of stations, but much work had to be done on the line from there to California.

Within two months the stock was purchased, many of them blooded and all above the average for speed and stamina. Eighty hardy riders were enrolled and sent to their stations. These men, aristocrats in their line, were paid from $100 to $150 a month. No one else in the great firm drew more, except the executives. Fully equipped, the road had 190 stations, 420 horses, 400 station men and assistants and eighty riders.

Great preparations for a gala opening day were made both in St. Joseph, Missouri, and in Sacramento, California. On April 3, 1860, the riders were scheduled to start with the mail in opposite directions. The mayor of St. Joseph was M. Jeff Thompson, an extravagantly likable fellow of the old river school. Mark Twain would write about him later as Colonel Sellers in *The Gilded Age*. Thompson liked tall gray beaver hats, ivory-handled pistols, tight pantaloons strapped under his instep and blue frock coats with brass buttons. On dress occasions he wore a great curved sword that hung from his belt by two straps and knocked against his knees. While still a young man, he had lost all the teeth in one side of his mouth. This permitted him to shut his jaws so that his head appeared as flat as a snake's. He used this deformity to good effect when haranguing his butternut constituents. A direct descendant of the Kentucky and Virginia oratorical school, he could thunder for internal improvements and cap the applause by folding up his face and bringing a roar of laughter from the crowd. Needless to say, he got the votes. A man who liked to do things, he had helped build the Hannibal & St. Joseph Railroad with a man later to become well known as a writer, Charles Dudley Warner. The first locomotive to be driven into St. Joe had M. Jeff Thompson at the throttle. Of course his real name was not Jeff. It was Merriwether. Back in Harpers Ferry, his birthplace, little Merriwether had liked to ride on the rattling scavenger-wagon driven by an old Negro named Jeff. The name had stuck to the little white boy.

Everybody liked to tell stories about the fabulous Thompsons but people liked the family, too. For the departure of the first pony express, Jeff Thompson prepared one of the speeches of his life. Newspapers all over the United States focused attention on St. Joseph. Russell and Majors both came up from Leavenworth. A special train, a locomotive and one car, was due on the Hannibal & St. Joseph with the dispatch bag from New York. Letters were wrapped in oiled silk to protect them from wet weather and horse sweat. The postage was $5.00 per ounce.

To the assembled multitude M. Jeff Thompson extolled the enterprise of Russell, Majors & Waddell, then closed his toothless jaws with the gesture of finality which the "bhoys" admired. Next, Majors, who had been talked into the enterprise against his better judgment, took the stand. A big executive, he thought in big terms and talked with sentences almost as long as the Overland Trail. He said:

Another, a more important, and a greater enterprise, which must soon reach its culmination, viz: the construction of the road upon which the tireless iron horse will start on his long overland journey, opening up as he goes the rich meadows of nature, the fertile valleys, and crowning the eminences of the rocky range with evidences of civilization and man's irresistible mania of progression; diversifying the prairies with the lowing cattle herds, and making them yet lovelier by the dwellings of the pioneer, cheered in his western pilgrimage by the loved ones of his household, and aided by the fair hands and bright eyes of woman. Of a truth, "the desert shall blossom as the rose."[4]

Across the hills the special train whistled. The locomotive chugged into town with its one car. The engineer had made a record run from Hannibal, averaging forty miles an hour. The mail messenger ran from the station to the post office. Then the broad doors of the Pike's Peak Livery Stable swung open. A bay race mare pranced out. On the street a short bandy-legged rider in embroidered red shirt, fringed breeches and silver spurs stood waiting. A cannon boomed—the signal to start. The jockey sprang to the saddle, cantered through the crowd to the post office and jumped to the ground. Mayor M. Jeff Thompson came out of the post office with a large square leather pad—the *mochila* for the mail. The pad was designed to hook over the horn and cantle of a saddle. In each corner a letter pocket was fastened with a small brass padlock. Mayor Thompson swung the *mochila* onto the saddle. The rider leaped on and galloped down to the wharf. The horse's hoofs thundered up the gangplank of a waiting steamboat. The ropes were cast off. The pilot's bell rang. Machinery began to rumble. The paddle wheels churned up the water and the boat left the dock.

People on the levee watched the steamboat puffing into the setting sun. At the far bank they saw the paddle wheels reverse and "backwater" for a good landing. They saw a rider gallop across the levee and race down the road, his shirt ballooning. Some may have noticed that the rider's clothes differed from those worn in St. Joe. They learned later that pony express men had a room on the boat. They changed their finery here, to be picked up when they came back for the grand ride into town again on the return trip. On the eventful evening of April 3, 1860, the crowd went home with M. Jeff Thompson's oratory ringing in their ears:

The mail must go. Hurled by flesh and blood across 2,000 miles of desolate space—Fort Kearney, Laramie, South Pass, Fort Bridger, Salt Lake City. Neither storms, fatigue, darkness, mountains or Indians, burning sands or snow must stop the precious bags. The mail must go.[5]

Nine days and twenty-three hours later the *mochila* with its locked pockets was delivered in California. Eleven days were required for the eastbound rider to reach St. Joe. In the Sierra Nevada Mountains a herd of mules was driven over the trail to trample down the snow ahead of the pony express.

At first each horse ran twenty to twenty-five miles, but this proved too long and the distance was cut in half. The average man rode seventy-five miles on six or seven horses. One day each week at every stage station across the continent a fresh horse must be saddled and waiting. The coming of the pony express was the event of the day. Attendants watched the road for hours as the time approached. Sometimes the relay horse was led back along the road to meet the incoming rider. In the desert a cloud of dust announced "the pony." At night the rider sounded a horn or whooped as he clattered down on the station. He loosened the *mochila* before arriving and leaped to the ground with it on his arm. He was allowed two minutes to change. After gulping a tin cup of water or a bite of bread, he swung the mail on the waiting horse. The fresh animal leaped away. The rider clutched the side of the saddle, leaped beside the flying hoofs and was thus tossed high in the air. At full speed he landed on the back of the running horse. All pony express riders learned this method of mounting and liked to display it. Many of the original riders dropped out after a few weeks of the exacting work. Remarkably few of them were killed. Seldom armed, they owed their safety to the speed of their mounts. Indian ponies could not overtake them. Only occasionally did an ambushed Indian hit such a fleeting mark.

The name of the pony express rider who left St. Joe on the initial run has been the cause of argument among historians. Tradition said that Johnnie Frey was his name. Claims were made with varying success for three other boys. The pony express was a private enterprise and no records are available. St. Joseph newspaper files were destroyed during the first months of the Civil War. Old diaries and letters failed to yield conclusive evidence. It was proved that Johnnie Frey was in town on the day the original pony express went out. He rode the horse that came in with the California mail eleven days later. The best evidence pointed to Frey as the first pony express rider, but scholars are slow to make dogmatic statements. Then, strangely enough, a contemporary newspaper file of *The Weekly West* was discovered. The departure of the first pony express was described in detail in the April 7, 1860, issue, and the rider's name was not Johnnie Frey. Instead, it was Johnson William Richardson.

The historians had a high old time censuring their colleagues for accepting circumstantial evidence and the memories of eyewitnesses years later, but the strangest angle of the investigation was yet to come. In October 1941 rider Richardson turned up himself, aged ninety-one. He said that he had not ridden the first lap of the pony express out of St. Joe. His brother, the manager of the livery barn, had put him on the horse for the ride down to the boat. There Johnnie Frey took the horse and mail from him.[6]

Perhaps the best-known express rider was "Pony Bob" Haslam. He made a famous ride in western Nevada when the Paiute were on the war trail. Haslam's regular run crossed the Sierras from California to Buckland's Station, later Fort Churchill, in Nevada. On the way, at Virginia City, he saw settlers fortifying against the Indians. Things looked bad ahead and there was no fresh horse for him to ride. Bob cantered off on his jaded mount. At the end of his run the next rider would not take the mail—ill from work, worry or fright. The superintendent offered Bob $50 to take the sick man's place. Within ten minutes Bob was off.

The first hitch was long, thirty-five miles to Carson Sink without a change. Here Bob got a fresh horse and rode to Cold Springs, thirty-seven miles beyond, and changed again. Thirty more miles put him at Smith's Creek, the end of the run. Bob delivered the mail to the next relay rider. He had ridden 190 miles, stopping only to change horses and to eat. He rested nine hours, then started back with the westbound mail. At Cold Springs he found charred logs and a dead station keeper. The Indians had done their work. Bob watered his fagged horse and set off down the trail toward the next station at Sand Springs. Night was coming and the sagebrush was tall enough in places to hide a mounted Indian. With the memory of the dead stationmaster in his mind, Bob watched his horse's ears for any warning that an Indian might be close at hand. He reached Sand Springs safely, told the station keeper what had happened and urged him to jump on a horse and come with him before the Indians arrived.

The two men clattered off together with the station horses. At Carson Sink they found the station men snugly forted with the horses inside the adobe buildings. They had seen fifty warriors and expected an attack momentarily. With plenty of food and a good spring of water near the house, they felt safe.

Haslam stayed until dark, about an hour. Then he slipped off into the night, with muffled hoofbeats pounding along the soft road. He arrived at Buckland's (Fort Churchill) only three and a half hours behind schedule. He was now back on his own route. He rested an hour and a half and went on toward the mountains. By the time he reached the end of his course west of the Sierras he had ridden 380 miles. He was tired, he said later, but the boss gave him $100 instead of $50.

Buffalo Bill is often referred to as a pony express rider. These statements stem from his publicity agents after William F. Cody became a famous showman. At the time of the pony express he was only fourteen years old. At that age he did work for Russell, Majors & Waddell as an office boy. Probably he carried messages on horseback to some of the partners, but no known contemporary records list him as a rider on the regular mail service.

Russell, Majors and Waddell, as has been said, were men of strict integrity. Majors and Waddell both feared God and operated their business conservatively, yet the nature of their business compelled them to hire wild and reckless men who could live with savages on their own terms. Some of their best stationmasters were outlaws. Yet the firm prohibited—on paper—drinking, gambling and swearing. Pony express riders pledged themselves as follows:

I, _____ _____, do hereby swear, before the Great and Living God, that during my engagement, and while I am an employe of Russell, Majors & Waddell, I will, under no circumstances, use profane language; that I will drink no intoxicating liquors; that I will not quarrel or fight with any other employe of the firm, and that in every respect I will conduct myself honestly, be faithful to my duties, and so direct all my acts as to win the confidence of my employers. So help me God.[7]

One of the most notorious division superintendents on the Overland Trail was Jack Slade. Born in Illinois of good parents, tradition says, he went west after killing a man. Elected captain of a wagon train, he quarreled with a teamster. The man beat Slade to the draw. Trapped, Slade reasoned with the teamster, said that their dispute was not great enough for either to lose his life. Why not throw down their guns and fight with fists? The man agreed and dropped his pistol, and Slade shot him dead. To escape punishment from his companions Slade fled and was forgotten for a while. Then he reappeared around the frontier forts and great tales of his deadly accuracy and courage began to circulate among travelers at overland stage stations and ferries. Russell, Majors & Waddell decided to employ him as superintendent of a division where outlaw employees were unmanageable. Slade brought order with a few quick shots at the right people, and his value to the firm became established. Next the division from Julesburg or Overland City—the South Platte Crossing—to Fort Laramie became troublesome. The stage was held up several times and robbed. Emigrant trains were plundered, and, strangely enough, these robberies occurred to parties shortly after they left Overland City. Evidently someone at the station was inspecting all travelers' outfits and marking the wealthy ones for plundering. Jules Reni was the superintendent, and evidence pointed to him as the leader of the freebooters.

Slade was assigned to Jules Reni's position, and moved down the line to take over. Jules was furious, and each man walked about Overland City watching for an opportunity to kill the other. At last Jules, from a hiding place behind a door, let Slade have both barrels from a shotgun. Slade replied with his six-shooter. The two men were carried to their lodgings. Jules recovered first. When able to stand on his feet, he left town. Slade got well shortly afterward and took charge of the division. He knew that Jules would probably come back some day if he lived. Slade warned henchmen to watch for him. One day four of them reported that they had caught Jules Reni. He was in a corral securely tied. Slade went out, recognized his old enemy, shot him where he lay and cut off his ears for pocket pieces. Slade was the law on his division.

Eight months after the pony express began its picturesque history, Abraham Lincoln was elected president. Since he was leader of a Northern party pledged to prevent the extension of slavery, people predicted that the South would revolt. News of Lincoln's success raced overland in eight days. His inaugural address, four months later, went across in seven days and seventeen hours, the best speed ever made by the pony express. News of the firing on Fort Sumter crossed in eight days and fourteen hours. The speed of these and other messages was important to the North's success in the war which now enveloped the nation. California had been admitted to the Union eleven years before as a free state, but it also had a minority in favor of the slaveholding South. Native Spanish-Californians constituted a dissatisfied, conquered group. To these might be added many emigrants who were having trouble patenting their land titles. These three groups might readily combine against the federal government.

A newly commissioned brigadier general, Edwin V. Sumner, the Bull of the Woods, who had recently been detailed to escort Lincoln from Springfield to Washington, was given the Western command. Orders commanding soldiers to return and defend the United States flew out on ponyback along the Overland Trail. The riders rushed on to deliver the latest orders to General Sumner. He was commanded to replace the evacuated overland forts with California volunteers. This withdrawal of able-bodied men gave the Confederate sympathizers a great advantage. At Virginia City, Nevada Territory, they raised the Confederate flag. General Sumner rebuilt Buckland's Station as Fort Churchill, put the Overland Road under martial law, collected arms and ammunition from suspected persons and thus nipped in the bud the little revolt designed to cut the Overland Trail.

As the horsemen shuttled back and forth, each the spearhead of a yellow shaft of dust, telegraph wires were laid from the East and from the West. Early in the summer of 1861, Fort Kearney was connected by wire with the Missouri. Pony express riders picked up messages there and delivered them at the western wire-end, then at Fort Churchill. In September the eastern telegraph was extended to Fort Laramie; in October wires from the Atlantic and the Pacific met[8] and the usefulness of the pony express was gone forever. Meantime, during September, the California elections disclosed the Golden State to be loyal to the Union. California's admission to statehood had helped to aggravate the Civil War, but she would stand firm in her conviction.

The coming of the Civil War profoundly affected another place on the Overland Road. St. Joseph, Missouri, with its railroad connection to the Mississippi, had become the biggest outfitting place for the Overland Trail. St. Joe was more accessible from the East than Kansas City, Leavenworth or Omaha. People prophesied that it would be the terminus of the overland railroad now on everyone's mind. Many citizens speculated in land, believing confidently that it would soon triple in value. Lincoln, shortly after his election, sent out a new postmaster to St. Joe. The town had many Confederate sympathizers. In order to prevent trouble an ordinance had ruled against flying any kind of flag. The new postmaster decided to raise the Stars and Stripes above the federal building, ordinance or no ordinance. A mob soon gathered—first to stare, then to hoot and throw rocks. According to a contemporary newspaper account, the mob started to attack the building intent on tearing down the flag. M. Jeff Thompson, whose term as mayor had expired, leaped on a wagon box and harangued the mob to keep its head and do nothing rash. The rowdies liked Thompson and they quieted down. Suddenly Thompson turned, climbed to the building next to the post office, ran across the roof to the flagpole and cut the flag down himself. At the Turnverein Hall the Germans had raised another American flag. The mob went there next and ordered it down. These acts in May 1861 were said to have prejudiced the Administration against St. Joseph as the terminus of the railroad. Descendants of the land speculators held a grudge against Thompson for three generations. Jeff's account in his memoirs of what he did that day does not differ materially from the newspaper report:

In the afternoon as the hour approached to hoist the flag over the Post Office the people of all parties began to collect. One of the employees of the post office asked me to go and drink with him; I went; another asked me to go with him; I went. As we returned, another met me and invited me, but, at this time I discovered that the flag was hoisted, and that they had been endeavoring to keep me away, and if possible, to get me drunk. They had gone just exactly too far, for, when I discovered their intentions, I had enough whisky in me to make me reckless, without intoxication. So, without consulting a soul, or intimating my intention, which was that instant formed, I drew my knife and pistol, ascended the rope ladder that they had used to the roof of the building, and amid cheers, groans, shouts and threats, I severed the halyards with my bowie, and the flag flew off into the street, and in an instant was torn into a thousand pieces.

That commenced a scene which might possibly be conceived but cannot be described. Hundreds rushed for the roof and over houses and every other way, all intent upon mischief; but, my resolution having conquered the liquor that I had just drunk, I was perfectly cool, and descended the ladder and walked away as if I was not an actor in the scene. The pole upon which the flag had been was torn down and brought to me. I ordered it thrown into the river, and away it went.

The Union men had now all fled to their homes, and several hundred terribly excited men were clamorous for mischief, and insisted that all other U. S. flags that were that day put out must be taken down. I had to lead them to control them, so marching towards the Turners Hall, I halted the crowd at Eighth and Messanie Streets and sent word to the Turner and German Rifle Company that had the Armory there, to take down the flag, or I would come for it.

The flag was taken down, and so were all the others in the city. I now ordered the men to their homes to await the signal . . .

Night had now fallen over the excited people, and all was quiet. I had gone too far now to recede. I had cut down the flag that I had once loved. I had, as yet drawn no blood from its defenders, but I was now determined to strike it down wherever I found it, and to cast my lot with my Southern brethren, who were building a new nation.[9]

---

1 William Lightfoot Visscher, *A Thrilling and Truthful History of the Pony Express* (Chicago, 1908) , 29.

2 LeRoy R. Hafen, *The Overland Mail, 1849-1869, Promoter of Settlement, Precursor of Railroads* (Cleveland, 1926) , 57.

3 Glenn D. Bradley, *The Story of the Pony Express* (Chicago, 1920) , 14.

4 *The Weekly West* (St. Joseph, Mo.) , April 7, 1860.

5 Autobiography of M. Jeff Thompson (MS in author's library) .

6 St. Joseph *News-Press*, Oct. 31, 1941.

7 Bradley, *The Story of the Pony Express*, 52.

8 Hafen, *The Overland Mail*, 187n., gives information concerning the progress of the telegraph across the continent.

9 Autobiography of M. Jeff Thompson.

Chapter 16

Mark Twain Follows the Trail

OON after the beginning of the Civil War Samuel Clemens learned that his brother Orion had been appointed Secretary of Nevada Territory. As an important official he offered Sam a job accompanying him as private secretary. The young man was delighted. The Clemens brothers packed their bags and went to St. Louis. There they took a boat for the six-day trip upriver to St. Joe. On the way Samuel Clemens learned that the Missouri was not the Mississippi. He prided himself on being a good pilot but he was not prepared for steamboating on the Big Muddy. The boat walked over jumbles of savage-looking snags. It bunted sand bars, backed up, bunted them again and finally walked across on the paddle wheels like crutches. Clemens thought the passengers might as well go to St. Joe by land but the patient Missouri captain said that the boat was "bully," it only needed a bigger wheel. Sam thought she needed stilts but did not say so out loud. At St. Joe, Sam and his brother hunted the Overland Stage office, site of the famous pony express departure a few months before. Tickets cost them $150 each and they were told that they could take only twenty-five pounds of baggage. They repacked and sent the surplus back to the boat. Like many tourists, they wanted to take something for every contingency. Sam's brother insisted on including a six-pound unabridged dictionary. Later they learned that they could buy dictionaries in California.

Early the next morning Sam and his brother, with a blanket or two, came to the stage station. The coach stood ready but it was loaded to the guards with sacks of mail. Some were lashed on the roof. One other passenger stood beside the vehicle. The Clemenses shook hands with Mr. George Bemis—a dismal fellow. The conductor and driver climbed up over the front boot, the three passengers climbed in on the mail. The six mules started and the coach lurched down to the dock. The passengers got out to watch the crossing and eyed one another's outfits. West of the Missouri the road rolled over green prairies, like the ocean after a storm. Here and there deep green patches of cultivated corn accentuated the limitless expanse of grass. The travelers, reclining among the mailbags, discussed one another's firearms. Sam Clemens carried a Smith & Wesson seven-shooter, his brother had a Colt that he carried loaded but without caps. Mr. Bemis had a double-action Allen "pepperbox," with six revolving barrels.

Every ten or twelve miles the stage stopped at a station to change mules. The passengers got out to stretch their legs and practice shooting. The conductor and driver both showed an interest in firearms. They looked curiously at Mr. Bemis' Allen and pronounced it thoroughly reliable. "If she didn't get what she went after," the stage driver remarked, "she would fetch something else." Sam Clemens pondered this remark solemnly. He stroked his broad mustache later when the Allen went out to get a deuce of spades nailed against a tree and fetched a mule standing thirty yards to one side. Mr. Bemis didn't want the mule, Clemens said, but the owner of the mule came out with a double-barreled shotgun and Bemis decided to buy it.

Sam noticed, too, that the conductor thought himself a humorous fellow. He said that the excessive amount of mail was "a little for Brigham . . . but the heft of it for the Injuns." Then he grimaced so that the travelers would know that he was joking.

After supper one night a talkative woman passenger got on and rode with them until an hour before daylight. Shortly thereafter the stage's thorough brace broke. Everyone got out in the dark and looked under the gears at the thorough brace, although Clemens, a steamboat pilot, did not know what to look for. The conductor said that he could fix things at once. The mailbags, he said, were addressed to the Indians. He would deliver them here. Clemens was sure that the conductor was indulging in another of his grimaces but it was too dark to see. Half or more of the mail was piled beside the road and the stage drove on. The bags not unloaded were laid between the seats. This left no place for the passengers to put their feet, but the conductor assured them they would be more comfortable lying down at ease. When they felt like it they could also climb on top of the stage and ride there. Traveling so, they passed over the Big Blue and the Little and Big Sandy. They noticed that the plains were very flat out here. The rolling prairies were left behind.

A hundred and eighty miles out of St. Joe they passed into the seven-year-old Territory of Nebraska. Sam Clemens found traveling at such a rapid pace exhilarating, with the stage curtains flapping in the breeze and arm loops waving back and forth. Once after breakfast the three passengers climbed onto the seat with the driver and let the conductor stretch out on the mailbags inside for a nap. The coach skimmed away and before long the travelers spied a "jackass rabbit," something new to Missourians. The Secretary of Nevada Territory cut loose with his Colt, Sam fired with his Smith & Wesson and Mr. Bemis let go a whole broadside from his Allen. The rabbit laid his long ears back on his body and stretched himself like a yardstick. A flash and a vanish, Clemens remembered. Long after the hare was out of sight, Sam said, they could still hear him whiz.

Every night the overland travelers put on their boots and clothes, wrapped up in their blankets and slept on the mailbags. In the morning, after nine o'clock, they began to undress for the heat of the day. The stage stations along this part of the Overland Trail were built of adobe with grass and weeds growing on the roofs. At each, bearded fellows came out with fresh mules. It was plain to Sam that they worshiped the driver—not his superior, the conductor, whom they treated with the same insolent tolerance they accorded Sam and his brother. The driver was the station men's idol. They hung on his every word, showed him every deference, slapped their thighs when he cracked a stale joke.

The stage stations were miserable hovels, many of them built hurriedly for the pony express early the preceding spring. They had no stoves and no floor except hard-packed earth. Station men dressed picturesquely in blue pantaloons with buckskin foxed on the seat and inside the legs. At mealtime these rough fellows drew up a stool, bench or box and ate with the passengers. Each place was set with a tin plate, knife, fork and pint cup. The driver sat at the head of the table with a chipped queens ware saucer. A cruet of vinegar graced the center of the greasy board, and all hands were served bread, bacon—a condemned army ration, Sam thought—and slumgullion. Clemens believed that the last was meant to be tea but it tasted more like dishwater, bacon grease and sand. This meal cost $1.00 a throw. The most startling thing to the Mississippi River pilot was the way the herders and station men addressed one another. Sam was amazed to hear men use the worst names in the docket as adjectives of friendship.

One afternoon the travelers saw a line of trees along the plains, marking the Platte. At 5:00 P.M. they drove into Fort Kearney, an adobe village with two two-story adobe blockhouses and several barns and barracks. Sam noted that they were 300 miles out of St. Joe. The next morning he climbed on the stage roof and sat with his legs dangling over the side. He saw his first prairie dog village, his first antelope and coyote. The mules scampered away with the coach and Sam felt thoroughly good. Years later he remembered the excitement of that ride.

Fort Kearney was the end of a division, and Sam Clemens began to notice the stage line's plan of operation. The driver changed every twelve hours. Conductors rode through to the end of the division. He learned, too, that each division had a superintendent—a man whom passengers seldom saw. Sam thought the conductors friendly and responsible. Not so the superintendents Clemens met, but he admitted that they were men to be respected. Absolute monarchs along the bit of road in their charge, they bought teams, built stations, repaired the road, did everything to get the stages through. Their employees were the roughest kind of men, many of them outlaws. A superintendent was always armed and ready to back an order with a bullet. Clemens heard that a man named Slade was the most deadly of them all.

At noon on the fifth day the stage pulled into Overland City—or Julesburg—at the crossing of the South Platte. The road to Denver—a three-year-old town—turned south here. The conductor told the passengers that they had an hour to eat dinner and look around. Sam and his brother walked up the street. The town was the strangest frontier settlement imaginable, crowded with emigrants, gamblers, Indian traders. Sam said that he and his brother felt like a couple of "meteoric people" who had been tossed into a new world.

The hour passed quickly and they were off again. The Platte at the ford looked flat and dismal with a few lonely trees along the banks. The stage splashed into the ford. Once or twice the passengers felt the wheels start to settle in the quicksand. A volley of oaths from the driver made the mules jump into their collars and the stage lurched forward. They got across, struggled up the bank and swung off merrily toward the setting sun. Sam sat with the driver, a sociable fellow, who said that Horace Greeley had gone over the Overland Road two years before. Greeley, the driver said, was always impatient about delays, eager to push ahead. At Carson City, the New York editor had told the driver, Hank Monk, that he must get across the mountains in short order to give a lecture. Hank cracked his whip and gave him the ride of his life through the mountains, spinning around curves with the hind wheels kicking gravel over the precipice. All the buttons were jolted off Greeley's coat and finally his head, white whiskers and all, shot through the top of the stage. He wasn't in such a hurry to keep his appointment as he had been. "Keep your seat, Horace," Hank Monk shouted over his shoulder as the stage lurched around another point of the mountain. "I'll get you there on time." "And you bet he did, too," the driver told Sam, "what was left of him!"[1]

The next morning just before dawn the stage broke down, a five-hour delay. Some campers by the road suggested a buffalo hunt. The three passengers accepted and rode away with them.

Sam said later that it was a memorable morning, galloping in the dewy freshness, but the hunt ended in disgrace. Mr. Bemis tried his Allen on a buffalo and the shaggy beast chased him two miles. Then Bemis forsook his horse and mounted a tree, the only one in several counties. Bemis was rescued by his friends but the experience left him in a sullen mood.

Back on the stage road, the coach was repaired and ready to go. The Clemens brothers climbed gaily on top and away they all went for Fort Laramie. The conductor said that they would meet the pony express sometime that day. The service was now provided twice weekly. Speed and frequency were doubly important with soldiers being drawn back to the States for war.

For hours Sam Clemens watched for the magic rider. The overland stage traveled the remarkable distance of 100 to 125 miles in twenty-four hours. The pony express went twice as fast. The romance and danger of such speed attracted all overland travelers. The conductor said that eighty riders were flying eastward and westward all the time across this barren wilderness. As yet Sam had missed seeing any of them. Always the daring horsemen had sped past in the night. The passengers had tried to see them by peeking out between the curtains, but they had heard only "a whiz and a hail, and the swift phantom of the desert was gone."[2] Now today they were to see a pony express rider in the light of day.

"Here he comes!" the driver yelled. Clemens remembered:

Away across the endless dead level of the prairie a black speck appears against the sky, and it is plain that it moves. . . . In a second or two it becomes a horse and rider, rising and falling, rising and falling—sweeping toward us nearer and nearer—growing more and more distinct, more and more sharply defined—nearer and still nearer, and the flutter of the hoofs comes faintly to the ear—another instant a whoop and a hurrah from our upper deck, a wave of the rider's hand, but no reply, and man and horse burst past our excited faces, and go swinging away like a belated fragment of a storm!

So sudden is it all, and so like a flash of unreal fancy, that but for the flake of white foam left quivering and perishing on a mail-sack after the vision had flashed by and disappeared, we might have doubted whether we had seen any actual horse and man at all, maybe.[3]

In time the stage spun through Scotts Bluff. The travelers saw and marveled at the sight of their first alkali—water soapy with it, whitewashed ground covered with the peculiar black alkali weed. Sam wrote about alkali in his notebook as a new wonder. The stage passed Fort Laramie in the dark. In the morning the passengers saw Laramie Peak, vast and solitary, looming in rich indigo among storm clouds. In the clear air the headland seemed to be only a short way beyond the sagebrush ridge west of the rocking stage. The travelers now entered dangerous Indian country. At the Laparelle Station the passengers heard that the keeper had recently fired four times at a skulking red man. The station man seemed provoked and blamed the Indian for not standing still long enough to be hit. Sam heard, too, that the last pony express rider had acquired a bullet hole through his jacket as he sped along in the dark. Filled with these stories and a dinner of condemned army bacon, the driver cracked his whip and the stage sped away. The conductor remarked that the Indians were not so bad up here as they were down South. He had come north with the Butterfield stages last spring, he said. Butterfield's Overland Mail Company had held a government contract to carry mail to California via Texas and New Mexico Territory. The Civil War made this impossible, and the firm had moved equipment and employees up onto the Russell, Majors & Waddell road.[4]

To Sam Clemens and his brother Orion the Indians were bad enough up here. The two watched thē distant cedars suspiciously. Did those shadows hide a party of lurking warriors ready to sweep out and surround them all? Sam looked thoughtfully at a bullet hole in the stage. He remembered that a station man had said that the bullet had hit the driver. The lurching sides and flapping curtains seemed a poor fortification. Dark settled over the travelers and, what was worse, the country became rougher. Indians might easily surround the horses here, pour a volley into the stage, kill the conductor and driver and then have the trapped passengers at their mercy. The passengers buttoned down the curtains and lay in the dark. Each man fondled his weapons. Above them they noticed that the conductor and driver were silent, apparently on the lookout. They spoke only at long intervals and then in low tones. Clouds covered the stars. Soon raindrops began to patter on the stage roof. Sam could hear only the grinding of the wheels in muddy gravel. He had a strange feeling that the stage was not moving; that it was standing still and being jolted and swayed. He knew better but the illusion was perfect. Occasionally one of his companions spoke. Then the other cut in with a sharp "Hark" and they sat in silence again, listening to the patter of the rain. At times they half-slept in stupor. Suddenly they heard a wild agonizing scream.

"Help! help! help!" Sam recognized the driver's voice. He was not ten steps from the side of the stage.

"Kill him! Kill him like a dog!" a rough voice said.

"I'm being murdered! Will no man lend me a pistol?"

"Look out! Head him off! head him off!" Two pistol shots rang out in the blackness. Sam Clemens and his friends lying on the mailbags in the coach heard many tramping feet surge around some object. They heard several heavy blows with a club. A voice appealed, "Don't, gentlemen, please don't. I'm a dead man!" Then a groan and another blow. The stage lurched forward and sped away in the night. It all happened in a few seconds.

The passengers, now fully awake, concluded that the trouble could not have been with Indians. Red men did not talk such good English. They called to the conductor for an explanation. "Tell you in the morning," he shouted back above the clatter of the wheels. Sam and his companions lighted their pipes, curled back a curtain to let out the smoke and began to talk. The new excitement banished thought of the wild Indians from their minds. The passengers never did learn the details of the dark night's tragedy other than that the stage driver who got off at the last station had been saying rough things about some

of the outlaws in that neighborhood. The conductor did not
have much sympathy for him. Only a fool would talk as he
had and then drive up without being prepared to defend himself.
"I tell you it's as much as Slade himself wants to do!"

The name of Slade aroused Sam Clemens' curiosity at once.
He had been hearing his name for miles. Now at last he was in
the dread man's division. This was more exciting and interesting
than the Indians. Two thirds of the talk on the run had been
about this man Slade. An outlaw among outlaws, he was the
bloodiest of them all, yet a most useful citizen in getting work
out of wild rogues. With Slade killing was not a sporting proposition. It was strictly business. Since he had outwitted and killed
the overland train driver he always got the advantage before
he shot. Sam heard that Slade had killed twenty-six people and
adopted the little boy of a family he had exterminated. People
said that Slade once sat in a room with friends. He saw coming a
man whom he disliked. "Gentlemen," said Slade, sighting his
revolver, "it is a good twenty-yard shot. I'll clip the third but-
ton on his coat,"[5] and he did. The guests all admired his accuracy and attended the funeral.

Sam Clemens rolled Slade stories around in his mind as the
stage rolled into the breakfast station. Seated at the table were
bearded and bepistoled roughs—ranchmen, mountain men and
station employees. The travelers took seats on a bench at one side
of the table. Sam took a seat beside a man who looked more gentlemanly than the others. He started to eat. In a few moments he
heard the men speak to the man at his elbow, the gentlemanly
fellow, as Slade. Sam never forgot that thrill. He suddenly became the proudest stripling who ever traveled to see strange
lands. Yet this beast who was said to have killed twenty-six men
was friendly and gentle-spoken. Sam watched him slyly. He did
not seem to differ in appearance from other men except that he
was rather wide across the cheekbones and his lips were pecu-
liarly thin and straight. The men bolted their food in silence
with a guilty air common among teamsters eating in public. The
coffee ran low and Slade reached for the pot. Then he saw that
Clemens' cup was empty. He offered the drink to the young

Courtesy, Union Pacific Railroad

UNION PACIFIC BRIDGE AT GREEN RIVER

THE COLUMBIA RIVER GORGE

man. Sam politely refused but Slade would not take "no" for an answer. Politely he filled Sam's cup. When all had finished, Slade came out to see the passengers off. He made some suggestions for rearranging the mail sacks in order that the passengers might be more comfortable. Then they drove away. For the rest of his life Sam Clemens remembered how Slade looked. Forever after, whenever Clemens saw a man with Slade's peculiar characteristics he unconsciously believed him a desperate character. A few years later Clemens learned that Slade was dead. He had become a drunkard, had moved to Montana and was hanged there by the vigilantes. Slade did not die bravely. His last moments were devoted to tears and prayers for mercy.

A short way beyond the breakfast station the stage came to a Mormon wagon train. Sam counted thirty-three whitetops. Coarsely clad men, women and children trudged beside them; others followed with a small drove of loose cattle. The Mormons, dusty, hatless and uncombed, looked very tired. They said that they had been on the road eight weeks, traveling 798 miles. The Clemens brothers had covered the same distance in eight days and three hours.

The stage crossed North Platte, spun along Sweetwater, passed Independence Rock and Devil's Gate. The Clemens boys felt themselves in the heart of the Rocky Mountains. They passed great flats or lakes of soda and alkali. The conductor told them that Mormons came here from Great Salt Lake City to gather these minerals. Great Salt Lake City! The boys felt far out West, indeed. That night they lay down to sleep rocking among the mailbags as in a cradle of romance. The night air tingled like none they had ever breathed back in Missouri—fresh, indescribably pure and soothing. In the morning they rolled up the stage curtains and beheld in the hazy distance a long array of misty mountain peaks. The rising sun gilded crag after crag and summit after summit. Then between these filmy fantasies they spied on the great flat ahead four log cabins. The road led to them and they knew this to be South Pass City. The leading—and only—citizen met them. With fresh mules they sped away. Two miles passed and Sam saw what he knew existed but never expected to

see and believe, banks of snow in midsummer. Yet there they
were. The approach to South Pass was not rugged but the travelers knew that they were far up in the sky. In the next few miles
many glittering peaks swung into view. Then the stagecoach
whirled into South Pass. On all sides he saw nature's monarchs,
ten, twelve and thirteen thousand feet high, crowned with snow.
Mountains and more mountains extended as far away as he could
see in the summer haze. The day was hot but the air was thin and
"air-conditioned" in the shade. From the rocking windows the
men watched a half-dozen storms playing in the purple mountains. A rag of cloud wrapped itself around a rocky dome, then
shred away and left the dome silvered with new white snow.

At last they came to the very summit of the Continental Divide. The conductor pointed to a spring which drained two
ways, into the Gulf of Mexico and the Pacific. Here, on this
ridgepole in the clouds, they overtook a long emigrant train,
many wagons, with haggard men, women and children. These
were not Mormons. They were Missourians like Sam Clemens
himself. Of all persons, Sam recognized an old school friend riding on a horse behind some livestock. The two boys had parted
last in a petty quarrel. That is, Sam had been leaning out a sec-
ond-story window with a watermelon and below him stood his
friend. Sam had been seized with an uncontrollable desire to
drop the watermelon on his friend's head. He had lost both a
good melon and a good friend. Now they met and spoke as
though nothing had come between them.

Since the beginning of the trip the travelers had been going
slowly uphill. Now they went down, spinning toward Green
River. The scenery was magnificent, with great mountains in the
distance. Near by they passed piles of white bones and upended
boards marking the graves of emigrants. A scrap heap of old iron
showed where the Mormons had burned one of the government
wagon trains in the "war" four years ago. At night, skulls along
the roadside glowed eerily; phosphate impregnated the bony tis-
sue. Once at midnight rain pattered on the stage roof. A deluge
followed, such as comes down only in a Western desert. The
travelers buttoned the curtains and reinforced the seams with

their spare clothing, but still the moisture filled the coach with a gray spray. Sam wondered how the conductor and driver outside could stand it. Little streams of water appeared on the mailbags and ran into puddles. The passengers' blankets became wet as sponges. The horses turned tail to the storm and soon it was plain that the stage was off the road. After a time the downpour stopped.

In a moderate drizzle the conductor got down with his lantern and hunted for the road. Small gulches across the desert floor gurgled brimful with chocolate-colored water. Suddenly the conductor disappeared, hurtling into a fourteen-foot wash, his lantern following him like a meteor. "Don't come here," he shouted frantically from the bottom.

"Think I'm a dam' fool?"[6] the driver replied sardonically.

The conductor climbed out and went back along the stage tracks in the mud. Twice he pointed out places where in the dark they had come within inches of catastrophe. An hour was lost finding the road.

On the morning of the tenth day out of St. Joe the stage swung down to the Green River flats. At the station the passengers ate the only good meal of the entire trip—hot biscuits, fresh antelope steak and coffee. The river was low in August and the stage forded the limpid stream. Extra teams pulled the load up the far bank. At five o'clock in the afternoon the mail coach rolled into Fort Bridger. Here they picked up an army sergeant traveling west. As evening shadows crept out from the mountains the sergeant regaled his companions with stories about military life out West, said that the most amusing story he knew was about Horace Greeley and Hank Monk. The passengers listened politely to the end.

In Echo Canyon, the next morning, Sam Clemens felt as though he were in a narrow street between tall buildings. He looked up at the enormous perpendicular walls 400 feet above the road and saw natural turrets that might have stood on medieval castles. At places ruins could be seen of fortifications built by the Mormons to repel the United States Army in 1858, but never used.[7] The road was good in the canyon and beside the Weber.

The stage seemed to fly along, with men and mailbags in solution under the curtains. A kindly Mormon got on the stage at one of the stations. He was affable and wanted to be hospitable to the strangers, said he had heard a very funny story—about Horace Greeley and Hank Monk. The two Clemens boys and Mr. Bemis listened to the tale again. At four o'clock in the afternoon the stage reached the summit of Big Mountain, only fifteen miles from Salt Lake City. Below them under an arched rainbow lay the stupendous panorama of Salt Lake Valley, gilded with the setting sun. The stage driver stopped his horses and gazed.

Half an hour later they pulled up at a Mormon stage station to change horses and eat supper. Sam was told that the proprietor was a Destroying Angel. He got his "shudder" ready, went in and was disappointed. The "Angel" proved to be a loud, profane old blackguard in a dirty shirt and no suspenders. One man in the room looked like a gentleman. He was Heber C. Kimball's son. A lot of slatternly women flitted back and forth with coffee-pots, bread, bowls of food slopping. These were the Angel's wives, Sam was sure. Had they been hired help they would not have tolerated the abusive language fired at them by the Angel. Clemens was not impressed with the West's peculiar institution. He knew he disliked slavery but he was used to that. Polygamy seemed to have no redeeming features.

Late that evening he reached Salt Lake City and unpacked at the Salt Lake House. This city in the mountains was, he thought, the only absolute monarchy in America. The three gentile travelers ate a fine supper, fresh meat, fowl and vegetables. Salt Lake City was as modern as any metropolis of its size back East. Good shops and stores lined the main street. Mr. Bemis remembered an errand and made an excuse for leaving the Clemenses. They strolled on without him, called on the acting governor of the territory and met many gentiles. Sam caught himself looking at everybody on the street and wondering, Is that a Mormon? He admired the neat shade trees and the water babbling down the gutters. Water sparkled in the orchards and gardens around every house. Salt Lake was different from any city he had ever seen, not a single unemployed person in it. Sam and his brother saw the Tithing House and the Mansion House and finally returned to their rooms at the hotel. Mr. Bemis came in about eleven o'clock. He was full of cheerfulness, talked loosely, hung his coat on the floor on one side of a chair and his vest on the floor on the other side, took off his trousers and piled them on the floor in front, then got in bed with his boots on. Clemens surmised that he was not only full of cheerfulness but also full of Valley Tan, a whisky of Mormon invention.

The next day the Clemenses made the acquaintance of a Mr. Street who was building the telegraph line from the Missouri River to California. As has been noted, the line was finished in the fall of 1861. Mr. Street told the Clemenses that he had subcontracted with several Mormons to get out telegraph poles for him. These men had gone to work, but when they were half finished they found that they were losing money on their contract. They left their poles on the ground and went home. Mr. Street said that he remonstrated but they told him that he could never prosecute them in a Mormon court in Utah. Street did not know what to do. He must get the wire stretched across the continent. A friend suggested that he see Brigham Young. Street went with little hope, but the President of the Church looked over the contracts, then ordered each man who had signed to come to his house. He lined them up and told them to comply with the contract that they had signed even if it impoverished every one of them. The men, Street said, went back to the job and the poles were being set. There would be a telegraph across the continent by fall. Mr. Street suggested that the Clemenses go with him to meet Brigham Young. The young men put on white shirts and called. They found Brigham a quiet, kindly, easy-mannered, dignified, self-possessed old gentleman of sixty. Sam thought that he "had a gentle craft in his eye that probably belonged there."[8]

The Clemens boys stayed in Salt Lake City two days. Sam heard and enjoyed many funny stories about polygamy; about the mistake Brigham made by giving one of his wives a $25 breastpin. The other wives heard about it and he paid $2,500 getting pins for all. Sam heard, too, that a woman came to Brigham once with a baby. She claimed to be his wife. Brigham looked at the child and thought it did look like him so he sent it to the Lion House, but when the baby was washed it turned out to be an Indian. Worse still were the stories about the economy Brigham tried to institute by putting all his wives in one bed ninety-six feet wide. They all snored and he could not sleep. Then, too, they all drew in their breath at once and a man could actually see the walls of the house contract. When they exhaled the walls swelled out, the rafters cracked and the shingles split. The stories Clemens heard about the Mormons seemed to him very different from the reticent people of the faith whom he met.

At the end of the two-day sojourn in Salt Lake City the Clemens brothers prepared for the last lap of the overland journey. Old travelers now, they knew what to take along for their own comfort, a good supply of bread, hard-boiled eggs and ham. So far the meals had been the only unpleasant thing on the trip. Now with the downgrade, a flying coach, peerless sunsets, alternate rainbows and thunderstorms, ham, eggs and a rank old delicious pipe, life should be superb. They left town in the evening and at eight o'clock the next morning they arrived at the remnant of Camp Floyd, forty-five miles from Salt Lake City. By four in the afternoon they had doubled the distance. Then they entered the hideous salt desert at dark.

The sun was just rising, a red ball behind the stage, when the passengers got out at the halfway station in the desert for breakfast. A few shacks and dripping casks stood desolately in the great flat, for all water had to be hauled to this outpost. The dawn wind was chilly, but an hour later the August sun beat down mercilessly. On all sides the endless desert lay parched and forlorn, an ocean dead and turned to ashes. The Clemens boys suffered with thirst and drank copiously from their canteens. By noon their water was gone. Outside, the lifeless solitude showed no bird, no insect, no reptile—space devoid of matter, a vacuum. Even the air seemed dead. The mules, evidently fagged, hauled the coach by a series of spurts. Under the driver's lash they tugged the vehicle ahead for a hundred yards, then stopped. Great clouds of dust rose around them and settled on the coach. The men's faces, eyebrows and mustaches became colorless with the gray powder, their clothes became dusty as millers'. The Clemens brothers were used to bowling along at eight and ten miles an hour, surrounded by inspiring scenery. They noticed grimly that here they were averaging only two and a quarter; and to add to their discomfort, the alkali began to burn their faces, chap their lips, redden their eyes. The sight of the next station late in the afternoon looked like paradise. For the first time, Sam said, he was glad that they had brought along the six-pound dictionary, but even it, unabridged as it was, failed to have suitable words to describe the desert journey.

In Nevada Territory Samuel Clemens noticed the savage Diggers who had helped reduce the Donner party and weaken them before the mountains had been reached. Along the stage route the Diggers loafed and begged at the stations, when they were not waylaying a lone emigrant or shooting from ambush at a flying pony express rider. A small, scrawny people, black as Negroes and caked with dirt, their only home was a tattered blanket thrown over a bush. They seemed to have no tribal life nor organization. For food they ate offal thrown out of the stage stations, supplemented with an occasional rabbit killed with their bows and arrows. The women collected grasshoppers and ground them into a meal that they prized highly. Samuel Clemens had never before seen such a low standard of living, but one of them asked him if he had heard a heap funny story about Horace Greeley and Hank Monk—so Mark Twain said.

The mountains that appeared above the western horizon as the stage approached Carson Sink were the most magnificent Clemens had yet seen. The days continued to be hot, but the nights were arctic. The high mountains were close and the trip was drawing to an end. East of the sink, and eighteen days' travel from St. Joe, the travelers came to the telegraph line that was being extended toward Salt Lake City. The new Secretary of Nevada Territory sent a message to the governor at Carson City. The next day the stage entered the pitiless desert that stretched forty miles to Carson Sink. The wheels sank from six inches to a foot in the hot sand. To save the mules the passengers got out and walked. The Carson desert from one end to the

other was strewn with bleaching bones, wrecked wagons and
rusting log chains. California emigrants, always on the point of
exhaustion when they reached this last stretch before the cool
green mountains, suffered their greatest casualties here.

The next stage station was known as "Ragtown." Ten miles
east of the stop the passengers saw a man lying by the road completely exhausted. They picked him up, lifted his limp body into
the stage and forced a little brandy between his lips. By dint of
much chafing of his arms they brought the poor fellow to life.
With grateful eyes he said that he could never repay them, but as
they appeared to be strangers to these parts he might at least
shorten one hour of their journey with an amusing story. Had
they ever heard about Horace Greeley and Hank Monk?

The Clemens boys had come to the end of their patience. They
had heard the bald-headed story from white men, Chinamen,
Mormons and Indians. It had been given to them flavored with
whisky, beer, cologne, sozodont, tobacco, garlic and grasshoppers. They did not want to hear it again. Mark Twain remembered that they remonstrated with the waif, asked him to for-
bear. The grateful invalid did so, but to all their sorrow. "In
trying to retain the anecdote in his system he strained himself and
died in our arms," so Mark Twain said.[9] And surely he would not
lie about it!

On the morning of the twentieth day out from St. Joseph the
Clemenses knew that their long journey was almost over. At
noon they expected to arrive at Carson City. The excursion had
been a great lark and they were sorry it was over. The country
around them was to be their new home. They examined it critically. The road ran, as usual, across a great desert with no tree
in sight, but the valley was walled with snow-clad mountains. In
the distance they saw wagon trains, alkali dust blowing from the
wheel ruts like smoke from a prairie fire. At last Carson City
was pointed out, a few spots against the great mountain miles
away.

In time they arrived in the board town, got out of the coach
and took their baggage. The stage moved on and left them alone.
The main street consisted of four or five blocks of frame build-

ings. The sidewalk was of boards. The young men introduced themselves at the stage station and walked toward the governor's mansion. On the way a man on horseback chatted with them and then cut his conversation short in the middle of a sentence to go over and start a shooting match with a man braiding a whiplash. This was the Clemenses' first introduction to Carson City and the end of their experience on the Overland Trail.

---

1 Mark Twain, *Roughing It* (New York, c1913) , I, 139.
2 *Ibid.*, 54.
3 *Ibid.*
4 J. V. Frederick, *Ben Holladay, The Stagecoach King* (Glendale, Calif., 1940) , 60-61.
5 Mark Twain, *Roughing It,* I, 67.
6 *Ibid.*, 89.
7 William Alexander Linn, *The Story of the Mormons* (New York, 1902) , 515.
8 Mark Twain, *Roughing It,* I, 97.
9 *Ibid.*, 142.

Chapter 17

Long-Eye and the Iron Horse

IGRATION over the road was heavy during the Civil War.
The year after Mark Twain's trip, 300 Mormon wagons
were counted crossing South Pass in one day. Eighty
went through on another day. During the same year 1862,
Russell, Majors & Waddell were sold out on foreclosure. The
pony express had helped bankrupt them. Their principal cred-
itor and onetime agent, Ben Holladay, bid in the firm's assets.
His first summer's operations were discouraging. With 110
coaches, 1,750 horses and mules and between four and five hundred men,[1] the line was threatened by Indians in serious numbers
for the first time. The Pike's Peak gold rush had driven out
many of the plains red men. These tribesmen had combined with
the northern Sioux and turned on the white invaders. For the
first time in plains Indian history, they began to raid in parties of
several hundred, not in little warrior bands of twenty or thirty.
Holladay moved his line 100 miles south to the Cherokee
Trail, the route taken later by the Union Pacific. The telegraph
wires were restrung in this lower country. Meanwhile, at deserted Fort Laramie, councils were called with the Indians in the
summer of 1863. The whites were particularly anxious to get a
right of way for a railroad to the Pacific. The Sioux refused to
come and talk. Chief Washakie of the Shoshoni agreed to let the
railroad pass.

In 1864 a gold rush to Montana swelled the number of draft
evaders and other emigrants trundling west. The red men struck

392

back like a tornado, raiding emigrant camps, burning stage stations. Julesburg was captured and looted twice—with soldiers in a near-by fort watching helplessly. In February 1865 General Grenville M. Dodge arrived in the West. He had taken a prominent part in the war and received severe wounds. The Western assignment came as a vacation but Dodge instilled new energy into the few troops stationed along the road. The winter of 1865 was unusually severe. Dodge made a few short sorties after the Indians but was unable to find them on the winter-locked plains. Regular freight service was resumed but everyone knew that the Indians were biding their time until green grass would let them fall on the long eastern stretch of the Overland Trail.

Grenville Dodge knew the Indians. They called him Long-Eye in the years before the war when he had surveyed a line west from Council Bluffs. To build a railroad to the Pacific was Dodge's great ambition in life. The war had come as a dirty job that must be done, but Dodge wanted to get back into civil engineering. He determined to strike at the Indians in the spring before they had time to strike at the road. While hunting hostiles, Dodge intended to scout for a roadbed across the continent. He prepared four columns to march into the northern buffalo ranges, one under General Alfred Sully and three under General Patrick E. Connor, a Californian who had won great renown in January 1863 by a hard winter march to Bear River where he defeated a large band of Shoshoni.

In April 1865 Dodge received word that Lincoln had been assassinated. With his staff, Dodge entrained for Springfield, Illinois, to take part in the burial ceremony. He had known the Martyr President before his election. The prospect of building a railroad to the Pacific had drawn the two men together. At that time Dodge had recommended Council Bluffs as the logical eastern terminus. He had speculated in land along the proposed route and urged Lincoln to buy some also. Two years later Lincoln had become President of the United States. Throughout the Civil War, Lincoln continued to press the importance of a transcontinental railroad. In 1862 a railroad bill had been introduced in Congress. Lincoln called his old friend Dodge from the front to discuss the measure. The act seemed generous enough. By it the government proposed to form a Union Pacific corporation which would be given ten sections of land and receive a loan of $16,000 for every mile of track it laid. In the foothills and mountains the subsidy was to increase to $32,000 and $48,000 per mile, respectively. The Union Pacific Company had only to raise sufficient capital to build the first forty miles. Then the subsidy would start. The government loan was to be secured by a first mortgage on the tracks and rolling stock.

In Springfield, General Dodge watched his troops guarding the sable-plumed hearse. He remembered Lincoln's great interest in the Union Pacific. Lobbyists from the Missouri River towns had clamored for the terminus and threatened to block passage of the Union Pacific act if not appeased. A compromise fixed the place of beginning at the hundredth meridian—Fort Kearney. Roads from Kansas City, Atchison, St. Joseph and Omaha might all build parallel feeders to this point.

General Dodge was determined then, and still was, that the road should commence at Omaha. With other stockholders in the Union Pacific he had started a branch road to Fort Kearney and hoped that it would become the main trunk. In January 1863 ground had been broken in Omaha. Businessmen in St. Louis and Kansas City had subscribed funds for a rival branch and had begun work ahead of the Dodge group. Fortunately for Dodge the money of the St. Louis-Kansas City promoters had soon been exhausted. Both companies were equally embarrassed. Railroads were a doubtful speculation and capital was drawn away on all sides by promises of gigantic war profits. Dodge recalled that Lincoln had been disappointed at the lack of interest in his railroad.

The funeral procession stopped in Oak Ridge Cemetery. Dodge watched his old friend's coffin being placed in a receiving vault. Dodge knew that even the stress of war had never diverted the President's attention from the transcontinental railroad. Lincoln had counted on the completion of the road as one of the achievements of his administration. The President had called Dodge to the White House again, this time from Vicksburg.

Dodge suspected that Lincoln intended to censure him but in Washington he learned that the President wanted more advice on the railroad to the Pacific. What could be done to interest capitalists?

The two men, both slow and deliberate thinkers, agreed that the subsidy would have to be increased, the land grant doubled. After the conference Dodge went at once to the Union Pacific's directors. He said that the President would back a request for more liberal payments. Congress must be asked for new legislation.

The second Union Pacific act of 1864 doubled the land grant and allowed the government to take a second instead of a first mortgage. Everyone knew that an eccentric financial genius, George Francis Train, had amused, shocked and finally interested capitalists in the new bill's possibilities. Train started life sweeping a Boston counting room and soon became head of the firm—so he claimed. Later as a clipper-ship king he opened counting rooms around the world. The construction of street railways in England interested him next. His idea of a cab on tracks to haul poor people at a moderate fee was revolutionary. In his successful business offices he attracted crowds with free champagne luncheons. He regaled them with songs and witty sallies against the status quo. The outbreak of the American Civil War had agitated his barbed tongue. Loudly he urged Ireland to join the North and fight Great Britain. Jailed occasionally for his unguarded utterances, he finally escaped to Canada as a stowaway. George Francis Train liked to be called a crank. He also enjoyed saying unpleasant things that were hard to answer. Journalists reported him to be a man who "talks on the stump like an embodied Niagara, composes songs to order by the hour as fast as he can sing them, . . . remembers every droll story from Joe Miller to Artemus Ward, is a born actor, is intensely in earnest, and has the most absolute and outspoken faith in himself and his future."[2]

George Francis Train had gone to the American financiers when they were afraid to finance the Union Pacific railroad and showed them that the act had possibilities not apparent in its innocent wording. The stockholders might organize a subsidiary company, a *Crédit Mobilier*, with interlocking directorate. This new firm could take all the subsidies offered by the government, lay the track with subcontracts and leave the road finished but financially strapped. The proposition was legal, logical and very profitable. Financiers signed their names on Train's subscription blanks. The Union Pacific began to lay rails and Mrs. George Francis Train attended President Lincoln's second inaugural ball in a gorgeous new dress, her hair powdered with gold.

General Dodge, at Lincoln's funeral, knew that the real Union Pacific railroad had not built forty miles of track since the second act was passed. Lincoln had always been willing to make great concessions to the builders provided the work pushed ahead. What would be the attitude of his successor, Andrew Johnson? General Dodge returned from Springfield to his headquarters. He soon learned that the new administration was not inclined to go ahead with Lincoln's railroad program nor even to prosecute vigorous operations against the Indians, which Dodge deemed necessary if the railroad was to be built. He was allowed 6,000 men and told that he must finish his Indian campaign by October 1865. The general organized his scant force to do what he could and changed his headquarters to Fort Kearney. He ordered his four columns into the buffalo range. In August, Dodge set off himself to learn why his army had failed to find the Indians. With a cavalry escort, twelve four-mule teams and two ambulances, he rode up the Platte. The Overland Road was choked with freight teams and emigrants' wagons, most of them headed for Denver with supplies. The general's column clattered into the ruined huts of much-raided Julesburg. A mountain man, Leon Pallady, stepped forward to greet the soldiers. The general hired him to guide the column to Fort Laramie. Pallady led the way up Lodge Pole Creek, across to Scotts Bluff and on to the fort where Dodge met another acquaintance of his plains-surveying days. Nick Janis was a renowned French squaw man reputed to have much influence with the Indians. He had a beautiful half-breed daughter who attracted the eye of dapper young Major McElroy. The Indians invited Dodge and his staff to a great feast in the council house. From the sutler's store, mess sergeants brought wines and canned goods but the main dish, the *pièce de résistance*, bubbled in a great caldron. All the officers dipped a ladle into the soup and pronounced the stew delicious. Dodge himself, always slow and dignified, took a second helping and smacked his lips beneath his broad mustache. He noticed a bone on his plate that looked like a hog's foot. "A squealer?" he asked the Frenchman beside him.

"No," Nick replied shaking his Indian hair, "a bowwow."

The soldiers looked at one another, then walked out of the building a trifle green with nausea. They were not used to the Indian delicacy, "puppy soup." But strangely enough, handsome Major McElroy sat unmoved and even called for more. He did not want to break up a party that associated him with the beautiful black-eyed half-breed.

The first week in September 1865 Dodge ordered his escort to proceed. His four columns, after a summer's campaign, had not found enough Indians to have a battle. Yet Dodge knew that the three confederated tribes were somewhere above, probably preparing to descend on the stage line any day. A battalion of Pawnee scouts commanded by Major Frank North, who had practically been raised in the tribe, had run down a few hunting parties and a large band of warriors had killed a lieutenant, Caspar Collins, at the bridge constructed where the old ferry on the upper Platte had been. The town of Casper, Wyoming, would later use his name with different spelling. On the whole, however, the campaign had accomplished nothing. Dodge decided to see the Powder River country himself before discontinuing operations. Major McElroy asked to be left behind. He wanted to stay by the dusky maiden with the blue-black braids, or better still, he wanted to take her along. Dodge would have none of it.

The column started. At the gate of Fort Laramie, Nick Janis stood beside his daughter watching the blue-clad horsemen. Major McElroy passed with bowed head. He would not look at them. The column wound north and west across the range to the head of Powder River. In these vast solitudes Dodge hoped to find the confederated Sioux, Cheyenne and Arapaho whom he knew to be organizing to resist the white men. On the sky line he saw signal smokes almost constantly but, like his four columns, he found no Indians. The size of the country and the enemy's ability to subsist indefinitely on buffalo convinced General Dodge that the red men could not be conquered with his small command. The Pacific railroad, Dodge's greatest interest always, had better be built farther south. The old Cherokee Trail across Wyoming evaded the bad Indian country and was shorter also.

Dodge was back at Fort Laramie with his escort by the middle of September 1865. For a day or two he rested, then started on an expedition that would be important to the future of the transcontinental railroad. On September 18[3] he led his little army south from Fort Laramie along the western mountains known then as the Black Hills. Leon Pallady still acted as guide and a detail of Pawnee scouts rode with the column. Dodge planned to ride south as far as Denver. By so doing he could examine every pass across the mountains into the Laramie plains. On the night of September 21, 1865, he encamped by Bear Creek. A hailstorm swept down from the mountains and blew his tents flat to the wet ground. The horses broke their hobbles and raced away. Pallady told Dodge that Indians had stampeded the horses. The Pawnee scouts rode in a circle around the muddy tracks and agreed. Then the stock was rounded up and the journey resumed. At Lodge Pole Creek, Dodge took Leon Pallady and a dozen picked cavalrymen and rode off up Cheyenne Pass toward the summit of the Laramie Mountains. The train was to follow along at the base of the hills as far as Crow Creek. Dodge had been watching the Black Hills with his telescope for a gap through to the west. From Cheyenne Pass he intended to ride down the top of the divide and thus discover a suitable defile to the Laramie plains if one existed. For three hours Dodge and his thirteen men picked their way along the ridge. Then Pallady reined his horse and pointed down the eastern slope. "Indians, and a lot of 'em," he said.

Dodge unsheathed his telescope and saw a large band of Crows on the mountainside between his little party and the distant train. "How many?" he asked Pallady, handing him the tube.

" 'Bout three hundred."

"Do they see us?"

"They've likely followed us all day," the guide concluded, "and aim to close in at night."

Dodge dismounted his men and moved in battle array down the slope toward the Indians. His objective was a patch of timber which he intended to fire as a signal to his men in the valley. The Indians deployed to meet the handful of whites. The soldiers reached the timber ahead of the Crows and started a smoke signal. Far below they watched the wagon train plodding along unmindful of their plight; evidently no one saw their signal. Soon the skirmish began. Bullets kicked up dirt across the battlefield. Dodge's men answered shot with shot and the telltale clouds of dust disclosed that the white men's guns shot the farther. The Indians noticed this too, and disappeared, but they were not retreating. Instead they came on under cover of rocks and gullies. Soon the smack of bullets told the white men that the invisible Indians were very close. Leon Pallady knew where to look for ambushed warriors. He knocked one out of hiding and killed two others' horses. His comrades admired his marksmanship but it was no time to be showing off. The whites reckoned that the red men had surrounded them. Moreover, the sun had set on their high position. Long shadows of the mountains flowed out on the plains below. Come dark, fourteen whites would be no match in close quarters for 300 Indians. Dodge ordered his men to build another signal fire. Surely the flames would be visible in the gloaming. Then Dodge turned his attention back to the men crouching behind boulders. Bullets cracked against the rocks with vicious regularity. Glancing shots hummed overhead, sharp as twanging guitar strings. Suddenly the firing stopped.

"Our men, the cavalry!" Pallady shouted as he pointed down a ravine. Dodge's signal fire had been seen at last. Soon the main body was among the forlorn hope. Men laughed and told about their narrow escapes. Dodge, with his telescope, watched the red men trailing off in the distance. He noticed that they dashed down a valley and vanished. The descent seemed to be more gradual than it appeared or horsemen could not ride down it at such speed. "Boys," Dodge said, "I think we've discovered a pass through which we can build the Union Pacific."[4]

The detail rode off on the Indians' trail and down the pass which was later to be crossed by the railroad between Cheyenne and Laramie.

The reconnaissance over, Dodge returned to the East. He wrote General Grant urging the War Department to initiate an active Indian campaign but learned that the administration was adamant. The Department of the Interior was also against aggressive measures. An old friend of Lincoln's sat in the Secretary's chair. Orville Hickman Browning, from Quincy, Illinois, had been intimate with the late President but also slightly contemptuous of him. He was more interested in establishing peace with the Indians than in building a railroad across the continent. His enemies maintained that his real motive was to build up patronage for his office, to create many Indian agencies for deserving party men. In any event, Browning allowed his wards to acquire rifles and soon they were as well armed as the soldiers.[5] The conquest of the plains and the construction of the Union Pacific railroad both seemed to be postponed indefinitely.

On April 24, 1866, General Dodge was in St. Joseph, Missouri. He met Thomas Durant, vice-president of the almost defunct Union Pacific. Durant asked Dodge to resign from the army and build the railroad. Durant had not got along with the chief engineer and was sure that Dodge could do the job. Dodge had been interested in the construction for years and made it the dream of his life. He knew that the company was in bad financial condition, that the *Crédit Mobilier* had received all the subsidies and that the government held a second mortgage on a pair of rusty rails that crossed about forty miles of plains. Dodge knew too that the new chief engineer, whoever he might be, would have trouble with Indians as well as finances. Dodge also knew Durant to be a man who was hard to get along with, but the general wanted the job more than anything else. The objections looked small to him. After all, he was very friendly with Grant and Sherman. They would help him with the Indians. Dodge told Durant, in his slow way, that he would take the job provided he be given absolute control. Durant agreed and the deal was closed.

Dodge asked for a leave of absence from the army. Grant objected. He wanted Dodge to try one more summer's campaign against the Indians. Then he relented and signed the request. Dodge tackled his railroad job like a general with a new command. He organized the engineering department on military lines, with centralized responsibility. He sent out surveying parties with heavily armed guards. To lay track he employed two brothers, General John Stephen Casement and his brother Dan. The Casement brothers assembled 1,000 laborers and 100 teams on the prairie west of Omaha. Dodge went out to see them. Camped like soldiers, the motley crew consisted of former Confederates and discharged Union veterans, Irish immigrants, bushwhackers and ex-convicts. Dodge was used to talking to the men under his command. He lined up the laborers and explained to them that they had enlisted for a new kind of warfare. In California another railroad company, the Central Pacific, was coming east. The governor of California, Leland Stanford, and financiers like Collis P. Huntington were pushing the western construction. That road was getting the same subsidies as the Union Pacific. The Californians would work hard but Dodge said that he expected his men to beat them at railroad building. True, the Westerners had a head start. As early as 1862 they had pushed their line up into the mountains and within ten months had built seventy miles,[6] but their money had run out and they were not yet to the top of the Sierras. The Union Pacific men, in plains country, would have fast going for six or seven hundred miles. Then the foothills would not be so bad as the California mountains. Surely the lion's share of the grading would go to the Union Pacific. The men cheered and set to work.

Dodge organized mule-drawn wagon trains—oxen were too slow—to go ahead to the mountains, cut ties and bridge timbers. Surveying crews drove stakes across the plains. On swells and hollows, miles ahead of the railhead, a dozen crews shoveled cuts and fills. Trainloads of rails were unloaded at St. Joe and sent upriver to Omaha by boat. Flatcars took the railroad iron out to the camps. Men carried the rails forward. Soon the sledges were ringing as the irons were spiked in place. Eastern newspapers began to carry stories about the building achievement—four rails laid in a minute, three miles of track built every day. The Casement brothers watched the work hour after hour and constantly perfected all movements. The men began to work with the enthusiasm of an athletic team.

"Moving towns" became a part of the construction. "Hell on Wheels," these headquarters were called. The first, at Fort Kearney, contained barracks for the laborers, gambling and drinking tents. A "Big Top," forty by a hundred feet, housed a brass band and dance floor with all the trimmings. The surveyors, fillers and graders had their own camps ahead but the majority of the laborers came back to Kearney each night on flatcars.

Soon the road had extended too far for workers to go and come each day. Another town, North Platte, at the forks of the river, was laid out and the false fronts, tent roofs and gambling tables from Kearney moved up the tracks. Next Julesburg became the site of Hell on Wheels. The women and their gambler friends, seated on the teetering fronts of their knocked-down houses, rolled into town on the "flats." Each railroad construction camp became a little rougher, a little more lawless than the last. At Julesburg a gang of camp followers decided to "jump" the area Casement had set off for the railroad's shops. The gamblers planned to take the best for themselves. Why let the big rich railroads have all the money? Dodge heard about it. He ordered Casement to go back to the railhead, restore order and take the area. Casement called for volunteers among the veterans in his work crew. He armed 100 of them and went to Julesburg. Three weeks later Dodge came along the line. "Are the gamblers quiet and behaving?" he inquired.

"You bet they are, General," Casement replied. "They're out there in the graveyard."[7]

In August 1866 the Indians began to raid the line. At Plum Creek, 200 miles west of Omaha, a band of warriors thundered around one of the freight trains and captured it. Dodge was at the end of the line ten miles beyond. He ran to his special car, an armored arsenal, and with twenty men and a locomotive puffed down the tracks. They found the freight train in flames with naked savages cavorting about on half-wild ponies. Dodge deployed his men as skirmishers and charged. The Indians galloped away. This was the first of twenty months of raiding along the right of way. What might Dodge expect when the railroad reached bad Indian country?

In October, back in Omaha, Dodge received a letter from Durant. The Union Pacific, as usual, was hard up for money. Durant stated that he was bringing a special trainload of prospective bond buyers with "a band, a caterer, six cooks, a photographer, three 'tonsorial artists,' a 'sleight-of-hand performer' and a printing press," along with great quantities of fancy foods and drinks.[8] Dodge prepared a camp for them at the Loup Crossing. A $50,000 bridge there was a marvel of engineering. Among the guests were George M. Pullman, Robert Todd Lincoln, the Marquis de Chambrun, Senators John Sherman and Ben Wade, also Mr. and Mrs. George Francis Train "and maid." The financial wizard could always be counted on to outdo any man.

The excursionists tripped down the car steps, helped the long-skirted ladies alight. Dodge served a great camp supper and planned a practical joke on his guests. Around great bonfires the Easterners danced on the bank of the stream where Narcissa and Marcus Whitman had caught up with the fur train thirty years before. At last the merrymakers all retired to the tents. Time had come for Dodge, the youthful major general, to have his fun. He had ordered a fireman to keep up steam in a locomotive. Now, in the dark, Dodge went to the engine, climbed in the cab and drove across to the Pawnee village. Major North and a platoon of Indian scouts came back with him. All slipped quietly into the capitalists' encampment, then raised the war whoop. In a moment pandemonium reigned. Ladies screamed, a few fainted. Then Dodge announced that it was all a hoax. With much laughter and dramatic Wild West bravado the tourists dressed and came out to shake hands with the Indians and sing around the campfires until breakfast time.

The special train carried its precious freight farther west across the plains. On the buffalo range the Easterners tried their luck at hunting. In the evening they returned, tired but happy. While red steaks sizzled on the fires, Durant negotiated his bonds. The Union Pacific's guests returned home and Dodge went back to work. He wrote Grant and Sherman for more soldiers to guard his crews, now that he had money to push the work again.

In the spring of 1867 Dodge's grading crews reached the Laramie plains. A new railroad, the Chicago and Northwestern was approaching Omaha and the problem of getting rails would soon be ended. The coming year promised to be one of great progress on the plains, but Dodge was disappointed. With spring came floods. The $50,000 bridge across the Loup collapsed. Miles of track behind the railhead washed away. And that was not all. The Indians began to attack here and there along a 500-mile line. Dodge's grading camp on the Laramie plains changed into a fortification. The overland stage stations for a distance of fifty miles were burned. Surveyors whipped back into camps reporting that Indians were pulling up their survey stakes. Dodge kept the bad news from the papers since it might prevent him from employing badly needed labor. Meanwhile he implored Grant and Sherman to send more men.

A few soldiers came out and the work went on. In June 1867 Grant wrote Dodge that General J. A. Rawlins, his chief of staff, was suffering from tuberculosis. Dodge suggested that the general come west and alleviate his malady in the high mountain air. Rawlins acted on the suggestion and Dodge looked forward to his visit. At last the inadequacy of the military on the plains would be known in high places.

General Rawlins arrived shortly before the railroad reached Cheyenne. He watched the tracklayers thrust the line steadily forward across the grasslands. Hundreds of carriages and wagons passed the construction crews to take up land ahead of the railroad. A mushroom village of some ten thousand people sprang up at Cheyenne. A great celebration was planned for July Fourth. All day long the liquor tents were crowded. Skyrockets and Roman candles illuminated the evening sky. General Rawlins delivered an oration. Civilization had come to the high plains! But at dawn a Cheyenne war party—a tribe whose name had been given to the new town—circled the metropolis swiftly as a flight of teal and disappeared. A few dead railroad graders lay sprawled on the ground, the only indication of the savage raid. Chief of Staff Rawlins could judge for himself the adequacy of his army.

Dodge considered calling a halt on railroad construction until more troops arrived, then changed his mind. If work stopped it might never start again. The administration, since Lincoln's death, had always opposed aid to the railroad. Dodge and Rawlins talked over the situation. They decided to establish an army post, Fort Fred Steele, where the railroad crossed the North Platte. General Steele had distinguished himself in the Civil War.

Dodge went with General Rawlins and his escort west of the North Platte across the endless sage flats. A division point would have to be selected here somewhere. Dodge said that he would name it Rawlins. Far beyond, on the desert where the Continental Divide crossed southern Wyoming, the party came to the haggard remnant of the surveying party routed by the Sioux. Still farther west they met another party of surveyors who announced that stakes for cuts and fills had been driven all the way to Green River. General Rawlins went back to Washington with a good knowledge of the road's progress and also of the hazards confronting construction crews.[9]

In the fall of 1867 Dodge went east also. He had been elected to Congress without campaigning. The railroad was graded past the place where he had had his brush with the Crows, and Hell on Wheels was being loaded for Cheyenne. Dodge went to Washington well satisfied, but heard before spring came that Vice-President Durant had changed the railroad division town from Cheyenne to Laramie. This would help a lot of new speculators but it would ruin Dodge's friends who had already speculated on blueprint lots in Cheyenne. The congressman packed his valise and boarded a train. At Laramie he learned that the rumor was fact. The prospective division town was booming, many tents and houses already set up in rows. The famous "Big Top" was lighted with gas flares, a band blared dance music. Gamblers had set up their tables. Dodge had seen the identical layout in Fort Kearney, Julesburg and North Platte. He had not expected to see it here.

In the dirt street between the tents and false-fronted buildings Dodge met Durant. The vice-president was the largest stockholder in the Union Pacific but Dodge had many friends who were opposed to him. The general decided to call for a showdown, to lay his cards on the table and see who really ran the Union Pacific. Dodge's friends controlled enough stock to make Durant uncomfortable. Dodge's personal friendship with Grant and Sherman was one of the road's great assets—and Grant was now a candidate for President. Moreover, the workmen were loyal to Dodge, at least Dodge thought so. He told Durant that the division town must be returned to Cheyenne. The vice-president backed down without a fight.

Dodge remained in the West to push the work. Congress would have to get along without him. The railhead moved across the North Platte near Fort Fred Steele and on to Benton—a town destined to disappear. By the middle of July 1868 the rails thrust their way out into the desert that marks the Continental Divide. In August surveying crews crossed Green River, pushed into Bear Valley and over the divide to Echo Canyon. They met Central Pacific linemen. Both crews were surprised. Neither believed that the other had advanced so rapidly.

Both crews were far in advance of their own railheads. Neither was willing to quit and both kept on in opposite directions on parallel lines. The Union Pacific act permitted either company to locate its right of way 300 miles ahead of construction. The act also specified that both roads should build until the rails met, but the act did not say that the rails must meet at the first opportunity. A $48,000 bonus and twenty sections of land went with every mile constructed out here, so both crews continued surveying parallel cuts and fills. Each railroad had confidence that its lobbyists in Congress would get its work accepted.

The Central Pacific employed Chinese laborers. Jack Casement had his toughs and many immigrant Irishmen. Grading gangs camped close together and sometimes fought with shovels and pick handles. Dynamite was placed in cuts and exploded when rival crews came by. As the workmen schemed to drive away their rivals, the owners got busy in Washington. The Californians had the inside track, for the Johnson administration looked on them with favor. Collis P. Huntington took advantage of his position and reported that the Union Pacific had been flimsily built, an unworkmanlike job done for the subsidies. Secretary of the Interior Browning, unfriendly to the Dodge-Grant-Sherman group, hesitated to pay the bonuses. The Union Pacific, still financially shaky, ran out of funds. Some of the directors wanted to give up and admit that they were whipped. Dodge and the Casement brothers rallied their forces and made the dirt fly.

All through the winter of 1868-1869 crews worked through the Wasatch canyons and in March the Union Pacific rails reached Ogden—a great victory, for Ogden was Salt Lake City's only outlet to the railroad. The Union Pacific had won the one great plum on the transcontinental line. But if Dodge felt elated he had not reckoned with Collis P. Huntington. True, Grant had been elected President of the United States but Huntington's friends in the Johnson administration were still in the saddle. Early in March 1869 Secretary Browning ordered bonds issued to the Central Pacific for construction work from Ogden to Promontory Point in Great Salt Lake.[10] This gave the Central Pacific an equal chance at the Salt Lake market in spite of the fact that their tracks were still far away.

This final blow, one of the last official acts of the retiring Johnson administration, might have ended the Union Pacific's battle with its rival, but Grenville Dodge was resourceful also. He bided his time until Grant took office on March 4, then went to his old army friend. Grant annulled Browning's order. Triumphantly Dodge set to work laying track toward Promontory Point—or beyond, if possible. Every mile meant $48,000, and construction on the Great Desert was cheap. Then Dodge went to see Collis P. Huntington, to spread the cards on the table before him as he had before Thomas Durant. Dodge offered to compromise with the California magnate. Parallel grading had been ridiculous. Parallel rail lines would ruin the Central Pacific. With Grant in the White House, Dodge said, the Union Pacific felt safe. Suppose they built all the way to the Pacific. With control of the Salt Lake outlet the Union Pacific could make the Central Pacific a branch line without a terminal. Surely the time had come to adjust differences, to agree on a place for the rails to meet. Besides, if the two roads did not agree, the government and the people might step in and regulate both corporations.

Huntington saw the danger. The Union Pacific had already won Ogden and the outlet to Salt Lake City. He agreed to set Promontory Point as the place of meeting provided that the Union Pacific lease a right of way over its tracks for Central Pacific trains to Ogden and thus give the California road an equal chance at the Salt Lake traffic. To this Dodge acceded. Thus Promontory Point was selected as the place of meeting and then began the most spectacular race of all, the sprint to the meeting place, a race strangely enough for notoriety, not for subsidy.

On April 1, 1869, the two railheads were almost equidistant from the junction point. The Central Pacific was fifty-four miles west of Promontory Point and the Union Pacific fifty-seven miles east. Each road had approximately 2,500 laborers—pick and shovel men, graders and tracklayers. Each road laid about five miles a day and tradition says that Thomas Durant lost a $10,000 bet that his men could lay ten miles of track a day. Both roads had to bring rails and ties for long distances. Some of the Central Pacific's rails came in ships around the Horn.

In May, Durant, leader of the anti-Dodge clique in the company, came west to take part in the ceremony of joining rails. West of Green River Durant's train was held up by infuriated contractors who demanded their pay from the company. Already they were hearing stories about the ample government funds absorbed by the *Crédit Mobilier*. The contractors and their workers decided to sidetrack the vice-president on their own account. Oliver Ames, president of the road, was leader of Durant's opponents. The news of his rival's predicament may have amused him but the prestige of the Union Pacific made it important that his enemy be taken from the clutches of the men. Moreover, a strike along the entire line from Omaha to Ogden seemed imminent. Ames wired Dodge in Salt Lake City to get the vice-president released. Dodge wired the soldiers at Fort Bridger to help him. The telegraph operator, sympathetic with the strikers, did not deliver the message. Dodge knew but one other alternative. He wired Ames to send $1,000,000—and send it quick. Ames complied. The company's debts were paid and Thomas Durant was allowed to trundle down the track in his private car to Ogden.

On May 2, 1869, the Central Pacific reached the place of meeting—winner of the race. The Union Pacific inched in slowly after the defeat and both sides waited for the great ceremony scheduled for May 10. Locomotives with private cars came up the tracks from the east and west and stopped head on. Between the panting engines the engineers, workmen and financiers—Huntington, Stanford, Dodge, Durant—met amid curious Mormons, Mexicans and Chinese, a few Indians and some Jewish peddlers. The telegraph wires were cleared for transmitting the ceremonies to distant cities. The last tie, a stick of polished laurel, was thrust beneath the rails. An official representative of Nevada handed Leland Stanford a golden spike and Thomas Durant a silver one. "To the iron of the East," he said impressively as the telegraphs ticked, "and the gold of the West, Nevada adds her link of silver to span the continent and wed the oceans."[11]

The golden spike was laid in place and an electric wire was attached to it. Stanford lifted a silver sledge and struck the spike, signaling to the entire nation that the road was completed. With more speeches the silver spike was driven. Then the tie was taken out and carried away to the private cars as a souvenir.

Crowds in cities all over the United States listened to the telegraph reproduce the driving of the golden spike. Men yelled and women waved their handkerchiefs as the electric needle clicked the death rattle of the Overland Road, shouted as though the end of the great trail was a great thing, yet no one who ever crossed with the covered wagons considered anything in life more worthy of remembrance.

1 J. V. Frederick, *Ben Holladay, The Stagecoach King* (Glendale, Calif., 1940), 177.

2 George Francis Train, *My Life in Many States and in Foreign Lands* (New York, 1902), 292.

3 J. R. Perkins, *Trails, Rails and War: The Life of General G. M. Dodge* (Indianapolis, 1929), 187.

4 *Ibid.*, 189.

5 *Ibid.*, 191.

6 *Ibid.*, 224.

7 *Ibid.*, 202.

8 *Ibid.*, 205.

9 Edwin L. Sabin, *Building the Pacific Railway* (Philadelphia, 1919), 153.

10 James G. Randall (ed.), *The Diary of Orville Hickman Browning (Collections of the Illinois State Historical Library*, XXII, Springfield, 1933), II, 242.

11 Perkins, *Trails, Rails and War*, 240.

EPILOGUE

The story of the Union Pacific after the line was completed is one of national development. Along the rails grew the states of Nebraska, Wyoming, Utah, Nevada and Idaho. The village of Fort Kearney sprang up at the railroad "whistling post"—not at the fort. North Platte became famous as the home and winter quarters of "Buffalo Bill's" Wild West Show. The old stage station at Julesburg grew into a division town, albeit the name was applied to four different sites. Laramie, as has been said, did not get the railroad shops, but it got the state university. South Pass and Fort Bridger, located to the right and the left of the railroad, sank back into the primitive. In 1883 a subsidiary of the Union Pacific built the Oregon Short Line from Granger, Wyoming, over to Bear Valley, down to Soda Springs, across the divide to the Port Neuf and to Pocatello, near old Fort Hall. Westward, down the Snake River, the Oregon Short Line followed the emigrant route to Boise, up Burnt Fork to Grande Ronde and across the Blue Mountains. Thus rails followed the entire Overland Trail.

During the year the golden spike was driven, 30,000 people went west on the Union Pacific. The next year almost 150,000 passengers rode the cars. Train travel was hot and dusty in summer, cold in winter. Sometimes buffalo stopped the locomotives. In the Sierras the scenery was marred by miles of snowsheds. Hour after hour passengers blinked at flickering slats. But seeing Yosemite and the Big Trees and the Golden Gate became the fashion for tourists. Yet always people who had crossed in the covered wagons looked patronizingly on late-comers. After all, it was something to have taken part in the longest overland migration in history.

In 1906 the Oregon Trail experienced a rebirth. In that year, in the era of Rough Riding "Teddy" Roosevelt, people were concerned about the vanishing frontier. Mass meetings discussed

411

preserving the forests, conserving wild life, saving the bison. Out in the State of Washington a seventy-six-year-old man with long white hair and beard started east with an ox team along the road he had traveled westward in 1852. He intended to stop at all the small towns, organize civic-minded citizens and enlist their help to mark the once famous trail. His trip elicited immediate response. In the East great crowds lined the roads to see him. He drove into New York City and stopped his ox team to be photographed in Wall Street. He went to Washington and shook hands with the great Rough Rider. Ezra Meeker had achieved his mission, but he had only begun to be famous as an overland pioneer. In 1916—aged eighty-six—he made the trip again in an automobile with a covered wagon top and camp outfit. The daring experiment of crossing the continent in a motor car, he said, was one of his ambitions in life. And it was an achievement, surely enough. The Lincoln Highway Association had not been organized until 1914, and people still wrote books about motoring from coast to coast. The dusty, rutted roads bore no resemblance to the modern highways tourists travel today on U. S. 40 to the Northwest or U. S. 30 through the Donner Pass to San Francisco.

With interest in the Overland Trail growing annually, Emerson Hough wrote a book entitled *The Covered Wagon*, which appeared serially in *The Saturday Evening Post*. The writer had made a name for himself as the author of articles on outdoor life, hunting, fishing and conservation. Although Hough already had several books to his credit, *The Covered Wagon* became much the most popular. A motion-picture magnate, James Cruze, decided to spend $800,000 to film the story. An entire frontier village and 400 covered wagons with oxen and horses were shipped to Nevada to be photographed. Ernest Torrence and Tully Marshall enacted the parts of mountain men—Marshall as Jim Bridger—and J. Warren Kerrigan that of the dashing hero. It soon became apparent to the producers that the wagon train was stealing the show from the actors. No man had personality enough to attract interest from the epic simplicity of trundling whitetops. Kerrigan, a trick horseman, tried to outdo himself and failed. The producers would not look. They had become interested in the spectacle of moving wagons and cared nothing for the actors.

The Covered Wagon, with accompanying strains of "Oh, Susanna," proved one of the most popular pictures of the silent screen, and with its success the Overland Trail became an American epic. The year following the picture's opening on Broadway, an aviation meet was held in Dayton, Ohio. An old biplane appeared in the western sky. It sailed down to the field, circled, came to the ground and taxied along the track before the grandstands. Two goggled figures sat in the tandem cockpit. They pulled off their helmets, and the crowd beheld white-haired Ezra Meeker, aged ninety-four. He had made his last trip, high in the air, above the Oregon Trail.

ACKNOWLEDGMENTS

The Overland Trail has led me to a continent of friends both living and long since dead. Those who crossed on the trail many years ago have talked to me in their journals. Many of the living who have been of great help in my understanding of the Overland Trail remain nameless.

A few friends have been extremely generous with their time and knowledge. LeRoy Hafen, my onetime boss and a past master in the Western field, has helped me greatly both with his books and with his prompt replies to my letters. At St. Joseph, I. R. Bundy assisted me in finding newspaper accounts of the disputed identity of the first pony express rider. At Fort Laramie, Thor Berson pointed out to me the site of the old fort and the converging roads. At Pocatello, Dr. Minnie Howard explained the diverse locations of the several Fort Halls on the near-by Indian reservation. Gaylord Sanford, who knows the flyways as well as the tortuous route of Snake River through the canyons, helped me with the local geography there. At La Grande, Charles H. Reynolds showed me the ruts of the old road and took me up into the Blue Mountains where the air smells of pines, moss and fern.

I want to express my gratitude to both D. L. Chambers and Harrison Platt of The Bobbs-Merrill Company. Their editorial assistance and technical advice are sources of constant satisfaction to a writer. In Springfield, Nira Irwin and James N. Adams have pulled me out of a hole once more by typing the entire manuscript with pony express speed. I want also to voice my appreciation of Margaret A. Flint's assistance in locating obscure titles in the extensive collection of overland material on the shelves of the Illinois State Historical Library.

To my wife, Mildred E. Monaghan, I owe one of those national debts that are never paid for her help on this book's voyage across the Overland Trail. Sitting, with sweet patience, on the sunbonnet side of the covered wagon seat, she has traveled the entire route to Oregon by car, by train and by manuscript. With an expert editorial eye she has discovered grammatical washouts and typographical chuckholes. Her companionship has made a rough road pleasant.

414

BIBLIOGRAPHICAL NOTE

The books written about the Overland Trail are endless. If they were placed at proper intervals across the continent, it is possible that a traveler might ride from the Missouri to the Pacific without getting out of sight of one of them. A suitable selection for an adequate understanding of the road is a formidable task. The first volume for every student is Henry R. Wagner's *The Plains and the Rockies: A Bibliography of Original Narratives of Travel and Adventures 1800-1865* (San Francisco, 1921), revised in 1937 by Charles L. Camp. Joseph Schafer's *A History of the Pacific Northwest* (New York, 1918) has long been a classic, and the volumes of H. H. Bancroft on Oregon and California, although outmoded in the form of presentation, remain bedrock sources in the field. Fred Lockley's *Oregon Trail Blazers* (New York, 1929) contains material on Robert Gray and the *Columbia* not found in other secondary sources. The volume prepared by the Federal Writers' Project on *The Oregon Trail: The Missouri River to the Pacific Ocean* (New York, 1939) gives modern distances from town to town along the trail, together with entertaining text and excellent illustrations. An M. A. dissertation by Jonathan T. Dorris, "The Oregon Trail," *Journal of the Illinois State Historical Society*, X, No. 4 (January, 1918), outlines the Meek, Barlow and Applegate roads omitted in the text. Julia Cooley Altrocchi's *The Old California Trail* (Caldwell, Idaho, 1945) describes traces of the trail a traveler may find today. The second printing has corrected a few minor details.

In the present study of the Overland Trail changing epochs have been described in terms of individuals. Thus some person or group has been selected in the different eras, and the reader crosses the continent with them. To do this, the journals of various members have been integrated, but a few general accounts of the period are necessary to color the background. For the chapter on the discovery and naming of the Columbia River, and for the sea-otter trade, two works have been used: Samuel Eliot Morison's *The Maritime History of Massachusetts* (Boston, 1921) and Stuart Ramsay Tompkins' *Alaska: Promyshlennik and Sourdough* (Norman, Okla., 1945). Samuel Flagg Bemis' *A Diplomatic History of the United States* (New York, 1936) has served for the Nootka Sound controversy and the later Oregon boundary disputes. Interesting details on the former may be found in W. R. Manning's "The Nootka Sound Controversy," *Annual Report of the American Historical Association,* 1904, 279-478.

Details of the cruise of the *Columbia* are presented best in John Boit's log of the voyage, published first in 1920 in Vol. LIII, 217-275, of the *Proceedings of the Massachusetts Historical Society,* and in Vol. XII, No. 1, of *The Washington Historical Quarterly.* A later printing in *The Quarterly of the Oregon Historical Society,* XXII, No. 4 (1921), [258]-351, is the most complete in text as well as footnotes. This account has been prepared by F. G. Young, who has benefited by the research and annotations by Edmond S. Meany, F. W. Howay and T. C. Elliott. The same issue of the Society's *Quarterly* also contains the "Remnant of the Official Log of the *Columbia,*" annotated by T. C. Elliott. Additional light on the leaders of the cruise may be found in "Captains Gray and Kendrick: the Barrell Letters," edited by F. W. Howay for *The Washington Historical Quarterly,* XII, No. 4 (October, 1921), 243-271. The important meeting with Vancouver's vessels is related in Captain George Vancouver's *A Voyage of Discovery to the Pacific Ocean* (4 vols., London, 1801). Edward L. Keithahn's *Monuments in Cedar* (Ketchikan, Alaska, 1945) assembles much data on the relations of early navigators with the natives and the rise of the totem pole culture.

The complete story of the Lewis and Clark expedition can be found in a few narratives. The account of Patrick Gass entitled *A Journal of the Voyages and Travels of a Corps of Discovery, under the Command of Capt. Lewis and Capt. Clarke* ... (Pittsburgh, 1807), the 1904 reprint with introduction by James Kendall Hosmer—a rarity like the former—and accounts written by Lewis and Clark themselves have been considered ample for this narrative. Every reader should use both Reuben Gold Thwaites's eight-volume edition, *Original Journals of the Lewis and Clark Expedition, 1804-1806* (New York, 1904), and Elliot Coues's four-volume edition of *History of the Expedition under the Command of Lewis and Clark* (New York, 1893). Thwaites gives an excellent description of the original manuscript, the various published editions, and explains the editorial problem of assembling the material. He prints both Lewis' and Clark's separate accounts of each day's events. Illustrations by Lieutenant Clark add realism to the publication. Elliott Coues's edition gives many editorial comments not to be found elsewhere. The spurious journal entitled *The Travels of Capts. Lewis & Clarke* (Philadelphia, 1809) is too vague in details about the expedition to mislead anyone.

Many side lights on river life at the beginning of the nineteenth century may be gained from other books. The writer has found H. M. Brackenridge's *Views of Louisiana, together with a Journal of a Voyage up the Missouri River, in 1811* (Pittsburgh, 1814) and the English translation of Prince Maximilian's *Travels in the Interior of North America* (London, 1843) invaluable. The latter is conveniently reprinted in Volumes XXII-XXV of Reuben Gold Thwaites's *Early Western Travels, 1748-1846* (Cleveland, 1906). Both authors describe the natives at a date slightly later than the Lewis and Clark period, but Indian culture was not changing sufficiently fast to distort the picture. Maximilian's descriptions of the Mandan villages and the customs of the peoples cannot be surpassed. A detailed account about Bird Woman, telling as much as is known of her entire life, her children, marriages and burial, may be found in Grace Raymond Hebard's *Sacajawea: A Guide and Interpreter of the Lewis and Clark Expedition* (Glendale, Calif., 1933).

For the Astorians, Washington Irving's two-volume *Astoria, or Anecdotes of an Enterprise beyond the Rocky Mountains* (Philadelphia, 1836, 1841) remains the old stand-by. In *The Discovery of the Oregon Trail* (New York, 1935) Philip Ashton Rollins has edited the journals of Wilson Price Hunt and Robert Stuart on their eventful trip east from Astoria. Gabriel Franchère, Canadian Frenchman who went to Astoria by sea, tells much about life at the fort in *Narrative of a Voyage to the Northwest Coast of America* (New York, 1854), an English translation of the original version published in 1820. The translation is reprinted conveniently in *Early Western Travels, 1748-1846*, edited by Reuben Gold Thwaites (Cleveland, 1904), VI, 167 ff.

Hiram M. Chittenden's three-volume *The American Fur Trade of the Far West* (New York, 1902, 1935, 1936) holds granite stature in the field. The author was able to interview people, since dead, who were familiar with the trade. His *History of Early Steamboat Navigation on the Missouri River* (New York, 1903) is virtually a fourth volume to his study.

The discovery of South Pass has been the source of much discussion. In addition to Rollins' *Discovery of the Oregon Trail*, noted above, Harrison Clifford Dale's edition of *The Ashley-Smith Explo-*

rations and the Discovery of a Central Route to the Pacific, 1822-1829 (Cleveland, 1918, revised 1941) is important and offers a detailed map of early Wyoming passes. There is also Donald McKay Frost's "Notes on General Ashley, the Overland Trail, and South Pass," *Proceedings of the American Antiquarian Society ... 1944*, LIV, part 2 (Worcester, Mass., 1945). Dale L. Morgan's *The Great Salt Lake* (Indianapolis, 1947) contains information of Etienne Provost not readily available elsewhere. Washington Irving's three-volume *Adventures of Captain Bonneville, or Scenes beyond the Rocky Mountains of the Far West* (London, 1837) is one of the underlying sources of the fur trade. Irving knew Bonneville personally and in consequence was subjected to polluted sources, which later investigators have analyzed. LeRoy Hafen and W. J. Ghent, in *Broken Hand, the Life Story of Thomas Fitzpatrick* (Denver, 1931), have resurrected one of the master mountain men. LeRoy Hafen and Francis M. Young, in *Fort Laramie and the Pageant of the West, 1834-1890* (Glendale, Calif., 1938), tell about the birth, growth and death of the great capital of the fur trade. In *The Pacific Northwest Quarterly*, XXXVII, No. 2 (April, 1946), 87-108, Merrill J. Mattes has an article, "Jackson Hole, Crossroads of the Western Fur Trade, 1807-1829," which describes with maps and pictures the confused bit of geography which baffled the early transcontinental travelers. British participation in the Oregon fur trade may be found readily in a biography by Robert C. Johnson, entitled *John McLoughlin: Patriarch of the Northwest* (Portland, Ore., 1935). Dr. McLoughlin's letters from Fort Vancouver, edited by E. E. Rich, were published in 1944 by the Champlain Society in Toronto. A doctoral dissertation, "The Hudson's Bay Company Claims, 1846-1869" (Urbana, Ill., 1934), by Ralph R. Martig, gives an excellent summary of the value of the various Canadian posts in the Oregon country. Howard R. Driggs has done much to focus attention on the Oregon Trail by editing and writing several Overland Trail volumes for broad and popular consumption.

In *The Washington Historical Quarterly*, III, No. 1 (October, 1908), 3-62, "A Contribution toward a Bibliography of Marcus Whitman," by Charles W. Smith, lists over two hundred titles. The cream of this material has been skimmed by Archer B. and Dorothy P. Hulbert for the Stewart Commission of Colorado College and the Denver Public Library Series entitled *Overland to the Pacific* (Denver, 1934-1941). Volumes V and VI contain biographies of Whitman and Samuel Parker, together with a report of Parker's western tour in 1835 and Oregon mission correspondence relating to Whitman's labors. These two volumes, so-called, are in reality five; the various parts are bound separately. Whitman's famous ride to save Oregon is "debunked" by E. G. Bourne in "The Legend of Marcus Whitman," *The American Historical Review*, VI, No. 2 (January, 1901), 276-300. As is so often the case, a revelation of this kind started a trend that discredited Whitman generally. This injustice is expiated in a measure by the Reverend Myron Eells in his *Marcus Whitman, Pathfinder and Patriot* (Seattle, 1909). Cornelius J. Brosnan gives a good picture of Whitman's colleague in *Jason Lee: Prophet of Oregon* (New York, 1932).

Source material on details of the life and adventures of Nathaniel Wyeth, edited by F. G. Young, may be found in "The Correspondence and Journals of Captain Nathaniel J. Wyeth, 1831-6," in *Sources of the History of Oregon* (Eugene, Ore., 1899), I, Part 3, 1-262. John Wyeth's pamphlet, "Oregon; or a Short History of a Long Journey" (1833), and J. K. Townsend's journal of the second Wyeth expedition are both reprinted in Volume XXI of *Early Western Travels, 1748-1846*, edited by Thwaites (Cleveland, 1905). John Ball's daughters, Kate Ball Powers, Flora Ball Hopkins and Lucy Ball, have compiled their father's "autobiography" as *John Ball, Member of the Wyeth Expedition to the Pacific Northwest, 1832; and Pioneer in the Old Northwest* (Glendale, Calif., 1925). Hall Kelley's journal, which discloses much of his petulant personality, has been edited by Fred Wilbur Powell as "Hall Jackson Kelley—Prophet of Oregon," *The Quarterly of the Oregon Historical Society*, XVIII, Nos. 1, 2, 3, 4 (March, June, September, December, 1917), 154, 93-139, 167-224, 271-295. Numerous petitions and pamphlets by Louis Tarascon bear witness of another man of the Kelley stamp who has been neglected by the historians. The importance of the publicists' agitations is considerably discredited by Archer Hulbert's collection of letters of recognized fur men describing the feasibility of a wagon road across the mountains, in *The Documentary Background of the Days of the First Wagon Train on the Road to Oregon* (Missoula, Mont., 1930). The best account of Miles Goodyear is found in Charles Kelly's and Maurice L. Howe's *Miles Goodyear: First Citizen of Utah, Trapper, Trader and California Pioneer* (Salt Lake City, 1937). Dale Morgan has added some important details in *The Great Salt Lake*, cited above. Fred Lockley's three-volume work remains basic for the *History of the Columbia River from The Dalles to the Sea* (Chicago, 1928).

The source materials on Father DeSmet's explorations along the Overland Trail are found in his letters published in *Early Western Travels*. The Jesuit's writings are badly organized. Often he did not mention certain facts until long after they had happened. His travels can be reconstructed from his own words only by breaking down his statements and synthesizing them. John Bidwell helps reconstruct the 1841 expedition with his description entitled "The First Emigrant Train to California," *The Century Magazine*, XIX (November, 1890), 116, but of course it must not be trusted like a contemporary source.

For Frémont, his own *Report of the Exploring Expedition to the Rocky Mountains in the Year 1842 and to Oregon and North California in the Years 1843-44 (U. S. Senate Report No. 174*, 28 Cong. 2d Sess., Washington, 1845)—written by his wife, perhaps—is certainly the best source as well as vivid reading. Allan Nevins' *Frémont, the West's Greatest Adventurer* (New York, 1928) remains the classic. Thomas Hart Benton, *Thirty Years' View* (New York, 1854-1856) is important to complete the picture. Many of Benton's separately printed speeches disclose the color of the man and his times. One especially, *Highway to the Pacific*, published in 1850, gives the senator's attitude toward the Overland Trail.

The great migration beginning with 1843 and ending with the driving of the golden spike in the Union Pacific Railroad is a vast field with a great many individual journals. To list them is beyond the purpose of these bibliographical notes. W. J. Ghent's *The Road to Oregon: A Chronicle of the Great Emigrant Trail* (London, 1929) is one of the best general accounts. Agnes C. Laut's *The Overland Trail: the Epic Path of the Pioneers to Oregon* (New York, 1929) is another summary by a recognized authority. Frémont, in his *Report*, described the 1843 migration as he saw it. Hafen and Young in their *Fort Laramie* give an important cross section. The New York *Herald* letters of Peter H. Burnett are easily available in *The Quarterly of the Oregon Historical Society*, III, No. 4 (December, 1902), 406 ff. Jesse Applegate's classic, "A Day with the Cow Column in 1843," may be found, edited by Joseph Schafer, in the same quarterly for December 1900 (Vol. I, No. 4), 372-383. A separate reprinting in 1934 was made by the Caxton Club of Chicago. The quaint description of the great tourist outing along the trail in 1843 is printed in "A Fragmentary Journal of William L. Sublette," edited by Harrison C. Dale, *Mississippi Valley Historical Review*, VI, No. 1 (June, 1919), 108 ff.

The Donner catastrophe, like the Great Migration, is the subject of a vast amount of source accounts. The most recent secondary accounts are built on the research of George R. Stewart, Jr., in *Ordeal by Hunger: The Story of the Donner Party* (New York, 1936). Bernard DeVoto has added to this account in *The Year of Decision, 1846* (Boston, 1943), with his own inimitable style. All readers interested in the event should sample J. Quinn Thornton's *Oregon and California in 1848* (New York, 1849). A good writer after the fashion of his time, Thornton was very close to the Donners and knew at firsthand much whereof he wrote. Lansford W. Hastings' *The Emigrants' Guide to Oregon and California* (Cincinnati, 1845) is essential for an understanding of the party's error. A reprint of it was made in Princeton in 1932.

Francis Parkman's account of his trip along the trail was originally printed as "The Oregon Trail, or a Summer's Journey out of Bounds," in *The Knickerbocker*, XXIX, No. 2 (February, 1847), 160 ff. Later printings in book form make very slight changes in the original text. I have used the magazine articles and Bernard DeVoto's *Year of Decision, 1846* for the small amount of space devoted to the Boston Brahmin in this book.

The Mormon field is another in which space requirements for this volume have necessitated a superficial treatment. The pioneer trip can be best reconstructed from *William Clayton's Journal: A Daily Record of the Journey of the Original Company of "Mormon" Pioneers from Nauvoo, Illinois, to the Valley of the Great Salt Lake* (Salt Lake City, 1921). An article by M. Hamlin Cannon, "Migration of English Mormons to America," *The American Historical Review*, LII, No. 3 (April, 1947), 436-455, adds much of the European background, but the author's disregard of the work of his colleagues is surprising.

A satisfactory summary of the Argonauts may be found in Owen Cochran Coy's *The Great Trek* (San Francisco, 1931). The author gives a series of maps showing the entire trail from the Missouri to the Pacific and a more detailed view of the trails from South Pass to central Nevada and the various California routes. A very large two-volume journal, copiously edited by Georgia Willis Read and Ruth Gaines, entitled *Gold Rush: The Journals, Drawings, and Other*

Papers of J. Goldsborough Bruff, Captain, Washington City and California Mining Association, April 2, 1849-July 20, 1851 (New York, 1944), makes very entertaining reading. Other invaluable contemporary accounts may be found in Peter H. Burnett's *Recollections and Opinions of an Old Pioneer* (New York, 1880), and Edwin Bryant's *What I Saw in California* (New York, 1848). Other journals that stand out among the multitude are Lorenzo Sawyer's *Way Sketches Containing Incidents of Travel across the Plains from St. Joseph to California in 1850* (New York, 1926); John Steele's *Across the Plains in 1850*, edited by Joseph Schafer (Chicago, 1930); and David DeWolf's "Diary of the Overland Trail, 1849," *Transactions of the Illinois State Historical Society*, No. 32 (1925), 183-222. The famous painter of overland scenes, William Henry Jackson, tells of his own trip across the road in 1866 in his autobiography, *Time Exposure* (New York, 1940). Best of all are the diaries and journals of James Clyman, published in the *California Historical Society Quarterly* (1925-1927), IV-VI, and in book form, with annotations by Charles L. Camp, as *James Clyman: American Frontiersman, 1792-1881* (San Francisco, 1928).

Frederic L. Paxson's *History of the American Frontier, 1763-1893* (Boston, 1924), written a quarter of a century ago, remains helpful as the over-all picture of certain phases of Western history. A completely satisfactory work on the pony express is yet to be written. William Lightfoot Visscher's *A Thrilling and Truthful History of the Pony Express* (Chicago, 1908), and Glenn D. Bradley's *The Story of the Pony Express* (Chicago, 1913, 1920, 1927, 1932), both contain much material that seems to be accurate, but neither is written according to present-day concepts of scholarship. Visscher's book has become a collector's item. Arthur Chapman's *The Pony Express: The Record of a Romantic Adventure in Business* (New York, 1932) is the best volume on the subject. A nearer approach to a scholarly job than anything else yet written, it makes interesting reading. Most of the unannotated quotations cited may be located by the context. The testimony of W. B. Richardson in 1941 necessitates a revision of Chapman's conclusions as to the first man to ride the express out of St. Joe. An important contribution on Buffalo Bill's activity in the pony express may be found in Richard J. Walsh's *The Making of Buffalo Bill* (Indianapolis, 1928).

Mark Twain's *Roughing It* (Chicago, 1872) is one of the classics which everyone reads. Important to his work is *Absalom Grimes,*

Confederate Mail Runner (New Haven, 1926), edited by Milo M. Quaife. Here the student may find Sam Clemens among the Confederate Rangers before he took his famous western trip.

Side lights on the Civil War on the plains just before the building of the Union Pacific Railroad, written from the red man's point of view, are available in George Bird Grinnell's *The Fighting Cheyennes* (New York, 1915) and in Grace R. Hebard's *Washakie: An Account of Indian Resistance of the Covered Wagon and Union Pacific* (Cleveland, 1930). Two standard works deal with the railroad's construction: Edwin L. Sabin's *Building the Pacific Railway* (Philadelphia, 1919) and Jacob R. Perkins' *Trails, Rails and War: The Life of General G. M. Dodge* (Indianapolis, 1929). The latter, more indefinite as to dates, has many of the characteristics of an "official" biography. George Francis Train exaggerates his own importance in financing the Union Pacific in his book *My Life in Many States and in Foreign Lands* (New York, 1902). To neutralize Train's own statements a student should read J. B. Crawford's *The Credit Mobilier of America; Its Origin and History* (Boston, 1880). An interesting contemporary account of the railroad's construction was published by the company with the title *Progress of the Union Pacific Railroad* (New York, 1868).

Of all the books written since the death of the Overland Trail, the most popular has probably been Emerson Hough's *The Covered Wagon*. An account of this book's filming may be found in *The Best Moving Pictures of 1922-23* (Boston, 1923), edited by Robert E. Sherwood. The famous picture was also described in *The American Review of Reviews* for June, 1923. Ezra Meeker wrote several books and pamphlets about his trips and efforts to erect markers along the Oregon Trail. A summary of his career by C. B. Galbreath was printed in the *Ohio Archaeological and Historical Quarterly*, XXXVI, No. 1 (January, 1927), 3-47.

INDEX